THE RELIGIOUS STUDIES
MONOGRAPH SERIES

The Words of Joseph Smith

The Words of Joseph Smith

The contemporary accounts of the
Nauvoo discourses of the Prophet Joseph

Compiled and edited by
Andrew F. Ehat and Lyndon W. Cook

With a Foreword by .
Truman G. Madsen

VOLUME SIX
IN THE RELIGIOUS STUDIES MONOGRAPH SERIES

Religious Studies Center
Brigham Young University
Provo, Utah

Library of Congress Catalog Card Number: 80-70806
ISBN 0-88494-419-0

Second Printing, 1981

Produced and Distributed by
BOOKCRAFT, INC.
Salt Lake City, Utah

Lithographed in the United States of America
PUBLISHERS PRESS
Salt Lake City, Utah

To
Lori and Lynette

Contents

Foreword

Truman G. Madsen

What did Joseph Smith teach? The attempt to answer usually leads Latter-day Saints to three publications: the written revelations of the Doctrine and Covenants and The Pearl of Great Price; the 7-volume *History of the Church*, and the compilation *Teachings of the Prophet Joseph Smith*, edited by Joseph Fielding Smith. But most of these documents are based on the journals, diaries, and notebooks of those who surrounded the Prophet. Some were appointed by him to fulfill the commission: "There shall be a record kept" (D&C 21). Some were making private notes for their own use.

Here for the first time in church literature, presented with almost photographic fidelity, are the original sources of all the discourses of Joseph Smith delivered during his climactic five years in Nauvoo. These discourses not only shed light on the standard works; they also provide teachings beyond the scope of those heretofore published. (In fact, many of these utterances were not available to the first-generation historians when they began their compilations.)

The collection presents Joseph Smith during the era when he was dealing with Church doctrine and organization in its ripest and fullest form. As is clear in the sermons of his last year, he was struggling with a sense of urgency to present "all the strongest doctrines in public," to roll off all the keys of responsibility on his brethren. He was trying to prepare the minds of the Saints to receive the truth even when it opposed their traditions. And literally and figuratively he sought to place upon the Church the capstone by finishing the temple and conferring upon the Saints within it the most sacred and glorious consummations of faith in the Lord Jesus Christ.

These 173 separable discourses were recorded by some 40 individuals. Probably still other contemporary records of the Prophet's discourses have not yet found their way into the Church Archives. But of these persons one can say they honored the commission of the Prophet (as recalled by Oliver B. Huntington) that they should "be prompt in keeping daily journals." They fulfill his prediction that their journals would be "sought after as history and scripture." In one classic admonition to the Twelve, he had said soberly, "The time will come, when, if you will neglect to do this thing, you will fall by the hands of unrighteous men." In lamentation that there were things already lost or never recorded, he said that without such records the "Great and glorious manifestations which have been made to us" could not be presented to the Church and to the world "with the same degree of power and authority" (*Teachings*, pp. 72-73).

Many of the full-bodied discourses of Joseph Smith can be traced to only one man, Wilford Woodruff. With an overwhelming conviction of his calling, he kept a faithful record of all the utterances of Joseph Smith he was present to hear. He could hardly sleep until he had taken his notes and transcribed them into a detailed account. Of his total effort B. H. Roberts wrote:

> Other men may found hospitals or temples or schools for the Church, or endow special divisions or chairs of learning in them; or they may make consecrations of lands and other property to the Church but in point of important service, and in placing the Church under permanent obligations, no one will surpass in excellence in permanence or largeness the service Wilford Woodruff has given to the Church of Jesus Christ in the new dispensation, by writing and preserving the beautiful and splendid journals he kept through sixty-three years—so far do the things of mind surpass material things (*Comprehensive History of the Church*, 7:355).

This volume is the product of a decade of careful, consistent cooperative effort by two superb researchers in Mormon origins: Andrew F. Ehat and Lyndon W. Cook. The result is in many ways a first: Every firsthand contemporary account of Joseph's Nauvoo discourses is included here. The origin-sources are reproduced with scrupulous fidelity to the original text, including stylistic abbreviations and grammatical and spelling errors. Because a text without a context can become a pretext, the editors have provided thorough bibliographic, biographical, and doctrinal commentary in their lengthy, but essential, footnotes. The compilation is in exact chronology and is cross-referenced to all scriptural passages to which the Prophet referred or alluded in his discourses. These in turn are cross-referenced to each other and are extensively indexed.

There are side benefits in having the entire collection and commentary under one cover: we see connections and relationships that otherwise are obscure; we see glimpses of the Prophet Joseph Smith as a common man who identifies himself with the grinding labor and sufferings of his people; we see how richly furnished was his mind and how receptive, malleable, and bold was its sweeping inspiration and yet how his very thought patterns were rooted in the New Testament—especially in Paul. (There are fewer allusions to the Old Testament, The Book of Mormon, and the Doctrine and Covenants.) We see something of the life-settings, the personalities, the needs, and even the crises surrounding many of his statements. We see humor and wit, we see trauma and prophetic vision. And through it all we see a man confident in his mission, assured of his divine calling—for all his light-hearted gregarious and social instincts, he was a man serious to the core.

The editors have done another service. Their careful footnoting and tracing of earlier authentic statements and later echoes affords the reader a fresh sense of the unfolding drama of the Restoration. The King Follett discourse, for example, which until now has seemed unprecedented, is here shown to be the outcome of earlier teachings. Its brilliance and stature emerge from its combining strands of prior insights of the Prophet into one majestic, comprehensive statement. Thus, the editors have done revelatory research on both the background and foreground of the discourses.

The book becomes a perennial instrument for interpreting and understanding later reminiscences and recollections about the Prophet and his sayings. It is also a hedge against folklore and fiction, and against the charge that one cannot trust the sources of Mormonism in its formative stages.

For teachers in all levels of Church administration and practice, for parents who are concerned to "go to the source" when counseling and guiding and testifying in the home, for students who seek a handbook of Mormon sources that will withstand careful scholarly scrutiny, for Latter-day Saints who wish to treasure up the fundamental teachings of the Restoration at their very fountainhead, and for all in or beyond the Church who have begun to recognize that in his high and inspired moments Joseph Smith passed on to this generation "gems for the sanctified," this book is not only useful, it is indispensable.

Introductory Essay

In the latter-day Restoration no individual stands taller than Joseph Smith, the Lord's prophet. As the first prophet of the last dispensation, he commands the respect and attention of all members of the Church. An early revelation received by Joseph Smith declared, "This generation shall have my word through you" (D&C 5:10), and no one would dispute the validity of this statement: the Prophet's teachings are the foundation of Mormon theology.

In recent years a greater sense of "getting to the sources" has marked Mormon historical writing. Serious students of Mormon history have sought to apply modern historical research methods to verify, firm up, and fill in the gaps of our seven-volume history. This approach has helped us understand and appreciate the efforts of early Church members in preserving our history. However, some have argued that the sources of official Church writings were altered to create faithful, but inaccurate history. Some have even argued that Joseph Smith's public teachings were not actually his but were created after his death—that Church historians took a free hand in creating or amplifying nonexistent or cryptic notes into full-blown discourses.

However, the following compilation of contemporary accounts of 173 known public discourses shows that all the Prophet's teachings during the Nauvoo period can be documented from original sources. Admittedly the reports of his discourses were incomplete, but having multiple accounts of many of the sermons allows one to compare and contrast what each reporter recorded of the Prophet's ideas. Thus, there is no evidence that Church historians who prepared Joseph Smith's discourses for publication went beyond a reasonable interpretation of the original recorded statements.

It is not our purpose to reconstruct how the Church historians, particularly George A. Smith, amalgamated the various versions of Joseph Smith's discourses in preparing them for publication. Suffice it to say that all available reports were synthesized into a single, coherent account. Of this process George A. Smith said, "The greatest care [was] taken to convey the ideas in the Prophet's style as near as possible; and in no case [was] the sentiment . . . varied that I know of; as I heard the most of his discourses myself, was on the most intimate terms with him, have retained a most vivid recollection of his teachings, and was well acquainted with his principles and motives" (Letter from George A. Smith to Wilford Woodruff, 21 April 1856).

Only those people who recorded Joseph Smith's teachings at the time could have preserved his doctrine and phraseology. One who desired to preserve the words of Joseph Smith was twenty-two-year old Franklin D. Richards. He began a personal record of the Prophet's teachings in 1843 and called it "Joseph's Words."

Because there were no mechanical devices for recording the Prophet's sermons, verbatim accounts of his words do not exist. Therefore, contemporary reports (almost always in the form of private notes and diaries) constitute the closest approximation of Joseph Smith's actual words.

This volume presents for the first time the original accounts of all Joseph Smith's public discourses given during the Nauvoo period. This includes records of previously unpublished sermons, contemporaneous reports not available when the Church historians finished their official reports of the discourses, and the originals of those used in the published accounts. The criterion for inclusion of a source in this work was whether that source was a contemporaneous record of a public discourse. While reminiscent accounts often contain much that is authentic, there is always the risk that recorders will make interpolations. Perhaps the clearest example of this problem is in reminiscent accounts of the Prophet's final public address—his address to the Nauvoo Legion. In reminiscent reports the Prophet is remembered as saying that the Saints will go to the Rocky Mountains to settle. However, according to contemporaneous records, he "called for all philanthropic men from Maine to the Rocky Mountains" to aid the Latter-day Saint people in overcoming mob oppression. Because we have selected only those sources that were unmistakably recorded at the time, the collection can serve as a standard against which to judge the myriad recollections.

The reports of Joseph Smith's sermons were copied and recopied by his disciples. For example, some of James Burgess's reports of the Prophet's discourses were copied from Willard Richards's "Pocket Companion," accounts Richards had earlier obtained from Wilford Woodruff and John Taylor. Later (probably while they were both clerks for the Prophet) William Clayton copied Richards's "Pocket Companion" records of discourses given in Nauvoo before Clayton arrived from England. William Clayton then added these teachings to his own collection of the Prophet's words that he recorded while Elders Richards, Woodruff, Taylor, and Burgess were in England. Even after Joseph Smith's death this sharing continued. James Harvey Glines, for example, copied some sayings of the Prophet from William Patterson McIntire's notebook. And Howard Egan recorded in Wilford Woodruff's private journal Joseph Smith's 28 April 1842 discourse to the Relief Society.

Aware of this sharing, we have analyzed each report and selected for inclusion in this volume the earliest reports available. Full bibliographic detail is noted the first time a source is used.

Without question, Willard Richards and Wilford Woodruff were the two most important reporters of Joseph Smith's sermons. Richards, who was appointed in December 1842 to record the Prophet's activities, reported in Joseph Smith's diary more than one-third of all the discourses we have reproduced. Wilford Woodruff, though having no special assignment, recorded more than twice the number of discourses reported by any other individual (except Willard Richards). Moreover, it is significant that half the discourses reported by Woodruff were recorded by no other person.

In terms of technique of recording, Willard Richards's entries in Joseph Smith's diary were, if not always dictated, written as if they had been dictated. However, Richards's reports of the Prophet's discourses in the diary are often cryptic and conceptually incomplete when compared with the well-rounded accounts by Woodruff. The disparity between the recording methods of these two men helps illustrate the problem of record-keeping in Nauvoo. Though both men knew some shorthand, neither was sufficiently skilled to take verbatim reports. Nevertheless, though their reports and the large number of companion reports of the Prophet's words comprised in this book are in this sense incomplete and lack some of his phraseology and personality, they do reflect Joseph Smith's mind and his doctrine.

Public discourse in Nauvoo occurred most often in the open air. While many meetings were held at or near private residences, in Joseph Smith's store, and on the rough floor of the Nauvoo Temple (still under construction), the majority were held in a grove. Usually the focal point of the meeting place was a portable platform called a "stand." Church leaders sat on the stand, and the audience sat on benches of split logs or on the ground. Rain and cold often precluded Sabbath meetings.

The physical strength required to preach from week to week to large open-air congregations was considerable. Naturally Joseph Smith was the preferred speaker at Sunday meetings, but occasionally he "used the boys' lungs," because his own constitution could not tolerate weekly use. For example, the day following the celebrated King Follett sermon, the Prophet was so worn out that he could speak only a few minutes. But he had given instructions to George J. Adams to speak. Rhoda Richards observed, "I heard brother Joseph by the mouth of brother Adams." On another occasion Willard Richards recorded that Joseph was sick because his lungs "were oppressed" and "overheated" from preaching the week before.

Before 1839 Sidney Rigdon stood as the public spokesman of Mormonism, having been so designated by revelation (D&C 100:9). But when he began to neglect this responsibility, in late 1839 Joseph Smith "came of age" in public discourse. After spending six months in a Missouri jail and seeing the entire Mormon population expelled from that state, the Prophet's desire for redress and justice compelled him to speak before national leaders. In many ways the

1839-40 trip to Washington, D.C., was a milestone in Joseph Smith's career, and of particular significance is the fact that on this occasion Joseph Smith himself did the speaking. And the Prophet did the preaching. It was not Sidney Rigdon (as in previous visits to the East Coast) but Joseph Smith who local newspapers and reporters announced would preach. It seems that sheer necessity and commitment of purpose compelled the Prophet to stand for himself and his people and defend his mission. Mathew L. Davis, a Washington correspondent who observed the Prophet at this time, stated,

> He is not an educated man: but he is a plain, sensible, strong minded man. Everything he says, is said in a manner to leave an impression that he is sincere. There is no levity, no fanaticism, no want of dignity in his deportment. . . . In his garb there are no pecularities; his dress being that of a plain, unpretending citizen.

Nor was the Prophet's desire solely to speak out for his people. By 1839 he had done a lot of thinking about the temple and the plan of the Kingdom as he alone then understood it. He had a keen desire to articulate these ideas to his people. His understanding was not yet complete, but there is no doubt that the seeds had been planted. From then on, he rarely spoke without making reference to some aspect of temple theology. And as he unfolded his vision of the Kingdom, his people yearned more and more for his words.

The Saints' anxiety to hear the Prophet is graphically described by Charlotte Haven, a non-Mormon, who visited Nauvoo in 1843. As she went for the first time to hear Joseph Smith preach, she was amazed at "such hurrying" at least two hours before the services were to commence. "One could have thought it was the last opportunity they would ever have to hear him." On another occasion, at the Nauvoo Temple, the Saints swarmed to hear Joseph Smith. Willard Richards recorded that nothing could be seen "from the stand but the heads and bodies of the congregation. They stood on the walls [of the uncompleted building] and the floor. It was one mass of Saints. To speak was literally to speak to the people, for there was nothing else to be seen."

At the Nauvoo lyceums the Prophet often spoke. On one of these occasions Mercy R. Thompson "heard him reprove the brethren for giving way to too much excitement and warmth in debate. I have listened to his clear and masterly explanations of deep and difficult questions. To him all things seemed simple and easy to be understood, and thus he could make them plain to others as no other man could." When English convert William Rowley first heard Joseph Smith speak, he wrote that he "knew he was listening to one that had not been taught of men so different were all his thoughts and language."

The authority and power with which the Prophet delivered a message was convincing. Even Willard Richards, who knew the Prophet's private life better than any other man, told his sister, following a public sermon on the resurrection, that he had "heard the sweetest sermon from Joseph he ever heard in his life." Charles Smith observed that when the Prophet spoke he "drew your soul out in love towards him."

Although his testimony was not borne in our traditional fashion, Joseph Smith did radiate a conviction of his own divine appointment. In 1843 he said, "If I had not actually got into this work, and been called of God, I would back out, but I cannot back out, I have no doubt of the truth." In Washington, D.C., in 1840, Joseph Smith affirmed that the Book of Mormon was "communicated to him, direct from heaven. If there was such a thing on earth, as the author of it, then he was the author of it; but the idea that he wished to impress was that he penned it as dictated by God."

So spoke Joseph Smith's contemporaries about his manner, authority, and conviction in public discourse. In the wake of the Prophet's martyrdom his influence continued to spread. Bathsheba W. Smith, the last living person who heard Joseph Smith's public and private teachings in every facet of the gospel, stated, "I never like to hear a sermon without hearing something of the Prophet, for he gave us everything, every order of the priesthood."

Acknowledgments

We are indebted to many individuals who have assisted either directly or indirectly in the preparation of this work. Materials used in this study were gleaned from the Church Archives, Historical Department of The Church of Jesus Christ of Latter-day Saints, Salt Lake City, Utah; Special Collections, Harold B. Lee Library, Brigham Young University, Provo, Utah; Manuscripts Division, J. Willard Marriott Library, University of Utah, Salt Lake City, Utah; and History Division, Library-Archives, Reorganized Church of Jesus Christ of Latter Day Saints, The Auditorium, Independence, Missouri. Thanks are given to the kind, talented staffs at these libraries. We especially remember the exceptional cooperation of James L. Kimball, Jr., at Church Archives. Chad Flake of Brigham Young University Library, Madelon Brunson and Patricia Roberts at the RLDS Library-Archives, and Della Dye of the University of Utah Library have also greatly assisted us in our work. Others who have contributed significantly are Dean C. Jessee, Ronald Watt, Lauritz Petersen, Ronald Esplin, Haybron Adams, William Slaughter, Gladys Noyes, and Linda Haslam.

We appreciate the painstaking efforts of Nancy Matthews, Julie Stokes, Stephen and Jeanine Ehat, Myron Decker, Blake Penrod, Anena Turner, and Kirk and Jacqueline Sherman, who assisted in the typing, proofreading, indexing, and final preparation of the book.

John N. Drayton, managing editor at Brigham Young University Press, has contributed significantly to the style and format of the text and the readability of the footnotes.

Donald Barney, manager of Seventy's Mission Bookstore, first recognized the importance of this study and worked for its publication.

Richard L. Anderson and James B. Allen, professors at Brigham Young University, gave encouragement and shared important materials used in this book.

We are particularly grateful to LaMar C. Berrett and Truman G. Madsen, directors in the Religious Studies Center at Brigham Young University, who over the years have given direction and constant encouragement, and have extended to us financial assistance that has substantially helped us in the preparation of this volume.

Finally, we are greatly indebted to our wives, Lori and Lynette, for their encouragement and long-suffering during the writing and preparation of this book.

Editorial Note

Every effort has been made to present a faithful copy of the original reports of Joseph Smith's discourses. By retaining original spelling, punctuation, and paragraphing we hoped to preserve the integrity of the documents. The footnotes provide biographical data on each individual mentioned in the text, doctrinal insights into many of the Prophet's teachings, historical background to each sermon, bibliographic information on each report, and references to scriptures the Prophet quoted but were not identified. Unless otherwise indicated, all discourses were delivered at Nauvoo, Illinois.

*   An asterisk is used to denote scriptural revisions made by Joseph Smith but not reflected in the manuscripts of the Inspired Translation of the Bible.

[ ]   The occasional use of brackets denotes the insertion by the editors of letters, words, or phrases for clarification.

{ }   Braces are used for two purposes: (1) to enclose in the original report words that are not the Prophet's but that give contextual background to his remarks and (2) to enclose words that come from the "Book of the Law of the Lord."

. . . Ellipses are used to delete from the text remarks made by individuals other than the Prophet. In no case are ellipses used to delete portions of Joseph Smith's discourses.

~~Joseph~~ Words struck out in the originals (e.g. recorder's errors) have been retained by drawing a line through the word(s).

(1) In footnotes the use of parentheses after the date of a discourse suggests that there is more than one discourse for that date. "(1)" denotes the first discourse, and "(2)" denotes the second discourse.

17 n 2 In the index a boldface page number following a name indicates the page on which is found a biographical note for that individual.

Abbreviations

History of the Church Joseph Smith, Jr. *History of The Church of Jesus Christ of Latter-day Saints,* ed. B. H. Roberts, 2nd ed. rev., 7 vols. (Salt Lake City: Deseret News, 1932-51).

Teachings *Teachings of the Prophet Joseph Smith.* Joseph Fielding Smith, comp. (Salt Lake City: Deseret Book Company).

Millennial Star	*The Latter-day Saints' Millennial Star*, 1840-1970. Manchester and Liverpool, England.
Times and Seasons	*Times and Seasons*, 1839-1846. Nauvoo, Illinois.
Lectures on Faith	*A Compilation Containing the Lectures on Faith*, N. B. Lundwall, comp. (Salt Lake City: n.p., n.d.).
Journal of Discourses	*Journal of Discourses*, 26 vols. (1851-1886) Liverpool, England.
JST	Joseph Smith Translation of the Holy Bible, entries contained in the Holy Bible published by The Church of Jesus Christ of Latter-day Saints, 1979 or The Holy Scriptures, A New Corrected Edition, The Reorganized Church of Jesus Christ of Latter Day Saints.
Journal History	Journal History of The Church of Jesus Christ of Latter-day Saints, Church Archives, Salt Lake City, Utah.

1839

1839

1839

27 June 1839 (Thursday).[1]
Willard Richards[2] Pocket Companion

Other important items of doctrines from
Joseph given in Commerce Ills
On the Doctrines of <u>Faith</u>
Faith comes by hearing the word of God[3] through the testimony of the Servants of God, that Testimony is always attended by the Spirit of prophecy & Revelation.

<u>Repentance</u>
Is a thing that cannot be trifled with every day. Daily transgression & daily repentance is not that which is pleasing in the sight of God—

Baptism
Is a holy ordinance preparatory to the reception of the Holy Ghost. It is the channel & Key by which the Holy Ghost will be administered The gift of the Holy Ghost by the laying on of hands cannot be received through the medium of any other principle. <u>than the principle of Righteousness</u>, for if the proposals are not complied with it is of no use but withdraws.

<u>Tongues</u>.
Were given for the purpose of preaching among those whose language is not understood as on the day of Pentecost &c[4], & it is not

necessary for tongues to be taught to the church particularly. for any man that has the Holy Ghost, can speak of the things of God in his own tongue, as well as to speak in another, for faith comes not by signs but by hearing the word of God.

The doctrine of the Resurrection of the Dead & Eternal Judgment are necessary to preach among the first principles of the gospel of Jesus Christ.[5]—

The Doctrine of Election

St Paul exhorts us to make our Calling & Election shure.[6] This is that sealing power spoken of by Paul in other places (See Eph I. 13.14. In whom ye also trusted, that after ye heard the work of truth; the gospel of your salvation, in whom also after that ye believed ye were sealed with that Holy Spirit of promise. Which is the earnest of our inheritance, until the redemption of the purchased possession unto the praise of his glory.) That we may be sealed up unto the day of redemption, this principle ought. (in its proper place[7]) to be taught, for God hath not revealed any thing to Joseph, but what he will make known unto the Twelve[8] & even the least Saint may know all things as fast as he is able to—bear them. for the day must come when no man need say to his neighbor know ye the Lord for all shall know him (who Remain) from the least to the greatest, How is this to be done? It is to be done by this sealing power & the other comforter spoken of which will be manifest by Revelation.[9] There is two Comforters spoken of is the Holy Ghost the same as given on the day of pentecost and that all Saints receive after faith. Repentance & Baptism. This first comforter or Holy Ghost has no other effect than pure inteligence. It is more powerful in expanding the mind enlightening the understanding & storeing the intellect with present knowledge of a man who is of the literal Seed of Abraham than one that is a gentile though it may not have half as much visible effect upon the body for as the Holy Ghost falls upon one of the Literal Seed of Abraham it is calm & serene & his whole soul & body are only exercised by the pure spirit of Inteligence; while the effect of the Holy Ghost upon a Gentile is to purge out the old blood & make him actually of the seed of Abraham. That man that has none of the blood of Abraham (naturally) must have a new creation by the Holy Ghost,[10] in such a case there may be more of a powerful effect upon the body & visible to the eye than upon an Israelite, while the Israelite at first might be far before the Gentile in pure inteligence

The other Comforter spoken of is a subject of great interest & perhaps understood by few of this generation, After a person hath faith in Christ, repents of his sins & is Baptized for the remission of his sins & received the Holy Ghost (by the laying on of hands) which is the first Comforter then let him continue to humble himself before God, hungering & thirsting after Righteousness. & living by every word of God & the Lord will soon say unto him Son thou shalt be exalted.[11] &c When the Lord has thoroughly proved him & finds that the man is determined to serve him at all hazard. then the man will find his calling & Election made sure[12] then it will be his privilege to receive the other Comforter which the Lord hath promised the saints as is recorded in the testimony of St John in the XIV ch from the 12th to the 27 verses Note the 16.17.18.21.23. verses. (16.vs) & I will pray the father & he shall give you another Comforter, that he may abide with you forever; (17) Even the Spirit of Truth;[13] whom the world cannot receive because it seeth him not, neither knoweth him; but ye know him; for he dwelleth with you & shall be in you.[14] (18) I will not leave you comfortless. I will come to you (21) He that hath my commandments & keepeth them, he it is that loveth me. & he that loveth me shall be loved of my father. & I will love him & will manifest myself to him (23) If a man Love me he will keep my words. & my Father will love him. & we will come unto him, & make our abode with him.

Now what is this other Comforter? It is no more or less than the Lord Jesus Christ himself & this is the sum & substance of the whole matter, that when any man obtains this last Comforter he will have the personage of Jesus Christ to attend him or appear unto him from time to time. & even he will manifest the Father unto him & they will take up their abode with him, & the visions of the heavens will be opened unto him & the Lord will teach him face to face & he may have a perfect knowledge of the mysteries of the kingdom of God, & this is the state & place the Ancient Saints arrived at when they had such glorious vision Isaiah, Ezekiel, John upon the Isle of Patmos, St Paul in the third heavens, & all the Saints who held communion with the general Assembly & Church of the First Born &c.[15]

The Spirit of Revelation[16] is in connection with these blessings. A person may profit by noticing the first intimation of the Spirit of Revelation for instance when you feel pure Inteligence flowing unto you it may give you sudden strokes of ideas that by noticeting it you may find it. fulfilled the same day or Soon. (I.E.) those things that were presented unto your minds by the Spirit of God will come to pass and thus by learning the Spirit of God. & understanding it you may grow into the principle of Revelation. until you become perfect in Christ Jesus

An Evangelist[17]

Is a patriarch even the oldest man of the Blood of Joseph or of the seed of Abraham, wherever the Church of Christ is established in the earth, there should be a patriarch for the benefit of the posterity of the Saints as it was with Jacob. in giving his patriarchal blessing unto his Sons &c.—[18]

Wilford Woodruff Journal[19]

I spent the day in Commerce in Council with the Presidency & Twelve we had an interesting day Joseph was president of the Council Brother Orson Hide[20] was restored to the Church and the quorum of the Twelve in full fellowship by a full vote of the Council. after making an humble Confession & acknowledgement of his Sins &c ⬡ ▨ ▥ ⊞ Among the vast number of the Keys of the Kingdom of God Joseph presented the following one to the Twelve for there benefit in there experience & travels in the flesh which is as follows. In order to detect the devel when he transforms himself nigh unto an angel of light. When an angel of God appears unto man face to face in personage & reaches out his hand unto the man & he takes hold of the angels hand & feels a substance the Same as one man would in shaking hands with another he may then know that it is an angel of God, & he should place all Confidence in him Such personages or angels are Saints with there resurrected Bodies, but if a personage appears unto man & offers him his hand & the man takes hold of it & he feels nothing or does not sens any substance he may know it is the devel, for when a Saint whose body is not resurrected appears unto man in the flesh he will not offer him his hand for this is against the law given him & in keeping in mind these things we may detec the devil that he decieved us not.[21]

2 July 1839 (Tuesday). Brigham Young[1] Dwelling, Montrose, Iowa Territory.[2]

Wilford Woodruff Journal

Then Joseph arose & presented some precious things of the

kingdom unto us in the power of the Holy Ghost, Yea precious principles that ought to be engraven upon our hearts & practiced in our lives. Some of which are as follows. Ever keep in exercise the principles of mercy & be ready to forgive our brother on the first intimations of repentance & asking forgiveness & should we even forgive our brother or our enemy before they ask it our heavenly father would be equally as merciful unto us. & also we ought to be willing to repent of & confess all of our own sins & keep nothing back, & let the Twelve be humble & not be exalted & beware of pride & not seek to excell one above another but act for each others good & honorably make mention of each others name in our prayrs before the Lord & before our fellow men, & not backbite & devour our brother. Why will not man learn Wisdom by precept & example at this late age of the world & not be oblieged to learn every thing we know by sad experiance. Must the new ones that are chosen to fill the places of those that are fallen of the quorum of the Twelve, begin to exhalt themselves untill they get so high that they will tumble over & have a great fall & go wallowing through the mud, mire, & darkness Judas like to the buffatings of Satan as several of the Twelve have done,[3] or will they learn wisdom & be wise (O God give them wisdom & keep them humble I pray) When the Twelve or any other witness of Jesus Christ stands befor the Congregations of the earth & they preach in the power & demonstration of the Holy Ghost & the people are asstonished & confounded at the doctrin & say that that man has preached a powerful discours a great sermon then let that man or those men take care that they do not asscribe the glory unto themselves but be careful that they are humble & asscribe the praise & glory to God & the Lamb for it is by the power of the Holy Priesthood & the Holy Ghost that they have power thus to speak. What art thou O man but dust & from wholm dost thou received thy power & blessings but from God, then O ye Twelve notice this ⊘━▤Key & be wise for Christ sake & your own souls sake. Ye are not sent out to be taught but to teach[4] let every man be sober be vigilent & let all his words be seasoned with grace[5] & keep in mind that it is a day of warning & not of many words.[6] Act honest before God & man beware of gentile sophestry such as bowing & scraping unto men in wholm you have no confidence be honest open & frank in all your intercourse with mankind

O ye Twelve and all saints, profit by this important Key ⊜▦ that in all your trials troubles &, temptations, afflictions bonds imprisonment & death See to it that you do not betray heaven, that you do not betray Jesus Christ, that you do not betray your Brethren, & that you do not betray the revelations of God whether in the bible, Book of Mormon, or Doctrine & Covenants or any of the word of God. Yea in all your kicking, & floundering see to it that you do not this thing lest innocent blood be found in your skirts & you go down to hell. We may ever know by this sign that there is danger of our being led to a fall & aposticy. When we give way to the devil so as to neglect the first known[indecipherable] but whatever you do do not betray your Friend. [See Appendix A.]

7 July 1839 (Sunday).[1]
Wilford Woodruff Journal

Joseph addressed us in few words & says remember brethren that if you are imprisiond Brother Joseph has been imprisiond before you. if you are placed whare you can ownly see your Brethren through the gates of a window while in Irons because of the gospel of Jesus Christ remember Brother Joseph has been in like[2] circumstances also after other similar remarks the meeting closed.

Before 8 August 1839 (1).[1]
Willard Richards Pocket Companion

<u>The Priesthood was.</u>
first given to Adam: he obtained the first Presidency & held the Keys of it, from generation to Generation; he obtained it in the creation before the world was formed as in Gen. 1, 26:28,—he had dominion given him over every living Creature. He is Michael, the Archangel, spoken of in the Scriptures,—Then to Noah who is Gabriel, he stands next in authority to Adam in the Priesthood; he was called of God to this office & was the Father of all living in his day, & To him was given the Dominion. These men held keys, first on earth, & then in Heaven.—The Priesthood is an everlasting principle & Existed with God from Eternity & will to Eternity, without beginning of days or end of years.[2] the Keys have to be brought from heaven whenever the Gospel is sent.—When they are revealed from Heaven it is by Adams Authority.

Dan VII Speaks of the Ancient of days, he means the oldest man, our Father Adam, Michael; he will call his children together, &

hold a council with them to prepare them for the coming of the Son of Man. He, (Adam) is the Father of the human family & presides over the Spirits of all men, & all that have had the Keys must stand before him in this great Council. This may take place before some of us leave this stage of action. The Son of Man stands before him & there is given him glory & dominion.—Adam delivers up his Stewardship to Christ, that which was deliverd to him as holding the Keys of the Universe, but retains his standing as head of the human family.[3]

The Spirit of Man is not a created being; it existed from Eternity & will exist to eternity. Anything created cannot be Eternal. & earth, water &c—all these had their existence in an elementary State from Eternity.[4] Our Savior speaks of Children & Says their angels always stand before my father.[5]

The Father called all spirits before him at the creation of Man & organized them. He (Adam) is the head, was told to multiply.[6] The Keys were given to him, and by him to others & he will have to give an account of his Stewardship, & they to him. The Priesthood is everlasting. The Savior, Moses, & Elias—gave the Keys to Peter, James & John on the Mount when they were transfigured before him.[7] The Priesthood is everlasting, without beginning of days or end of years, without Father, Mother &c,—

If there is no change of ordinances there is no change of Priesthood. Wherever the ordinances of the Gospel are administered there is the priesthood. How have we come at the priesthood in the last days? They it came down, down in regular succession. Peter James & John had it given to them & they gave it up. Christ is the Great High priest; Adam next.—Paul speaks of the Church coming to an innumerable company of Angels, to God the Judge of all, the Spirits of Just men made perfect, to Jesus the mediator of the New Covenant, &c. Heb XII, 23. I saw Adam in the valley of Ah-dam-ondi-Ahman[8]—he called together his children & blessed them with a Patriarchal blessing. The Lord appeared in their midst, & he (Adam) blessed them all, & foretold what should befall them to the latest generation—See D.C. Sec III 28,29 par[9]—This is why Abraham[10] blessed his posterity: He wanted to bring them into the presence of God. They looked for a city, &c.[11]—Moses sought to bring the children of Israel into the presence of God, through the power of the Pristhood, but he could not.[12] In the first ages of the world they tried to establish the same thing—& there were Elias's raised up who tried to restore these very glories but did not obtain them. But (Enoch did for himself & those that were with Him, but not for the world. J.T.[13]) they prophesied of a day when this Glory would be revealed.—Paul spoke of the Dispensation of the fulness of times, when God would gather together all things in one &c &.[14] Those men to whom these Keys have been given will have to be there. (I.E. when Adam shall again assemble his children of the Priesthood, & Christ be in their midst) the Ancient of Days come &c &c J.T.) And they without us cannot not be made perfect.[15] These men are in heaven, but their children are on Earth. Their bowels yearn over us. God sends down men for this reason, Mat. 13. 41. & the Son of man shall send forth his Angels &c—All these authoritative characters will come down & join hand in hand in bringing about this work—The Kingdom of heaven is like a grain of mustard seed. the mustard seed is small but brings forth a large tree, and the fowls lodge in the branches The fowls are the Angels,[16] the Book of Mormon perhaps, these Angels come down combined together to gather their children, & gather them. We cannot be made perfect without them, nor they without us when these things are done the Son of man will descend, the ancient of Days sit.—We may come to an innumerable company of Angels have communion with & receive instruction from them.—Paul told about Moses's proceedings. Spoke of the Children of Israel being baptized,[17] &c, he knew this & that all the ordinances, & blessings were in the Church. Paul had these things; & we may have the fowls of the heaven lodge in the branches &c. The horn made war with the Saints, & overcame them &c, until the Ancient of Days came, judgment was given to the Saints of the Most High, from the Ancient of Days—the time came that the Saints possessed the kingdom—this not only makes us ministers here but in Eternity. Salvation cannot come without revelation, it is in vain for anyone to minister without it.

No man is a minister of Jesus Christ, without being a Prophet. No man can be the minister of Jesus Christ, except he has the testimony of Jesus & this is the Spirit of Prophecy.[18] Whenever Salvation has been adminsitered it has been by Testimony. Men at the present time testify of Heaven & of hell, & have never seen either—& I will say that no man knows these things without this. Men profess to prophecy. I will prophecy that the signs of the coming of the Son of Man are already commenced, one pestilence will dessolate after another, we shall soon have war & bloodshed.[19] The Moon will be turned to blood.[20] I testify of these things, & that the coming of the Son of Man is nigh even at your doors.—If our Souls & our bodies are not looking forth for the coming of the Son of Man, & after we are dead if we are not looking forth, &c we shall be among those who are calling for the rocks to fall upon us &c[21]—The hearts of the children will have to be turned to the fathers, & the fathers to the children living or dead to prepare them for the coming of the Son of Man. If Elijah did not come the whole earth would be smitten.[22] There will be here & there a stake &c. For the gathering of the Saints Some may have cried peace, but the Saints & the world will have little peace from henceforth. Let this not hinder us from going to the Stakes, for God has told us to flee not dallying, or we shall be scattered, one here, another there.[23] There your children shall be blessed & you in the midst of friends where you may be blessed. &c The Gospel net gathers of every kind.[24] I prophecy that the man who tarries after he has an opportunity of going will be aflicted by the Devil. Wars are at hand we must not delay, but we are [are we?] not required to Sacrifice.[25] We ought to have the building up of Zion as our greatest object.—when wars come we shall have to flee to Zion, the cry is to make haste. The last revelation says ye shall not have time to have gone over the Earth until these things come.[26] It will come as did the cholera,[27] war, & fires burning earthquake, one pestilence after another &c until the Ancient of Days come then judgment will be given to the Saints.

Whatsoever you may hear about me or Kirtland, take no notice of,[28] for if it be a place of refuge the Devil will use his greatest efforts to trap the Saints. You must make yourselves acquainted with those men, who, like Daniel pray three times a day to the house of the Lord.[29]—Look to the Presidency &c. & receive instruction. Every man who is afraid, covetous &c will be taken in a snare.—The time is soon coming when no man will have any peace but in Zion & her Stakes.[30] I saw men hunting the lives of their own sons, & brother murdering brother, women killing their own daughters & daughters seeking the lives of their mothers. I saw armies arrayed against armies I saw blood, desolations, & fires &c,—The Son of Man has said that the mother shall be against the daughter, & the daughter against the mother &c, &c,—these things are at our doors.[31] They will follow the Saints of God from City to City—Satan will rage & The Spirit of the Devil is now enraged, &c I know not how soon these things will take place, and with a view of them shall I cry peace? No! I will lift up my voice & testify of them. How long you will have good crops, & the famine be kept off. I do not know. When the fig tree leaves, know then that the summer is nigh at hand.[32] we may look for Angels &c. & recieve their ministering but we are to try the spirits & prove them.[33] for it is often the case that men make a mistake in regard to these things.

God has so ordained that when he has communicated by vision no vision [is] to be taken but what you see by the seeing of the eye or what you hear by the hearing of the ear—When you see a vision &c pray for the interpretation if you get not this, shut it up.[34]—There must be certainty in this matter. An open vision will manifest that which is more important. Lying Spirits are going forth in the Earth.

There will be great manifestation of Spirit both false & true. &c. Being born again comes by the Spirit of God through ordinances.[35] An angel of God never has wings. Some will say that they have seen a Spirit, that he offered them his hand, but they did not touch it. This is a lie. First it is contrary to the plan of God A Spirit cannot come but in glory.[36] An angel has flesh and bones, we see not their glory. The Devil may appear as an angel of light. Ask God to reveal it, if it be of the Devil, he will flee from you, if of God he will manifest himself or make it manifest, we may come to Jesus & ask him. he will know all about it.—If he comes to a little child, he will adapt himself to the Language & capacity of a little child.—There is no Gold nor Silver &c.[37] it is false, all is plain in heaven; every Spirit or vision or Singing is not of God. The Devil is an orator, &c: he is powerful: he took our Savior onto a pinnacle of the temple, & kept him in the wilderness for forty days.[38] The gift of discerning spirits will be given to the presiding Elder, pray for him. that he may have this gift[39] Speak not in the Gift of tongues without understanding it, or without interpretation, The Devil can speak in Tongues. The Adversary will come with his work, he can tempt all classes, Can speak in English or Dutch.—Let no one speak in tongues unless he interpret except by the consent of the one who is placed to preside, then he may discern or interpret or another may. Let us seek for the Glory of Abraham, Noah, Adam, the Apostles have communion with these things and then we shall be among that number when Christ comes.

Before 8 August 1839 (2).[1]
Willard Richards Pocket Companion

Parables

Behold a sower went forth to Sow &c Our Savior is the Sower; the people are the world; the harvest is the end of the world; the reapers are the angels[2]

The end of the world is not come, consequently the Harvest. The harvest cannot come without Angels;[3] The Son of Man is to send forth his Angels. The Son of man Said that the Saints shall judge the world & Angels.[4]—God has revealed himself. when they come up before God they will be asked did this Angel perform this or that. that he was sent to do. if not they will be judged—The world judg—

Some fell among thorns &c—

God sows—The enemy comes & sows parties divisions, heresies; Shall we kill them?[5] No, not till harvest—The end of the world. The Son of God will do as he ever has done from the beginning. Send forth his Angels. If the reapers do not come, the wheat cannot be Saved. Nothing but Kingdom being restored, can save the world. Like unto a treasure hid in a field. This figure is a representation of the [kingdom] in the last days.[6] Michael==Adam. Noah. I am Gabriel—Well says I. Who are you? I am Peter, the angel flying through the midst of heaven Moroni delivered the Book of Mormon.[7] The pearl of great price is the inheritance prepared for the Saints.[8] Sell all you have got, purchase &c. What is the end of the world? the destruction of the wicked.[9] The Angels have begun to be revealed. They shall bind up the testimony Like unto a merchant man buying goodly Pearls A net that gathers of every kind. The wheat gathers in of every kind Those who hold Keys were more concerned about their children than themselves. It happens to be our Lot to live in a day when this takes place.

Before 8 August 1839 (3).[1]
Willard Richards Pocket Companion

It is the privilege of the Children of God to come to God & get Revelation. XIV John [verse 1] Let not your heart be troubled &c, [verse 2] There are a great many Mansions in my Father's house. I am going to prepare one for you rather Better than common. It is the privilege of the Sons of God to inherit the same Mansion &c. When any person receives a vision of Heaven, he sees things that he never thought of before.[2] if we should tell of different glories as Paul did, in my fathers house there are Many Mansions, every Man that receives the Gospel receives that inheritance that the Apostles did. [verse 9] Everyone that hath seen me hath seen the Father. [verse 12] He that believeth, any person that believes the works I do shall he do also & greater works [verse 13] The Father could not be glorified in the Son [verse 13] on any other principle than we coming to God, asking, receiving, heavens open visions &c.—They are done away because of unbelief—[verse 16] I will pray the Father & he shall send you another Comforter. There is one Comforter [i.e. the Holy Ghost] & another Comforter to abide with you forever, reach to things within the vail, know that you are Sealed. If you get it, it will stand by you forever. How is it obtained? Keep my commandments & I will pray &c.—[verse 17] It is a privilege to view the Son of Man himself, he dwelleth with you & shall be in you, his spirit shall be in you.[3] [verse 18] I will not have you comfortless, I will come to you, abide with you forever, Seal you up to Eternal life. [verse 19] Yet a little while & you shall see me no more, but ye see me.—[verse 21] He that hath my commandments & keepeth them, he it is that loveth me &c.—I will manifest myself to him. if he does not he has not told the truth. I will put promises in your hearts, that will not leave you that will Seal you up. We may come to the general assembly & church of the first born, Spirits of Just men made perfect, unto Christ. The innumerable company of Angels are those that have been resurrected from the dead. the Spirits of Just men made perfect are those without bodies.[4] It is our privilege to pray for & obtain these things. [verse 22] How wilt thou manifest thyself to us & not to the world? evidently knowing that it would be so that he would manifest himself.[5] There was no cholera, no mobs, before this came. I told them that rejoiced in Mobs that they should have them, they have since come in torrents. they did not receive the testimony of the Servants of the Son of God. [verse 23] If a man love me he will keep my words, & my father will love him, & We both me & my father will take our abode with him.[6] There are certain characters that walked with God, saw him, conversed about heaven &c. [verse 26] but the comforter that I will send, (not the other comforter) shall teach you all things.—who?—He that loveth me &c—This shall bring all things to remembrance whatsoever things I have said unto you, he shall teach you until ye come to me & my father. God is not a respecter of persons, we all have the same privilege. Come to God weary him until he blesses you &c—we are entitled to the same blessings, Jesus, revelations, Just Men &—Angels &c. &c. not Laying again the doctrine of Christ go on unto perfection. Obtain that holy Spirit of promise—Then you can be sealed to Eternal Life.[7]

22 September 1839 (Sunday).[1]
Joseph Smith Diary, by James Mulholland[2]

Attended & presided at meeting—Spoke concerning the other Comforter &c &c &c.[3]

29 September 1839 (Sunday). Old Homestead.[1]
Joseph Smith Diary, by James Mulholland

Meeting at own house (After others had spoken I spoke and explained concerning uselessness of preaching to the world about great judgements but rather to preach the simple gospel—Explained concerning the coming of the Son of Man &c that all will be raised to meet him, but the righteous will remain with him in the cloud whilst all the proud and all that do wickedly will have to return to the earth and suffer his vengeance which he will take upon them this is the second death &c &c[2]

Also it is a false idea that the saints will escape all the judgements whilst the wicked suffer—for all flesh is subject to suffer—and "the righteous shall hardly escape"[3] still many of the Saints will escape—for the just shall live by faith[4]—Yet many of the righteous shall fall a prey to disease to pestilence &c by reason of the weakness of the flesh and yet be saved in the Kingdom of God So that it is an unhallowed principle to say that such and such have transgressed because they have been preyed upon by disease or death for all flesh is subject to death and the Saviour has said—"Judge not" lest ye be judged."[5]

5 October 1839 (Saturday).[1]
Times and Seasons 1 (December 1839):30

The President then spoke at some length upon the situation of the Church, the difficulties they had had to contend with, and the manner in which they had been led to this place;[2] and wished to know the views of the brethren whether they wished to appoint this a stake or not, stating that he believed it to be a good place and suited for the saints. It was then unanimously agreed upon, that it should be appointed a stake and a place of gathering for the saints.

6 October 1839 (Sunday Morning).[1]
Times and Seasons 1 (December 1839):30-31

After some remarks from the President respecting observing order and decorum during conference, Elder Lyman Wight,[2] spoke as to the duties of Priests, Teachers, &c.

President J. Smith, Jr. then spoke as to appointing a Patriarch and other matters connected with the well being of the church. Having now got through the business matters, the President proceeded to give instructions to the Elders respecting preaching the gospel, and pressed upon them the necessity of getting the spirit, so that they might preach with the Holy Ghost sent down from heaven, to be careful in speaking on those subjects which are not clearly pointed out in the word of God, which lead to speculation and strife.

7 October 1839 (Monday Morning).[1]
Times and Seasons 1 (December 1839):31

Conference met pursuant to adjournment.

The President spoke at some length to the Elders, and explained many passages of scripture . . . .

After having referred the business not gone into, to the high council; the president then returned thanks to the conference for their good attention and liberality; and having blessed them in the name of the Lord, the conference was dismissed.

1839 NOTES

27 June 1839

1. See *History of the Church*, 3:371-81, and *Teachings*, pp. 148-51. Wilford Woodruff's account of this discourse is here published for the first time. While the following two accounts of the 27 June 1839 discourse do not parallel one another, there is, nevertheless, sufficient reason to believe that the date is accurate for both reports. Whereas Woodruff's account is dated, Willard Richards's Pocket Companion account is not. John Taylor was undoubtedly the recorder of the account found in the Pocket Companion, which would have been copied by Richards in England. John Taylor's notes may well confirm the date of the discourse as 27 June 1839, but his notes have not been found, if in fact they still exist. The best evidence that 27 June 1839 is the accurate date is the fact that Wilford Woodruff, with George A. Smith, assigned it that date when they included the discourse in the "Manuscript History of the Church." Unlike the "Before 8 August 1839 (1)" discourse, which Woodruff and Smith refused to date, they confidently placed the date 27 June 1839 on the Pocket Companion account. Moreover, Woodruff admits that his notes of the discourse were incomplete, that he recorded only some of the "vast number Keys of the Kingdom" given by the Prophet on that occasion. The day before this discourse was given such matters were being discussed by the Brethren, in Joseph Smith's absence, as revealed in Woodruff's journal under date of 26 June 1839. Clearly the discourse made a deep impression on those who heard it, as well as on Willard Richards, who later copied it into his Pocket Companion. This discourse probably encouraged Brigham Young and Willard Richards to write "Election and Reprobation" for the *Millennial Star* (vol. 1, no. 9).

2. Willard Richards (1804-54) was converted to the Church in 1836. He was ordained an apostle in England in April 1840 and served as a scribe to the Prophet 1841-44.

3. Romans 10:17.* Regarding the "Spirit of Prophecy and Revelation" that accompanies the "testimony of the Servants of God," see Ephesians 1:17; 2 Peter 1:5-9; Revelation 19:10; Alma 5:46-47; 6:8; 8:24; 9:21; 10:12; 13:26; 17:3; 23:6; 43:2; 45:10; Helaman 4:12; 3 Nephi 3:19; D&C 8:2-3; 11:25; 107:30-31; 113:10.

4. Acts 2:1-13.

5. Hebrews 6:1-2. In this statement Joseph Smith emphasized that the doctrines of resurrection and eternal judgment should be taught as part of the fundamental articles of faith by the missionaries. He repeatedly referred to and amplified this theme in discourses during the Nauvoo period. See also D&C 19:4, 8-9, 21-22 (1-24).

6. It is possible that Joseph Smith said, "St *Peter* exhorts us to make our Calling and Election sure": the phraseology is Peter's not Paul's (2 Peter

1:10). On the other hand, Joseph does say in the next sentence that when Paul speaks of the sealing power (2 Corinthians 1:20-22; Ephesians 1:13-14; 4:30), he is speaking of the doctrine of making our calling and election sure. More significant, however, is the fact that this is the first record we have of a discourse by the Prophet Joseph on this doctrine using Peter's words "calling and election sure." To be sure the general concept was taught as early as 1834 because Oliver Cowdery says that the Saints "make their calling and election sure" when they "obtain the promise from the Lord of glory ('hear his voice . . . [and receive] a promise from his mouth') that their salvation was sealed that their election was sure" (see *The Evening and The Morning Star* 2 [June 1834]:167). Furthermore, in 1835 Joseph Smith wrote to his uncle Silas to convince him that revelation was still necessary, reasoning that the modern Saints had to hear an audible voice from the Lord by revelation to know that their salvation was secure, just as their ancient counterparts had received such assurances by revelation. However, in this letter Joseph Smith made no allusion to Peter's "calling and election" wording (Oliver R. Smith, ed., *Six Decades in the Early West: The Journal of Jesse Nathaniel Smith; Diaries of a Mormon Pioneer, 1834-1906*. 3d ed. [Provo, Utah: Jesse N. Smith Family Association, 1970], pp. 3-4). These instructions by the Prophet Joseph on making one's calling and election sure reminded Heber C. Kimball (who undoubtedly was present at this meeting) of an experience just two months previous. He recorded in his journal, "[On 6 April 1839] the following words came to my mind, and the Spirit said unto me, 'write,' which I did by taking a piece of paper and writing on my knee as follows: . . . 'Verily I say unto my servant Heber, thou art my son, in whom I am well pleased; for thou art careful to hearken to my words, and not transgress my law, nor rebel against my servant Joseph Smith, for thou hast a respect to the words of mine anointed, even from the least to the greatest of them; therefore thy name is written in heaven, no more to be blotted out for ever, because of these things" (Heber C. Kimball Journal, Library-Archives, the Historical Department of The Church of Jesus Christ of Latter-day Saints, Salt Lake City, Utah [hereafter referred to as Church Archives]).

7. As Joseph Smith here defines it, making one's calling and election sure is the crowning achievement of a life of righteous devotion. However, the Prophet apparently senses that if this concept is too commonly taught it could easily generate within the Church a misguided devotion to a principle that could divert the Saints' energy from the equally important principle of selfless devotion to others. Seeking blessings for oneself only is contrary to the principle that "He that loseth his life for my sake shall find it" (Matthew 10:39).

8. The nature of the presiding authority of the Quorum of the Twelve Apostles developed over several years. In 1835, when they were first organized, they were recognized as special missionaries with jurisdiction limited to the areas where there were no organized stakes. In 1841, after their return from Great Britain, the Twelve were appointed a position next

to the First Presidency in settling the Saints in the stakes of Zion. Given the roles of Brigham Young and Heber C. Kimball (senior members in the Twelve) in organizing and moving the Saints from Missouri to Quincy, Illinois, when the Prophet was in Liberty Jail, this statement (in 1839) seems to foreshadow the later development.

9. Joseph Smith asked rhetorically how the Lord's restatement (D&C 84:98) of Jeremiah's great prophecy on the last days (Jer. 31:31-34) was to be fulfilled. He answered that it will be fulfilled when the Saints' callings and elections are made sure and when they receive the Second Comforter.

10. 2 Corinthians 5:17.

11. John 6:27, 66-71 (cf. JST John 6:27); 14:12-15; 17:2-3; Acts 13:48; Romans 6:23; 2 Corinthians 1:20-22; 1 Timothy 6:12; 2 Timothy 4:6-8; Titus 1:1-3; Hebrews 11:2, 4-6, 13, 26-27, 33, 39-40; 2 Peter 1:10-11, 19; 1 John 1:1-3; 2:25 (20-27); 3:15; 5:11-13 (1-20); Revelation 7:1-3; 14:1-5; 2 Nephi 31:20; Enos 5-8, 27; Mosiah 5:15; 26:20; Helaman 10:4-10; 3 Nephi 28:3, 10 (1-15); Mormon 2:19; Ether 12:37 (19-40); Moroni 10:34; D&C 53:1; 59:23; 68:12; 76:50-53, 58, 70 (50-70); 77:8-9, 11; 131:5-6; 132:7, 19-24, 26-27; 46-50, 59-60; Moses 1:4, 25-26; 5:4-11; 6:34 (26-36), 52-68; 7:27, 62-64; Abraham 2:6-11 (cf. Genesis 22); JST Genesis 9:21-23; JST Genesis 14:26-35 (cf. Alma 13); and, JST 1 John 3:9. See also the Apocrypha, 2 Esdras 2:33-48.

12. 2 Peter 1:10.

13. D&C 93:26 also identifies Jesus Christ with the title normally assigned to the Holy Ghost, namely, the Spirit of Truth.

14. Verse 20 of this chapter of John indicates that when a man receives the blessings of the Second Comforter, as Joseph Smith defines them in this discourse, then, "At that day ye shall know that I am in my Father, and ye in me, and I in you." See the same idea in D&C 88:49-50, 66-69.

15. Isaiah 6; Ezekiel 1, 40-47; the book of Revelation; 1 Corinthians 12:1-4; and Hebrews 12:22-24. Regarding the last passage on the "Church of the Firstborn," see also D&C 76:50-54, 67, 94, 102, and 118 (114-119); 78:20-21; 88:3-5; 93:21-22; and 129.

The theme of the "other Comforter" as the personal appearance of the Savior to those faithful saints *after* they have made their calling and election sure was a prevalent theme not only in Joseph Smith's discourses throughout the remainder of his life, but also in the scriptures he previously recorded. See 2 Nephi 1:15; 2:3; 10:2-3; 25:13; Mosiah 27:30; 3 Nephi 19:14-36; Mormon 1:15; Ether 3:6-16; 9:22; 12:39; D&C 67:10; 76:5-10, 22-25, 114-19; 84:18-27; 88:3-5, 67-69, 75; 93:1; 97:16; 101:23, 38; 103:20; 107:18-20, 49, 53-57; 109:5, 12; and 110:1-10. See also D&C 130:3.

16. D&C 8:2-3. See scriptural references listed in note 3, this discourse. In regard to the assertion that the Spirit of Revelation is in connection with

the blessings of Calling and Election and the Second Comforter, Joseph Smith later stated that making one's calling and election sure was "by revelation and the spirit of prophecy" (D&C 131:5).

17. Ephesians 4:11; D&C 107:39-57.

18. Genesis 48 and 49.

19. Wilford Woodruff (1807-98). Baptized in December 1833, Woodruff was ordained an apostle in 1839 and in 1889 became the fourth president of the Church.

20. Orson Hyde (1805-78) was converted to the Church in 1831 and was ordained an apostle in 1835. In 1841, as a special assignment from the Prophet, he dedicated the land of Israel for the return of the Jews.

21. The morning after the visitations from the angel Moroni (21-22 September 1823), Joseph Smith went to the side of the hill Cumorah to unearth the plates he had seen in his vision. As he later told Oliver Cowdery, on the road to Cumorah he became fixed and determined to obtain the plates for wealth and prestige and not for the glory of God. Only after attempting unsuccessfully three times to remove the plates from the stone box in which they were enclosed did he become aware that Moroni was present. The angel indicated that he was permitted by God to be led by this evil spirit so that from that time forth he would always know the difference between a true spirit and an evil spirit. This was only a beginning of his instructions in the gift of discerning spirits (D&C 46:15-16, 23, 27). Subsequent revelations through Joseph Smith gave greater detail concerning keys to detecting the adversary. D&C 50:30-35 gave instructions that if after prayer a spirit would not manifest itself, the individuals involved would have power to rebuke the spirit. Joseph Smith had experience himself with this type of manifestation. On the banks of the Susquehanna River, Michael appeared to intervene and detect the devil when he appeared as an angel of light (D&C 128:20), indicating another dimension to this question of detection. Because the adversary apparently can take light and truth away from the disobedient (D&C 93:39), he can attempt to pass as an angel of glory (2 Corinthians 11:14; D&C 129:8; Moses 1:2, 9, 11-25). As indicated in this discourse, Joseph Smith therefore revealed additional keys of detection. Far from saying that when the instructions of this discourse were followed, the adversary's only recourse was to attempt to return the handshake, in a December 1840 discourse Joseph says, "The Devil . . . will either shrink back . . . or offer his hand." He will not remain absolutely still if he is tested. On 28 April 1842, the Prophet revealed to the Relief Society, and on 1 May 1842 to the Nauvoo populace, that there was another dimension for determining whether manifestations and revelations were approved by God. There were "keys of the kingdom," he said to a Sunday audience of the saints in the Grove, "certain signs and words by which false spirits and personages may be

detected from true, which cannot be revealed to the Elders till the Temple is completed . . . . There are signs . . . the Elders must know . . . to be endowed with the power, to finish their work and prevent imposition" (1 May 1842 discourse). Three days later Joseph Smith revealed these sacred keys to nine men—in accordance with his plans as announced to the Relief Society just six days before (28 April 1842). To these men he taught the keys of prayer and detection whereby all false documents, revelations, or manifestations could be tested (*Times and Seasons* 5 [15 September 1844]:649-50 and Letter of Orson Hyde, George A. Smith, and Ezra T. Benson to Brigham Young, dated 5 April 1849, Brigham Young Collection, Church Archives). They were so sacred that when Heber C. Kimball wrote to fellow apostle Parley P. Pratt just a few weeks later, he said that Joseph had taught them some precious things on the priesthood that would cause his soul to rejoice if he knew them, but that Joseph had given instructions that these keys not be written about. Heber concluded his description of the newly revealed endowment by saying that Parley would have to come to Nauvoo to receive the instruction for himself (Letter of Heber C. Kimball to Parley P. Pratt, 17 June 1842, Church Archives). Parley arrived in Nauvoo on 7 February 1843, and although the Prophet made him wait ten months before giving him his endowment (2 December 1843), after only two days he partially satisfied Parley's curiosity by giving him the instructions contained in D&C 129—the same instructions as given in this discourse, 27 June 1839 (see also Joseph Smith Diary, 9 February 1843, Church Archives). George A. Smith, who received his endowment with Parley P. Pratt in December 1843, and who also was a witness to all the dimensions of Joseph's teachings on this subject, later said, "There was no point upon which the Prophet Joseph dwelt more than the discerning of Spirits" ("Minutes of Meetings held in Provo City," 28 November 1869, Church Archives). This may be true because the Prophet insisted that true religion was one of individual participation in revelation from God but that in their zeal many could be deceived.

2 July 1839

1. Brigham Young (1801-77) was baptized in 1832 and ordained an apostle in 1835. He became the second President of the Church in 1847.

2. See *History of the Church*, 3:383-85, and *Teachings*, pp. 155-56.

3. The Prophet is referring to Thomas B. Marsh, William E. M'Lellin, and Luke and Lyman Johnson. Initially, in 1838, Orson Hyde sided with Marsh in opposing the Prophet, but by now Hyde had been reinstated.

4. D&C 43:15.

5. Colossians 4:6.

6. D&C 63:58.

7 July 1839

1. The following instructions, probably given to members of the Quorum of the Twelve Apostles prior to their leaving for England, are here published for the first time.

2. An obvious allusion to the Prophet's Missouri incarceration from November 1838 to April 1839.

Before 8 August 1839 (1)

1. See *History of the Church*, 3:385-92, and *Teachings*, pp. 157-62. Although this discourse is given the date 2 July 1839 in *Teachings*, the original compilers of the "Manuscript History of the Church," George A. Smith and Wilford Woodruff, had insufficient documentation to place a precise date on the report. They chose, instead, to give it an approximate date of "about this time" (see *History of the Church*, 3:385). In the absence of conclusive evidence, there is no reason to assume that this discourse should be dated 2 July 1839. Because the initials "J.T." appear in two separate notes in this discourse (as recorded in Willard Richards's Pocket Companion), it is probable that it was recorded by John Taylor. Furthermore, because John Taylor and Wilford Woodruff left for England on 8 August 1839, we have simply assigned the date "Before 8 August 1839" to the discourse.

2. Alma 13:7-9; D&C 84:17 (1-17); Abraham 1:2-4; JST Hebrews 7:3.

3. Daniel 7:9-14, 21-22, 27 (1-28); D&C 29:26-28; 78:16 (13-16); 116; and, 128:18.

4. D&C 93:29, 30, 33 (29-35). Whether one believes that the spirit of man is a special act of creation at the time of birth (as in Catholic theology) or that man's spirit had a premortal existence *beginning* at the time of the Creation (as in some Protestant theology), the creation of the spirit of men is viewed as essentially a creation *ex nihilo*—out of nothing. Joseph Smith rejected the *ex nihilo* concept very early (D&C 93:29, 30, 33 (29-35); a 6 May 1833 revelation); nevertheless, this discourse contains his first public reference to the concept, which received its closest attention in the celebrated King Follett sermon (7 April 1844). Here the Prophet extends his discussion of *ex nihilo* creation to the self-existence of all matter. According to Joseph Smith, God did not utterly transcend existence by creating from nothing time, space, and matter; rather, these things always existed: He is composed of matter, occupies space, and lives in an eternity of time. During the Nauvoo period, Joseph Smith repeatedly discussed this and thus implicitly dealt with the ultimate questions of reality—the question of the existence of God, the nature of man, and the problem of evil and suffering.

5. Matthew 18:10.

6. Before this discourse, no published scriptures of the Church had fully synthesized Joseph Smith's apparently well developed concept of the premortal existence of mankind. To be sure, the Book of Mormon and the Doctrine and Covenants contained elements of the concept, but not until 1842 would the book of Abraham be published, which tells of Abraham's vision of the premortal condition of the human family (see Abraham 3:22-4:1). Thus this discourse is a very significant statement of theology on the part of the Prophet when taken in conjunction with his previously recorded scriptures on this subject (in chronological order): 2 Nephi 2:17-18; 9:8-9, 16; Mosiah 3:6; Alma 13:2-5; Moses 1:33-34; D&C 29:28, 36-40, 42; Moses 3:4-5; 4:1-4; 5:6-7, 24; 76:25-28, 44; 93:29, 30, 33, 38.

7. Matthew 17:1-13.

8. "Ah-dam" stands for Adam. Orson Pratt speaks of an uncanonized revelation Joseph Smith received in which the Lord revealed words of Adam's language including the word Ahman used in this name-title of the land where Adam dwelt (*Journal of Discourses* 26 vols. [Liverpool, England: F. D. Richards, *et al.*, 1854-86], 2:342). The above pronunciation of Adam (as "Ah-dam") is interesting, given that in Hebrew the first syllable in the name Adam is pronounced with an umlaut-a sound (that is, aw-dawm'), rather than the short sound as in our anglicized form.

9. D&C 107:53-57 in our present edition of the Doctrine and Covenants.

10. It seems probable that Joseph Smith said "Adam," but the recorder of this sermon wrote "Abraham." On the other hand, the name recorded might be correct, in which case the Prophet might possibly be providing insight to Hebrews 11:8-10* beyond what is explicitly stated in that passage of scripture.

11. Hebrews 11:8-10. See also "Church of the First Born" passages in 27 June 1839, note 15.

12. Exodus 19, 20; D&C 84:19-25. See also JST Exodus 34:1-2.

13. The initials "J. T." undoubtedly stand for John Taylor. John Taylor (1808-87) was baptized in 1836 and was ordained an apostle in December 1838. He became the third President of the Church in 1880.

14. Ephesians 1:10.

15. Hebrews 11:40. A year and a half later this passage of scripture was used as a proof-text for the validity of the doctrine of Baptism for the Dead. This application of Hebrews 11:40 makes it difficult to know whether the ordinance of Baptism for the Dead had yet been revealed to Joseph Smith, though aspects of the Doctrine of Salvation for the Dead had previously been revealed. See D&C 137.

16. The insight that the "fowls" in Matthew 13:31-32* represent "angels" is consistent with other interpretations the Savior gave in this chapter; there is no explicit explanation of the Mustard Seed parable. This is an example of the Prophet's amplifying the text of the Bible beyond what is recorded in the manuscripts of his translation of that book.

17. 1 Corinthians 10:1 (1-4).

18. Revelation 19:10. See also the scriptures listed in 27 June 1839, note 3.

19. D&C 38:29-31; 45:63-75; 86; 87; 131:12-13. Joseph Smith's certainty that the signs of the Second Coming had commenced may have had its basis in Moroni's 1823 instructions that these signs were soon to be fulfilled.

20. On the night of 21-22 September 1823, when the angel Moroni appeared to Joseph Smith he quoted Joel's prophecy regarding the moon's turning into blood, and told Joseph "that this was not yet fulfilled, but was soon to be." (See Joel 2:31 and JS-H 1:41.)

21. Regarding the ability of those in the Spirit World to witness the second coming of the Savior, see Revelation 1:7; 6:12-17; and, D&C 88:92-110.

22. Malachi 4:5-6.

23. D&C 42:64; 45:68; 133:12-13.

24. Matthew 13:47-50. See also *Teachings*, p. 102.

25. Psalm 50:5. See also *Lectures on Faith* 6:9.

26. The Prophet may be alluding to a presently unknown revelation or simply expressing his awe at the magnitude of the work to be accomplished before the Second Coming.

27. Cholera is a term applied to a wide variety of acute diarrheal diseases of short duration. Very common in Asia, it was, for example, between 1898 and 1907 responsible for at least 370,000 deaths. Oliver Cowdery, who watched the spread of Cholera, believing it to be a sign of the last days, reported that an outbreak in India in 1817 spread to England by 1830 and finally to America by 1832 (*The Evening and The Morning Star* 2 [September 1834]:189).

28. This appears to be a reference to the failure of the Kirtland Bank and to certain lawsuits in which Joseph Smith was involved.

29. Daniel 6:10.

30. D&C 45:69.

31. Matthew 10:35.

32. Matthew 24:32-33.

33. 1 John 4:1. See 27 June 1839, note 21 and *Teachings*, pp. 202-15.

34. Daniel 8:26; D&C 76:47 (40-49). See also 27 June 1839, note 21.

35. D&C 52:14-20; 84:19-25; Moses 6:57-68; JST Exodus 34:1-2.

36. In a later address Joseph Smith clarified this observation on the glory of spirits when he said, "Spirits can only be revealed in flaming fire, or glory. Angels have advanced farther—their light and glory being tabernacled, and hence appear in bodily shape" (9 October 1843 discourse). See 27 June 1839, note 21.

37. Revelation 21:21 (17-21).

38. Matthew 4:5.

39. D&C 46:23, 26.

Before 8 August 1839 (2)

1. The following report in Willard Richards's Pocket Companion was undoubtedly recorded by John Taylor. It is here published for the first time.

2. Matthew 13:3, 24-30, 36-43; D&C 86. See also *Teachings*, pp. 97-8, 100-101.

3. The Second Coming must come in a period of modern revelation when angels appear again. Matthew 13:39-42, and *Teachings*, pp. 101-102.

4. Matthew 19:27-30; Luke 22:24-30; 1 Corinthians 6:1-3.

5. This is, of course, a paraphrase of the question the angels asked of the Savior (Matthew 13:28-30).

6. Matthew 13:44. See *Teachings*, p. 101.

7. Revelation 14:6-7 apparently refers to several angels conferring their keys and knowledge of the gospel to Joseph Smith.

8. Matthew 13:45-46; D&C 88:107.

9. Joseph Smith first distinguished between the words *world* and *earth* (a distinction not made in the King James Version of the Bible) in 1832 when he translated Matthew 24 (see JS-M 1:4, 55; see also the 5 January 1841 discourse: "The world and earth are *not* synonymous terms. The world is the human family." By this reasoning the "end of the world" would mean "the end of the wicked part of the human family.").

Before 8 August 1839 (3)

1. The following report in Willard Richards's Pocket Companion was undoubtedly recorded by John Taylor. It is here published for the first time.

2. Isaiah 64:4; 2 Corinthians 2:9; D&C 76:10.

3. It is confusing to speak of Christ's dwelling within those sealed up unto eternal life, yet the Savior says that *after* we enjoy the blessings of the Second Comforter, "then shall [you] know that . . . I am the true light that is in you, and that you are in me" (D&C 88:50). The same is said in John chapter 14: "At that day [when you receive the Second Comforter] ye shall know that I am in my Father, and ye in me, and I in you" (see also JST Luke 10:23).

In John 14:17 Christ is also speaking of himself as the source of truth. Similarly, he declared to Joseph Smith, "I am the Spirit of Truth" (D&C 93:26). However, the Savior and the Holy Ghost work in perfect oneness when bestowing these, the highest spiritual blessings of mortality, for the Savior said of the Holy Ghost, "He shall glorify me: for he shall receive of mine, and shall shew it unto you" (John 15:14). The emphasis in John 14:16-17 is the concept that the Savior has been appointed by the Father to be our ultimate source of comfort and truth.

4. This appears to be the first time Joseph Smith in a sermon explicitly distinguished between the terms *angels* and *spirits of just men made perfect* as used in Hebrews 12:22-24 (see D&C 129 and 27 June 1839, note 15).

5. That is, Joseph Smith found verse 22 conclusive evidence that the apostles understood clearly that Jesus was referring to himself (and not to the Holy Ghost) when he spoke of "another Comforter."

6. See 2 April 1843 discourse (Joseph Smith Diary by Willard Richards); D&C 130:2.

7. In a certain limited sense, a sense Joseph Smith used many times, the phrase "Holy Spirit of Promise" has reference to the concept of "making your calling and election sure" or "being sealed up unto eternal life" (D&C 88:3-5). Thus, when the *Holy Spirit* (who was the one appointed by the Father to give final sanctioning authority for all priesthood blessings) receives authorization from Jesus Christ to unmistakably "seal" the *promise* of eternal life on a worthy individual, he is placing the seals on the highest gospel ordinances in his office as Holy Spirit of Promise (D&C 132:7). The Prophet expressed this concept in his poetic rendition of D&C 76 (v. 53):

> For these overcome, by their faith and their works,
>   Being tried in their life-time, as purified gold,
> And seal'd by the spirit of promise, to life,
>   By men called of God, as was Aaron of old.

(*Times and Seasons* 4 [1 February 1843]:84).

22 September 1839

1. See *History of the Church*, 4:10. Not in *Teachings*.

2. James Mulholland (1804-39) was born in Ireland and was converted to the Church in Upper Canada. He served as Joseph Smith's scribe 1838-39.

3. The "&c &c &c" used to conclude this brief reference of Joseph Smith's discourse suggests that the topic "the other Comforter" was a theme which the Prophet was discussing often at this time. Three of the six discourses reported thus far contain this theme. The theme is taken from John 14.

29 September 1839

1. See *History of the Church*, 4:11 and *Teachings*, pp. 162-63. The "Old Homestead" was the Prophet's first residence at Nauvoo. Located on Water Street, block 155, it was also known as the "Old Log House."

2. D&C 88:95-104. See also discourse dated "Before 8 August 1839 (1)," note 21.

3. D&C 63:34.

4. Habakkuk 2:4; Romans 1:17; Galatians 1:11.

5. Matthew 7:1.

5 October 1839

1. See *History of the Church*, 4:12. Not in *Teachings*. The following remarks were made at the October 1839 General Conference of the Church.

2. Members of the Church first became aware of Nauvoo in October or November 1838 when Israel Barlow, who with other Saints had fled northeastward towards Quincy, Illinois from Far West, Missouri. But losing his way arrived at the Des Moines River in Iowa. Crossing the Mississippi River Barlow came to old Commerce, Illinois and found Isaac Galland, owner of several parcels of land in Lee County Iowa as well as Commerce. Not authorized to make purchases for the Church, Elder Barlow directed his course downstream to Quincy. Subsequently, an exploring party was sent to examine Galland's lands. But while some Church leaders were in favor of gathering to Commerce, Illinois, and Lee County, Iowa, others suggested that the membership of the Church should scatter among the various counties in Illinois and elsewhere. In the meantime, Joseph Smith, who was incarcerated in Missouri, learned of Galland's offer and counseled the brethren to purchase the properties. When Joseph Smith escaped from Missouri law enforcement officers on 16 April 1839 he went immediately to Quincy arriving there on 22 April. At a council meeting held two days later, on 24 April 1839, it was resolved that "President Joseph Smith, Jun., Bishop Knight, and Brother Alanson Ripley, visit Iowa Territory immediately, for the purpose of making a location for the Church" (*History of the Church*, 3:336). Properties at Commerce were purchased from Isaac Galland on 30 April 1839, and immediately thereafter the Saints began to settle the area (see Lyndon W. Cook, "Isaac Galland—Mormon Benefactor." *Brigham Young University Studies* 19 [Spring 1979]:267-70).

6 October 1839

1. See *History of the Church*, 4:13. Not in *Teachings*. The following remarks were made at the October 1839 General Conference of the Church.

2. Lyman Wight (1796-1858) was baptized in 1830. He was ordained one of the Quorum of Twelve Apostles in April 1841.

7 October 1839

1. See *History of the Church*, 4:13-15. Not in *Teachings*. The following remarks were made at the October 1839 General Conference of the Church.

1840

1840

1840

1 January 1840 (Wednesday). Philadelphia, Philadelphia County, Pennsylvania.[1]
Times and Seasons 1 (May 1840): 104

We had a conference here the first of Jan. 1840, J. Smith, Jr. S. Rigdon,[2] Orson,[3] P.P. Pratt,[4] and many other elders, were present. The minutes of the above, I will send to you as soon as convenient.[5] J. Smith, jr. bore testimony to the coming forth of the book of mormon which was the means of doing much good.[6]

13 January 1840 (Monday Afternoon). Philadelphia, Philadelphia County, Pennsylvania.[1]
Philadelphia Branch Minutes[2]

Brother Joseph Smith Jr. dilated at some length on the offices of the Priesthood and on the duties of Elder, Bishops, Priests, &c. and directed it should be entered on the minutes as the injunction of the Presidency that travelling Elders should be especially cautious of incroaching on the ground[3] of stationed & presiding Elders and rather direct their efforts to breaking up and occupying new ground and that the Churches generally refuse to be burthened with the support of unprofitable and dilatory labourers.

25 January 1840 (Saturday). Brandywine, Chester County, Pennsylvania.[1]
Times and Seasons 1 (March 1840): 79

On Saturday last (Jan. 25) a conference of elders was held in the Brandywine branch; pres't. Joseph Smith Jr. being present, was called to preside, and James Rodeback[2] appointed clerk. Two elders and two priests were ordained; great harmony prevailed in the meeting, and much important instruction was given to the elders and members present by pres't. Smith. The saints in that place appear determined to keep the commandments of God; and the visit of brother Smith among them, I trust has tended much to strengthen, and confirm them in the faith of the everlasting gospel.

5 February 1840 (Wednesday Evening). Washington, D.C.[1]
History of the Church, 4:78-80

Washington, 6th February, 1840.

My Dear Mary:—I went last evening to hear "Joe Smith," the celebrated Mormon, expound his doctrine. I, with several others, had a desire to understand his tenets as explained by himself. He is not an educated man; but he is a plain, sensible, strong minded man. Everything he says, is said in a manner to leave an impression that he is sincere. There is no levity, no fanaticism, no want of dignity in his deportment. He is apparently from forty to forty-five years of age,[2] rather above the middle stature, and what you ladies would call a very good looking man. In his garb there are no peculiarities; his dress being that of a plain, unpretending citizen. He is by profession a farmer, but is evidently well read.

He commenced by saying, that he knew the prejudices which were abroad in the world against him, but requested us to pay no respect to the rumors which were in circulation respecting him or his doctrines. He was accompanied by three or four of his followers. He said, "I will state to you our belief, so far as time will permit." "I believe," said he, "that there is a God, possessing all the attributes ascribed to Him by all Christians of all denominations; that He reigns over all things in heaven and on earth, and that all are subject to His power." He then spoke rationally of the attributes of

Divinity, such as foreknowledge, mercy &c., &c. He then took up the Bible. "I believe," said he, "in this sacred volume. In it the 'Mormon' faith is to be found. We teach nothing but what the Bible teaches. We believe nothing, but what is to be found in this book. I believe in the fall of man, as recorded in the Bible; I believe that God foreknew everything, but did not foreordain everything; I deny that foreordain and foreknow is the same thing. He foreordained the fall of man; but all merciful as He is, He foreordained at the same time, a plan for redemption for all mankind. I believe in the Divinity of Jesus Christ, and that He died for the sins of all men, who in Adam had fallen." He then entered into some details, the result of which tended to show his total unbelief of what is termed *original sin*. He believes that it is washed away by the blood of Christ, and that it no longer exists. As a necessary consequence, he believes that we are all born pure and undefiled. That *all* children dying at an early age (say *eight* years) not knowing good from evil, were incapable of sinning; and that all such assuredly go to heaven. "I believe," said he, "that a man is a moral, responsible, free agent; that although it was foreordained he should fall, and be redeemed, yet after the redemption it was not foreordained that he should again sin. In the Bible a rule of conduct is laid down for him; in the Old and New Testaments the law by which he is to be governed, may be found. If he violates that law, he is to be punished for the deeds done in the body.

I believe that God is eternal. That He had no beginning, and can have no end. Eternity means that which is without beginning or end. I believe that the *soul* is eternal; and had no beginning; it can have no end. Here he entered into some explanations, which were so brief that I could not perfectly comprehend him. But the idea seemed to be that the soul of man, the spirit, had existed from eternity in the bosom of Divinity; and so far as he was intelligible to me, must ultimately return from whence it came. He said very little of rewards and punishments; but one conclusion, from what he did say, was irresistible—he contended throughout, that everything which had a *beginning* must have an *ending*; and consequently if the punishment of man *commenced* in the next world, it must, according to his logic and belief have an *end*.[3]

During the whole of his address, and it occupied more than two hours, there was no opinion or belief that he expressed, that was calculated, in the slightest degree, to impair the morals of society, or in any manner to degrade and brutalize the human species. There was much in his precepts, if they were followed, that would soften the asperities of man towards man, and that would tend to make him a more rational being than he is generally found to be. There was no violence, no fury, no denunciation. His religion appears to be the religion of meekness, lowliness, and mild persuasion.

Towards the close of his address, he remarked that he had been represented as pretending to be a Savior, a worker of miracles, etc. All this was false. He made no such pretensions. He was but a man, he said; a plain, untutored man; seeking what he should do to be saved. He performed no miracles. He did not pretend to possess any such power. He closed by referring to the Mormon Bible, which he said, contained nothing inconsistent or conflicting with the Christian Bible, and he again repeated that all who would follow the precepts of the Bible, whether Mormon or not, would assuredly be saved.

Throughout his whole address, he displayed strongly a spirit of charity and forbearance. The Mormon Bible, he said, was com-municated to him, *direct from heaven*. If there was such a thing on earth, as the author of it, then he (Smith) was the author; but the idea that he wished to impress was, that he had penned it as dictated by God.

I have taken some pains to explain this man's belief, as he himself explained it. I have done so because it might satisfy your curiosity, and might be interesting to you, and some of your friends. *I have changed my opinion of the Mormons*. They are an injured and much-abused people. Of matters of *faith*, you know I express no opinon.

Affectionately your husband,
M. L. Davis.[4]

Christian Advocate and Journal (6 March 1840)[5]

A delegation of the "Mormons" having been in this city [Washington] some time, to seek remuneration of congress for their Missouri losses, Joseph Smith ("Jo Smith" as known to fame) has held one or two meetings here. I dropped in a little while on the evening of the 4th instant[6] to see and hear. The Prophet, or inspired penman, (whichever title he prefers, for he averred to the meeting that he was inspired to write the golden Bible, or the "Book of Mormon," a copy of which he held in his hand,) is a stout, square-built man of about thirty or thirty-five years of age, of prepossessing manner, and *look*, and *shrewd* mind. He has evidently a good English education, and is an energetic, impassioned speaker. The doctrines he professes in Washington are similar to those of the Campbelites of the west, laying great stress on baptism "FOR" the remission of sins. He quotes from the New Testament readily in his addresses. He took good care, as there was an intelligent congregation, including several members of congress, present, to say but little about the "Book of Mormon." He averred, however that nobody wrote it but him, and that it contained nothing contrary to the Bible, or its virtue. In describing the sufferings of his followers in Missouri he was somewhat eloquent, as he has a good voice for the pathetic.

1 March 1840 (Sunday).[1]
John Smith Diary[2]

Sabbath March 1st ... visited my aged Br Joseph who has been sick all winter found him very low went to meeting Joseph ~~gave~~ spoke to the people was much interested.

6 April 1840 (Monday).[1]
Times and Seasons 1 (April 1840):92

The president rose and made some observations on the business of the conference; exhorted the brethren who had charges to bring against any individual to be charitable; and made some very appropriate remarks respecting "pulling out the beam in their own eyes, that they might see clearly the mote which was in their brothers eye."[2]

7 April 1840 (Tuesday).[1]
Times and Seasons 1 (April 1840):92-93

The President called upon the Clerk to read the report of the Presidency and High council, with regard to their proceedings in purchasing lands and securing a place of gathering for the saints.

The report having been read, the President made some observations respecting the pecuniary affairs of the church, and requested the brethren to step forward and assist in liquidating the debts on the town plot, so that the poor might have inheritances.

He then gave some account of his mission to Washington city, in company with President Rigdon and Judge Higbee,[2] the treatment they received and the action of the Senate on the memorial which was presented to them.[3]

8 April 1840 (Wednesday Afternoon)[1].
Times and Seasons 1 (April 1840): 94

Conference met pursuant to adjournment, after singing the President arose and read the 3d chap. of John's Gospel after which prayer was offered by elder Erastus Snow.[2]

The President commenced making observations on the different subjects embraced in the chapter particularly on the 3d, 4th, 5th verses illustrating it with a very beautiful and striking figure, and throwing a flood of light on the subjects which were brought up to review.[3]

He then spoke to the elders respecting their mission, and advised those who went into the world, to preach the gospel, to leave their families provided for, with the necessaries of life; and to teach the gathering as set forth in the Holy scriptures.[4]

That it had been wisdom to, for the greater body of the church to keep on this side of the river, in order that a foundation might be established in this place, but that now, it was the privilege of the saints to occupy the lands in the Iowa, or wherever the spirit might lead them.[5]

That he did not wish to have any political influence, but wished the saints to use their political franchise to the best of their knowledge.

He then stated that since Elder Hyde had been appointed to visit the Jewish people, he had felt an impression that it would be well for Elder John E. Page[6] to accompany him on his mission.

30 July 1840 (Thursday).[1]
John Smith Diary

Thurs 30 Went to Nauvoo attend fast & Prayer Meeting for the

Purpose of calling on the lord that he would pacify the Elements &c that health may be restored to the Saints. Joseph said that inasmuch as the Saints will leaving of Speaking evil of one another & not Speaking evil of the Seer which Speaking evil of the archangel or the holy Keys which he held & the archangel & if the church would cease from these bickerings & murmerings & be of one mind the Lord would visit them with health & every needed good, for said he this is the voice of the Spirit. furthermore if the Saints are sick or have sickness in their families, and the Elders do not prevail every family should get power by fasting & prayer & anointing with oil & continue so to do their sick shall be healed this also is the voice of the Spirit.

9 August 1840 (Sunday). Lee County, Iowa Territory.[1]
John Smith Diary

Sabath 9 Joseph & Hyrum[2] commenced delivering a course of lectures to the Church in Iowa upon the first Principles of the gospel.[3] More particularly the Ressurrection from the dead & eternal Judgement also the Doom of Murderers & Adulterers &c.[4]

15 August 1840 (Saturday).[1]

[The first discourse by Joseph Smith on baptism for the dead]

16 August 1840 (Sunday). Lee County, Iowa Territory.[1]
John Smith Diary

Sunday 16th Joseph & Hyrum meet with us today Spoke upon Eternal Judgement or continued their Lectures

30 August 1840 (Sunday). Lee County, Iowa Territory.[1]
John Smith Diary

Sabath 30 Joseph Smith Jr continued his discourse on eternal Judgement and the eternal duration of matter.[2]

3 October 1840 (Saturday Morning).[1]
Times and Seasons 1 (October 1840):185

The president arose and stated that there had been several

depredations committed on the citizens of Nauvoo, and thought it expedient that a committee be appointed, to search out the offenders, and bring them to justice. . . . The president then rose, and stated that it was necessary that something, should be done with regard to Kirtland, so that it might be built up; and gave it as his opinion, that the brethren from the east might gather there, and also, that it was necessary that some one should be appointed from this conference to preside over that stake.[2]

3 October 1840 (Saturday Afternoon).[1]
Times and Seasons 1 (October 1840):186

The president then spoke of the necessity of building a "House of the Lord" in this place.[2]

4 October 1840 (Sunday Morning).[1]
Times and Seasons 1 (October 1840):186

President Joseph Smith jr. then arose and delivered a discourse on the subject of baptism for the dead, which was listened to with considerable interest, by the vast multitude assembled.

5 October 1840 (Monday Morning).[1]
Original Manuscript, in hand of Robert B. Thompson[2]

In order to investigate the subject of the Priesthood so important to this as well as every succeeding generation, I shall proceed to trace the subject as far as I possibly can from the Old and new Testament.

There are two Priesthoods spoken of in the Scriptures, viz the Melchisadeck and the Aaronic or Levitical Altho there are two Priesthoods, yet the Melchisadeck Priesthood comprehends the Aaronic or Levitical Priesthood[3] and is the Grand head, and holds the highest Authority which pertains to the Priesthood the keys of the Kingdom of God in all ages of the world to the latest posterity on the earth and is the channel through which all knowledge, doctrine, the plan of salvation and every important matter is revealed from heaven.[4] Its institution was prior to "the foundation of this earth or the morning stars sang together or the Sons of God shouted for joy,"[5] and is the highest and holiest Priesthood and is after the order of the Son [of] God, and all other Priesthoods are only parts, ramifications, powers and blessings belonging to the same and are held controlled and directed by it. It is the channel through which the Almighty commenced revealing his glory at the beginning of the creation of this earth and through which he has continued to reveal himself to the children of men to the present time and through which he will make known his purposes to the end of time— Commencing with Adam who was the first man who is spoken of in Daniel as being the "Antient of days" or in other words the first and oldest of all, the great grand progenitor of whom it is said in another place he is Michael because he was the first and father of all, not only by progeny, but he was the first to hold the spiritual blessings,[6] ~~the plan~~ to whom was made known the plan of ordinances for the Salvation of his posterity unto the end,[7] and to whom Christ was first revealed, and through whom Christ has been revealed from heaven and will continue to be revealed from henceforth. Adam holds the Keys of the dispensation of the fulness of times, i.e. the dispensation of all the times have been and will be revealed through him from the begining to Christ and from Christ to the end of all ~~world~~ the dispensations that have [been and] are to be revealed

Ephesians 1st Chap 9 & 10 verses. "Having made known unto us the mystery of his will, according to his good pleasure which he has purposed in himself that in the dispensation of the fulness of times he might gather together in one all things in Christ both which are in heaven and which are on earth in him" Now the purpose in himself in the winding up scene of the last dispensation is, that all things pertaining to that dispensation should be conducted precisely in accordance with the preceeding dispensations. And again, God purposed in himself that there should not be an eternal fulness until every dispensation should be fulfilled and gathered together in one and that all things whatsoever that should be gathered together in one in those dispensations unto the same fulness and eternal glory should be in Christ Jesus, therefore he set the ordinances to be the same for Ever and ever and set Adam to watch over them to reveal them from heaven to man or to send Angels to reveal them[8] Heb 1 Chap. 16 verse. Are they not all ministring spirits sent forth to minister to those who shall be heirs of Salvation. These angels are under the direction of Michael or Adam who acts under the direction of Christ.

From the above quotation we learn that Paul perfectly understood the purpose of God in relation to his connexion with man, and
that glorious and perfect order which he established in himself
whereby he sent forth power revelations and glory. God will not
acknowledge that which he has not called, ordained, and chosen. In
the begining God called Adam by his own voice See Genesis 3 Chap
9 & 10 verses. And the Lord called unto Adam and said unto him
where art thou, and he said I heard thy voice in the garden and I was
afraid because I was naked and hid myself. Adam received commandments and instruction from God. this was the order from the
begining: that he received revelations, Commandments, and
ordinances at the begining is beyond the power of controversy,
else, how did they begin to to offer Sacrifices to God in an acceptable
manner? And if they offered sacrifices they must be authorized by
ordination. We read in Gen 4th Chap. v. 4 That Abel brought of the
firstlings of the flock and the fat thereof and the Lord had respect to
Abel and to his offring. And again Heb 11 Chap 4 verse. By Faith
Abel offered unto God a more excellent Sacrifice than Cain by which
he obtained witness that he was righteous God testifying of his gifts
and by it he being dead yet speaketh. how doth ye yet speak? Why
he magnified the Priesthood which was confired upon him and
died a righteous man, and therefore has become a ~~righteous man~~ an
angel of God by receiving his body from the dead,[9] therefore
holding still the keys of his dispensation and was sent down from
heaven unto Paul to minister consoling words & to commit unto
him a knowledge of the mysteries of Godliness and if this was not
the case I would ask how did Paul know so much about Abel and
why should he talk about his speaking after he was dead. How that
he spoke after he was dead must be, by being sent down out of
heaven, to administer. This then is the nature of the priesthood,
every man holding the presidency of his dispensation and one man
holding the presidency of them all even Adam, and Adam receiving
his presidency and authority from Christ, but cannot receive a
fulness, untill Christ shall present. the kingdom to the Father which
shall be at the end of the last dispensation.[10] The power, glory, and
blessings of the priesthood could not continue with those who
received ordination only as their righteousness continued,[11] for
Cain also being authorized to offer sacrifice but not offering it in
righteousness, therefore he was cursed. It signifies then, that the

ordinances must be kept in the very way God has appointed, otherwise their priesthood will prove a cursing instead of a blessing.[12] If Cain had fulfilled the law of righteousness as did Enoch he could have walked with God all the days of his life and never failed of a blessing. Gen [5:22] And Enock walked with God after he begat Mathusalah 300 years and begat Sons and Daughters and all the days of Enoch were 365 years and Enoch walked with God and he was not for God took him. Now this Enoch God reserved unto himself that he shoud not die at that time and appointed unto him a ministry unto terrestiral bodies of whom there has been but little revealed, He is reserved also unto the presidency of a dispensation. and more shall be said of him and terrestrial bodies in another treaties[13] He is a ministring Angel to minister to those who shall be heirs of Salvation and appered unto Jude as Abel did unto Paul. therefore Jude spoke of him 14 & 15 verses in Jude. and Enoch the seventh revealed these sayings. Behold the Lord cometh with ten thousand of his saints Paul was also aquainted with this character and received instructions from him. Heb 11 Chap. 5 ver By Faith Enoch was translated that he should not see death, and was not found because God had translated him for before his translation he had this testimony that he pleased God. But without faith it is impossible to please God, for he that cometh to God must believe that he is, and that he is a revealer[14] to those who diligently seek him.

Now the doctrine of translation is a power which belongs to this priesthood, there are many things which belong to the powers of the priesthood and the keys thereof that have been kept hid from before the foundation of the world.[15] they are hid from the wise and prudent to be revealed in the last times many may have supposed that the doctrine of translation was a doctrine whereby men were taken immediately into the presence of God and into an Eternal fulness but this is a mistaken idea. There place of habitation is that of the terrestrial[16] order and a place prepared for such characters, ~~he had in~~ he held in reserve to be ministring angels unto many planets, and who as yet have not entered into so great a fulness as those who are resurrected from the dead. See Heb 11 Chap part of the 35 verse "others were tortured not accepting deliverance that they might obtain a better resurrection" Now it was evident, that there was a better resurrection or else God would not have revealed it unto Paul wherein then can it be said a better ressurection? This distinction is made between the doctrine of the actual ressurrection and the doctrine of translation, the doctrine of translation obtains deliverance from the tortures and sufferings of the body but their existence will prolong as to their labors and toils of the ministry before they can enter into so great a rest and glory, but on the other hand those who were tortured not accepting deliverance received an immediate rest from their labors, See Rev [14:13] And I heard a voice from heaven saying blessed are the dead who die in the Lord for from henceforth they do rest from their labors and their works do follow them—They rest from their labors for a long time and yet their work is held in reserve for them, that they are permitted to do the same works after they receive a ressurection for their bodies, but we shall leave this subject and the subject of the terresteal bodies for another time in order to treat upon them more fully[17] The next great grand patriarch who held the Keys of the priesthood was Lamech[18] See Gen 5 Chap 28 & 29 verses—And Lamech lived 182 years and begat a Son and he called his name Noah saying this same shall comfort us concerning our work and the toil of our hands because of the ground which the Lord has curst. "The priesthood continued from Lamech to Noah Gen 6 Chap 13 verse. And God said unto Noah the end of all flesh is before me, for the earth is filled with violence through them, and behold I will destroy them with the earth," thus we behold the Keys of this priesthood consisted in obtaining the voice of Jehovah[19] that he talked with him in a familiar and friendly manner, that he continued to him the Keys, the Covenants, the power and the glory with which he blessed Adam at the beginning and the offring of Sacrifice which also shall be continued at the last time, for all the ordinances and duties that ever have been required by the priesthood under the direction and commandments of the Almighty ~~in the last dispensation at the end thereof~~ in any of the dispensations, shall all be had in the last dispensation.[20] Therefore all things had under the Authority of the Priesthood at any former period shall be had again—bringing to pass the restoration spoken of by the mouth of all the Holy Prophets. ~~Malachi 3 then shall the sons of Levi offer unto the Lord an acceptable offring~~" then shall the sons of Levi offer an acceptable sacrifice to the Lord Se[e] Malichi 3 Chap. 3&4 And he shall sit as a refiner and purifier of Silver; and he shall purify the sons of Levi, and purge them as gold and silver, that they may offer unto the Lord

It will be necessary here to make a few observations on the doctrine, set forth in the above quotation, As it is generally supposed that Sacrifice was entirely done away when the great sacrife was offered up—and that there will be no necessity for the ordinance of Sacrifice in future, but those who assert this, are certainly not aquainted with the duties, privileges and authority of the priesthood. or with the prophets The offering of Sacrifice has ever been connected and forms a part of the duties of the priesthood. It began with the prieshood and will be continued untill after the coming of Christ from generation to generation—We freequently have mention made of the offering of Sacrifice by the servants of the most high in antient days prior to the law of moses, See[21] which ordinances will be continued when[22] the priesthood is restored with all its authority power and blessings. Elijah was the last prophet that held the keys of this priesthood, and who will,[23] before the last dispensation, restore the authority and delive[r] the Keys of this priesthood in order that all the ordinances may be attended to in righteousness.

It is true that the Savior had authoritity and power to bestow this blessing but the Sons of Levi were too predjudi[ced][24]

And I will send Elijah the Prophet before the great and terrible day of the Lord &c &c.

Why send Elijah because he holds the Keys of the Authority to administer in all the ordinances of the priesthood and without the authority is given the ordinances could not be administered in righteousness.[25]

It is a very prevalent opinion that in the ~~sacrifices of~~ sacrifices which were offered were entirely consumed, this was not the case if you read Leviticus [2] Chap [2-3] verses you will observe that the priests took a part as a memorial and offered it up before the Lord, while the remainder was kept for the ~~benefit~~ maintenance of the priests.[26] So that the offerings and sacrifices are not all consumed upon the Alter, but the blood is sprinkled and the fat and certain other portions are consumed These sacrifices as well as every ordinance belonging to the priesthood will when the temple of the Lord shall be built and the Sons Levi be purified be fully restored and attended to then all their powers ramifications ramifications and blessings—this ~~the Sons of Levi shall be purified.~~ ever was and will exist when the powers of the Melchisid Priesthood are sufficiently manifest.[27] Else how can the restitution of all things spoken of by all the Holy Prophets be brought to pass ~~be brought to pass~~[28] It is not to be understood that, the law of moses will be established again with all it rights and variety of ~~ceremonies,~~ ceremonies, this had never been spoken off by the prophets but those things which existed prior Mose's day viz Sacrifice will be continued[29]—It may be asked by some what necessity for Sacrifice since the great Sacrifice was offered? In answer to which if Repentance Baptism and faith ~~were necessary to Salvation~~ existed prior to the days of Christ what necessity for them since that time[30]—

The priesthood has descended in a regular line from Father to Son through their succeeding generations

See Book of Doctrine & Covenants [107:40-52].[31]

December 1840.[1]
Extracts from William Clayton's Private Book

A Key by Joseph Smith Dec
1840—W[illiam].C[layton].[2]

If an Angel or spirit appears offer him your hand; if he is a spirit from God he will stand still and not offer you his hand. If from the Devil he will either shrink back from you or offer his hand,[3] which if he does you will feel nothing, but be deceived.

A good Spirit will not decieve.

Angels are beings who have bodies and appear to men in the form of man.

1840 NOTES

1 January 1840

1. Not in *History of the Church* or *Teachings*. Joseph Smith left Nauvoo for Washington, D.C., on 29 October 1839 to lay before Congress the grievances of the Saints who were expelled from Missouri. After spending nearly a month at the capital, the Prophet went to Philadelphia, where he occupied several days "preaching and visiting from house to house, among the brethren and others" (*History of the Church*, 4:47). On 23 December 1839, the Prophet's birthday, Joseph presided at the organizing of a branch of the Church in Philadelphia. He may well have spoken on this occasion, but we have not found any record. Following are accounts of four discourses in the D.C. area, two at Philadelphia, one at Brandywine, and two variants of a discourse in Washington. Joseph Smith spoke publicly on several other occasions during this visit to the east, and further research may turn up records of them. It is known, for example, that Joseph Smith visited a branch of the Church in Monmouth County, New Jersey, in late December 1839 (see *History of the Church*, 4:49). George Woodward, who was present on the occasion, remembered that the Prophet preached at a meeting "upon astronomy and told where God resided. It was very interesting" (St. George Temple Minute Book, p. 45 [11 January 1900] Church Archives).

2. Sidney Rigdon (1793-1876) was baptized in 1830. He served as a counselor to Joseph Smith in the Presidency from 1832-44.

3. Orson Pratt (1811-81) was baptized in 1830 and ordained an apostle in 1835.

4. Parley P. Pratt (1807-57) was baptized in 1830 and ordained an apostle in 1835.

5. If the minutes were in fact sent, they were not published in the *Times and Seasons*.

6. Parley P. Pratt left an account of this discourse in his *Autobiography*: "While visiting with brother Joseph in Philadelphia, a very large church was opened for him to preach in, and about three thousand people assembled to hear him. Brother Rigdon spoke first, and dwelt on the Gospel, illustrating his doctrine by the Bible. When he was through, brother Joseph arose like a lion about to roar; and being full of the Holy Ghost, spoke in great power, bearing testimony of the visions he had seen, the ministering of angels which he had enjoyed; and how he had found the plates of the Book of Mormon, and translated them by the gift and power of God. He commenced by saying: 'If nobody else had the courage to testify of so glorious a message from Heaven, and of the finding of so glorious a record, he felt to do it in justice to the people, and leave the event with God.' The entire congregation was astounded; electrified, as it were, and over-

whelmed with the sense of the truth and power by which he spoke, and the wonders which he related. A lasting impression was made; many souls were gathered into the fold. And I bear witness, that he, by his faithful and powerful testimony, cleared his garments of their blood (Parley P. Pratt, Jr., ed., *Autobiography of Parley Parker Pratt, One of the Twelve Apostles of the Church of Jesus Christ of Latter-day Saints* [Salt Lake City:Deseret Book Co., 1961], pp. 298-99).

13 January 1840

1. The following report is here published for the first time.

2. The Philadelphia Branch Minutes are located in the Library-Archives of the Reorganized Church of Jesus Christ of Latter Day Saints, the Auditorium, Independence, Missouri.

3. Because the presiding officer of a branch of the Church was a proselyting missionary, and because he was supported by the congregation while he was in their area, it was only reasonable that such an injunction be given by the Presidency of the Church.

25 January 1840

1. Not in *History of the Church* or *Teachings*. The *History of the Church*, 4:77 records, "About this time I visited the Saints at Brandywine, where I spent some days, and returned to Philadelphia."

2. James Rodeback (1807-75) was a native of Chester County, Pennsylvania, where he joined the Church. He moved to Utah in 1852 and was a prominent figure in Cedar City, Utah.

5 February 1840

1. Not in *Teachings*. The original source of the following report is presently unavailable. The letter was undoubtedly published in the *New York Enquirer* because Davis was the Washington correspondent for that newspaper. It seems highly unlikely that Church historians would have obtained a copy of a private letter from Davis to his wife. Richard L. Anderson has made a thorough search without success, to find this report in the *New York Enquirer*. But because there are missing numbers during this period, it does not preclude the possibility that the report was published in that paper.

2. Actually Joseph was only 34 years old.

3. See discourse dated "Before 8 August 1839 (1)," note 4.

4. Mathew Livingston Davis (1773-1850) was a journalist. Remembered for his long association with Aaron Burr, Davis was a Washington

correspondent for the *New York Enquirer* at the time the Prophet gave this discourse.

5. This report is here published for the first time in LDS sources, and we are indebted to Richard L. Anderson for making it available to us. The author of the report is unnamed, but he dated the article, "Washington, D.C., Feb. 20, 1840."

6. According to the Mathew L. Davis account, the discourse was delivered on the evening of 5 February 1840. Davis's account was written the following day, 6 February, and is undoubtedly more accurate in its dating than the present report which was prepared nearly three weeks later, on 20 February 1840.

1 March 1840

1. This report is here published for the first time. Although *History of the Church*, 4:89, indicates that the Prophet did not arrive home from Washington, D.C., until 4 March 1840, John Smith's diary is probably accurate in dating this account: it was contemporaneously written and the date given was indeed a Sunday.

2. John Smith (1781-1854) was the Prophet's uncle. He was baptized in 1832 and was appointed president of the Nauvoo Stake in October 1844, after Joseph's death.

6 April 1840

1. See *History of the Church*, 4:105. Not in *Teachings*. The *History of the Church* entry is based on the *Times and Seasons* account given in the text. The following remarks were made at the April 1840 General Conference of the Church.

2. Matthew 7:3-5.

7 April 1840

1. See *History of the Church*, 4:106-7. Not in *Teachings*. The *History of the Church* entry is based on the *Times and Seasons* account given in the text. The following remarks were made at the April 1840 General Conference of the Church.

2. Elias Higbee (1795-1843). He was baptized in 1832 and served as a member of the Nauvoo Temple Committee.

3. The Saints' petition to the United States Senate and House of Representatives for redress of their Missouri grievances is published in *History of the Church*, 4:24-38. The report of the Senate Judiciary Committee on the petition is found in *History of the Church*, 4:90-92. In summary the

report stated, "The case presented for . . . investigation is not such a one as will justify or authorize any interposition by this government."

8 April 1840

1. See *History of the Church*, 4:109. Not in *Teachings*. The *History of the Church* entry is based on the *Times and Seasons* account given in the text. The following remarks were made at the April 1840 General Conference of the Church.

2. Erastus Snow (1818-88) was baptized in 1833 and served numerous preaching missions 1836-44. He was ordained an apostle in 1849.

3. John 3:3-5.

4. A great number of passages of scripture dealing with the gathering of Israel were prominently used when this subject was presented. Representative passages include the following: Deuteronomy 30:1-5; Psalm 107:1-7; Isaiah 2:2-5; 5:25-26; 11:11-12; 43:5-7; 54:7-8; 61:4; Jeremiah 3:12-15, 18; 16:14-16; 31:7-17; 33:7-11; 34:31-34; Ezekiel 20:34-35, 42; 37:21-27; Amos 9:14-15; Matthew 24:31. See also *Teachings*, pp. 79-80, 83-89, 94-102 for letters Joseph Smith wrote on the principle of the gathering of Israel.

5. In May and June 1839 Church land agents purchased nearly 20,000 acres of land in Lee County, Iowa. Although it appears that the Prophet's desire in 1839 was to have the Saints settle on the Iowa side of the Mississippi River, opportunities subsequently allowed the Saints to acquire large parcels of land at Nauvoo, and the choice was made to build up the Illinois side. With the headquarters now firmly established, Joseph Smith is counseling the Saints to occupy the Iowa lands or "whenever the spirit might lead them" in the vicinity of Nauvoo.

6. John E. Page (1799-1867) was baptized in 1833. He was ordained a member of the Quorum of the Twelve Apostles in December 1838.

30 July 1840

1. The following report is here published for the first time.

9 August 1840

1. The following report is here published for the first time.

2. Hyrum Smith (1800-44). The Prophet's elder brother Hyrum was baptized in 1830 and was appointed Church Patriarch and Assistant President of the Church in 1841.

3. The first principles of the Gospel are defined as faith in Jesus Christ, repentance, baptism by immersion for the remission of sins, and the laying

on of hands for the gift of the Holy Ghost. As demonstrated in this discourse, the Prophet Joseph said it is necessary that the doctrines of resurrection and eternal judgment be preached as part of the first principles (Hebrews 6:1-2; see also 27 June 1839, note 5).

4. While this is the first explicit reference to the Prophet's teaching the doctrine of eternal judgment regarding murderers and adulterers, no text is provided. Undoubtedly, he taught on this occasion what he taught the Saints in Nauvoo on 16 May 1841 (see *Times and Seasons* report in this volume). See also 27 June 1839, note 5.

15 August 1840

1. On 10 August 1840 Seymour Brunson, member of the Nauvoo High Council, died in Nauvoo. The Prophet took the occasion of his funeral, on 15 August 1840, to deliver the first discourse on the doctrine of baptism for the dead (see *History of the Church*, 4:231). In a letter to John Taylor dated 9 November 1840, Heber C. Kimball provided the following additional background for this discourse. "Semer Bronson is gon. David Paten came after him. the R[o]om was full of Angels that came after him to waft him home, he was burred [buried] under arms. the Procession, that went to the grave was judged to be one mile long, and a more joyfull Season She [Vilate Kimball] Ses She never Saw be fore on the account of the glory that Joseph set forth" (Letter courtesy of Buddy Youngreen).

Although there is no known contemporary text for this discourse, Simon Baker (1811-63) left the following reminiscent account with the Historian's Office: "I was present at a discourse that the prophet Joseph delivered on baptism for the dead 15 August 1840. He read the greater part of the 15th chapter of Corinthians and remarked that the Gospel of Jesus Christ brought glad tidings of great joy, and then remarked that he saw a widow in that congregation that had a son who died without being baptized, and this widow in reading the sayings of Jesus 'except a man be born of water and of the spirit he cannot enter the kingdom of heaven,' and that not one jot nor tittle of the Savior's words should pass away, but all should be fulfilled. He then said that this widow should have glad tidings in that thing. He also said the apostle was talking to a people who understood baptism for the dead, for it was practiced among them. He went on to say that people could now act for their friends who had departed this life, and that the plan of salvation was calculated to save all who were willing to obey the requirements of the law of God. He went on and made a very beautiful discourse" (Journal History, under date, Church Archives).

16 August 1840

1. The following report is here published for the first time. This Sunday discourse was one of at least three delivered by the Prophet to the Saints in Lee County, Iowa, in August 1840.

30 August 1840

    1. This report is here published for the first time.

    2. See discourse dated "Before 8 August 1839 (1)," note 4.

3 October 1840 (1)

    1. See *History of the Church*, 4:204. Not in *Teachings*. The *History of the Church* entry is based on the *Times and Seasons* account given in the text. The following remarks were made at the October 1840 General Conference of the Church.

    2. Almon W. Babbitt was chosen president of the stake at Kirtland.

3 October 1840 (2)

    1. See *History of the Church*, 4:205. Not in *Teachings*. The *History of the Church* entry is based on the *Times and Seasons* account given in the text. The following remarks were made at the October 1840 General Conference of the Church.

    2. As in each of the Saints' gathering places before Nauvoo—in Kirtland, Independence, and Far West—temple sites were selected and dedicated. Therefore, it is not surprising that three and a half months *before* D&C 124 was received authorizing the building of and approving of site selection for a temple, Joseph Smith began to speak of the necessity of such a structure in Nauvoo.

4 October 1840

    1. See *History of the Church*, 4:206. Not in *Teachings*. The *History of the Church* entry is based on the *Times and Seasons* account given in the text. The following account mentions a discourse that Joseph Smith delivered at the October 1840 General Conference of the Church.

5 October 1840

    1. See *History of the Church*, 4:207-212 and *Teachings*, pp. 166-173. The original source for the reports of this discourse in *History of the Church* and *Teachings* is the account given in this text. This discourse is apparently the only discourse for which the Prophet ever prepared a text. He did not personally deliver this "Treatise on Priesthood," but had his scribe, Robert B. Thompson, read it to the Saints assembled in general conference. The dictation of the text by the Prophet has a fascinating background. We are indebted to Howard Coray, another of Joseph's clerks at the time, for the following account preserved in his autobiography (Special Collections, Brigham Young University):

One morning, I went as usual, into the Office to go to work: I found Joseph sitting on one side of a table and Robert B. Thompson on the opposite side, and the understanding I got was that they were examining or hunting in the manuscript of the new translation of the Bible for something on Priesthood, which Joseph wished to present, or have read to the people the next Conference: Well, they could not find what they wanted and Joseph said to Thompson "put the manuscript one side, and take some paper and I will tell you what to write." Bro. Thompson took some foolscap paper that was at his elbow and made himself ready for the business. I was seated probably 6 or 8 feet on Joseph's left side, so that I could look almost squarely into Joseph's left eye — I mean the side of his eye. Well, the Spirit of God descended upon him, and a measure of it upon me, insomuch that I could fully realize that God, or the Holy Ghost, was talking through him. I never, neither before or since, have felt as I did on that occasion. I felt so small and humble I could have freely kissed his feet.

Much like the Prophet's dictated revelations, this text has few editorial changes. Furthermore, the document demonstrates the Prophet's knowledge of the scriptures. With no Bible at hand, he accurately cited and dictated the text of fourteen scriptural passages. Only twice did the Prophet not remember the chapter and verse of a passage. Nevertheless, he quoted those passages accurately. In this important address the Prophet makes many important statements on Temple Priesthood the day after announcing plans for the construction of the Nauvoo Temple.

2. Robert Blashel Thompson (1811-41). Baptized by Parley P. Pratt in Upper Canada in 1836. Scribe for the Prophet 1839-41.

3. In the 5 January 1841 discourse, Joseph stated, "All priesthood is Melchizedeck; but there are different portions or degrees of it" (see D&C 107:1-20).

4. "What was the power of Melchisedick?" Joseph Smith asked in his 27 August 1843 discourse. "Twas not P. of Aaron &c. [but it was the power of] a king & a priest to the most high God. [That priesthood was] a perfect law of Theocracy, holding keys of power & blessings, [and] stood as God to give laws to the people, administering endless lives to the sons and daughters of Adam."

5. Job 38:7 (1-7).

6. In the discourse dated "Before 8 August 1839 (1)," Joseph Smith states, "The Priesthood was first given to Adam: he obtained the First Presidency and held the Keys of it from generation to generation; he obtained it in the creation before the world was formed" (spelling and punctuation standardized).

7. Moses 5:1-12; 6:4-9, 45-68.

8. In the discourse dated "Before 8 August 1840 (1)," Joseph Smith stated, "The Keys [of the Priesthood] have to be brought from heaven whenever the Gospel is sent. When they are revealed from Heaven it is by Adam's authority" (spelling and capitalization standardized).

9. See 27 June 1839, note 21.

10. D&C 29:22-32; 76:98, 106-8.

11. D&C 121:34-37, 41-42.

12. The Law of Sacrifice authorized as a legitimate offering to the Lord the offering of the "first fruits of the field." Therefore, Cain was following the proper form when he offered sacrifice. The reason he was cursed was not, as is generally supposed, because he violated the forms of sacrifice, but because he did not offer his sacrifice with a righteous heart.

13. Only a brief mention of this subject is made during the Prophet's 3 October 1841 discourse a year later, and no lengthy "treatise" has ever been found on the "doctrine of translation." It is a subject the Prophet was uniquely qualified to clarify. For in the scriptures revealed through him, he had much to say on this subject—certainly more than is given in the King James Version of the Bible. See, for example, Alma 45:18-19; 3 Nephi 28; 4 Nephi 14, 37; Mormon 8:10-12; 9:22; Ether 12:17; D&C 7; 49:8; 50:26-30; 77:7-11, 14; 84:25, 98-100; 107:48-49, 57; 110:13-16; 129:1-3; 130:4-7; 133:52-56; Moses 6:32-34; 7:13; 16-23, 27, 61-69; JST Genesis 9:21-25; 13:13; 14:25-36.

14. This change in Hebrews 11:6*—the change of the word *rewarder* to the word *revealer*—is not found in the manuscript of Joseph Smith's Translation of the Bible.

15. Much evidence suggests that Joseph Smith considered the doctrine of translation to be an outgrowth of the highest blessings of the priesthood. For example, JST Genesis 14:25-36, is a clear statement of the relationship of the highest powers of the priesthood and the blessing of "translation." There are also other allusions by Joseph Smith in this discourse to certain elements of priesthood doctrine—teachings as he put it "that have been kept hid from before the foundation of the world . . . from the wise and prudent"—ordinances not previously performed in this dispensation that would be institutionalized in the Church by way of the temple endowment. For example, the Prophet alludes to the reinstitution of the Law of Sacrifice—that part administered by the Melchizedek Priesthood before the Law of Moses. Moreover, it is clear by this discourse that Joseph Smith expected to reinstitute the priesthood vestments (as described in Exodus 28 and 29) and the restoration of the Levitical Order of the Priesthood sufficient to fulfill Malachi 3:3-4 (see D&C 2).

16. The term *terrestrial order* suggests the Mormon definitions of "telestial" life (the present earthly order) and "celestial" existence (the highest state of resurrected life).

17. See note 13 of this discourse.

18. Apparently Joseph Smith reasoned that because biblical chronology indicated that Noah was not a contemporary of Adam, the keys of Adam's dispensation fell to Noah's father, Lamech.

19. D&C 107:18, 19. Three months after this discourse, Joseph Smith received a revelation specifically requiring that he teach Hyrum Smith and William Law certain "keys by which they could ask and receive" (D & C 124:95, 97). In the 1879 edition of the Doctrine and Covenants, Orson Pratt indicated that these keys were "the order of God for receiving revelations"—the keys to the oracles of God. Because these keys were part of the endowment ordinances not revealed until a year and a half later, and because they were not to be reduced to writing until there was a temple repository (something not accomplished until 1877), we are therefore dependent either upon those who received these ordinances or those who knew second-hand for any of the otherwise unrecorded details of Joseph Smith's revelations on temple ordinances. Apostle Charles C. Rich was one of the latter category of second-hand preservers of Joseph's revelations on the temple ordinances and who obviously was sensitive to the propriety of discussing endowment ordinances. Nevertheless, he publicly gave this very important account of the revelation of these keys of the priesthood, during a stake conference meeting in Idaho in 1878. "It was a long time after the Prophet Joseph Smith had received the keys of the kingdom of God, and after Hyrum and others had received many blessings, that the Lord gave Joseph a revelation, to show him and others how they could ask for and receive certain blessings. We read in the revelations of St. John, that [of] the white stone [as follows:] 'and in the stone a new name, which no man knoweth save him that receiveth it.' Joseph tells us [in D&C 130:10-11] that this new name is a key-word, which can only be obtained through the endowments. This is one of the keys and blessings that will be bestowed upon the Saints in these last days, for which we should be very thankful" (*Journal of Discourses*, 19:250).

Two years after this October 1840 discourse, Joseph Smith, according to George A. Smith's interpretation of the Prophet's meaning, told the Relief Society on 28 April 1842 (six days before the endowment was first given) that he was about to deliver "the keys of the Priesthood to the Church, and said that the faithful members of the Relief Society should receive them with their husbands, that the Saints whose integrity has been tried and proved faithful, might know how to ask the Lord and receive an answer" (*Teachings*, p. 226). While the original minutes are not this explicit, no doubt George A. Smith felt justified in amplifying the meaning of the text based on his personal experience with the Prophet in sacred meetings when the temple ordinances were administered. His wife, Bathsheba W. Smith, left on record several statements indicating the Prophet's public reference to this concept. On one occasion she said of Joseph Smith, "When speaking in one of our general fast meetings, he said that we did not know how to pray to have our prayers answered. But when I and my husband had our endowments . . . Joseph Smith presiding, he taught us the order of prayer" (*Juvenile Instructor* 27 [1 June 1892]:345). Notwithstanding G. A. Smith's interpretation, there is evidence that prior to 19 January 1841 the Prophet had thought long on the question of keys of access to God. For example, in 1833 the Prophet taught the brethren of the School of the Prophets "how to get revelation." Also in 1835, Joseph Smith taught the Father of Lorenzo Young how to get the spiritual power to heal his son. "Join in prayer," the Prophet said, "one by mouth and the others repeat after him in unison . . . [then] continuing the administration in this way until you receive a testimony that he will be restored" ("Biography of Lorenzo Dow Young," *Utah Historical Quarterly* 14:45). But three months after these instructions were given, the Prophet received the keys of the sealing power from Elijah. Apparently based on a maturing appreciaton of the authority Elijah bestowed upon him, the Prophet six years later stated that "For him to whom these keys [of Elijah] are given there is no difficulty in obtaining" revelation (see D&C 128:10-11). Thus, based on the authority he received of Elijah, Joseph Smith conferred the keys of the priesthood in the endowment 4 May 1842 (see *History of the Church*, 5:1-2 or *Teachings*, p. 137, and 28 April 1842, notes 6, 12, 1 May 1842, notes 2 and 4 and note 15, this discourse).

20. See note 15 of this discourse.

21. See for example, Genesis 4:3-5; 8:20-22; 11:7-8; 13:3-4; 22:1-19; Moses 5:4-8; Abraham 2:17-21; the book of Abraham Facsimile 2, figure 2.

22. The use of the word *when* rather than the word *because* is interesting. According to his own diary, Elijah appeared to him on 3 April 1836 and delivered these keys (Joseph Smith Diary, Church Archives, D&C 110:13-16). Apparently in his mind it was not sufficient that he alone had these keys and this power, but he intended by way of ordinances to confer a portion of this power on others who were faithful, thereby actually bringing about the restoration of all things. For example, in D&C 132:45-46, where by revelation Joseph Smith is reassured that he received the keys of the binding and loosing power of Elijah, the Lord says, "For I have conferred upon you the keys and power of the priesthood, wherein I restore all things, *and make known unto you all things in due time.*" These keys of access to God (D&C 128:10-11) held in all their fulness by the President of the Church, enable the "least member" in the Church to have power in his priesthood (See *Teachings*, p. 137). It was not enough to Joseph Smith to be a king and a priest unto the Most High, but he insisted that his people be a society of priests "as in Paul's day, as in Enoch's day" through the ordinances of the temple (see 30 March 1842 discourse). Throughout the remainder of his Nauvoo

experience, Joseph Smith taught and emphasized the importance of the temple ordinances, ordinances that would bestow upon members of the Church the knowledge and power he foreshadows in this discourse (see note 15).

23. Interesting use of "will" rather than "has." See note 22, this discourse.

24. Joseph Smith was already recognizing the difficulty he would have attempting to introduce all the knowledge and ordinances he had received by revelation. Undoubtedly the recently announced doctrine of baptism for the dead challenged the faith of some. Likewise also, he had only recently begun to preach the practice of plural marriage, which met with decided opposition. It was these and other doctrinal developments that would try the faith of many saints and fly in the face of their prejudices. Often throughout the remainder of his life, Joseph Smith would lament that many Saints were unwilling to accept the glorious things revealed to him from heaven.

25. Despite the restoration of the authority of the Aaronic Priesthood (by John the Baptist; Joseph Smith-History 1:69-72) and the apostleship (by Peter, James and John; Joseph Smith-History 1:72), there were ordinances of the priesthood that could not be performed unless administered by the power and authority of Elijah.

26. That is, as food for the priests.

27. See note 15, this discourse.

28. Acts 3:19-21.

29. For example, Genesis 3:21; 4:2-7 (see note 12, this discourse); 8:20-21 are sacrifices after the order of the Melchizedek Priesthood (see Mosiah 13:27-35).

30. Unlike the King James Version of the Bible, the scriptures revealed through Joseph Smith include the ordinances of baptism for the remission of sins and the gift of the Holy Ghost by the laying on of hands as authentic Old Testament ritual. See for example, 2 Nephi 31 in the Book of Mormon, and Moses 6:51-68 of the Joseph Smith Translation of the Bible.

31. Abraham 1:2-4, 31; and 2:7-11.

December 1840

1. The following report is here published for the first time. William Clayton, an English convert, arrived in Nauvoo 24 November 1840.

2. William Clayton (1814-79). A convert from England, Clayton was given numerous clerical assignments in Nauvoo, including recording the Prophet's sermons and assisting with his correspondence.

3. Unlike other versions of these instructions given by Joseph Smith from 1839 to 1843, this account indicates that the Devil is not compelled to "offer his hand." Apparently Joseph Smith believed that the Devil had sense enough to avoid obvious detection but that unlike "a spirit from God," he would not remain motionless (Moses 1:11-23; 4:6; see also 27 June 1839, note 21).

1841

1841

1841

5 January 1841 (Tuesday). Old Homestead.[1]
Extracts from William Clayton's Private Book

By Joseph, Jany. 5th 1841, at
the organization of a school of
instruction.

Description of Paul—He is about 5 foot high; very dark hair; dark complection; dark skin; large Roman nose; sharp face; small black eyes, penetrating as eternity; round shoulders; a whining voice, except when elevated and then it almost resembles the roaring of a Lion. He was a good orator, but Doctor Benentt[2] is a superior orator, and like Paul is active and deligent, always employing himself in doing good to his fellow men.

By Joseph, January 5th, 1841
Answer to the question, was the
Priesthood of Melchizedeck taken
away when Moses died.[3]

All priesthood is Melchizedeck; but there are different portions or degrees of it. That portion which brought Moses to speak with God face to face was taken away; but that which brought the ministry of angels remained.[4] All the Prophets had the Melchizedeck Priesthood and was ordained by God himself.

The world and earth are not synonymous terms.[5] The world is the human family. This earth was organized or formed out of other planets which were broke up and remodelled and made into the one on which we live.[6] The elements are eternal. That which has a begining will surely have an end. Take a ring, it is without beginning or end; cut it for a beginning place, and at the same time you will have an ending place.

A key, every principle proceeding from God is eternal, and any principle which is not eternal is of the Devil. The sun has no beginning or end, the rays which proceed from himself have no bounds, consequently are eternal. So it is with God. If the soul of man had a beginning it will surely have an end.[7] In the translation, "without form and void" it should read "empty and desolate." The word "created" should be formed or organized.[8]

Observations on the Sectarian God.

That which is without body or parts is nothing. There is no other God in heaven but that God who has flesh and bones. John 5—26, "As the father hath life in himself, even so hath he given the son to have life in himself". God the father took life unto himself precisely as Jesus did.[9] The first step in the salvation of men is the laws of eternal and self-existent principles. Spirits are eternal. At the first organization in heaven we were all present and saw the Savior chosen and appointed, and the plan of salvation made and we sanctioned it.[10] We came to this earth that we might have a body and present it pure before God in the Celestial Kingdom. The great principle of happiness consists in having a body. The Devil has no body, and herein is his punishment. He is pleased when he can obtain the tabernacle of man and when cast out by the Savior he asked to go into the herd of swine showing that he would prefer a swines body to having none.[11] All beings who have bodies have power over those who have not. The devil has no power over us only as we permit him; the moment we revolt at anything which comes from God the Devil takes power.

This earth will be rolled back[12] into the presence of God and crowned with Celestial Glory.[13]

McIntire Minute Book[14]

Subject first—Discused By D. C. Smith;[15] also this preciple practized By many the Blessings & Results of the same he said the priciple would Bind the Harts of Man together & give them confidence in each other & as John says thy word is truth; so he says if we keep his word shall all be actuated By the same principles be as one man; & as angels are obedient to the same word we shall have Concorse to them & also to all the Heavnly throng; Joseph said to D. C. Smith that to be free from the Coruptions of the Earth that meant the speaker should all ways speak in his Natureal tone of voice; & Not to keep in one loud strain; But to act without affectaton[16] Next Subject was—Did the Lord God make the Earth out of Nothing; By D. Ells.[17] say he God did not make the earth out of Nothing; for it is contrary to a Rashanall [rational] mind & Reason. that a something could be Brought from a Nothing; also it is contry to the principle & Means by witch God does work; for instance; when God formed man, he made him of something; the Dust of the Earth, & he allways took a somthing to afect a something Else; oft he takes man to scorge his fellow man, or watter to Destroy man—or fire to Distroy Man or angels for istance the angel that went forth & Distroyed a hundred thousand one knigt Joseph Smith said to D Ells, & to the Congregation that he for a lenth of time, thought on phreknoleagee [phrenology][18]; & that he had a Revalation. the Lord Rebuking him sharply in Crediting such a thing; & further said there was No Reality in such a science But was the works of the Devil; he also said the Lord had told him that Bro. Law[19] would Do well, he would Go & preach the Gospel he also said as for his own knowledge the Earth was made out of sumthing for it was impossible for a sumthing to be made out of Nothing fire, air, & watter are Eternal Existant principles which are the Composition of which the Earth-has been Composed; also ~~this~~ Earth has been organized out of portions of other Globes that has ben Disorganized; in tistimoney that this Earth was Not the first of Gods work; he quoted a passage from the testament where Jesus said all things that he had saw the father Do he had done & that he done Nothing But what he saw the father do John the 5th [verse 19][20] he also said in testimony of the situation the saints in the presence of God. that they had flesh & bones & that was the agreement in Eternity to come here & take on them tabernacles & the Differance Between us & Satin in that Respect is that he fell & had Not opertunity to Come in the flesh—& that he allways is striving to get others as miserable as himself—[21]

12 January 1841 (Tuesday). Amos Davis Home.[1]
McIntire Minute Book

Tuesday the 12th at Mr. Davises[2]—1st Subject Education By Mr —— he said a people whose minds were Culavated & Maners Refined By Education—that they had Great & precious Ejoyments that Ignorant had Not 2d Subject was vice By Mr stout[3] he said Murder theft & the Like came from indulgances in this principle—Joseph—said that some things were Eavils that did not come under the Head of vise; for instance one Nation would come against an other it would be an Eavil on the Nation was come aganst yet it would not be a vice for them to Repell[4]————Virtue was 3d subject 4th subject the Gospel By Mr Badlum[5] he lectors on it till he Comes the Laying on the hands for the Holy Ghost—then Joseph—takes it up & ads the Resurection & Eternal Judgment[6] in the Eternal Judgment there is many things to know & to under stand in Gods Judging for instance Peter said David had not yet ascend to heaven & that he was a Murderer & that His soul was in Hell is plainly told By Peter in acts 2d ch.[7] Petter shews plainer it in the 3d of acts that a murderer could Not be Redmed intill he would send Jesus Christ which before was preached unto you &.c[8]—that is that faith Repentance & Baptizm would not save them untill the[y were] scourged in hell or paid the Last farthing.[9]

19 January 1841 (Tuesday).[1]
McIntire Minute Book

Next Meeting—Joseph said that before foundation of the Earth in the Grand Counsel that the Spirits of all Men ware subject to opression & the express purpose of God in Giveing it a tabernicle was to arm it against the power of Darkness[2]—for instance Jesus said Get behind me Satan[3] Also the apostle said Resist the Devil & he will flee from you.[4]

2 February 1841 (Tuesday).[1]
McIntire Minute Book

Next Meeting—Joseph said the Lord said that we should build our house[2] to his name that we might be Baptized for the Dead—But if we Did it Not we should be Rejected & our Dead with us & this Church should Not be excepted [accepted].[3]

9 February 1841 (Tuesday).[1]
McIntire Minute Book

Joseph said in answer to Mr stout[2] that Adam Did Not Comit sin in [e]ating the fruits for God had Decred that he should Eat & fall—But incomplyance with the Decree he should Die—only he should Die was the saying of the Lord therefore the Lord apointed us to fall & also Redeemed us—for where sin a bounded Grace did Much more a bound[3]—for Paul says Rom—5.10 for if—when were enemys we were Reconciled to God by the Death of his Son, much more, being Reconciled, we shall be saved by his Life—

16 February 1841 (Tuesday).[1]
McIntire Minute Book

Next Meetting . . . Joseph said Concerning the Godhead it was Not as many imagined—three Heads & but one body, he said the three were separate bodys[2]—God the first & Jesus the Mediator the 2d & the Holy Ghost & these three agree in one & this is the maner we Should aproach God in order to get his blessings[3] & he also said Every Man were st stimulated by a certain Motive, to act motive preceeds action & if we want to know ourselves this is the Key to Examin the motive what it is, & the fact will be manifest.

23 February 1841 (Tuesday).[1]
McIntire Minute Book

Next Metting . . . Joseph said he Never wanted to hear a man snore Louder than he could shout in battle—he Did Not want a man say O Joseph how I Love you &c. & when the time of Danger come forsake him.[2]

2 March 1841 (Tuesday).[1]
McIntire Minute Book

Next Meeting W Soby[2] on true friendship—he said true Friendship was such as a Man Laying Down his Life for his Friend. Joseph said there was a Diferance Between the vengance that Belongeth to the Lord[3], & a man Defending himself[4] or friend—of the Mamon of unrighteousness[5] Joseph said the Majority of man Kind was agn'st & true a [man] must Lavish His goods on all around him & out of them he will find freinds in the hour of Distress for those that have been made Ritch By the Benevalance of their Rich freind of them there will be some that will do you good in affliction—

9 March 1841 (Tuesday).[1]
McIntire Minute Book

Subject 1st on the Gospel By father Cole[2] he Said that Some thought that He Difered from president Smith Concerning the time of the Giving of the Holy Ghost—as teach that all men receive the Holy Ghost before Baptizem[3]—Joseph said we Do not take Notice of things as they Read them—or they might know things as they Read them—he quotes rather 2d Repent & be Baptized &c—& ye Shall Receive the Gift of the Holly Ghost—Now said he (taking up his Cap & presenting to Prd Law)[4] in Giveing you this Gift is not giving myself. However there is a prist-Hood with the Holy Ghost & Key—the Holy Ghost over shadows you & witness unto you of the authority & the Gifts of the Holly Ghost—he said was the provence of the Father to preside as the Chief or President—Jesus as the Mediator & Holy Ghost as the testator or witness[5]—the Son Had a Tabernicle & so had the father[6] But the Holly Ghost is a personage of spirit without tabernicle the Great God has a name By wich He will be Called which is Ahman[7]—also in asking have Referance to a personage Like Adam for God made Adam Just in his own Image Now this a key for you to know how to ask & obtain.[8]

Next was Robinson[9] in the Gospel he spoke of Adam pertaking of the forbiden fruit & so on—Joseph said a person ought always take his subject along—for instance Jesus in all his Doctrines & pariables set it forth Like a tree or Mustard Stock Comencing at the foundation or Root thence up to the first Branch & out along it then back to the body of the tree or subject & thence to the Next Branch & so—on Now as to Adam the Lord said in the Day thous Shalt Eat there of thou shalt shurely Die Now the Day the Lord has Refferance too is spoken of by Petter a thousand of our years is with the Lord as one Day[10] &c at the time the Lord said this to Adam there was No mode of Counting time By Man, as man Now Counts time.[11]

16 March 1841 (Tuesday).[1]
McIntire Minute Book

Next Meeting ... Joseph Said th they wiked will Not all be Distroyed at the Coming of Christ & also there will be wiked During the Melenium[2]—for instance Isaiah says the Days of an infant shall be as the age of a tree[3] also Zarch.—says all who Does Not Come up year by year with their Gifts to the preasts of the tabernicle that No Rain shall fall upon them—& that Jesus will be a Resident on the Earth a thousand [years] with the Saints is Not the Case but will Raign over the saints & come Down & instruct as he Did the 5 hundrd Brethern[4] (1st Cor. 15) & those of the first Resurrection will also Raign with him over the saints—then after the Little Season is Expired & the Earth underGoes its Last Change & is Gloryfyed then will all the meek inherit the Earth wherein Dwelleth Righteous[5]—he says satan Cannot Seduce us by his Enticements unles we in our harts Consent & yeald—our organization such that we can Resest the Devil If we were Not organized so we would Not be free agents.[6]

21 March 1841 (Sunday). Vinson Knight Home.[1]
Howard and Martha Coray Notebook

Sermon 2nd

~~On the death of Judge Higbee~~ delivered in the latter part of the winter ~~about~~ just before he took Laws[2] store at the House of Bishop Knight[3] year 1841

Joseph Smith read the 3 chap Malachi dwelt with emphasis upon the Levitical priesthood and the promise concerning them

Took up Jhon shewed him to be a Levite[4] and proceed The voice of one crying in the wilderness prepare ye the way of the Lord and make his paths straight[5] Now it was written that the priests lips should keep knowledge and to them should the people seek for understanding[6] and above all the law binds them and us to receive the word of the Lord at the hands of the Levites[7] therefore Jhon being Lawful heir to the Levitical Priesthood the people were bound to receive his testimony. Hence the saying the Kingdom of heaven suffereth violence and the violent take it by force[8] after Jhon had been testifying of Jesus for some time Jesus came unto him for baptism Jhon felt that the honor of baptizing his master was too great a thing grater than he could claim and said I have need to be baptized thee and comest thou to me Jesus repled thus it behooveth us to fulfill all righteousness[9] thus signifying to Jhon the claim of the Aronic priesthood which holds the Keys of entrance into the Kingdom.[10] Then the three signs which were given were conclusive[11] The dove which sat upon his shoulder was a sure testimony that he was of God Brethren be not deceived ~~an~~ nor doubtful of this fact a spirit of a good man or an ~~angell~~ from heaven who has not a body will never undertake to shake hands with you for he knows you cannot perceive his touch and never will extend his hand but any spirit or body that is attended by a dove you may know to be a pure spirit[12] Thus you may in some measure detect ~~them~~ the spirits who may come unto you[13] Jhon was great in that he baptized Jesus an for this cause Jesus saith "Among them that are born of women there hath not risen a greater than Jhon the baptist[14] But again he says ~~the~~ from the ~~coming~~ days of Jhon the Batist till the Kingdom of Haven suffereth violence and the violent taketh it by force[15]

Jesus as I said could not enter except by the administration of Jhon. Although Jhon was not a restorer but a forerunner[16] It was not the Lawful priests who rejected jesus but the self made priests Those who were priests lawfully received the Saviour in his station which was given him by the Law All the Authority that we have is from Jhon The Law is not changed nor the ordinances The keys of ushering into the Kingdom were given to Peter James & Jhon.[17]

Malachi 4th [3rd] chap And he shall purify the sons of Levi &c yes brethren the Lord will purify the sons of Levi good or bad for it is through them that blessings flow to Israel and as Israel once was baptized in the cloud and in the sea[18] so shall God as a refiners fire and a Fullers soap ~~Purge~~ purify the sons of Levi and purge them as Gold and as silver & then and not till then shall the offering of Judah & Jerusalem be pleasant unto the Lord as in days of old and as in former years[19]

And he shall witness against all iniquity as saith Malachi and shall sorely chastize those who are gone astray, but still he saith I am God I change not therefore ye sons of Jacob are not consumed return thou unto me and I will return unto thee[20] The Lord will begin by revealing the House ~~House~~ of Israel among the gentiles and those who have gone from the ordinances of God shall return unto the keeping of all the law and observing his judgments and statutes to do them[21] Then shall the law of the Lord go forth from Zion and the word of the Lord to the priests and through them from Jerusalem[22]

And I prophecy that the day will come when you will say Oh that we had given heed but look now upon our public works the store schoolhouse for instance the Simoon of the Desert has passed over it the people will not hearken nor hear And bondage Death and destruction are close at our heels The Kingdom will not be broken up but ~~Judgements awaits man~~ we shall be scattered and driven gathered again & then dispersed reestablished & driven abroad and so on until the Ancient of days shall sit and the kingom and power thereof shall the be given to the Saints and they shall ~~the~~ possess it forever and ever,[23] which may God hasten for Christs sake Amen.

McIntire Minute Book

Sabath Meeting—Joseph Read the 2 & 3d Chapters of Malichi & stated that there was a preistHood Confered upon the sons of Levi throughout the Jenerations of the Jews, & he also said they was born heirs to that prestHood[24] By Linage or Decent & held the Keys of the first principles of the Gospel—for this—he quoted concerning Jesus coming to John to be Baptized of Jhon that he (Jesus) Might Enter into the Kingdom as Jhon held the Keys, suffer it to be so now[25] &c he also Brought up Zacharias pleading with the Lord in the temple that he might have seed so that the preistHood might be preserved[26]

he also prophesyed that all those that made Light of the Revalations that was Given and him & his words—would ere Long Cry & Lement (when the servent of God would be imprizened) say O!! that we had harkened to the words of God & the Revelattions Given—But all opertunity is Cut of from them.

28 March 1841 (Sunday).[1]
McIntire Minute Book

Next Meeting Meeting on sunday Joseph Reads the 38th Ch—of Job. in the book he says is a Great Display of human Nature—it is very Natureal for a man when he sees his fellow man afflicted his Natureal conclusion is that he is sufering the Rath of an angry God & turn from him in haste not knowing the purpose of God[2] he says the spirit or the inteligence of men are self Existant principles he before the foundation this Earth—& quotes the Lords question to Job "where wast thou when I laid the foundation of the Earth"[3] Evidence that Job was in Existing somewhere at that time he says God is Good & all his acts is for the benifit of infereir inteligences— God saw that those intelegences had Not power to Defend themselves against those that had a tabernicle therefore the Lord Calls them togather in Counsel & agrees to form them tabernicles so that he might Gender the Spirit & the tabernicle togather so as to create sympathy for their fellowman—for it is a Natureal thing with those spirits that has the most power to bore down on those of Lesser power so we see the Devil is without a tabernicle & the Lord as set bo[u]nds to all Spirits & hence Come the Saying thou son of David why art thou Come to torment us before the time, & Jesus Comanded him to Come out of the Man & the Devil besought him that he might Enter in a herd of swine Near by (for the Devil knew they were a Coveitous people & if he Could Kill their Hogs that would Drive Jesus out of their Coasts & he then would have tabernicle enough) & Jesus—permitted him to Enter into the swine.[4]

30 March 1841 (Tuesday).[1]
McIntire Mintute Book

Next meeting Lecyum 1st—Stewart[2] an Equality in property & in knoledge Joseph said that an Equality would Not answer for he says if we were eaquel in property at present in six months we would be worse than Ever for there is too many Dishonest men amongst us who has more injenity to threat the Rest &c

E. Robinson[3] spoke on the other comforter in the 14 & 16 of John & that to all man kind for he shall [re]prove the world of sin & Righteous & of Judgment &c[4] Joseph said he would Corect in the translation[5] it ought to Read thus & he shall Remind the world of sin & of Righteous & of Judgment & this Comforter Reminds of the these things through the servants of the Lord—But the other Comforter spoken of By John is Jesus himself that is to Come & take up his aboad with them.[6]

6 April 1841 (Tuesday Morning). Temple Site.[1]
Times and Seasons 2 (15 April 1841): 382

The first presidency superintended the laying of the Chief Corner Stone on the south east corner of the building, which done, Prest. J. Smith, arose and said, that the first corner stone of the Temple of Almighty God was laid, and prayed that the building might soon be completed, that the saints might have an habitation to worship the God of their fathers.

7 April 1841 (Wednesday Morning). Temple Site.[1]
Times and Seasons 2 (15 April 1841): 386-87

Gen. Bennett[2] then read the revelations from "The Book of the Law of the Lord,"[3] which had been received since the last general Conference, in relation to writing a proclamation to the kings of the earth, building a Temple in Nauvoo, the organization of the church &c.[4]

Pres. Jos. Smith rose and made some observations in explanation of the same, and likewise of the necessity which existed of building the Temple, that the saints might have a suitable place for worshiping the Almighty, and also the building of the Nauvoo Boarding House, that suitable accomodations might be afforded for the strangers who might visit this city.[5]

8 April 1841 (Thursday). Temple Site.[1]
Times and Seasons 2 (15 April 1841):387-88

At an early hour this morning the different quorums, who had previously been organized, came to the ground and took their seats as follows: the First Presidency, with the presidents of the quorums on the stand; the High Council, on the front of the stand; the High Priesthood on the front to the right of the stand; the Seventies immediately behind the high preisthood; the Elders in the front, to the left; the Lesser Priesthood on the extreme right.[2]

On motion; Resolved: that this session of Congress continue until Sunday evening.

Pres't. J. Smith declared the rule of voting, to be a majority in each quorum,[3] exhorted them to deliberation, faith and prayer, and that they should be strict, and impartial in their examinations. He then told them that the presidents of the different quorums would be presented before them for their acceptance or rejection. . . .

Pres't. Joseph Smith presented the building Committee of the "House of the Lord," to the several quorums collectively, who were unanimously received.[4]

Pres't. Smith observed, that it was necessary that some one should be appointed to fill the quorum of the twelve, in the room of the late Elder David W. Patten,[5] whereupon, Pres't. Rigdon nominated Elder Lyman Wight to that office, which was unanimously accepted. . . .

[P.M.] Pres't. Rigdon delivered a discourse to the conference on the subject of "Baptism for the dead" which was set forth in a manner new and interesting, and with an eloquence peculiar to the speaker, which was listened to with intense interest by the assembly.

Gen. Bennett made some very appropriate observations in continuation of the subject.

Pres't Smith likewise followed on the same subject, threw considerable light on the doctrine which had been investigated.

9 April 1841 (Friday Morning). Temple Site.[1]
Times and Seasons 2 (15 April 1841):388

Pres't. J. Smith made some observations respecting the duty of the several quorums, in sending their members into the vineyard,[2] and also stated, that labor on the Temple would be as acceptable to the Lord as preaching in the world.

Pres't. Smith then stated that it was necessary that some one should be appointed to collect funds for building the Temple. . . .

Pres't J. Smith then stated that he should resign the meeting to the presidency of the Stake, and the president of the High Priest Quorum.[3]

McIntire Minute Book

Joseph said to the presidents of the quorums that they should see that No man go out to preach unless their family, was amply Provided for; and if not provided for stay untill they are, this is Done to put up the Barrs against those that mearly Join the Church &

Get ordained & Get their familys struck in her & Go out & Glut themselves while the Church has their familys to Keep.

11 April 1841 (Sunday Afternoon). Temple Site.[1]
Times and Seasons 2 (15 April 1841):388

Pres't. Joseph Smith then addressed the assembly and stated, that in consequence of the severty of the weather, the saints had not received as much instruction as he desired and that some things would have to be laid over until the next conference—as there were many who wished to be baptized, they would now go to the water and give opportunity to any who wished to be baptized of doing so.[2]

25 April 1841 (Sunday Morning). Near Temple.[1]
Alexander Neibaur Journal[2]

Showery fornoon; went to the preaching in the open air, a fine spot of land near the Temple—a platform for the speakers, seats prepared for the congregation. Br. Bennett[3] spoke first in respect to his profession, all caracter being injured by some of those who prefesset to be Saints. Br. Law[4] followed on the principles of righteousness & unrighteousness, there having been some depratations being committed by some that once had been Saints but was cut off from the Church for misconduct. Elder Joseph the Prophet followed in very strong language determined to put down all iniquity.

9 May 1841 (Sunday).[1]
William Clayton Journal

Joseph preached on his side[2] on baptism for the dead (see Record.)[3]

Alexander Neibaur Journal

Fine day. Elder Joseph Smith preached from 9th Romans on the principles of Election.

16 May 1841 (Sunday Morning). Meeting Ground.[1]
Times and Seasons 2 (1 June 1841): 429-430

The indications of the morning promised a beautiful day. At 10 o'clock A.M. a large concourse of the saints assembled on the meeting ground and were addressed by Pres. Joseph Smith, who spoke at considerable length. He commenced his observations by remarking that the kindness of our Heavenly Father, called for our heartfelt gratitude. He then observed that satan was generally blamed for the evils which we did, but if he was the cause of all our wickedness, men could not be condemned. The devil cannot compel mankind to evil, all was voluntary.— Those who resist the spirit of God, are liable to be led into temptation, and then the association of heaven is withdrawn from those who refuse to be made partakers of such great glory—God would not exert any compulsory means and the Devil could not; and such ideas as were entertained by many were absurd.[2] The creature was made subject to vanity, not willingly, but Christ subjected the same in hope[3]—we are all subject to vanity while we travel through the crooked paths, and difficulties which surround us. Where is the man that is free from vanity? None ever were perfect but Jesus,[4] and why was he perfect? because he was the son of God,[5] and had the fulness of the Spirit,[6] and greater power than any man.[7]— But, notwithstanding our vanity, we look forward with hope, (because "we are subjected in hope,")[8] to the time of our deliverance.

He then made some observations on the first principles of the gospel, observing that many of the saints who had come from different States and Nations, had only a very superficial knowledge of these principles, not having heard them fully investigated. He then briefly stated the principles of faith, repentance, and baptism for the remission of sins, which were believed by some of the religious societies of the day, but the doctrine of laying on of hands for the gift of the holy ghost, was discarded by them.

The speaker then referred them to the 6th chap. of Heb. 1. and 2. verses, "not laying again the foundation of repentance from dead works &c., but of the doctrines of baptism, laying on of hands, the resurrection and eternal judgment &c." The doctrine of eternal judgment was perfectly understood by the apostle, is evident from several passages of scripture. Peter preached repentance and baptism for the remission of sins to the Jews,[9] who had been led to acts of violence and blood, by their leaders, but to the Rulers he said, "I would that through ignorance ye did it, as did also *those ye ruled*."— Repent, therefore, and be converted that your sins may be blotted out, when the times of refreshing (redemption), shall come from the presence of the Lord, for he shall send Jesus Christ, who before was preached unto you &c."[10] The time of *redemption* here had reference to the time, when Christ should come; then and not till then would their sins be blotted out. Why? Because they were murderers, and no murderer hath eternal life.[11] Even David, must wait for those times of refreshing, before he can come forth and his sins be blotted out; for Peter speaking of him says, "David hath not yet ascended into Heaven, for his sepulchre is with us to this day:"[12] his remains were then in the tomb. Now we read that many bodies of the saints arose, at Christ's resurrection, probably all the saints, but it seems that David did not.[13] Why? because he had been a murderer.

If the ministers of religion had a proper understanding of the doctrine of eternal judgment, they would not be found attending the man who had forfeited his life to the injured laws of his country by shedding innocent blood; for such characters cannot be forgiven, until they have paid the last farthing.[14] The prayers of all the ministers in the world could never close the gates of hell against a murderer.

The speaker then spoke on the subject of election, and read the 9th chap. in Romans, from which it was evident that the election there spoken of was pertaining to the flesh, and had reference to the seed of Abraham, according to the promise God made to Abraham, saying, "In thee and in thy seed all, the families of the earth shall be blessed."[15] To them belonged the adoption, and the covenants &c.[16] Paul said, when he saw their unbelief I wish myself accursed— according to the flesh—not according to the spirit.[17]

Why did God say to Pharoah, "for this cause have I raised thee up?"[18] Because Pharoah was a fit instrument—a wicked man, and had committed acts of cruelty of the most atrocious nature.

The election of the promised seed still continues, and in the last days, they shall have the priesthood restored unto them, and they shall be the "Saviors on mount Zion"[19] the "ministers of our God,"[20] if it were not for the remnant which was left,then might we be as Sodom and as Gomorah.[21]

The whole of the chapter had reference to the priesthood and the house of Israel; and unconditional election of individuals to eternal life was not taught by the apostles.[22]

God did elect or predestinate, that all those who would be saved, should be saved in Christ Jesus, and through obedience to the gospel; but he passes over no man's sins, but visits them with correction, and if his children will not repent of their sins, he will discard them.

This is but a very imperfect sketch of a very interesting discourse, which occupied more than two hours in delivery, and was listened to with marked attention by the vast assembly present.

Extracts from William Clayton's Private Book

Remarks by Joseph, May 16th, 1841.

There are three independent principles—the spirit of God, the spirit of man, and the spirit of the devil. All men have power to resist the devil. They who have tabernacles have power over those who have not. The doctrine of eternal judgment[23] Acts 2-41 Peter preached repent and be baptized in the name of Jesus Christ for the remission of sins, &c but in Acts 3-19 he says "Repent and be converted that you sins may be blotted out when the time of redemption shall come and he shall send Jesus," &c. Remission of sins by baptism was not to be preached to murderers. All the priests in christendom might pray for a murderer on the scaffold forever, but could not avail so much as a gnat towards their forgiveness. There is no forgiveness for murderers. They will have to wait until the time of redemption[24] shall come and that in hell. Peter had the keys of eternal judgment[25] and he saw David in hell and knew for what reason, and that David would have to remain there until the resurrection at the coming of Christ. Romans 9—all election that can be found in the scripture is according to the flesh and pertaining to the priesthood.

William Clayton Journal

I went over the river to hear Joseph Election and Eternal judgement (see Record).[26]

30 May 1841 (Sunday).[1]
Alexander Neibaur Journal

J. Smith preached from the last 2 Ch Cronicls.

13 or 20 June 1841 (Sunday). In Front of Temple.[1]
Juliet Courier and *Times and Seasons* 2 (2 August 1841): 498.

On Sunday I attended one of their meetings, in front of the Temple now building, and one of the largest buildings in the state. There could not have been less than 2,500 people present, and as well appearing as any number that could be found in this or any state. Mr. Smith preached in the morning, and one could have readily learned, then, the magic by which he has built up this society, because, as we say in Illinois, "they believe in him," and in his honesty.

25 July 1841 (Sunday Afternoon). Grove.[1]
Manuscript History of the Church

I followed him [Sidney Rigdon], illustrating the subject of the resurrection by some familiar figures.

16 August 1841 (Monday Afternoon).[1]
Times and Seasons 2 (1 September 1841):521-22

President Joseph Smith now arriving proceeded to state to the conference at considerable length, the object of their present meeting, and in addition to what President [Brigham] Young had stated in the morning, said that the time had come when the twelve should be called upon to stand in their place next to the first presidency,[2] and attend to the settling of emigrants and the business of the church at the stakes, and assist to bear off the kingdom victoriously to the nations;[3] and as they had been faithful, and had borne the burden in the heat of the day that it was right that they should have an opportunity of provididing something for themselves and families, and at the same time relieve him so that he might attend to the business of translating.[4]

22 August 1841 (Sunday). At the Stand.[1]
Manuscript History of the Church

I preached at the Stand on Wars & desolations that await the nations.

5 September 1841 (Sunday). At the Stand.[1]
Manuscript History of the Church

I preached to a large congregation at the Stand, on the Science and practice of Medicine, desiring to persuade the Saints to trust in God when sick, and not in an arm of flesh, and live by faith and not by medicine, or poison;[2] and when they were sick, and had called for the Elders to pray for them, and they were not healed, to use herbs and mild food.[3]

2 October 1841 (Saturday Afternoon). Meeting Ground.[1]
Times and Seasons 2 (15 October 1841):576-77

P.M. Pres. Joseph Smith opened by calling on the choir to sing a Hymn—sung 18th Hymn.[2] The President then read a letter from Br. O. Hyde giving an account of his journeys and success in his mission,[3] which was listened to with intense interest; and the conference, by vote, expressed their approbation of the style and spirit of said letter. The President then made remarks on the inclemency of the weather and the uncomfortable situation of the saints with regard to a place of worship, and a place of public entertainment[4] . . . .

Br. L Wight then addressed the conference on the importance of order and uniformity of instruction, and, of unanimity of effort to spread the work of the kingdom. Pres. Joseph Smith then made some corrections of doctrine in quoting a passage from 1 Cor. 12,28[5] showing it to be a principle of order or gradation in rising from one office to another in the Priesthood.

3 October 1841 (Sunday Morning). Meeting Ground.[1]
Times and Seasons 2 (15 October 1841):577-78

Sunday 3rd, A. M. Conference assembled and was called to

order by President Marks,[2] and divine service commenced by the choir singing Hymn 274,[3] and prayer by Br. H. C. Kimball.[4]

President Joseph Smith, by request of some of the Twelve, gave instructions on the doctrine of Baptism for the Dead; which was listened to with intense interest by the large assembly. The speaker presented "Baptism for the Dead" as the only way that men can appear as saviors on mount Zion.[5] The proclamation of the first principles of the gospel was a means of salvation to men individually, and it was the truth,[6] not men that saved them; but men, by actively engaging in rites of salvation substitutionally, became instrumental in bringing multitudes of their kin into the kingdom of God. He explained a difference between an angel and a ministering spirit; the one a resurrected or translated body,[7] with its spirit, ministering to embodied spirits—the other a disembodied spirit, visiting and ministering to disembodied spirits. Jesus Christ became a ministering spirit, while his body laying in the sepulchre, to the spirits in prison; to fulfil an important part of his mission, without which he could not have perfected his work or entered into his rest.[8] After his resurrection, he appeared as an angel to his disciples &c.[9] Translated bodies cannot enter into rest until they have undergone a change equivalent to death.[10] Translated bodies are designed for future missions. The angel that appeared to John on the Isle of Patmos was a translated or resurrected body.[11]—Jesus Christ went in body, after his resurrection, to minister to translated[12] and resurrected[13] bodies. There has been a chain of authority and power from Adam down to the present time.[14] The only way to obtain truth and wisdom, is not to ask it from books, but to go to God in prayer and obtain divine teaching.[15] It is no more incredible that God should *save* the dead, than that he should *raise* the dead. There is never a time when the spirit is too old to approach God. All are within the reach of pardoning mercy, who have not committed the unpardonable sin, which hath no forgiveness, neither in this world, nor in the world to come. There is a way to release the spirit of the dead; that is, by the power and authority of the Priesthood— by binding and loosing on earth.[16]

This doctrine appears glorious, inasmuch as it exhibits the greatness of divine compassion and benevolence in the extent of the plan of human salvation. This glorious truth is well calculated to enlarge the understanding, and to sustain the soul under troubles, difficulties, and distresses.

For illustration the speaker presented, by supposition, the case of two men, brothers, equally intelligent, learned, virtuous and lovely, walking in uprightness and in all good conscience, so far as they had been able to discern duty from the muddy stream of tradition, or from the blotted page of the book of nature. One dies, and is buried, having never heard the gospel of reconciliation, to the other the message of salvation is sent, he hears and embraces it, and is made the heir of eternal life.[17] Shall the one become a partaker of glory, and the other be consigned to hopeless perdition? Is there no chance for his escape? Sectarianism answers, "none! none!! none!!!" Such an idea is worse than atheism. The truth shall break down and dash in pieces all such bigoted Pharisaism; the sects shall be sifted, the honest in heart brought out, and their priests left in the midst of their corruption. The speaker then answered the objections urged against the Latter Day Saints for not admitting the validity of sectarian baptism, and for withholding fellowship from sectarian churches.[18] It was like putting new wine into old bottles and putting old wine into new bottles. What, new revelations in the old churches! New revelations knock out the bottom of their bottomless pit. New wine into old bottles!—the bottles burst and the wine runs out. What, Sadducees in the new church! Old wine in new leathern bottles will leak through the pores and escape; so the Sadducee saints mock at authority, kick out of the traces, and run to the mountains of perdition, leaving the long echo of their braying behind them.[19]

The speaker then contrasted the charity of the sects, in denouncing all who disagree with them in opinion, and in joining in persecuting the saints, with the faith of the saints, who believe that even such may be saved[20] in this world and in the world to come, (murderers and apostates excepted.)

This doctrine, he said, presented in a clear light, the wisdom and mercy of God, in preparing an ordinance for the salvation of the dead, being baptized by proxy, their names recorded in heaven,[21] and they judged according to the deeds done in the body.[22] This doctrine was the burden of the scriptures. Those saints who neglect it, in behalf of their deceased relatives, do it at the peril of their own salvation.[23]

The dispensation of the fulness of times will bring to light the things that have been revealed in all former dispensations, also other things that have not been before revealed.[24] He shall send Elijah the prophet[25] &c., and restore all things in Christ.[26]

The speaker then announced, "There shall be no more baptisms for the dead, until the ordinance can be attended to in the font of the Lord's House; and the church shall not hold another general conference, until they can meet in said house. *For thus saith the Lord!*"[27]

Jonathan Dunham Diary[28]

Comm at 9 agan Continued unt 5 P.M. A commandment from the Lord that there should no more Conference be held until the house of the Lord should be finished Adjourned with out day or date.[29]

4 October 1841 (Monday Morning). Meeting Ground.[1]
Times and Seasons 2 (15 October 1841):579

Monday 4th A.M. Conference opened by the choir singing hymn 183[2] and prayer by Bro. Geo. Smith.[3]

Pres't. Joseph Smith made a lengthy exposition of the condition of the temporal affairs of the church, the agency of which had been committed to him at a general conference in Quincy—explaining the manner that he had discharged the duties involved in that agency, and the condition of the lands and other property of the church.[4]

5 October 1841 (Tuesday Afternoon). Meeting Ground.[1]
Times and Seasons 2 (15 October 1841):579

P.M. Conference opened by the choir singing hymn 104,[2] and prayer by Bro. O. Pratt.

Bro. O. Pratt read to the conference, the minutes of a special conference held in the city of Nauvoo Aug. 16th 1841.[3]

Pres't. Joseph Smith made remarks explanatory of the importance of the resolutions and votes passed at that time.

7 November 1841 (Sunday). Meeting Ground Near Temple.[1]
Wilford Woodruff Journal

7th Sunday I first called upon Br Joseph with some of the Twelve from thence to B. Young from thence to the meeting ground near the Temple whare I found many hundreds of Saints Elder W<u>m</u> Clark[2] preached about 2 hours when Br Joseph arose & reproved him as pharisaical & hypocritical & not edifying the people Br Joseph then delivered unto us an Edifying address showing us what temperance faith virtue, charity & truth was he also said if we did not accuse one another God would not accuse us & if we had no accuser we should enter heaven he would take us there as his backload if we would not accuse him he would not accuse us & if we would throw a cloak of charity over his sins he would over ours for Charity coverd a multitude of sins & what many people called sin was not sin & he did many things to break down superstition[3] & he would break it down he spoke of the curse of ham for laughing at Noah while in his wine but doing no harm.[4]

14 November 1841 (Sunday). At Temple.[1]
Wilford Woodruff Journal

Joseph preached to a large congregation at the Temple.

12 December 1841 (Sunday Morning). Brother Snider's Home.[1]
Wilford Woodruff Journal

Joseph preached in the forepart of the day at Br Sniders[2] & had an interesting meeting.

19 December 1841 (Sunday). Old Homestead.[1]
Wilford Woodruff Journal

Joseph the Seer arose & read a Chapter in the New Testament containing the parable of the vine & its branches & explained much to our edification[2] & said, "if we kept the commandments of God we should bring forth fruit & be the friends of God & know what our

Lord did, "Some say Joseph is a fallen Prophet because he does not bring forth more of the word of the Lord"[3] "Why does he not do it" are we able to receive it No (says he) not one in this room, he then chastized us for our wickedness & unbelief knowing that whom the Lord loveth he chasteneth[4] & scourgeth every son & daughter whom he receiveth & if we do not receive chastizements then are we bastards & not Sons. On revelation he said "A man would command his son to dig potatoes, saddle his horse but before he had done either tell him to do something els this is all considered right "But as soon as the Lord gives a commandment & revokes that decree & commands something els then the prophet is considered fallen &c"[5] Because we will not receive chastizment at the hand of the Prophet & Apostles the Lord chastizeth us with sickness & death "Let not any man publish his own righteousness for others can do that for him." sooner let him confess his sins & then he will be forgiven & he will bring forth more fruit when a man is chastized he gets angry & will not endure it. The reason we do not have the secrets of the Lord revealed unto us is because we do not keep them but reveal them,[6] we do not keep our own secrets but reveal our difficulties to the world even to our enemies then how would we keep the secrets of the Lord Joseph says I can keep a secret till dooms day He spoke of love what greater love hath any man than that he lay down his life for his friend[7] then why not fight for our friend untill we die & many other things of interest was spoken.

1841 NOTES

5 January 1841

1. See *Teachings*, pp. 180-81. The original source for the report of this discourse in *Teachings* is William Clayton's Private Book as found in this text. This discourse is the only entry in *Teachings* for which Joseph Fielding Smith did not provide a source. The following lecture, separately recorded by William Clayton and William P. McIntire, was delivered at the Nauvoo Lyceum. The lyceum met every Tuesday, at different locations in Nauvoo, for several months beginning 5 January 1841. William P. McIntire's account is here published for the first time.

2. John Cook Bennett (1804-67) was elected mayor of Nauvoo one month from the time of this discourse. He was five feet five inches tall and weighed one hundred forty-two pounds. He also fit the Prophet's description of Paul in his patriarchal blessing. It states, "[Thou] shalt be like unto Paul," and he was also told "Turn not aside from the truth for the popularity of the world; but be like Paul." Finally he was promised, "When thou shalt reason . . . it shall be like Paul reasoning with Felix, and they shall tremble when they hear thy words" (*History of the Saints; or, an Expose of Joe Smith and the Mormons.* [Boston: Leland & Whiting, 1842], p. 43). Unfortunately, Bennett did not live up to these expectations. He was excommunicated from the Church in 1842 for teaching that illicit intercourse was condoned by Church leaders.

3. Apostle John Taylor was the person who first asked this question. However, when the answer was given, Elder Taylor, with others of the Twelve, was in England, and he was never apprised of the Prophet's explanation. Nevertheless, Joseph Smith assured Elder Taylor that he had received the Holy Spirit and challenged him pointedly: "Now listen to the dictates of that spirit and cultivate it, and it will become a spirit of revelation" (L. John Nuttall Diary, 3 August 1881, Special Collections, Harold B. Lee Library, Brigham Young University, Provo, Utah; hereafter referred to as BYU Special Collections). As a test of this promise to John Taylor specifically, and of Mormon theology generally, Elder Taylor's later independent speculations on this "unanswered" question are fascinating. Mormonism has no *Summa Theologica*. Notwithstanding this, the following example of independent yet consistent doctrinal affinity can be multiplied. In a meeting of the First Presidency and the Quorum of the Twelve Apostles held in Salt Lake City 22 April 1849, John Taylor asked President Brigham Young, "If Elijah, David, Solomon and the Prophets had the High Priesthood, how it was, [because] the Lord took it away with Moses." The question was discussed at length and finally "Prest Young said he did not know, but wished he did." John Taylor then offered his feelings on the question. The minutes record, "Brother Taylor thought perhaps the Lord conferred it himself upon some at times whom he had considered

worthy, but not with permission for them to continue it down upon others" ("Record of the Acts of the Quorum of the Twelve Apostles," 1849 Record Book, p. 39, Church Archives). Based on a combination of theological considerations—Mormonism's conception of translated and angelic beings before Christ's resurrection, the necessity of the laying on of hands for priesthood conferral, and a hint of the possibility of God's direct intervention contained in D&C 84:12 and (remotely) in JST Genesis 14:28-29—it is conceivable that both Joseph Smith and John Taylor could independently come to the same conclusion. However, if after 1849 John Taylor ever read the answer to his question (it was first published in 1882, in F. D. Richards' *Compendium*), he no doubt would have considered it an evidence that the Prophet's promise had been fulfilled.

4. D&C 13; 84:18-28; 107:18-20.

5. See discourse dated "Before 8 August 1839 (2)," note 9.

6. The William P. McIntire account of this discourse indicates that the subject of *ex nihilo* creation was one of the major topics of discussion during this inaugural lyceum meeting. Joseph Smith had previously discussed this subject (see discourse dated "Before 8 August 1839 (1)," note 4).

7. See discourse dated "Before 8 August 1839 (1)," note 4.

8. Genesis 1:1-2*. There were remarkable changes in these two passages in the manuscripts of Joseph Smith's translation of the Bible, but the alterations here mentioned were not made in 1830. They were included, however, in the creation account published with the book of Abraham (4:1-2).

9. This is the first mention by the Prophet Joseph Smith of the extremely important concept in Mormon theology that God the Father once had a mortal probation and was resurrected with a body of flesh and bones. It might be assumed by some today that this concept should have been obvious to most saints given the revelations received before this time. Yet this first explicit reference to the idea is most important for at least one reason. The following syllogistic argument used today for Mormonism's concept that God the Father once lived on an earth was not used or understood by the early Saints. The basic reasoning used today is as follows: All men are raised with their physical bodies in the resurrection (Alma 40:23, printed in 1830). Jesus, the Son of God and the great prototype (John 14:6-9), was the express image of his Father (Hebrews 1:3) and was resurrected with (Luke 24:30-39) and retained (3 Nephi 11:14-17, printed in 1830; Acts 1:11) his corporeal body. In the celestial resurrection men can become gods (D & C 76:58 [51-58], 1832 revelation). Therefore, God the Father must have a body of resurrected flesh and bones that he obtained following his own earth life.

That this reasoning was not apparent to the early saints may be demonstrated through the example of Lorenzo Snow. Perhaps no one in the history of the Church, except Joseph Smith has popularized this concept more than Lorenzo Snow. As an expert missionary he undoubtedly knew all the scriptures to which reference was made. Moreover, while in England in 1839, he claimed to have received special revelation in which he learned that "As man now is, our God once was; As God now is, so man may be, and thus unfolds our destiny." Notwithstanding all this, in a letter written to a "Respected Sister," two years later (about the time of this discourse by Joseph Smith) he said that the Father and the Son were spirits (Lorenzo Snow Letters, Call number Ms/f/562/item 12, pp. 40-45, Church Archives). It is possible that Elder Snow did not wish to assert something that he would have to explain, especially since in 1839 Apostle Brigham Young told him not to teach the concept of a once-mortal God until he heard the Prophet Joseph teach it. Nevertheless, the letter belies a spontaneous willingness to express the nature of the Godhead as he then understood it. Here, very early in the Nauvoo period of Church History, we find the Prophet launching out in a new area of doctrine that would be crucial to and interrelated with many other doctrines that made Nauvoo a quantum increase of light. Clearly the Nauvoo era was distinct from its Kirtland underpinnings. For an excellent and well-researched discussion of this question, see Van Hale, "The Doctrinal Impact of the King Follett Discourse," *Brigham Young University Studies* 18 (Winter 1978): 209-225.

10. A journal entry recorded by William Clayton in 1845 may be evidence that not only did Clayton copy this discourse into his Private Book, but that he also was the original reporter. Clayton had arrived in Nauvoo only six weeks before, on 24 November 1840, and no doubt this discourse would have impressed him. In 1845 he recorded in his journal an entry demonstrating his interest in this subject: "It has been a doctrine taught by this church that we were in the Grand Council amongst the Gods when the organization of this world was contemplated and that the laws of government were all made and sanctioned by all present and all the ordinances and ceremonies decreed upon" (Andrew F. Ehat, " 'It Seems Like Heaven Began on Earth': Joseph Smith and the Constitution of the Kingdom of God." *Brigham Young University Studies* 20 [Spring 1980]:269). See also 27 June 1839, note 6.

11. Matthew 8:28-34.

12. "President [Brigham Young] gave it as his opinion that the Earth did not dwell in the sphere in which it did when it was created, but that it was banished from its more glorious state or orbit of revolution for man's sake" ("Record of Acts of the Quorum of the Twelve Apostles," 1849 Record Book, p. 41, Church Archives). This and other statements like it probably had their origin with teachings of the Prophet Joseph Smith.

13. D&C 77:1; 88:17-26; 130:9; Moses 7:48, 49, 54, 58, 61-65, 67 (48-67).

14. William Patterson McIntire (1813-82) was a native of Pennsylvania.

Baptized in 1836, he worked as a tailor in Nauvoo. McIntire's Minute Book is in the Church Archives.

15. Don Carlos Smith (1816-41), Joseph Smith's brother, baptized in 1830. He edited thirty-one issues of the *Times and Seasons*.

16. Joseph Smith was concerned with the rhetorical and oratorical practices of his day. He detested the affectation and hypocrisy of the many flamboyant speakers. He spoke of the Holy Ghost as "calm and serene," "natural," and "edifying." When in Liberty Jail, he said, "A fanciful and flowery and heated imagination beware of; because the things of God are of deep import; and time, and experience, and careful and ponderous and solemn thoughts can only find them out" (*Teachings*, p. 137). For another of the Prophet's statements on speaking skills, see the 9 March 1841 discourse.

17. Dr. Josiah Ells came to Nauvoo in 1840. He was one of a company, under the command of Charles C. Rich, that attempted to rescue the Prophet Joseph Smith from his Dixon, Illinois, arrest in June 1843.

18. Many Saints have had an attraction to phrenology—the alleged analysis of character and mental faculties by studying the form of the skull (see Davis Bitton and Gary L. Bunker, "Phrenology among the Mormons," *Dialogue* [Spring 1974]:43-61). Unfortunately, members of the Church have been unaware of the revelation to Joseph Smith on this psuedoscience, and have misinterpreted his indifference toward the practice.

19. William Law (1809-92) was baptized in Upper Canada in 1836 and two weeks after this discourse was appointed by revelation (D&C 124:91) a counselor to Joseph Smith in the First Presidency. Rejecting certain of the Prophet's teachings (particularly plural marriage), Law left the Church in 1844. The revelation referred to also confirms the Prophet's announcement that William Law should go on a mission (D&C 124:88).

20. Unlike the William Clayton account of this discourse, the McIntire account shows how Joseph Smith used John 5:19 to shift from a discussion of the creation of the earth to a discussion of the nature of God.

21. 2 Nephi 2:18, 27.

12 January 1841

1. This report of the Prophet's remarks at the Nauvoo Lyceum is here published for the first time.

2. Amos Davis (1813-72). A prominent merchant and land owner in Nauvoo, Davis was baptized in 1840, but he did not migrate west with the Saints. He lived in Commerce, block 14, lot 3.

3. Undoubtedly Hosea Stout (1810-89). He was baptized in 1838, and in January 1844 he was appointed chief of police in Nauvoo.

4. Alma 48:10-25; D&C 98:13-48.

5. Alexander Badlam (1808-94), an early convert to Mormonism, was a commissioned officer of the Illinois State Militia. He assisted in the election of the general officers of the Nauvoo Legion in 1841.

6. See 27 June 1839, note 5.

7. Acts 2:34.

8. Acts 3:19-21.

9. Matthew 5:26.

19 January 1841

1. This report of the Prophet's remarks at the Nauvoo Lyceum is here published for the first time.

2. See the text of the 5 January 1841 discourse at note 11.

3. Luke 4:8.

4. James 4:7.

2 February 1841

1. This report of the Prophet's remarks at the Nauvoo Lyceum is here published for the first time.

2. That is, the Nauvoo Temple.

3. D&C 124:26-35.

9 February 1841

1. This report of the Prophet's remarks at the Nauvoo Lyceum is here published for the first time.

2. Hosea Stout.

3. Romans 5:20.

16 February 1841

1. This report of the Prophet's remarks at the Nauvoo Lyceum is here published for the first time.

2. See 9 March 1841, note 5.

3. 1 John 5:7-8; Matthew 18:19-20; D&C 124:95-97. Undoubtedly the Prophet knew what he was going to teach Hyrum Smith and William Law as

a result of D&C 124:95, 97. In addition to his allusion to this subject, the 9 and 21 March 1841 discourses also refer to these keys. It is interesting that Joseph Smith was not commanded to teach these keys to the other members of the First Presidency, namely Sidney Rigdon and John C. Bennett. When the Prophet first revealed these keys on 4 May 1842 Hyrum Smith and William Law were present, but Sidney Rigdon and John C. Bennett were conspicuously absent.

23 February 1841

1. This report of the Prophet's remarks at the Nauvoo Lyceum is here published for the first time.

2. Obviously still smarting from betrayals by some of his brethren while in Kirtland, Ohio and Far West, Missouri, the Prophet also expressed this idea in his 2 July 1839 discourse: "Whatever you do, do not betray your Friend."

2 March 1841

1. This report of the Prophet's remarks at the Nauvoo Lyceum is here published for the first time.

2. Leonard Soby was appointed a member of the Nauvoo High Council on 8 April 1841. After the Prophet's death he was disfellowshipped for supporting Sidney Rigdon's claim that he was Joseph Smith's successor.

3. Deuteronomy 32:35, 41, 43 (15-43).

4. Alma 48:10-25; D&C 98:13-48.

5. Luke 16:9-13.

9 March 1841

1. This report of the Prophet's remarks at the Nauvoo Lyceum is here published for the first time.

2. Austin Cowles was appointed counselor to William Marks in the Nauvoo Stake Presidency on 29 March 1841. Opposed to the Prophet's practice of plural marriage, Cowles sided with William Law and other dissenters.

3. Acts 2:37-38; Acts 10:44-48 (1-48); D&C 20:37.

4. William Law, counselor in the First Presidency.

5. There is an undated but nearly identical statement "By Joseph" recorded in the William Clayton Private Book. It states, "[An] Everlasting covenant was made between three personages before the organization of

this earth and relates to their dispensation of things to men on the earth. These personages according to Abraham's record are called God the first, the Creator; God the second, the Redeemer; and God the third, the Witness or Testator" ("Extracts from Wm Clayton's Private Book," pp. 10-11, L. John Nuttall Collection, BYU Special Collections).

6. See 5 January 1841, note 9.

7. See discourse dated "Before 8 August 1839 (1)," note 8.

8. This is a very significant early public reference by the Prophet to the concept of approaching the Lord by the use of key words and through the priesthood. See 5 October 1840 discourse, note 19.

9. Undoubtedly Ebenezer Robinson (1816-91). He was baptized in 1835 and was editor and publisher of the *Times and Seasons*.

10. Genesis 2:17 (Moses 3:17; Abraham 3:4 [4-9]; 5:12, 13; Facsimile 2, figures 1 and 4); 2 Peter 3:8.

11. Abraham 5:13 (cf. Revelation 10:5-6).

16 March 1841

1. This report of the Prophet's remarks at the Nauvoo Lyceum is here published for the first time.

2. As President Joseph Fielding Smith has pointed out (*Teachings*, p. 268 n), revelation through Joseph Smith applies the term *wicked* (D&C 84:53 [49-53]) to individuals who in other revelations are referred to as the "honorable men of the earth" (D&C 76:75). Apparently those who, as President Smith says, are "without Gospel ordinances" are "wicked." They are tolerable for the millennial, terrestrialized earth; however, this ultimate sense of the term *wicked* will eventually apply when terrestrial individuals are prevented from entering the celestialized, glorified permanent residence of Christ (D&C 130:9). See note 4, this discourse.

3. Isaiah 65:20-22.

4. Zechariah 14:16-19; Revelation 5:10* (20:4, 6); 1 Corinthians 15:6. In December 1842 Joseph Smith made essentially the same statement. As published in the *History of the Church*, 5:212 (or *Teachings*, p. 268), the statement is somewhat equivocal: "They ["Christ and the resurrected Saints"] will not probably dwell upon the earth, but will visit it when they please, or when it is necessary to govern it." However, neither the McIntire account here presented nor the original source for the *History of the Church* are as tentative. In the Prophet's diary kept by Willard Richards, the statement reads, "Christ & the Resurrected saints will reign over the earth, but not dwell on the earth visit it when they please or when necessary to govern it" (Joseph Smith Diary, 30 December 1842, Church Archives).

5. Revelation 20:3; D&C 43:22; 88:17-26; 110:16; 130:9; Matthew 5:5.

6. Genesis 2:17; Moses 3:17; 7:32; Abraham 5:12, 13; 2 Nephi 2:11-27.

21 March 1841

1. The following reports by Martha Jane Knowlton Coray and William P. McIntire are here published for the first time.

2. William Law's store on Water Street, block 148.

3. Vinson Knight (1804-42) was converted to the Church in 1834 and appointed a bishop in Nauvoo. Knight lived on Main Street, block 126.

4. Luke 1:5; D&C 84:27.

5. Matthew 3:3.

6. Malachi 2:7.

7. Leviticus 10:10-11 (9-11); Deuteronomy 17:9-13 (8-13); 33:10 (8-11).

8. Matthew 11:12.

9. Matthew 3:14-15 (13-17).

10. D&C 84:26-27.

11. Matthew 3:13-17. Undoubtedly, the three signs referred to in the text are (1) the opening of the heavens and the Holy Ghost, a personage in the form of a man, descending; (2) the appearance of a dove; and (3) the voice of the Father saying "This is my Beloved Son."

12. This is the only reference in all of the Prophet's teachings that the appearance of a dove signifies the presence of a "pure" or "true" spirit messenger. See 27 June 1839, note 21.

13. See 27 June 1839, note 21.

14. Luke 7:28.

15. Matthew 11:11-12.

16. JST Matthew 17:10-14.

17. Matthew 17:1-3 (cf. 16:19; 18:18 [7-20]).

18. 1 Corinthians 10:1 (1-4).

19. Malachi 3:2-4 (1-4).

20. Malachi 3:5-7.

21. Ezekiel 36:21-27; Isaiah 49:22-23 (cf. 1 Nephi 22).

22. A combination of Isaiah 2:3 and the scriptures cited in note 7, this

discourse (cf. Malachi 3:3-4).

   23. Daniel 7:9, 14, 21-22, 27 (1-28).

   24. Exodus 40:15.

   25. Matthew 3:15 (13-17).

   26. Luke 1:8* (5-11) (cf. 1 Chronicles 24:10, 19). Zacharias, of the order of Abia, had a turn—the rare opportunity—to officiate in the priest's office in the temple. The Prophet here asserts that Zacharias, in the authority and wearing the robes of the Levitical priesthood, wrestled with the Lord to obtain the promise of a son. Because of respect to Zacharias's keys, God sent the angel Gabriel. See 23 July 1843, note 21 and 5 October 1840, note 19.

28 March 1841

   1. The following report by William P. McIntire is here published for the first time.

   2. See Joseph Smith's statement (in the discourse dated 29 September 1839) that such thinking is "an unhallowed principle."

   3. Joseph Smith quoted Job 38:4 as an evidence of the premortal existence of man. See discourse dated "Before 8 August 1839 (1)," note 4.

   4. Matthew 8:28-34.* See discourse dated 5 January 1841.

30 March 1841

   1. The following remarks made at the Nauvoo Lyceum are here published for the first time.

   2. Either Urban Van Stewart (1817-98) or Levi Stewart (1812-78).

   3. Ebenezer Robinson.

   4. John 16:8-11.

   5. John 16:8.*

   6. Ebenezer Robinson made the error of thinking that the "Other Comforter"mentioned in John 14:16-25 was the Holy Ghost. See note 5 of discourse dated "Before 8 August 1839 (3)."

6 April 1841

   1. See *History of the Church*, 4:329. Not in *Teachings*. The *History of the Church* entry is based on the *Times and Seasons* account. The cornerstones of the Nauvoo Temple were laid at the April 1841 General Conference of the Church.

7 April 1841

1. See *History of the Church,* 4:339. Not in *Teachings.* The *History of the Church* entry is based on the *Times and Seasons* account. The following remarks were made at the April 1841 General Conference of the Church.

2. John Cook Bennett.

3. Begun between 19 January 1841 and 7 April 1841, the "Book of the Law of the Lord" was a compilation of revelations, letters, and journal entries of the Prophet. The very first entry in the record was the revelation referred to in this discourse, D&C 124. Beginning in December 1841, tithes and other donations (particularly those for the temple) were also recorded in the "Law of the Lord."

4. The text refers to D&C 124. Regarding the proclamation to the kings of the earth, the revelation specified that Robert B. Thompson and John C. Bennett should assist in its writing and dissemination. However, Thompson's premature death and Bennett's apostasy precluded either contributing to the project. Although several attempts were made to write this document, it was not until the spring of 1844 that any work was accomplished. In 1863 William W. Phelps reported that he was specially commissioned in May 1844 to write the "great proclamation" under the direction of the Prophet, and that he had in his possession 22 manuscript pages which Joseph Smith had approved. He lamented, however, that the project was dropped after the martyrdom. In 1845, the Quorum of the Twelve Apostles essentially fulfilled the instructions of D&C 124 by publishing their proclamation to the kings of the world. See *Proclamation of the Twelve Apostles of the Church of Jesus Christ of Latter-day Saints. To all the kings of the world; to the President of the United States of America; to the governors of the several states and to the rulers and peoples of all nations* . . . [New York, Prophet Office, 1845].

5. The "Boarding House" was another name for the Nauvoo House. Begun in October 1841, the building was intended to be a prestigious hotel for the accommodation of prominent public figures. After the Prophet's death, the edifice was left unfinished.

8 April 1841

1. See *History of the Church,* 4:340-41. Not in *Teachings.* The *History of the Church* entry is based on the *Times and Seasons* account. The following remarks were made at the April 1841 General Conference of the Church.

2. On this occasion the voting to sustain Church leaders was done in order of priesthood groupings. The Priesthood quorums had only recently been reorganized as a result of D&C 124.

3. Voting was, generally speaking, unanimous among the Latter-day Saints, although during the Prophet's lifetime a more democratic spirit prevailed. On this occasion a simple majority was all that was required for the passing of proposals.

4. The Temple Building Committee consisted of Elias Higbee, Alpheus Cutler, and Reynolds Cahoon.

5. David W. Patten (1799-1838) was baptized in 1832 and ordained an apostle in 1835. He was shot and killed while attempting to rescue three kidnapped Mormons near Far West, Missouri.

9 April 1841

1. See *History of the Church*, 4:342. Not in *Teachings*. The *History of the Church* entry is based on the *Times and Seasons* account. The following remarks were made at the April 1841 General Conference of the Church. William P. McIntire's report is here published for the first time.

2. Though the published minutes of the conference are vague, the McIntire report given below preserves the Prophet's instructions regarding the financial obligations of missionaries.

3. At this time in the history of the Church (unlike today), the president of the stake and the president of the high priests quorum were not the same person (see D&C 124:133-34).

11 April 1841

1. See *History of the Church*, 4:343. Not in *Teachings*. The *History of the Church* entry is based on the *Times and Seasons* account. The following remarks were made on the final day of April 1841 General Conference.

2. That is, those who wished to be baptized for remission of sins, for the restoration of health, and for the dead.

25 April 1841

1. The following report by Alexander Neibaur is here published for the first time.

2. Alexander Neibaur (1808-76), born in Ehrenbriesten, France (now Germany), was baptized by Isaac Russell in Preston, England, in April 1838. In 1841 he came to Nauvoo, where he practiced dentistry. The Neibaur Journal is located in the Church Archives.

3. Dr. John Cook Bennett.

4. William Law.

9 May 1841

1. The following report by William Clayton was first published in James B. Allen and Thomas G. Alexander, eds., *Manchester Mormons: The Journal of William Clayton 1840 to 1842* (Santa Barbara and Salt Lake City: Peregrine Smith, 1974), p. 212. The Alexander Neibaur account is here published for the first time.

2. In other words, Nauvoo. At the time, William Clayton was residing in Lee County, Iowa.

3. The document "Extracts from William Clayton's Private Book," undoubtedly was prepared and given this title by William Clayton. The original is not known to be in existence; however, L. John Nuttall and Joseph F. Smith made copies of a record by this title. The Joseph F. Smith copy is the more inclusive of the two, but neither contains a discourse on baptism for the dead nor one dated 9 May 1841. On the other hand, both contain the 16 May 1841 discourse Clayton copied into his "Record." Thus, the "Record" may have been the "Private Book" from which the "Extracts from William Clayton's Private Book" was prepared. If true, possibly Clayton did not feel his report of the 9 May 1841 discourse was significant enough to include in the "Extracts" document.

16 May 1841

1. See *History of the Church*, 4:358-60, and *Teachings,* pp. 187-89. The reports of this discourse found in *History of the Church* and *Teachings* have their source in the *Times and Seasons* account. The first of the two William Clayton accounts is here published for the first time. The latter was first published in James B. Allen and Thomas G. Alexander, eds., *Manchester Mormons: The Journal of William Clayton 1840 to 1842,* (Santa Barbara and Salt Lake City: Peregrine Smith, 1974), p. 213.

2. Genesis 2:17; Moses 3:17; 7:32; Abraham 5:12, 13; 2 Nephi 2:11-27. In Clayton's version of this discourse, he records Joseph Smith as saying, "There are three independent principles—the spirit of God, the spirit of man, and the spirit of the devil. All men have power to resist the devil." This statement on human individuality and the Prophet's teachings on the self-existence of human individuality combine to form the basis of a unique Mormon view of the problem of evil and suffering. While Joseph Smith nowhere gave an extended, systematic statement on theodicy, yet this view of absolving God of the problem is much different than the approach used in orthodox Christian theology (see discourse dated "Before 8 August 1839 (1)," note 4).

3. Romans 8:20.

4. Romans 3:23; 2 Corinthians 5:21; Hebrews 4:15; 1 Peter 2:21-25; D&C 45:4.

5. Matthew 27:43; Luke 22:70; John 5:25; 9:35-37; 10:36; 11:4 are passages in which Jesus referred to himself as the Son of God.

6. D&C 93:4-17.

7. John 17:2.

8. Romans 8:20.

9. Acts 2:37-38.

10. Acts 3:17-21.

11. 1 John 3:15.

12. Acts 2:34.

13. Matthew 27:52-53. See also Helaman 14:25-26; 3 Nephi 23:9-13.

14. Matthew 5:26.

15. Genesis 12:3; 18:8; 22:18; 26:4-5; D&C 110:12; Abraham 2:9-11.

16. Romans 9:4.

17. Romans 9:3.

18. Romans 9:17. See also Exodus 9:16 (15-17).

19. Obadiah 21.

20. Isaiah 61:6 (1-6).

21. Romans 9:27-29.

22. To Joseph Smith unconditional election of the House of Israel to eternal life was a repulsive Calvinist doctrine of predestination. Founded in the doctrine of human depravity, this notion asserted that God in his almighty wisdom had elected some men to eternal salvation and relegated others to eternal torment. Joseph Smith believed that the Saints might make their calling and election sure through the righteous use of free agency.

23. See 27 June 1839, note 5.

24. Acts 3:19-21.

25. Matthew 16:19 (13-20). Cf. D&C 132:46. See 10 March 1844, note 23.

26. See 9 May 1841, note 3.

30 May 1841

1. The following account by Alexander Neibaur is here published for the first time.

13 or 20 June 1841

1. See *History of the Church*, 4:381. Not in *Teachings*. The *History of the Church* entry is based on the *Times and Seasons* account.

25 July 1841

1. Not in *Teachings*. The original source for this entry is most probably the "Book of the Law of the Lord." The Prophet's remarks on the resurrection were made at the conclusion of a "general" funeral sermon by Sidney Rigdon.

16 August 1841

1. See *History of the Church*, 4:403, and *Teachings*, p. 190. The source for entries in *History of the Church* and *Teachings* is the *Times and Seasons* account. The following remarks were made by Joseph Smith at a special conference held in Nauvoo. The purpose of the meeting was to "select men of experience to send forth into the vineyard, take measures to assist emigrants who may arrive at the places of gathering, and prevent impositions being practiced upon them by unprincipled speculators" (see *History of the Church*, 4:402).

2. See 27 June 1839, note 8.

3. This is an interesting foreshadowing of the role that the Quorum of the Twelve would assume at Joseph's death. Language such as this undoubtedly made it easier for the Twelve to succeed to the Presidency.

4. That is, the translation of both the Bible and the Book of Abraham.

22 August 1841

1. Not in *Teachings*. The original source for this entry is most probably the "Book of the Law of the Lord." The "Stand" was a platform upon which Church leaders sat and from which they addressed the congregation. The audience sat on benches of split logs or on the grass. This portable meeting house, normally set up in a grove, could be conveniently moved from place to place according to need and circumstance.

5 September 1841

1. See *Teachings*, p. 190. The original source for this account is most probably the "Book of the Law of the Lord."

2. An obvious allusion to calomel and other "heroic" medicines of the day. See 13 April 1843, notes 16 and 17.

3. D&C 42:43.

2 October 1841

1. See *History of the Church*, 4:424. Not in *Teachings*. The *History of the Church* entry is based on the *Times and Seasons* account. The following remarks were made at the October 1841 General Conference of the Church.

2. The hymn sung was "Jesus from Whom All Blessings Flow."

3. Orson Hyde had been sent by the Prophet to Jerusalem to dedicate the land of Palestine for the return of the Jews.

4. A reference to the Prophet's desire to build the Nauvoo Temple and Nauvoo House.

5. At a previous conference (see 16 July 1841) the Prophet Joseph announced a significant increase of authority that the Twelve Apostles were to exercise. In citing this passage of scripture, he seemed to reinforce this new development: "And God hath set some in the church, first apostles, secondarily prophets, thirdly teachers."

3 October 1841

1. See *History of the Church*, 4:424-26, and *Teachings*, pp.191-93. The *History of the Church* and *Teachings* entries for this discourse have their source in the *Times and Seasons* account. The Jonathan Dunham account is here published for the first time. The following discourse on baptism for the dead was delivered at the October 1841 General Conference of the Church.

2. William Marks (1792-1872). Baptized by 1835, Marks was a man of means and influence. He was appointed president of the Nauvoo Stake in 1839.

3. "Come, Let Us Anew Our Journey Pursue" was the hymn that was sung.

4. Heber C. Kimball (1801-68) was baptized in 1832 and ordained an apostle in 1835.

5. Obadiah 21.

6. More than two years before Joseph Smith first preached the doctrine of baptism for the dead, he publicly announced, "All those who have not had an opportunity of hearing the Gospel, and being administered unto by an inspired man in the flesh, must have it hereafter, before they can be finally judged." *Elders Journal* 1 (July 1838):43.

7. See 5 October 1840, note 13.

8. 1 Peter 3:18-20; 4:6.

9. For example, Luke 24:36-39; D&C 129:2.

10. That is, translated individuals are still mortal. See Mormon's perplexity regarding the nature of translated beings in 3 Nephi 28. In verse 15 he seems convinced that they are immortal; in verse 17 he does not know whether they were immortal or not. Finally, in verses 36-40 he indicates that he had learned by revelation that they were still mortal and would have to undergo a final change in order "to be received into the kingdom of the Father to go no more out." See 5 October 1840, note 13.

11. Revelation 1:10-20; 19:9-10; 22:8-9.

12. Apparently the City of Enoch (Moses 7:62-64, 69).

13. We have no account of Christ's ministry to resurrected beings following his resurrection.

14. D&C 84:6-18, 25-28; 93:6-17; 27:8, 12-13.

15. D&C 88:118.

16. Isaiah 22:22 (Revelation 3:7-12); Matthew 16:19; 18:18; Helaman 10:7; D&C 110:16; 132:46.

17. Titus 3:7.

18. D&C 22.

19. JST Matthew 9:18-23.* David Osborn confirms these teachings in a reminiscent account of what is probably this discourse.

"Joseph's explanation of this saying of the Savior. 'No man putteth new wine into old bottles—but new wine must be put into new bottles, lest the bottles break and the wine be spilt etc.' He said the Jews anciently used bottles made of the skins of sheep and other animals. The wine when new would ferment and swell so would a new bottle stretch and swell, but to put new wine into an old one that had stretched all it could, the bottle was liable to burst and spill the wine. He explained the new wine to represent new revelation. He said he had seen this saying of the Savior's exemplified in this church many times by those who had been gathered out of other churches. Who were so full of ancient revelation on the Bible that when a little more was given they could not find room for it, consequently it was lost to them. They would turn away and leave the church" (David Osborn Journal, Church Archives).

20. Here we find a hint about the distinction between the terms *salvation* and *exaltation*. The use of the term *salvation* for all those resurrected except the sons of perdition may be found in D&C 76:43 (42-44). However, fewer than two years after this discourse, Joseph recorded his revelation on eternal marriage, wherein angels inherit the Celestial Kingdom but are without "exaltation" (D&C 132:17).

21. Revelation 20:12-13; D&C 128:6-9.

22. Revelation 20:12-13.

23. It should be borne in mind that the policy regarding baptisms for the dead allowed that ordinance work be done (1) for those who were direct ancestors; (2) for those who were known personally by their descendants; and (3) for those believed to have accepted the gospel in the Spirit World. Under these criteria, the Saints were required to do ordinance work for at most three or four generations. Subsequent revelation has added to this responsibility. Statements of Joseph Smith on these criteria may be found in D&C 137:5-9 and *Teachings*, p. 179.

24. See 5 October 1840, note 15.

25. Malachi 4:3-4; Joseph Smith-History 1:38-39 (D&C 2); D&C 110:13-16.

26. This is important confirmation by Joseph Smith that the appearance of Elijah in the Kirtland Temple completed the restoration of all the keys of the priesthood. See D&C 132:45-48.

27. Prior to this time, baptisms for the dead were being performed in the Mississippi River and local streams. The baptismal font in the basement of the Nauvoo Temple was completed on 8 November 1841, and baptisms for the dead were commenced on Sunday, 21 November 1841. Wilford Woodruff reported that a large congregation assembled to witness the baptism of about forty persons on that occasion (Wilford Woodruff Journal, 21 November 1841, Church Archives).

28. Jonathan Dunham (1800-1845) was Nauvoo high policeman and major-general in the Nauvoo Legion.

29. That is, they adjourned without establishing a date for the next general conference. (The next general conference was held on 6 April 1842.)

4 October 1841

1. See *History of the Church*, 4:427. Not in *Teachings*. The *History of the Church* entry for this discourse has its source in the *Times and Seasons* account. The following remarks were made at the October 1841 General Conference of the Church.

2. "Alas! And Did My Savior Bleed!" was the hymn that was sung.

3. George A. Smith (1817-75) was Joseph Smith's cousin. He was baptized in 1832 and ordained an apostle in April 1839.

4. See 5 October 1839, note 2.

5 October 1841

1. See *History of the Church*, 4:428. Not in *Teachings*. The entry in the *History of the Church* for this discourse has its source in the *Times and Seasons*

account. The following remarks were made at the October 1841 General Conference of the Church.

2. "My Soul is Full of Peace and Love" was the hymn that was sung.

3. See report of discourse dated 16 August 1841.

7 November 1841

1. See *History of the Church*, 4:445-46, and *Teachings*, pp. 93-94. The Wilford Woodruff Journal is the source for the entry in *History of the Church* and *Teachings*.

2. William Ogelby Clark was born 25 June 1817 at Madison, Jefferson County, Indiana. A seventy, Clark served a mission in Iowa and Illinois in 1844.

3. 1 Peter 4:8.

4. Genesis 9:18-27.

14 November 1841

1. See *History of the Church*, 4:448. Not in *Teachings*. The Wilford Woodruff Journal is the source for the entry in *History of the Church*.

12 December 1841

1. See *History of the Church*, 4:470. Not in *Teachings*. The Wilford Woodruff Journal is the source for the entry in *History of the Church*.

2. John Snider (1800-1875). Converted in Toronto in 1836, Snider was a member of the Nauvoo House Association.

19 December 1841

1. See *History of the Church*, 4:478-79, and *Teachings*, pp. 194-95. The Wilford Woodruff Journal is the source for the entries in *History of the Church* and *Teachings*.

2. John 15:1-8.

3. D&C 82:4. See 5 October 1840, note 24.

4. Hebrews 12:5-11.

5. D&C 58:30-33. See also D&C 56:1-7.

6. Alma 12:9-11; Ether 4:1-7.

7. John 15:13.

1842

1842

16 January 1842 (Sunday). Old Homestead.[1]
Manuscript History of the Church

 I preached at my own house morning and evening, illustrating the nature of Sin, and shewing that it is not right to sin that grace may abound.[2]

30 January 1842 (Sunday). Old Homestead.[1]
Manuscript History of the Church

 I preached at my house morning and evening, concerning the different Spirits, their operations, designs—&c.

27 February 1842 (Sunday).[1]
Manuscript History of the Church

 Engaged in Counselling the Saints.

6 March 1842 (Sunday). Orson Spencer's Home.[1]
Manuscript History of the Church

 I preached at Elder Orson Spencer's[2] near the Temple.

17 March 1842 (Thursday). Upper Room, Red Brick Store.[1]
Nauvoo Relief Society Minutes

The meeting was address'd by Prest. Smith, to illustrate the object of the Society[2]—that the Society of Sisters might provoke the brethren to good works in looking to the wants of the poor—searching after objects of charity, and in administering to their wants—to assist by correcting the morals and strengthening the virtues of the ~~female~~ community, and save the Elders the trouble of rebuking; that they may give their time to other duties &c: in their public teaching.

Prest. Smith further remark'd that an organization to show them how to go to work would be sufficient. He propos'd that the Sisters elect a presiding officer to preside over them, and let that presiding officer choose two counsellors to assist in the duties of her office—that he would ordain[3] them to preside over the Society—and let them preside just as Presidency, preside over the church: and if they need his instruction ask him, will give it from time to time.

Let this Presidency serve as a constitution[4]—all their decisions be considered law, and acted upon as such.

If any Officers are wanted to carry out the designs of the Institution, let them be appointed and set apart,[5] as Deacons, Teachers, &C. are among us.

The minutes of your meetings will be precedent for you to act upon—your Constitution—and law.

He then suggested the propriety of electing a Presidency to continue in the office during good behavior, or so long as they shall continue to fill the office with dignity &C.,—like the first Presidency of the Church.

Motioned by Sister Whitney[6] and seconded by Sister Packard[7] that Mrs. Emma Smith[8] be chosen President—passed unanimously.

Mov'd by Prest. Smith, that Mrs. Smith proceed to choose her Counsellors, that they may be ordain'd to preside over this Society, in taking care of the poor, administering to their wants, and attending to the various affairs of this Institution.

The Presidentess Elect, then made choice of Mrs. Sarah M. Cleveland[9] and Mrs. Elizabeth Ann Whitney for Counsellors.

President Smith read the Revelation to Emma Smith, from the book of Doctrine and Covenants;[10] and stated that she was ordain'd at the time the Revelation was given,[11] to expound the scriptures to all; and to teach the female part of community; and that not she alone, but others, may attain to the same blessings.—[12]

The 2d Epistle of John, 1st verse, was then read to show that respect was there had to the same thing, and that why she was called an Elect lady is because elected to preside.

. . . [After John Taylor had ordained the presidency] Prest. Smith then resumed his remarks and gave instruction how to govern themselves in their meetings—when one wishes to speak, address the chair—and the chairman responds to the address.

Should two speak at once, the Chair shall decide who speaks first, if anyone is dissatisfied, she appeals to the house.

When one has the floor, [she] occupies [it] as long as she pleases &C.

Proper manner of address is Mrs. Chairman or President and not Mr. Chairman &C.

A question can never be put until it has a second

When the subject for discussion has been fairly investigated; the chairman will say, are you ready for the question? &c.

Whatever the majority of the house decide upon becomes a law to the Society.

Prest. Smith proceeded to give counsel: do not injure the character of anyone—if members of the Society shall conduct [themselves] improperly, deal with them, and keep all your doings within your own bosoms; and hold all characters sacred—

. . . [After a discussion to determine the official name of the society, Joseph Smith said] I now declare this society organized with president and counsellors and according to parliamentary usage, and all who shall hereafter be admitted into this society must be free from censure and received by vote.

Manuscript History of the Church

I assisted in commencing the organization of "The Female {Relief Society of Nauvoo" in the "Lodge Room." Sister Emma Smith, President, and Sisters Elizabeth Ann Whitney and Sarah M.

Cleveland Counsellors. I gave much instruction, read in the New Testament,[13] and Book of Doctrine and Covenants[14] concerning the Elect Lady, and shewed that the elect meant to be elected to a certain work &c and that the revelation was then fulfilled by Sister Emma's election to the Presidency of the Society, she having previously been ordained to expound Scriptures}[15] Emma was blessed, and her counselors were ordained by Elder John Taylor.

20 March 1842 (Sunday Morning). Grove, West Side of Temple.[1]
Wilford Woodruff Journal

A large assembly of Saints gather together at an early hour to hear a discours deliverd upon the Subject of Baptism by Joseph the Seer; but as a young child[2] was dead & his corpes presented in the assembly it called for many remarks from The speaker upon death & the resurrection which were in the highest degree interesting & his remarks upon Baptism was truly glorious to the believer in Jesus Christ. The following is a brief synopsis of some of the items presented in the discours

The Speaker read the 14ch Revelations. And sayes "we have again the warning voice sounded in our midst which shows the uncertainty of human life. And in my leasure moments I have meditated upon the subject, & asked the question Why is it that infants innocent children are taken away from us esspecially those that seem to be most intelligent beings" Answer "This world is a vary wicked world & it is a proverb that the world grows weaker & wiser; but if it is the case the world grows more wicked & corrupt. In the early ages of the world A ritheous man & a man of God & intelligence had a better chance to do good to be received & believed than at the present day. but in these days such a man is much opposed & persecuted by most of the inhabitants of the earth & he has much sorrow to pass through, hence the Lord takes many away even in infancy that they may escape the envy of man. The sorrows & evils of this present world & they were two pure & to lovly to live on Earth, Therefore if rightly considered we have, instead of morning we have reason to rejoice, as they are deliverd from evil & we shall soon have them again,[3] What chance is their for infidelity[4] when we are parting with our friends almost daily none at all The infidel will grasp at evry straw for help untill death stares him in the face & then his infidelity takes its flight for the realities of the eternal world are resting upon him in mighty power & when evry earthly support & prop fail him. He then sensibly feels the eternal truths of the immortality of the soul Also the doctrin of baptizing Children or sprinkling them or they must welter in Hell is a doctrin not true not supported in Holy writ & is not consistant with the Character of God The moment that Children leave this world they are taken to the bosom of Abraham The ownly difference between the old & young dying is one lives longer in heaven & Eternal light & glory than the other & was freed a little sooner from this miserable wicked world Notwithstanding all this glory we for a moment loose sight of it & mourn the loss but we do not mourn as those without hope.[5] (We should take warning & not wait for the deathbed to repent) As we se the infant taken away by death, so may the youth & middle aged as well as the infant suddenly be called into eternity, Let this then proove as a warning to all not to procrastinate repentance or wait till a death bed,[6] for it is the will of God that man should repent & serve him in health & in the strength & power of his mind in order to secure his blessings & not wait untill he is called to die.

"My intention (says the speaker) was to have treated upon the subject of Baptism, But having a case of death before us I thought it proper to refer to that subject. I will now however say a few words upon ~~that subject~~ Baptism as intended God has made certain decreas which are fixed & unalterable for instance God set the sun, the moon, the stars in the heavens, & give them their laws conditions, & bounds which they cannot pass except by his command, they all move in perfect harmony in there sphere & order[7] & are as wonders, lights & signs[8] unto us. The sea also has its bounds which it cannot pass God ~~has~~ set many signs in the earth as well as in heaven[9] for instance the oaks of the forrest the fruit of the tree, the herb of the field all bear a sign that seed hath been planted there, for it is a decree of the Lord that evry tree fruit or herb baring seed should bring forth after its kind & cannot come forth after any other law or principle.[10] upon the same principle do I contend that Baptism is a sign ordained of God for the believer in Christ to take upon himself in order to enter into the Kingdom of God, "for except you are born of the water & the spirit you cannot enter into the Kingdom of God.[11] Saith the Savior as It is a sign of command which

God hath set for man to enter into this ~~kingdom of God~~ those who seek to enter in any other way[12] will seek in vain for God will not receive them neither will the angels acknowledge their works as accepted, for they have not taken upon themselves those ordinances & signs which God ordained for man to receive in order to receive a celestial glory, & God has decreed that all ~~that~~ who will not obey his voice shall not escape the damnation of hell, what is the damnation of hell, to go with that society who have not obeyed his commands Baptism is a sign to God, to angels to heaven that we do the will of God & there is no other way beneath the heavens whareby God hath ordained for man to come ~~to God~~ & any other course is in vain. God hath decreed & ordained that man should repent of all his sins & Be Baptized for the remission of his sins then he can come to God in the name of Jesus Christ in faith then we have the promise of the Holy Ghost[13]

What is the sign of the healing of the sick? the laying on of hands, is the sign or way marked out by James[14] & the custom of the ancient saints as ordered by the Lord & we should not obtain the blessing by pursuing any other course except the way which God has markd out. What if we should attempt to get the Holy Ghost through any other means except the sign or way which God hath appointed should we obtain it certainly not all other means would fail The Lord says do so & so & I will bless so & so their is certain key words[15] & signs belonging to the priesthood which must be observed in order to obtain the blessings The sign of Peter was to repent & be baptized for the remission of sins, with the promise of the gift of the Holy Ghost & in no other way is the gift of the Holy Ghost obtained.[16] Their is a difference between the Holy Ghost & the gift of the Holy Ghost. Cornelius received the Holy Ghost before he was Baptized[17] which was the convincing power of God unto him of the truth of the gospel but he could not receive the gift of the Holy Ghost untill after he was Baptized, & had he not taken this sign ordinances upon him the Holy Ghost which convinced him of the truth of God would have left him untill he obeyed those ordinances & received the gift of the Holy Ghost by the laying on of hands according to the order of God he could not have healed the sick or command an evil spirit to come out of a man[18] & it obey him, for the spirit might say to him as he did to the sons of Scava Peter I know & Christ I know but who are ye[19]

It matereth not whether we live long or short after we come to a knowlede of these principles & obey them, I know that all men will be damned if they do not come in the way which God has appointed.

As concerning the resurrection I will merly say that all men will come from the grave as they lie down, whether old or young their will not be added unto their stature one cubit neither taken from it.[20] All being raised by the power of God having the spirit of God in their bodies & not blood[21] Children will be enthroned in the presence of God & the Lamb with bodies of the same stature that were on earth,[22] Having been redeemed by the Blood of the Lamb they will there enjoy a fulness of that light Glory & intelligence which is received in the celestial kingdom of God "blessed are the dead who die in the Lord, for they rest from their labours & their works do follow them[23]

The speaker before closing called upon the vast assembly before him to humble themselves in faith before God & in mighty prayer & fasting to call upon his Holy name untill the elements were purified over our heads & the earth sanctified under our feet that the inhabitants of this city may escape the power of the disease pestilence & destroyer that rideth upon the face of the earth & that the holy spirit of God may rest upon this vast multitude

At the close of the meetg President Smith informed the congregation that he should attend to the ordinance of Baptism in the ~~his to~~ river near his house at 2 oclock.

27 March 1842 (Sunday). Grove Near Temple.[1]
Wilford Woodruff Journal

Sunday 27 This was an interesting day A large assembly met in the grove near the Temple Br Amisa Lyman[2] addressed the assemby & made many interesting remarks. He was followed by Joseph the Seer who made some edifying remarks concerning Baptism for the dead. He said the Bible supported the doctrine "why are ye Baptized for the dead if they dead rise not &c"[3] if their is one word of the Lord that supports the doctrin it is enough to make it a true doctrin Again if we can baptize a man in the name of the Father of the Son & of the Holy Ghost for the remission of sins it is just as much our privilege to act as an agent & be baptized for the remission of sins for & in behalf of our dead kindred who have not herd the gospel or fulness of it.

30 March 1842 (Wednesday). Upper Room, Red Brick Store.[1]
Nauvoo Relief Society Minutes

Pres. Joseph Smith arose—spoke of the organization of the society. Said he was deeply interested that it might be built up to the Most High in an acceptable manner—that its rules must be observed—that none should be received into the society but those who were worthy. Proposed that the society go into a close examination of every candidate—that they were going too fast—that the society should grow up by degrees; should commence with a few individuals—thus have a select society of the virtuous, and those who will walk circumspectly. Commended them for their zeal but said some times their zeal was not according to knowledge. One principal object of the institution was to purge out iniquity—said they must be extremely careful in all their examinations or the consequences would be serious. Said all difficulties which might and would cross our way must be surmounted, though the soul be tried, the heart faint, and hands hang down—must not retrace our steps. That there must be decision of character aside from sympathy. That when instructed we must obey that voice, observe the constitution,[2] that the blessings of heaven may rest down upon us. All must act in concert or nothing can be done, that the society should move according to the ancient Priesthood, hence there should be a select society, separate from all the evils of the world, choice, virtuous and holy.[3] Said he was going to make of this society a kingdom of priests as in Enoch's day—as in Paul's day—that it is the privilege of each member to live long and enjoy health.[4] Pres. Smith proposed that the brethren withdraw that the society might proceed to business—that those wishing to join might have their names presented at the next meeting.

7 April 1842 (Thursday Afternoon). Grove.[1]
Times and Seasons 3 (15 April 1842):761-63

Conference met, Pres't. Joseph Smith had the several quorums put in order, and seated:[2] he then made some very appropriate remarks concerning the duties of the church, the necessity of unity of purpose in regard to the building of the houses,[3] and the blessings connected with doing the will of God; and the inconsistency folly and danger of murmuring against the dispensations of Jehovah.

He said that the principal object of the meeting was to bring the case of Elder Page before them, and that another object was to choose young men, and ordain them, and send them out to preach, that they may have an opportunity of proving themselves, and of enduring the tarring and feathering and such things as those of us who have gone before them, have had to endure.

. . . Pres't. J. Smith then arose and stated that it was wrong to make the covenant referred to by him;[4] that it created a lack of confidence for two men to covenant to reveal all acts of secrecy or otherwise to each other—and Elder Page showed a little grannyism. He said that no two men when they agreed to go together ought to separate, that the prophets of old would not and quoted the circumstance of Elijah and Elisha iii Kings 2 chap. when about to go to Gilgal, also when about to go to Jericho, and to Jordan, that Elisha could not get clear of Elijah, that he clung to his garment until he was taken to heaven and that Elder Page should have stuck by Elder Hyde, and he might have gone to Jerusalem, that there is nothing very bad in it, but by the experience let us profit; again, the Lord made use of Elder Page as a scape goat to procure funds for Elder Hyde.

. . . Pres't. J. Smith spoke upon the subject of the stories respecting Elder Kimball and others, showing the folly and inconsistency of spending any time in conversing about such stories or hearkening to them, for there is no person that is acquainted with our principles would believe such lies, except Sharp[5] the editor of the "Warsaw Signal." Baptisms for the dead, and for the healing of the body must be in the font, those coming into the church and those rebaptized[6] may be done in the river.

A box should be prepared for the use of the font, that the clerk may be paid, and a book procured by the monies to be put therein by those baptized, the remainder to go to the use of the Temple.

Wilford Woodruff Journal

Rainy in the fore part of the day conferance opened at 1 oclock

President J. Smith H. Smith Wm Law & the Twelve took the stand & opened meeting & spoke upon a variety of subjects & called upon those who wished to be ordained to the office of an Elder to come forward & have their names taken many came forward.

8 April 1842 (Friday). Grove.[1]
Wilford Woodruff Journal

Conference opened at 10 oclock Elder L. Wight Presidents J Smith & Hyarm Smith & others spoke. . . . In the afternoon Elders Amasa Lyman & Wm Smith[2] occupied the stand in the afternoon & was followed by Joseph with a few remarks & the Conference closed.

9 April 1842 (Saturday Morning). Grove.[1]
Wilford Woodruff Journal

9th The Saints in Nauvoo assembled at the house of President Marks[2] at an early hour in the morning to pay their last respects to the Body of Ephraim Marks[3] son of President Marks who died on the evening of the 7th A large procession formed two by two & walked to the grove a larger concorse assembled President Joseph Smith spoke upon the occasion with much feelings & interst among his remarks he said it is a vary solumn & awful time I never felt more solumn it calles to mind the death of my oldest Brother who died in New York[4] & my youngest Brother Carloss Smith who died in Nauvoo[5] It has been hard for me to live on earth & see those young men upon whome we have leaned upon as a support & comfort taken from us in the midst of their youth, yes it has been hard to be reconciled to these things I have some times felt that I should have felt more reconciled to have been called myself if it could have been the will of God, yet I know we ought to be still & know it is of God & be reconciled all is right it will be but a short time before we shall all in like manner be called. It may be the case with me as well as you Some has supposed that Br Joseph Could not die but this is a mistake it is true their has been times when I have had the promise of my life to accomplish such & such things, but having accomplish those things I have not at present any lease of my life I am as liable to die as other men[6] I can say in my heart that I have not done any thing against Ephraim Marks that I am sorry for & I would ask any of his companions if they have done any thing against him that they are sorry for or that they would not like to meet at the bar of God if so let it prove as a warning to all men to deal justly before God & with all men then we shall be clean in the day of judgment When we loose a near & dear friend upon whom we have set our hearts we can never feel the same afterwards knowing that if we set our hearts upon others they may in like manner be taken from us President Smith made many other interesting remarks & left it for President Rigdon to close.

10 April 1842 (Sunday Morning). Grove.[1]
Wilford Woodruff Journal

A pleasant morning A large Congregaton of Saints met at the grove President William Law addressed the asembly for about 1 hour Then Joseph the Seer arose in the power of God reproved & rebuked wickedness before the people in the name of the Lord God He wished to say a few words to suit the condition of the general mass And I shall speak with authority of the prieshood in the name of the Lord God which shall prove a savior of life unto life or of death unto death.

Notwithstanding this congregation profess to be saints yet I stand in the midst of all characters and classes of men If you wish to go whare God is you must be like god or possess the principles which God possesses for if we are not drawing towards God in principle we are going from him & drawing towards the devil, yes I am standing in the midst of all kinds of people Search your hearts & see if you are like god, I have searched mine & feel to repent of all my sins, we have theives among us Adulterers, liars, hypocritts, if God should speak from Heaven he would Command you not to steal, not to commit Adultery, not to covet, nor deceive but be faithful over a few things[2] As far as we degenerate from God we desend to the devil & loose knowledge & without knowledge we cannot be saved & while our hearts are filled with evil & we are studying evil their is no room in our hearts for good or studying good, is not God good, Yes then you be good. if he is faithful then you be faithful Add to your faith virtue to virtue knowledge.[3] & seek for evry good thing the church must be cleansed & I proclaim against all iniquity. A man is saved no faster than he gets knowledge for if he does not get knowledge he will be brought into captivity by some evil power in the other world as evil spirits will have more knowlede & consequently more power than many men who are on the earth.[4] hence it needs Revelation to assist us & give us knowledge of the things of God. What is the reason that the Priest of the day do not get Revelation They ask ownly to consume it upon their lust[5] their hearts are corrupt & they cloke their iniquity by saying that their is no more Revelations But if any Revelations are given of God they are universally opposed by the priest & christendon at large for it reveals their wickedness & abominations many other remarks of interest were made by the speaker I truly felt in my own heart that it was a profitable meeting.

Manuscript History of the Church

I preached in the grove, and pronounced a curse {upon all adulterers and Fornicators, and unvirtuous persons and those who have made use of my name to carry on their iniquitous designs}.[6]

24 April 1842 (Sunday). Near Temple.[1]
Manuscript History of the Church

Preached {on the hill, near the Temple concerning the building of the temple, and pronounced a curse on the Merchants and the rich, who would not assist in building it}.[2]

28 April 1842 (Thursday Afternoon). Upper Room, Red Brick Store.[1]
Nauvoo Relief Society Minutes

President Smith arose and said that the purport of his being present on the occasion was, to make observations respecting the priesthood,[2] and give instructions for the benefit of the Society that as his instructions were intended only for the Society; he requested that a vote should be taken on those present who were not members, to ascertain whether they should be admitted—He exhorted the meeting to act honestly and uprightly in all their proceedings inasmuch as they would be call'd to give an account to

Jehovah. All hearts must repent—be pure and God will regard them and bless them in a manner that could not be bless'd in any other way—

... Committee retired and Prest. J. Smith arose and call'd the attention of the meeting to the 12th chap of 1st Co. "Now concerning spiritual gifts" &C.—said that the passage which reads "No man can say that Jesus is the Lord but by the holy ghost," should be translated, No man can know &C[3]

He continued to read the Chap and give instructions respecting the different offices, and the necessity of every individual acting in the sphere allotted him or her; and filling the several offices to which they were appointed—Spoke of the disposition of man, to consider the lower offices in the church dishonorable and to look with jealous eyes upon the standing of others—that it was the nonsense of the human heart, for a person to be aspiring to other stations than appointed of God—that it was better for individuals to magnify their respective callings,[4] and wait patiently till God shall say to them come up higher.

He said the reason of these remarks being made was, that some little things was circulating in the Society, that some persons were not going right in laying hands on the sick, &C.[5] Said if he had common sympathies, would rejoice that the sick could be heal'd, that the time had not been before, that these things could be in their proper order—that the Church is not now organiz'd in its proper order, and cannot be until the Temple is completed.[6] Prest. Smith continued the subject by adverting to the commission given to the ancient apostles "Go ye into all the world" &C.[7] No matter who believeth; these signs such as healing the sick, casting out devils &C. should follow all that believe whether male or female. He ask'd the Society if they could not see by this sweeping stroke that werein they are ordained, it is the privilege of those set apart[8] to administer in that authority which is conferr'd[9] on them—and if the sisters should have faith to heal the sick, let all hold their tongues, and let every thing roll on.

He said if God has appointed him, and chosen him as an instrument to lead the church, why not let him lead it through? why stand in the way, when he is appointed to do a thing? Who knows the mind of God? Does he not reveal things differently from what we expect?[10] He remarked that he was continually rising—altho' he had every thing, bearing him down, standing in his way and opposing—after all he always comes out right in the end.

Respecting the females laying on hands, he further remark'd, there could be no devil in it if God gave his sanction by healing— that there could be no more sin in any female laying hands on the sick than in wetting the face with water It is no sin for any body to do it that has faith, or if the sick has faith to be heal'd by the administration.

He reproved those that were dispos'd to find fault with the management of concerns—saying that if he undertook to lead the church he would lead it right—that he calculats to organize the church in proper order &C.

President Smith continued by speaking of the difficulties he had to surmount ever since the commencement of the work in consequence of aspiring men, "great big Elders" as he called them who had caused him much trouble, whom he had taught in the private counsel; and they would go forth into the world and proclaim the things he had taught them; as their own revelations— said the same aspiring disposition will be in this Society, and must be guarded against—that every person should stand and act in the place appointed, and thus sanctify the Society and get it pure—

He said he had been trampled under foot by aspiring Elders, for all were infected with that spirit, for instance P. Pratt O. Pratt, O. Hyde and J. Page had been aspiring—They could not be exhalted but must run away as though the care and authority of the church were vested with them—He said we had a subtle devil to deal with and could only curb him by being humble.

He said as he had this opportunity, he was going to instruct the Society and point out the way for them to conduct, that they might act according to the will of God—that he did not know as he should have many opportunities of teaching them—that they were going to be left to themselves—they would not long have him to instruct them—that the church would not have his instruction long, and the world would not be troubled with him a great while, and would not have his teachings[11]—He spoke of delivering the keys to this society and to the Church—that according to his prayers God had appointed him elsewhere[12]

He exhorted the sisters always to concentrate their faith and prayers for, and place confidence in those whom God has appointed to honor, whom God has plac'd at the head to lead—that we should arm them with our prayers—that the keys of the kingdom are about to be given to them, that they may be able to detect every thing false—as well as to the Elders[13]

He said if one member become corrupt and you know it; you must immediately put it away. The sympathies of the heads of the church have induc'd them to bear with those that were corrupt in consequence of which all become contaminated—you must put down iniquity and by your good example provoke the Elders to good works—if you do right no danger of going too fast; he said he did not care how fast we run in the path of virtue. Resist evil and there is no danger. God, man, angels and devils can't condemn those that resist every thing that is evil as well might the devil seek to dethrone Jehovah, as that soul that resists every thing that is evil.

The charitable Society—this is according to your natures—it is natural for females to have feelings of charity—you are now placed in a situation where you can act according to those sympathies which God has planted in your bosoms. If you live up to these principles how great and glorious—if you live up to your privilege the angels cannot be restrain'd from being your associates—

Females, if they are pure and innocent can come into the presence of God, for what is more pleasing to God than innocence; you must be innocent or you cannot come up before God.[14] If we would come before God let us be pure ourselves. The devil has great power—he will so transform things as to make one gape at those who are doing the will of God—You need not be teasing men for their deeds, but let the weight of innocence be felt which is more mighty than a millstone hung about the neck. Not war, not jangle, not contradiction, but meekness, love purity, these are the things that should magnify us. Achan[15] must be brough to light—iniquity must be purged out—then the vail will be rent and the blessings of heaven will flow down—they will roll down like the Mississippi river. This Society shall have power to command Queens in their midst—I now deliver it as a prophecy that before ten years shall roll around, the queens of the earth shall come and pay their respects to this Society—they shall come with their millions and shall contribute of their abundance for the relief of the poor—If you will be pure, nothing can hinder.[16]

After this instruction, you will be responsible for your own sins. It is an honor to save yourselves—all are responsible to save themselves.

Prest. Smith, after reading from the above mentioned chapter, Continued to give instruction respecting the order of God, as established in the church; saying every one should aspir only to magnify his own office &C.

He then commenc'd reading the 13 chapter,[17] "Though I speak with the tongues of men" &C. and said don't be limited in your views with regard to your neighbors' virtues, but be limited towards your own virtues, and not think yourselves more righteous than others; you must enlarge your souls toward others if you [w]ould do like Jesus, and carry your fellow creatures to Abrams bosom. He said he had manifested long suffering and we must do so too—Prest. Smith then read, "Though I have the gift of prophecy" &C. He then said though one should become mighty—do great things—overturn mountains &C should then turn to eat and drink with the drunken; all former deeds would not save him—but he would go to destruction!

As you increase in innocence and virtue, as you increase in goodness, let your hearts expand—let them be enlarged towards others—you must be longsuffering and bear with the faults and errors of mankind. How precious are the souls of man! The female part of community are apt to be contracted, in their views. You must not be contracted but you must be liberal in your feelings.

Let this Society teach how to act towards husbands, to treat them with mildness and affection. When a man is borne down with trouble—when he is perplexed, if he can meet a smile, [not] an argument—if he can meet with mildness, it will calm down his soul and smoothe his feelings. When the mind is going to despair it needs a solace.

This Society is to get instruction through the order which God has established—thro' the medium of those appointed to lead—and I now turn the key to you in the name of God and this Society shall . rejoice and knowledge and intelligence shall flow down from this time—this is the beginning of better days to this Society.[18]

When you go home never give a cross word, but let kindness, charity and love, crown your works henceforward. Don't envy sinners—have mercy on them, God will destroy them—Let your labors be confined mostly to those around you to your own circle, as far as knowledge is concerned, it may extend to all the world, but your administrations, should be confin'd to the circle of your immediate acquaintances and more especially to the members of the society.

Those ordain'd to lead the Society, are authoriz'd to appoint to different offices as the circumstances shall require.[19]

If any have a matter to reveal, let it be in your own tongue. Do not indulge too much in the gift of tongues, or the devil will take advantage of the innocent. You may speak in tongues for your own comfort but I lay this down for a rule that if any thing is taught by the gift of tongues, it is not to be received for doctrine.[20]

Prest. S. then offered instruction respecting the propriety of females administering to the sick by the laying on of hands—said it was according to revelation—&C.[21] Said he never was placed in similar circumstances, and never had given the same instruction.

He clos'd his instruction by expressing his satisfaction in improving the opportunity.

The spirit of the Lord was pour'd out in a very powerful manner, never to be forgotten by those present on that interesting occasion.

Manuscript History of the Church

At two o'clock P.M. I met {the members of the "female Relief Society" and after presiding at the admission of many new members gave a lecture on the Priesthood shewing how the sisters would come in possession of the privileges, blessings, and gifts of the Priesthood, and that the signs should follow them, such as healing the sick, casting out devils[22] &C and that they might attain unto these blessings by a virtuous life and conversation and diligence in keeping all the commandments}.[23]

1 May 1842 (Sunday). Grove.[1]
Manuscript History of the Church

I preached in the grove on the keys of the Kingdom,[2] Charity[3] &c The keys are certain signs and words by which false spirits and personages may be detected from true, which cannot be revealed to the Elders till the Temple is completed[4]—The rich can only get them in the Temple—the poor may get them on the Mountain top as did Moses.[5] The rich cannot be saved without Charity, giving to feed the poor when and how God requires as well as building. There are signs in heaven, earth, and hell, the Elders must know them all to be endowed with power, to finish their work and prevent imposition.[6] The devil knows many signs but does not know the sign of the Son of Man, or Jesus. No one can truly say he knows God[7] until he has handled something, and this can only be in the Holiest of Holies.

26 May 1842 (Thursday). Upper Room, Red Brick Store.[1]
Nauvoo Relief Society Minutes

Prest. Smith rose; read the 14th Chap. of Ezekiel—Said the Lord had declared by the prophet that the people should each one stand for himself and depend on no man or men in that state of corruption of the Jewish Church—that righteous persons could only deliver their own souls—applied it to the present state of the church of Latter Day Saints—Said if the people departed from the Lord, they must fall—that they were depending on the prophet hence were darkened in their minds from neglect of themselves[2]—envious toward the innocent, while they afflict the virtuous with their shafts of envy.

There is another error which opens a door for the adversary to enter. As females possess refined feelings and sensitiveness; they are also subject to an over much zeal which must ever prove dangerous, and cause them to be rigid in a religious capacity— Should be arm'd with mercy notwithstanding the iniquity among us. Said he had been instrumental in bringing it to light— melancholy and awful that so many are under the condemnation of the devil & going to perdition With deep feeling said that they are our fellows—we lov'd them once. Shall we not encourage them to reformation?

We have not forgiven them seventy times—perhaps we have not forgiven them once.[3] There is now—a day of salvation to such as repent and reform—they should be cast out from this Society yet we should woo them to return to God lest they escape not the damnation of hell!

When there is a mountain top there is also a valley—we should act in all things as a proper medium to every immortal spirit.

Notwithstanding the unworthy are among us, the virtuous should not from self importance grieve and oppress needlessly those unfortunate ones, even these should be encourag'd to hereafter live to be honored by this Society who are the best portions of community. Said he had two things to recommend to the Society, to put a double watch over the tongue. No organiz'd body can exist without this at all. All organiz'd bodies have their peculiar evils, weaknesses and difficulties—the object is to make those not so good, equal with the good and ever hold the keys of power which will influence to virtue and goodness. Should chasten and reprove and keep it all in silence, not even mention them again, then you will be established in power, virtue and holiness and the wrath of God will be turn'd away. One request to the Prest. and Society that you search yourselves—the tongue is an unruly member[4]—hold your tongues about things of no moment, a little tale will set the world on fire. At this time the truth on the guilty should not be told openly[5]—Strange as this may seem yet this is policy. We must use precaution in bringing sinners to justice lest in exposing their heinous sins, we draw the indignation of a gentile world upon us (and to their imagination justly too)

It is necessary we hold an influence in the world and thus spare ourselves an extermination; and also accomplish our end in spreading the gospel in holiness in the earth.

If we were brought to desolation, the disobedient would find no help. There are some who are obedient yet man cannot steady the ark[6]—my arm cannot do it—God must steady it. To the iniquitous show yourselves merciful. I am advis'd by some of the heads of the church to tell the Relief Society to be virtuous—but to save the Church from desolation and the sword beware, be still, be prudent, Repent, reform but do it in a way to not destroy all around you. I do not want to cloak iniquity—All things contrary to the will of God, should be cast from us, but dont do more hurt than good with your tongues—be pure in heart—Said Jesus ye shall do the work which ye see me do[7]—Jesus designs to save the people out of their sins. These are the grand key words[8] for the Society to act upon.

If I were not in your midst to aid and council you, the devil would overcome you. I want the innocent to go free—rather spare ten iniquitous among you than than condemn one innocent one. "Fret not thyself because of evil doers,"[9] God will see to it.

1 June 1842 (Wednesday). Grove.¹
Manuscript History of the Church

I attended a political meeting in the Grove, for the nomination of County officers, for the County at large, in which I concurred, with the exception of the Candidate for the Sheriffalty and spoke in favor of the proceedings.²

5 June 1842 (Sunday).¹
The Wasp (11 June 1842)

The Prophet, Joseph Smith, delivered a powerful discourse, last Sabbath, to an attentive audience of about 8000, in this city. The subject matter was drawn from the 32nd and 33rd chapters of Ezekiel, wherein it was shown the Old Pharoah was comforted, and greatly rejoiced, that he was honored as a kind of King Devil over those uncircumcised nations, that go down to hell for rejecting the word of the Lord, withstanding his mighty miracles, and fighting the saints:—The whole exhibited as a pattern to this generation, and the nations now rolling in splendor over the globe, if they do not repent, that they shall go down to the pit also, and be rejoiced over, and ruled over by Old Pharoah, King Devil of mobocrats, miracle rejecters, saint killers, hypocritical priests, and all other fit subject to fester in their own infamy.—Spring water tastes best right from the fountain.

9 June 1842 (Thursday). Grove.¹
Nauvoo Relief Society Minutes

Prest. Smith opened the meeting by pray'r and proceeded to address the congregation on the design of the Institution—said it is no matter how fast the Society increases if all are virtuous—that we must be as particular with regard to the character of members as when the Society first started—that sometimes persons wished to put themselves into a Society of this kind, when they do not intend to pursue the ways of purity and righteousness, as if the society could be a shelter to them in their iniquity.

Prest. S. said that henceforth no person shall be admitted but by presenting regular petitions signed by two or three members in good standing in the Society—Who ever comes in must be of good report.

Said he was going to preach mercy Supposing that Jesus Christ and angels should object to us on frivolous things, what would become of us? We must be merciful and overlook small things.

Respecting the reception of Sis. Overton,[2] Prest. Smith [said] it grieves me that there is no fuller fellowship—if one member suffer all feel it by union of feeling we obtain pow'r with God. Christ said he came to call sinners to repentance and save them. Christ was condemn'd by the righteous Jews because he took sinners into his society—He took them upon the principle that they repented of their sins. It is the object of this Society to reform persons, not to take those that are corrupt, but if they repent we are bound to take them and by kindness sanctify and cleanse from all unrighteousness, by our influence in watching over them. Nothing will have such influence over people, as the fear of being disfellowshipp'd by so goodly Society as this. Then take Sis. O. as Jesus received sinners into his bosom.

Sis. O. In the name of the Lord I now make you free, and from this hour any thing should be found against you

Nothing is so much calculated to lead people to forsake sin as to take them by the hand and watch over them with tenderness. When persons manifest the least kindness and love to me, O what pow'r it has over my mind, while the opposite course has a tendency to harrow up all the harsh feelings and depress the human mind.

It is one evidence that men are unacquainted with the principle of godliness, to behold the contraction of feeling and lack of charity. The pow'r and glory of godliness is spread out on a broad principle to throw out the mantle of charity. God does not look on sin with allowance, but when men have sin'd there must be allowance made for them.

All the religious world is boasting of its righteousness—it is the doctrine of the devil to retard the human mind and retard our progress by filling us with self righteousness—The nearer we get to our heavenly Father the more are we disposed to look with compassion on perishing souls to take them upon our shoulders and cast their sins behind our back. I am going to talk to all this Society—if you would have God have mercy on you, have mercy on one another.

Prest. S. then referr'd them to the conduct of the Savior when he was taken and crucified &C.

He then made a promise in the name of the Lord saying, that soul that has righteousness enough to ask God in the secret place for life every day of their lives shall live till three score years and ten—We must walk uprightly all day long—How glorious are the principles of righteousness! We are full of selfishness—the devil flatters us that we are very righteous, while we are feeding on the faults of others—We can only live by worshipping our God—all must do it for themselves—none can do it for another. How mild the Savior dealt with Peter saying "when thou art converted, strengthen thy brethren"[3] at another time he said to him "lovest thou me?" "Feed my sheep"[4]—If the sisters love the Lord let them feed the sheep and not destory them. How oft have wise men & women sought to dictate Br. Joseph by saying "O if I were Br. Joseph I would do this and that" but if they were in Br. Joseph's shoes, they would find that men could not be compell'd into the kingdom of God, but must be dealt with in long suff'ring and at the last we shall save them. The way to keep all the saints together and keep the work rolling is to wait with all longsuff'ring till God shall bring such character to justice. There should be no license for sin, but mercy should go hand in hand with reproof.

Sisters of the Society, shall there be strife among you? I will not have it—You must repent and get the love of God. Away with selfrighteousness. the best measure or principle to bring the poor to repentance is to administer to their wants—the Society is not only to relieve the poor but to save souls.

Prest. S. then said that he would give a lot of land to the Society by deeding it to the Treasurer, that the Society may build houses for the poor. He also said he would give a house frame not finished—said that Br. Cahoon will move it on to the aforesaid lot, and the Society could pay him by giving Orders on the store—that it was a good plan to set those to work who are owing widows and thus make an offsett. &C. &C.

18 June 1842 (Saturday). Near Temple.[1]
Wilford Woodruff Journal

The Citizens of Nauvoo Both Male & female assembled near the Temple for a general meeting many thousands were assembled

Joseph the seer arose & spoke upon several subjects Among other subjects he spoke his mind in great plainness concerning the iniquity & wickedness of Gen John Cook Bennet, & exposed him before the public[2] He also prophesied in the Name of the Lord concerning the merchants in the City that if they with the rich did not open their hearts & contribute to the poor that they would be Cursed by the hand of God & be Cut off from the land of the living, The main part of the day was taken up upon the business of the agricultural & manufacturing society,[3] if we have a charter granted us by the Legislator of the State for that purpose & the time has come for us to make use of that Charter, it is divided into stock of $50 dollars each share, any person owning one share become a member of the society a stock-holder, each share is entitled to one vote this is esstablished with a view of helping the poor arangments were entered into to commence operations immediately

Also Joseph commanded the Twelve to organize the Church more according to the Law of God that is to require of those that come in to be settled according to their Council & also to appoint a committee to wait upon all who arive & make them welcome & council them what to do B Young, H.C. Kimball G A. Smith & Hyrum Smith was the committee appointed to wait upon emigrants & settle them.[4]

21 June 1842 (Tuesday). Temple Stand.[1]
Wilford Woodruff Journal

A large meeting was again assembled & addressed by President Smith concerning emigration agriculturall & Manufacturing persuits & was followed by the Twelve & others.

3 July 1842 (Sunday Morning). Grove.[1]
The Wasp (9 July 1842)

Joseph Smith delivered one of his interesting and sublime discourses. The congregation, which listened with almost breathless attention, was very large, numbering probably 8 or 10,000. The subject matter was drawn from the prophecies of Daniel which foretold that the God of heaven would set up a kingdom in the last days, &c.[2] It was so satisfactorily done, that it was a pity that the world of great men, sectarians and all, could not have been present, to take a few lessons of common sense from Jo's mouth, (as Bennett[3] of the [New York] Herald would say) that they might come to understanding and save themselves, as well as talk about saving the heathen.

Wilford Woodruff Journal

Sunday was an interesting day about six thousand persons assembled at the place of meeting in Nauvoo & was addressed by Joseph the Seer much to our edifycation. He read the 7th ch of Daniel & explained about the Kingdom of God set up in the last days & said many things which were truly edifying.

4 July 1842 (Monday).[1]
The Wasp (9 July 1842)

Several very appropriate speeches were made before the Legion[2] was dismissed. Gen. Smith's was able and satisfactory; setting forth the conduct, harmony and union of our citizen soldiers, in their true light.

15 July 1842 (Friday Morning). Grove.[1]
Manuscript History of the Church

It was reported early in the morning that Elder Orson Pratt was missing.[2] I caused the Temple hands and the principle men of the City to make search for him. After which a meeting was called at the Grove, and I gave the public a general outline of John C. Bennett's conduct.

22 July 1842 (Friday Morning). Meeting Ground.[1]
Times and Seasons 3 (1 August 1842): 869

The meeting was called to order by the chairman [Orson Spencer], who stated the object of the meeting to be to obtain an expression of the public mind in reference to the reports gone abroad, calumniating the character of Pres. Joseph Smith. Gen. Wilson Law[2] then rose and presented the following resolution.

Resolved—That, having heard that John C. Bennett was circulating many base falsehoods respecting a number of the citizens of Nauvoo, and especially against our worthy and respected Mayor, Joseph Smith, we do hereby manifest to the world that so far as we know him to be a good, moral, virtuous, peaceable and patriotic man, and a firm supporter of law, justice and equal rights; that he at all times upholds and keeps inviolate the constitution of this State and of the United States.

A vote was then called and the resolution adopted by a large concourse of citizens, numbering somewhere about a thousand men. Two or three, voted in the negative.

Elder Orson Pratt then rose and spoke at some length in explanation of his negative vote.[3] Pres. Joseph Smith spoke in reply—

24 July 1842 (Sunday Afternoon). Grove.[1]
Manuscript History of the Church

This morning at home sick—Attended meeting at the Grove in the afternoon and spoke of brother Miller's[2] having returned with the good news that Bennett could not be able to accomplish his designs.

27 July 1842 (Wednesday). Grove.[1]
Manuscript History of the Church

Attended meeting at the Grove and listened to the Electioneering Candidates,[2] and spoke at the close of the meeting.

27 August 1842 (Saturday Evening). Old Homestead.[1]
Eliza R. Snow Journal[2]

Pres. S. was at home and met in the large drawing room with a respectable number of those considered trustworthy—counsel'd them to go out forthwith to proclaim the principles of truth.

29 August 1842 (Monday Morning). Grove Near Temple.[1]
Manuscript History of the Church

Near the close of Hyrum's[2] remarks I went upon the Stand. I was rejoiced to look upon the Saints once more, whom I have not seen for about three weeks.³ They also were rejoiced to see me, and we all rejoiced together. My sudden appearance on the Stand under the circumstances which surrounded us, caused great animation and cheerfulness in the Assembly. Some had supposed that I had gone to Washington, and some that I had gone to Europe, while some thought I was in the City; but whatever difference of opinion had prevailed on this point, we were now all filled with thanksgiving and rejoicing. When Hyrum had done speaking I arose and congratulated the brethren and Sisters on the victory I had once more gained over the Missourians. I had told them {formerly about fighting the Missourians, and about fighting alone. I had not fought them with the Sword, or by carnal weapons; I had done it by stratagem, by outwitting them, and there had been no lives lost, and there would be no lives lost if they would hearken to my Council. Up to this day God had given me wisdom to save the people who took Council. None had ever been killed who abode by my Council. At Hauns Mill the brethren went contrary to my Council; if they had not, their lives would have been spared.⁴ I had been in Nauvoo all the while, and outwitted Bennett's associates,⁵ and attended to my own business in the City all the time. We want to whip the world mentally and they will whip themselves physically. The brethren cannot have the tricks played upon them that were done at Kirtland and Far West, they have seen enough of the tricks of their enemies and know better. Orson Pratt has attempted to destroy himself and caused all the city almost to go in search of him.⁶ Is it not enough to put down all the infernal influence of the devil, what we have felt and seen, handled and evidenced of this work of God? But the Devil had influence among the Jews after all the great things they had witnessed to cause the death of Jesus Christ by hanging him between heaven and earth. O. Pratt and others of the same class caused trouble by telling stories to people who would betray me, and they must believe those stories because his Wife told him so! I will live to trample on their ashes with the souls of my feet. I prophecy in the name of Jesus Christ that such shall not prosper, they shall be cut down in their plans. They would deliver me up Judas like, but a small band of us shall overcome. We dont want or mean to fight with the sword of the flesh, but we will fight with the broad Sword of the Spirit.⁷ Our enemies say our Charter and writs of Habeas Corpus are worth nothing. We say they came from the highest authority in the State and we will hold to them. They cannot be disannulled or taken away.[8] I then told the brethren I was going to send all the Elders away, and when the Mob came there would only be women and chldren to fight and they would be ashamed. I dont want you to fight but to go and gather tens, hundreds, and thousands to fight for you. If oppression comes, I will then shew them that there is a Moses and a Joshua amongst us; and I will fight them, if they dont take off oppression from me. I will do as I have done this time. I will run into the woods. I will fight them in my own way. I will send brother Hyrum to call conferences everywhere throughout the States and let documents be taken along and show to the world the corrupt and oppressive conduct of Boggs,[9] Carlin,[10] and others, that the public may have the truth laid before them. Let the Twelve send all who will support the character of the Prophet, the Lord's anointed, and if all who go will support my character, I prophecy in the name of the Lord Jesus, whose servant I am, that you will prosper in your missions. I have the whole plan of the kingdom before me, and no other person has.[11] And as to all that Orson Pratt, Sidney Rigdon, or George W. Robinson[12] can do to prevent me, I can kick them off my heels, as many as you can name, I know what will become of them. I concluded my remarks by saying I have the best of feelings towards my brethren, since this last trouble began, but to the Apostates and enemies, I will give a lashing every opportunity and I will curse them}.[13] During the address an indescribable transport of good feeling was manifested by the Assembly and about 380 Elders volunteered to go immediately on the proposed Mission.

31 August 1842 (Wednesday). Grove.[1]
Nauvoo Relief Society Minutes

Prest. Joseph Smith opened the meeting by addressing the Society. He commenced by expressing his happiness and thankfulness for the privilege of being present on the occasion. He said that great exertions had been made on the part of our enemies, but they had not accomplished their purpose—God had enabled him to keep out of their hands—he had war'd a good warfare inasmuch as he had whip'd out all of Bennett's host[2] his feelings at present time were that inasmuch as the Lord Almighty had preserv'd him to day.

He said it reminded him of the Savior, when he said to the pharisees, "Go ye and tell that fox, Behold I cast out devils, and I do cures today and tomorrow, and the third day I shall be perfected." &C.[3]

He said he expected the heavenly Father had decreed that the Missourians shall not get him—if they do, it will be because he does not keep out of the way.

Pres. S. continued by saying, I shall triumph over my enemies—I have begun to triumph over them at home and I shall do it abroad—All those that rise up against me will feel the weight of their iniquity upon their own heads—Those that speak evil are abominable characters and full of iniquity. All the fuss and all the stir against me, is like the jack in the lantern, it cannot be found. Altho' I do wrong, I do not the wrongs that I am charg'd with doing—the wrong that I do is thro' the frailty of human nature like other men. No man lives without fault. Do you think that even Jesus, if he were here would be without fault in your eyes? They said all manner of evil against him—they all watch'd for iniquity. How easy it was for Jesus to call out all the iniquity of the hearts of those whom he was among? The servants of the Lord are required to guard against those things that are calculated to do the most evil—the little foxes spoil the vines[4]—little evils do the most injury to the church If you have evil feelings and speak of them to one another, it has a tendency to do mischief—these things result in those evils which are calculated to cut the throats of the heads of the church.

When I do the best I can—when I am accomplishing the greatest good, then the most evils are got up against me. I would to God that you would be wise. I now counsel you, if you know any thing, hold your tongues, and the least harm will be done.

The Female Relief Society has taken the the most active part in my welfare—against my enemies—in petitioning to the Governor[5]—these measures were all necessary—Do you not see that I foresaw what was coming beforehand? by the spirit of prophecy?—all had an influence in my redemption from the hand of my enemies.

If these measures had not been taken, more serious consequences would have resulted.

I have come here to bless you. The Society has done well—their principles are to practice holiness. God loves you and your prayers in my behalf shall avail much—let them not cease to ascend to God in my behalf. The enemy will never get weary, I expect he will array everything against me—I expect a tremendous warfare. He that will war the christian warfare will have the angels of devils and all the infernal powers of darkness continually array'd against him. When wicked and corrupt men oppose, it is a criterion to judge if a man is warring the christian warfare. When all men speak evil of you, blessed are ye, &C.[6] Shall a man be considered bad when men speak evil of him? No! If a man stands and opposes the world of sin, he may expect all things array'd against him.

But it will be but a little season and all these afflictions will be turned away from us inasmuch as we are faithful and are not overcome by these evils. By seeing the blessings of the endowment rolling on and the kingdom increasing and spreading from sea to sea, we will rejoice that we were not overcome by these foolish things.[7]

Prest. S. then remark'd that a few things had been manifested to him in his absence respecting the baptism for the dead, which he should communicate next Sabbath if nothing should occur to prevent.[8]

Prest. S. then addressed the throne of grace.

Prest. S. said he had one remark to make respecting the baptism for the dead to suffice for the time being, until he has opportunity to discuss the subject to greater length—that is, all persons baptiz'd for the dead must have a Recorder present, that he may be an eye witness to testify of it.[9] It will be necessary in the grand Council, that these things be testified let it be attended to from this time lest if there is any lack it may be at the expense of our friends—they may not come forth &C.

25 September 1842 (Sunday). Grove.[1]
Manuscript History of the Church

At the Grove. Spoke more than two hours, chiefly on the subject of my persecution.

William Mendenhall Diary[2]

Joseph Smith the Prophet preached again from the Stand on the 19 Chapter of 1st Kings.[3]

Wilford Woodruff Journal

Br Joseph appeared upon the stand & addressed the Saints much to their edification though quite unexpectedly to them.[4]

29 October 1842 (Saturday Morning). Red Brick Store.[1]
Manuscript History of the Church

Saturday, 29.—About 10 {in the forenoon I rode up and viewed the Temple. I expressed my satisfaction at the arrangements, and was pleased with the progress made in that sacred edifice. After conversing with several of the brethern and shaking hands with numbers who were very much rejoiced to see their Prophet again,[2] I returned home, but soon afterwards went over to the Store, where a number of brethren and Sisters were assembled who had arrived this morning from the neighborhood of New York, Long Island &c After Elders Taylor, Woodruff, and Samuel Bennett,[3] had addressed the brethren and Sisters, I spoke to them at considerable length, shewing them the proper course to pursue, and how to act in regard to making purchases of land &c.

I shewed them that it was generally in consequence of the brethren disregarding or disobeying counsel that they became dissatisfied and murmured; and many when they arrived here were dissatisfied with the conduct of some of the Saints because every thing was done perfectly right, and they get mad and thus the devil gets advantage over them to destroy them. I told them I was but a man, and they must not expect me to be perfect; if they expected perfection from me, I should expect it from them; but if they would bear with my infirmities and the infirmities of the brethren, I would likewise bear with their infirmities. I told them it was likely I would have again to hide up in the woods but they must not be discouraged but build up the city, the Temple &c. When my enemies take away my rights, I will bear it and keep out of the way, but if they take away your rights, I will fight for you. I blessed them and departed}.[4]

1842 NOTES

16 January 1842

1. See *History of the Church*, 4:494. Not in *Teachings*. The original source for this account is most probably the "Book of the Law of the Lord."

2. Romans 5:20.

30 January 1842

1. See *History of the Church*, 4:510. Not in *Teachings*. The original source for this account in most probably the "Book of the Law of the Lord."

27 February 1842

1. See *History of the Church*, 4:518. Not in *Teachings*. The original source for this entry is most probably the "Book of the Law of the Lord." It is possible that this entry does not refer to a public address by the Prophet, but is here included since the "counseling" occurred on the Sabbath, and the use of the term *Saints* implies a large group.

6 March 1842

1. See *History of the Church*, 4:543. Not in *Teachings*. The original source for this reference is probably the "Book of the Law of the Lord," p. 89.

2. Orson Spencer (1802-55) was baptized in 1841 and elected mayor of Nauvoo in February 1845.

17 March 1842

1. Reference to this meeting is mentioned in *History of the Church*, 4:552-53. Not in *Teachings*. The account by Willard Richards is here published for the first time. First recorded into the "Book of the Law of the Lord," p. 91, these minutes were later transcribed into the Nauvoo Relief Society Minutes. The occasion on which the following remarks were made was the organization of the Nauvoo Relief Society. The "Red Brick Store," also known as Joseph Smith's store, was located on Water Street, block 155. The store opened for business on 5 January 1842 but did not remain under the Prophet's management continuously. In the upper level of the building was a large meeting room called the "Lodge Room" or the "General Business Office." This chamber accommodated a variety of meeting functions—city council meetings, court proceedings, Masonic meetings, Church councils, administering priesthood ordinances, and so on.

2. The term *Society* is used consistently throughout the Nauvoo Relief Society minutes to mean identically "Relief Society."

3. Regarding the "ordination" of Emma Smith and her counselors as the presidency of the Nauvoo Relief Society, and the implicit understanding they had that this ordination was not a conferral of priesthood but the conferral of presiding authority and keys over the sisters, the following explanation is pertinent:

"On the occasion of the organization of the Relief Society, by the Prophet Joseph Smith at Nauvoo, I was present Sister Emma Smith was elected president and Sisters Elizabeth Ann Whitney and Sarah M. Cleveland her Counselors. The Prophet Joseph then said that Sister Emma was named in the revelation recorded in the Book of Doctrine and Covenants concerning the Elect Lady, and furthermore that she had been ordained to expound the Scriptures. By my request my Secretary Elder L. John Nuttall read to you relative to this meeting from the 'Book of the Law of the Lord,' at your Conference held June 19th, ult., which explained what was then done.

The ordination then given did not mean the conferring of the Priesthood upon those sisters yet the sisters hold a portion of the Priesthood in connection with their husbands. (Sisters Eliza R. Snow and Bathsheba W. Smith, stated that they so understood it in Nauvoo and have looked upon it always in that light.)

As I stated, at that meeting, that I was called upon by the Prophet Joseph and I did then ordain Sisters Whitney and Cleveland, and blessed Sister Emma and set her apart. I could not ordain these sisters to anything more or to greater powers than had been conferred upon Sister Emma who had previously been ordained to expound the Scriptures, and that Joseph said at that time, that being an elect lady had its significance, and that the revelation was then fulfilled in Sister Emma being thus elected to preside over the Relief Society" (*The Woman's Exponent* 9 [1 September 1880]:53).

4. Unlike other institutions, the Nauvoo Relief Society was not to have a written constitution. The voice of the presidency of the society and the decisions of its membership (recorded in their minutes) served as a living constitution.

5. There was no attempt to differentiate between the terms *set apart* and *ordain* during this period.

6. Elizabeth Ann Whitney (1800-1882) was the wife of Newel K. Whitney. She was first counselor to Emma Smith in the Nauvoo Relief Society.

7. Sophia Packard (1800-1858). Wife of Noah Packard.

8. Emma Smith (1804-79) was Joseph Smith's wife. She was baptized in 1830 and was (at this meeting) appointed the first Relief Society president in Nauvoo.

9. Sarah Merietta Kingsley Cleveland, born 20 October 1788, was a native of Becket, Berkshire, Massachusetts. Although a faith-

ful member of the Church and a plural wife of the Prophet Joseph Smith, Sarah remained with her non-Mormon husband, John Cleveland, in Quincy, Illinois, after the Mormon exodus.

10. D&C 25.

11. D&C 25:7-9. The revelation was given in July 1830.

12. D&C 25:16.

13. 2 John 1.

14. D&C 25:3, 7-10.

15. Emma was ordained at the time of the reception of D&C 25—July 1830. See text of this discourse at note 11. See also notes 3 and 11 of this discourse. The braces enclose the words that come from the "Book of the Law of the Lord."

20 March 1842

1. See *History of the Church*, 4:553-57, and *Teachings*, pp. 196-201. The Wilford Woodruff Journal account is the source for the entries in *History of the Church* and *Teachings*. The Prophet originally intended to preach a Sabbath sermon on baptism for the dead, but he altered his plans when an infant corpse (Marian Lyon) was laid before him.

2. Marian Lyon (1839-42). Daughter of Windsor P. and Sylvia Lyon.

3. According to a revelation received by Joseph Smith on 21 January 1836, "All children who die before they arrive at the years of accountability are saved in the celestial kingdom of heaven" (D&C 137:10).

4. Infidelity in the sense of lacking faith that there is a God.

5. D&C 42:45.

6. Alma 34:31-35.

7. Moses 3:9; D&C 88:36-38, 42-45; 93:30; 77:3.

8. Genesis 1:14-15.

9. Moses 6:63.

10. Genesis 1:11-12, 20-21, 24-25.

11. John 3:5.

12. John 10:1-6; 2 Nephi 9:41; 31:21.

13. Regarding the signifying to the angels of man's willingness to obey his covenants, see D&C 63:54; 38:12; 89:21; 132:17-19. Regarding the first principles of the gospel and the promise of the Holy Spirit as signs of entering into the covenants, see Mark 16:16; Acts 2:37-39.

14. Mark 16:17-18; James 5:14-15.

15. See 1 May 1842, note 2.

16. Acts 2:37-40.

17. Acts 10:44-48 (25-48).

18. Mark 16:15-18.

19. Acts 19:15 (13-16). Rather than "Peter I know," it should have been "Paul I know."

20. Alma 40:21-23.

21. 1 Corinthians 15:50 (40-56); Job 19:25-27.

22. From the time of this discourse to within three months of his death, Joseph Smith apparently taught that children would not grow after the resurrection. However, of all the Prophet's Nauvoo discourses, only in the case of the Wilford Woodruff account of the "King Follett" discourse (7 April 1844) is there an explicit statement that children will "never grow" after the resurrection. For example, William Clayton, a year before the King Follett, recorded the words of the Prophet on this subject. "I asked the Prest.," Clayton records in his journal 18 May 1843, "wether children who die in infancy will grow. He answered 'No, we shall receive them precisely in the same state as they died ie no larger. They will have as much intelligence as we shall but shall always remain separate and single.' " Undoubtedly, William Clayton's report of the King Follett is, on this subject, so brief because he remembered the Prophet's personal teachings to him a year before. All accounts, as the above William Clayton diary entry, do exclude the possibility of growth of the body *in* the grave, but there is no contemporary record that the Prophet taught that there would be growth after the resurrection. Even as late as 12 May 1844, when the subject comes up again, the Prophet did not explicitly teach otherwise (see Thomas Bullock and Samuel W. Richards reports). Nevertheless, Brigham Young, Wilford Woodruff, Lorin Walker, Agnes Smith and Joseph and Isabella Horne recalled years later that Joseph Smith afterwards said there would be growth in the resurrection (Wilford Woodruff Journal, 31 January 1861, Church Archives; *History of the Church*, 4:556-57; *Improvement Era* 21 [February 1918]:571-73; and, Wilford Woodruff to Samuel Roskelley, 6 June 1887, microfilm of typed copy from "Family Record Book," Samuel Roskelley Papers, Utah State University Library, Logan, Utah).

23. Revelation 14:13.

27 March 1842

1. See *History of the Church*, 4:568-69, and *Teachings*, p. 201. The Wilford Woodruff Journal account is the source for the entries in *History of the Church* and *Teachings*.

2. Amasa Lyman (1813-77) was baptized in 1832 and ordained an apostle in 1842.

3. 1 Corinthians 15:29.

30 March 1842

1. See *History of the Church*, 4:570, and *Teachings*, pp. 201-02. The source for the entries in *History of the Church* and *Teachings* is the Nauvoo Relief Society Minutes, kept by Eliza R. Snow.

2. See 17 March 1842, note 4.

3. According to Joseph Smith, unanimity of feeling and purpose and the entering of covenants of righteousness and virtue were aspects of the ancient order of the priesthood. See next note and *History of the Church*, 5:1-2 (or *Teachings*, p. 137).

4. In preparing this discourse for publication, the original compilers changed the word *society* (see 17 March 1842, note 2) to *Church* (Joseph Smith Papers, Box 4 folder 4, Church Archives). This change obscured the important fact that these minutes demonstrate that at least a month before he gave endowment ordinances in their fulness for the first time (4 May 1842), Joseph Smith intended that women would receive ordinances promising them that they would be queens and priestesses in eternity. Moreover, Joseph Smith conveyed the impression that husbands and wives would receive the fulness of the priesthood blessings, through which they would be promised life as long as it would be desirable to them (see 5 October 1840, note 13). That the conferral of these ordinances would not be a conferral of priesthood is expressed best by Elder James E. Talmage in this classic and ever-timely statement:

> In the restored Church of Jesus Christ, the Holy Priesthood is conferred, as an individual bestowal, upon men only, and this in accordance with Divine requirement. It is not given to woman to exercise the authority of the Priesthood independently; nevertheless, in the sacred endowments associated with the ordinances pertaining to the House of the Lord, woman shares with man the blessings of the Priesthood. When the frailities and imperfections of mortality are left behind, in the glorified state of the blessed hereafter, husband and wife will administer in their respective stations, seeing and understanding alike, and co-operating to the full in the government of their family kingdom. Then shall woman be recompensed in rich measure for all the injustice that womanhood has endured in mortality. Then shall woman reign by Divine right, a queen in the resplendent realm of her glorified state, even as exalted man shall stand, priest and king unto the Most High God. Mortal eye cannot see nor mind comprehend the beauty, glory, and majesty of a righteous woman made perfect in the celestial kingdom of God (James E. Talmage, "The Eternity of Sex." *Young Woman's Journal* 25 [October 1914]: 602-03).

7 April 1842

1. See *History of the Church*, 4:583-86. Not in *Teachings*. The source for the *History of the Church* entry is the *Times and Seasons* account. The following remarks were made by the Prophet at the April 1842 General Conference of the Church. Wilford Woodruff's report is here published for the first time.

2. That is, the priesthood quorums sat in order according to the gradations of offices in the priesthood.

3. Namely, the Nauvoo Temple and the Nauvoo House.

4. The text refers to repeated covenants made by Orson Hyde and John E. Page relative to their mission to Jerusalem. They covenanted to "stand by each other while on the mission; that if they were insulted, or imposed upon they would stand by each other even unto death, and not separate unless to go a few miles to preach a sermon; that all monies should go into one purse" (*Times and Seasons* 3 [15 April 1842]: 761-62).

5. Thomas Coke Sharp (1814-94), a native of New Jersey, was the most feared and hated anti-Mormon in Illinois. Trained as a lawyer, Sharp was editor of the rabid anti-Mormon *Warsaw Signal*.

6. Concerning the use of the baptismal font for rebaptisms and the healing of the body, see D. Michael Quinn, "The Practice of Rebaptism at Nauvoo," *Brigham Young University Studies* 18 (Winter 1978), pp. 226-32.

8 April 1842

1. *History of the Church*, 4:586, which is based on *Times and Seasons* (15 April 1842), does not mention that the Prophet spoke at this session of April 1842 General Conference. Not in *Teachings*. Wilford Woodruff's report is here published for the first time.

2. William Smith (1811-93), the Prophet's younger brother, was baptized in 1830 and was ordained as apostle in 1835.

9 April 1842

1. See *History of the Church*, 4:586-87, and *Teachings*, pp. 215-16. The Wilford Woodruff Journal account is the source for *History of the Church* and *Teachings*.

2. William Marks, president of the Nauvoo Stake.

3. Ephraim Marks, son of William and Rosanna Marks, died 7 April 1842.

4. Alvin Smith (1798-1823). Joseph Smith's eldest brother.

5. Don Carlos Smith died in Nauvoo 7 August 1841.

6. See D&C 5:22; 6:29-30 and *Teachings*, p. 90. See also 28 April 1842, note 11.

10 April 1842

1. See *History of the Church*, 4:587-88, and *Teachings*, pp. 215-17. The introductory statement from the Manuscript History of the Church (published below), was taken from the "Book of the Law of the Lord," p. 93. The Wilford Woodruff Journal is the source for the text of the discourse in *History of the Church* and *Teachings*.

2. Matthew 25:21.

3. 2 Peter 1:5-7.

4. At this time the subject of detecting evil spirits apparently occupied the Prophet's mind very much. Only a few days before, as managing editor of the *Times and Seasons*, he had published a lengthy treatise entitled "Try the Spirits" (5 [1 April 1842]:743-48). Within three weeks, he would twice refer to this subject in public discourse (see 28 April 1842, note 13, and 1 May 1842, note 4). These public teachings reflected his private thought and revelations concerning the endowment ordinances, in which a fuller knowledge of this subject was first communicated on 4 May 1842 (*History of the Church*, 5:1-2, or *Teachings*, p. 137). See also 27 June 1839, note 21.

5. James 4:3.

6. The words enclosed in braces are from the "Book of the Law of the Lord."

24 April 1842

1. See *History of the Church*, 4:601. Not in *Teachings*. The original source for the following report is the "Book of the Law of the Lord," p. 94.

2. The words enclosed in braces are from the "Book of the Law of the Lord."

28 April 1842

1. See *History of the Church*, 4:602-07, and *Teachings*, pp. 223-29. The introductory statement from the Manuscript History of the Church (published below), is from the "Book of the Law of the Lord," p. 94. The original source for the text of the discourse in *History of the Church* and *Teachings* is the Nauvoo Relief Society Minutes, kept by Eliza R. Snow.

2. At the end of the two previous meetings of the Relief Society, held 14 and 19 April, ladies who were ill were administered to by the Relief

Society presidency. During the meeting of 19 April, for example, "Mrs. Durfee bore testimony to the great blessing she received when administered to after the close of the last meeting, by Emma Smith and Counselors Cleveland and Whitney. She said she never realized more benefit through any administration, [and] that she was healed and thought the sisters had more faith than the brethren" (Relief Society Minutes, 19 April 1842, Church Archives). This caused some members of the society to question the propriety of women anointing with oil and laying on hands, thinking this was only a priesthood function. At this meeting, however, the Prophet explained that this was entirely appropriate. He sympathized with those who did not understand his larger vision of the situation. He said "that the time had not been before, that these things could be in their proper order—that the Church is not now organized in its proper order, and cannot be until the Temple is completed." In the Temple women would with oil and by the laying on of the hands confer on their sisters blessings of greater eternal significance than the beautiful but single effect of healing an illness.

3. 1 Corinthians 12:3.*

4. D&C 84:33-39.

5. See note 2, this discourse.

6. In the Kirtland Temple in 1836, after attending to the ordinance of the washing of the feet, Joseph Smith said he had "completed the organiza-tion of the church, and ... [had given] all the necessary ceremonies" (*History of the Church*, 2:432 or *Teachings*, p. 110). However, four days later, he was given greater keys of authority and knowledge which he did not confer on the leaders of the Church until the Nauvoo period (see D&C 110). So while the Prophet's statement made in Kirtland refers to the finalization of all offices within the Church priesthood structure and sets the basic structure of temple ordinances, the Prophet's statement to the Relief Society referred to here in this discourse portends that the same priesthood organi-zation as finalized in Kirtland would be endowed with the greater keys and knowledge as revealed later to Joseph Smith by Elias and Elijah. This greater knowledge eventually effected a considerable enlarging of the scope and meaning of temple ordinances, transforming the Kirtland Temple ordi-nances to their Nauvoo counterparts *without* changing the order of these ordinances (see *History of the Church*, 2:309 or *Teachings*, p. 91). This can be demonstrated by listing the ordinances. In the following listing of the nine temple ordinances performed for the living, those ordinances found in both temples are not italicized and those ordinances either formalized in or unique to the Nauvoo period are italicized:

(1) washing of the body (*wording of the ordinance set*), (2) *sealing the washing*, (3) anointing *the body* with oil (compare number 8), (4) sealing the anointing (*wording set*), (5) *Aaronic portion of the endowment*, (6) *Melchizedek portion of the endowment*, (7) *marriage for time and eternity*, (8) *anointing with oil* (compare number 3), and (9) washing of feet.

The above listing is based entirely on the published *History of the Church*. See *History of the Church* 2:379-82, 391-92, 429, and 432 (Kirtland Period); 5:1-2; 7:541-42, 547, 552-53, 562, 566, and 576 (Nauvoo Period). See also note 2, this discourse and note 21, 27 August 1843.

7. Mark 16:15-18.

8. See 17 March 1842, note 3.

9. That is, the authority conferred upon them when they are given the gift of the Holy Ghost (Mark 16:18).

10. Isaiah 55:8-9.

11. Bathsheba W. Smith recollected that the Prophet himself opened the meeting with prayer. She remembered that in his prayer "his voice trembled very much." Joseph then addressed the Relief Society and said, "According to my prayer I will not be with you long to teach and instruct you; and the world will not be troubled with me much longer" (*Juvenile Instructor* 27:345). The minutes of this meeting do not indicate who gave the opening prayer. See next note and 1 May 1842, note 4.

12. "Keys," apparently meaning the keys of the kingdom, used in the next paragraph (at note 13; see also 1 May 1842, note 4). Apparently because the record says that the "keys" would be given both to the Relief Society members and to the Church, and the "keys of the Kingdom" referred to were to be given in the endowment, George A. Smith felt justified in amplifying this text as follows (italicized words are the amplifications):

"He spoke of delivering the keys *of the Priesthood* to the Church and *said that the faithful members of* the Relief Society *should receive them in connection with their husbands,* that *the Saints whose integrity has been tried and proved faithful, might know how to ask the Lord and receive an answer; for* according to his prayers, God had appointed him elsewhere" (*History of the Church*, 4:604, or *Teachings*, p. 226). For further explanation, see 5 October 1840, note 19.

13. The context of this statement clearly indicates that Joseph Smith intended first to give "the keys of the kingdom" to the leaders of the Church before giving them to the "Elders." (His foreboding comments (at note 11) certainly imply that he was afraid they would be lost from the earth if he did not confer them on others before his death.) The "keys of the kingdom" that enable the possessor to "detect every thing false" are the keys given in the endowment ordinances (see his next public discourse, given 1 May 1842). Six days after this discourse to the Relief Society, he gave the endowment for the first time in this dispensation (*History of the Church*, 5:1-2, or *Teachings*, p. 137). Given that Joseph's main reason for talking to the Relief Society that day was to instruct them that women "would come in possession of the privileges, blessings and gifts of the Priesthood . . . such as healing the sick [and] casting out devils" (see note 21, this discourse), and given that

"casting out devils" would be done by the "keys of the kingdom," Joseph Smith therefore intended even before he first gave these ordinances that women would receive the endowment.

14. Hebrews 12:14; D&C 93:1.

15. Joshua 7.

16. The hope that Nauvoo, its temple and hotel would attract such visitors was based upon D&C 124. Nauvoo's surrounding communities, however, forced the Saints to leave Illinois four years later. Thus the Saints were absolved of finishing these projects following their expulsion in 1846 (D&C 124:53 [49-54]).

17. 1 Corinthians 13.

18. Rather than "I now turn the key in your behalf," the minutes read "I now turn the key to you" (*History of the Church*, 4:607, or *Teachings*, pp. 228-29). So while they were to "get instruction through the order of God . . . thro' the medium of those appointed to lead," nevertheless, the Prophet conceived that the Relief Society was worthy of significant autonomy. They "should be anxiously engaged in a good cause, and do many things of their own free will, and bring to pass much righteousness" (D&C 58:27).

19. See note 17. See also text at notes 3-5 of 17 March 1842.

20. See text of the 27 June 1839 discourse at note 4.

21. Based on D&C 42:43, the published version of this paragraph has been amplified. Those words not in the original text are italicized. "President Smith then *gave* instruction respecting the propriety of females administering to the sick by *the prayer of faith*, the laying on of hands, *or the anointing of oil*; and said it was according to revelation *that the sick should be nursed with herbs and mild food, and not by the hand of an enemy. Who are better qualified to administer than our faithful and zealous sisters, whose hearts are full of faith, tenderness, sympathy and compassion. No one.*"

22. Mark 16:15-18. See notes 2, 12 and 13, this discourse.

23. The words enclosed in braces are from the "Book of the Law of the Lord," p. 94.

1 May 1842

1. See *History of the Church*, 4:608. Not in *Teachings*. The original source for this account is the "Book of the Law of the Lord," p. 94.

2. In these two sentences the Prophet defines the "keys of the kingdom" as "certain signs and words . . . [to] be revealed . . . [in] the Temple." This is an important evidence of his understanding of the

endowment ordinances. Based on this statement, the ordinances of the endowment would be far more significant than what was given during the Kirtland period. See 28 April 1842, notes 6, 12, and 13, and discourse of 20 March 1842, text at note 15.

3. Assuming that the Prophet repeated elements of what he had taught the sisters of the Relief Society three days before, he probably quoted from 1 Corinthians 13.

4. Three days before, the Prophet indicated that he was about to give the endowment to the leaders of the Church. He also said that he would eventually bestow these ordinances upon the "Elders." Here it is clarified that the "Elders" would have to await the completion of the Nauvoo Temple before they would be permitted to receive these blessings. He, however, had two related reasons for administering these ordinances outside the temple before its dedication. The first reason he gave was that he was commanded of God to introduce the ordinances, and the second was that he had premonitions that he might be dead before the temple's completion. Evidence for the first reason is found in D&C 124:95, 97 and George Miller's letter to the *North Islander* dated 26 June 1855 in H. W. Mills, "De Tal Palo Tal Astilla," *Annual Publications—Historical Society of Southern California* 10 (Los Angeles: McBride Printing Company, 1917):120-21. Evidence for the second reason is found in the minutes of his 28 April 1842 discourse and Bathsheba W. Smith's recollection of possibly this very Relief Society meeting in "Recollections of the Prophet Joseph Smith," *Juvenile Instructor* 27 (1 June 1892):345; Lucius N. Scovil letter to the Editor, *Deseret News Semi-Weekly*, 15 February 1884, p. 2; and the affidavit of Justus Morse dated 23 March 1887 in Charles A. Shook, *The True Origin of Mormon Polygamy* (Cincinnati: The Standard Publishing Company, 1914), p. 170. In regard to the more specific aspect of this referenced sentence, namely "the keys" of detection, see 27 June 1839, note 21, and 28 April 1842, note 13.

5. Given that three days after this discourse the Prophet would administer the ordinances of the complete endowment for the first time (see *History of the Church*, 5:1-2, or *Teachings*, p. 137), Joseph Smith's comment that Moses received the endowment is fascinating—particularly in light of a remarkable alteration to Exodus 34:1-2 in Joseph Smith's Translation. Undoubtedly, if, at this stage of Joseph Smith's thinking, he had been asked, "What was taken away when Moses died?" he would not have answered, "the Endowment ordinances as they were given in Kirtland." Those ordinances there administered were identical for the Aaronic and Melchizedek Priesthoods (again see *History of the Church*, 5:1-2 or *Teachings*, p. 137). Based on his 5 January 1841 response to this question, his answer probably would have been the Melchizedek Priesthood portion of the endowment that could have brought Israel to see God face to face was taken away, but the keys of the Aaronic portion of the endowment that brought the ministry of angels remained. Moreover, the sacred vestments of the

priesthood shown by the pattern of God for the Levitical order of the temple service (Exodus 28, 39, and 40:1-33) were not restored in Kirtland, but were given in Nauvoo.

6. See 27 June 1839, note 21 and note 4, this discourse.

7. John 17:3; 1 John 1:1-3; 3 Nephi 11:14-17; D&C 45:51-53; 50:45; 64:10; 84:98 (see 27 June 1839, note 9); 93:1; 132:22-24; JST Matthew 7:33 "Ye never knew me" and JST Matthew 25:11 "Ye know me not."

26 May 1842

1. See *History of the Church*, 5:19-21, and *Teachings*, pp. 237-39. The source for the entries in *History of the Church* and *Teachings* is the Nauvoo Relief Society Minutes, kept by Eliza R. Snow.

2. Numbers 11:29 (1-33).

3. Matthew 18:22 (21-22).

4. James 3:5-8.

5. Undoubtedly, reference is here being made to John C. Bennett. Bennett's immoralities had come to the attention of the Prophet, but the latter, acting on a bleak hope of possible reformation of Bennett deferred publicly exposing his counselor in the First Presidency.

6. 1 Chronicles 13:9-12.

7. John 14:12.

8. In this setting the phrase *Key words* was used with reference to "principles" and "teachings" rather than "signs" and "words" as used on 1 May 1842. Cf. 1 May 1842, note 2.

9. Psalm 37:1.

1 June 1842

1. See *History of the Church*, 5:21. Not in *Teachings*. The original source for the following entry is most probably the "Book of the Law of the Lord."

2. The choice of sheriff was William Backenstos. The other officers chosen as candidates were Dr. J. F. Charles for the Senate, Mark Aldridge and Orson Pratt for representatives, Sidney Rigdon for school commissioner, Hiram Kimball for county commissioner, and Daniel H. Wells for coroner. See *The Wasp* (4 June 1842).

5 June 1842

1. See *History of the Church*, 5:22. Not in *Teachings*. The *History of the Church* account is based on *The Wasp* (11 June 1842).

9 June 1842

1. See *History of the Church*, 5:23-25, and *Teachings*, pp. 239-42. These entries are based on the Nauvoo Relief Society Minutes, kept by Eliza R. Snow.

2. Mahala Overton was the wife of Jacob Morris. They were married 9 December 1843 in Nauvoo.

3. Luke 22:32 (31-34).

4. John 21:15-17.

18 June 1842

1. See *History of the Church*, 5:34-35. Not in *Teachings*. The original source for *History of the Church* is the Wilford Woodruff Journal.

2. This appears to be the first public announcement in Nauvoo of John C. Bennett's licentious conduct. The Prophet made every effort to help Bennett amend his ways, but "seeing no prospects of any satisfaction" the Church withdrew the hand of fellowship from him. After his excommunication Bennett pleaded earnestly that he not be exposed publicly, which Joseph Smith agreed to, but when Bennett abruptly left Nauvoo, began traducing the Prophet's character, and threatened to join forces with anti-Mormons from Missouri, Joseph Smith had no recourse but to unmask Bennett's past.

3. The Nauvoo Agricultural and Manufacturing Association was incorporated by the state of Illinois in February 1841. The purpose of the association was for the "promotion of agriculture and husbandry in all its branches, and for the manufacture of flour, lumber, and such other useful articles as are necessary for the ordinary purposes of life." Joseph Smith, Sidney Rigdon, and William Law, the commissioners, were to receive subscriptions and distribute capital stock (*Times and Seasons*, 2[15 March 1841]: 355-56).

4. See 16 August 1841, note 2.

21 June 1842

1. See *History of the Church*, 5:35. Not in *Teachings*. The *History of the Church* entry is from the Wilford Woodruff Journal.

3 July 1842

1. See *History of the Church*, 5:56. Not in *Teachings*. The *History of the Church* entry is based on *The Wasp* (9 July 1842) and probably on an entry from the "Book of the Law of the Lord." The Wilford Woodruff account is here published for the first time.

2. Daniel 2:44; 7:9-14, 22-27.

3. James Gordon Bennett (1795-1872) was editor of the *New York Herald* and a well-known public figure.

4 July 1842

1. See *History of the Church*, 5:56-57. Not in *Teachings*. The *History of the Church* account is either a reconstruction of the details of the occasion based on *The Wasp* (9 July 1842) or taken from an entry in the "Book of the Law of the Lord." The salient points of this Independence Day celebration were the appearance of the Nauvoo Legion on parade and addresses by Joseph Smith, General Swazy, and others. The *History of the Church* offers the following insight: "At the close of the day General Smith expressed his entire satisfaction in an animated speech, in which he illustrated the design of the organization of the Legion, viz., to yield obedience to the institutions of our country, and protect the Saints from mobs, after which leave was given for strangers to address the Legion, when General Swazey, of Iowa, expressed his friendly feelings towards Nauvoo, and his gratification at the good discipline of the Legion" (*History of the Church*, 5:57).

2. That is, the Nauvoo Legion.

15 July 1842

1. See *History of the Church*, 5:60-61. Not in *Teachings*. The following account is most probably taken from the "Book of the Law of the Lord."

2. "I remember well the excitement which existed at the time," Ebenezer Robinson later reflected, "as a large number of the citizens turned out to go in search for [Orson Pratt]." Apostle Pratt had been told Joseph Smith wanted Orson's wife as his own plural wife and John C. Bennett was accused of having committed adultery with his wife. Both men denied these charges. "Under these circumstances his mind temporarily gave way, and he wandered away, no one knew where ... [the searchers] fearing lest he had committed suicide. He was found some 5 miles below Nauvoo, sitting on a rock, on the bank of the Mississippi river, without a hat" (Ebenezer Robinson, "Items of Personal History of the Editor," *The Return*, Vol. 2, No. 11 [November 1890]). Orson Pratt became more embittered towards the Prophet and a month later was excommunicated from the Church. In January 1843, however, he learned that he had made his judgment from information gained from a "wicked source." After a reconciliation with the Prophet and after the Church's move westward, Orson Pratt became the Church's expert spokesman for the doctrine of plural marriage, giving the first published discourse on the subject. Subsequently he was sent to Washington, D.C. to publish the reasons the Church advocated this principle. The title of his periodical, *The Seer*, demonstrated whom he ultimately believed regarding his earlier dilemma—Joseph the Seer.

22 July 1842

1. *History of the Church*, 5:70-71, refers to this meeting but does not indicate that the Prophet addressed the congregation nor that Orson Pratt objected to the resolution. Not in *Teachings*. The *History of the Church* account comes from *Times and Seasons* 3(1 August 1842): 869.

2. Wilson Law (1807-77) was baptized and ordained an elder in Nauvoo. He was brigadier-general in the Nauvoo Legion. Wilson was William Law's brother.

3. See 15 July 1842, note 2.

24 July 1842

1. See *History of the Church*, 5:82. Not in *Teachings*. The original source for the following account is most probably the "Book of the Law of the Lord."

2. George Miller (1794-1856) was baptized in August 1839, and was appointed president of the Nauvoo House Association. The text has reference to Miller's assignment to go to Quincy, Illinois, and Jefferson City, Missouri, to confer with public officials regarding rumors that another demand was being issued by Missouri Governor Reynolds to extradite the Prophet.

27 July 1842

1. See *History of the Church*, 5:82. Not in *Teachings*. The original source for this entry is most probably the "Book of the Law of the Lord."

2. This would have been some last minute campaigning: the state election was held the first Monday of August 1842.

27 August 1842

1. Not in *History of the Church* or *Teachings*. The following report, misdated in the diary 28 August 1842, was first published by Maureen Ursenbach Beecher, "Eliza R. Snow's Nauvoo Journal," *Brigham Young University Studies* 15[Summer 1975]:398.

2. Eliza Roxcy Snow (1804-87) was baptized in 1835. Universally recognized as "Zion's Poetess," she was sealed to the Prophet 29 June 1842. The Eliza R. Snow Journal is located at Church Archives.

29 August 1842

1. See *History of the Church*, 5:137-39. Not in *Teachings*. The original source for the following report is the "Book of the Law of the Lord," pp. 183-84.

2. Hyrum Smith's remarks.

3. Joseph Smith and Orrin Porter Rockwell were arrested in Nauvoo by two sheriffs from Adams County, Illinois, on 8 August 1842. A requisition for the Prophet (and Rockwell), issued by Governor Thomas Reynolds of Missouri on 22 July 1842, charged the Prophet with being an accessory before the fact to an assault with intent to kill ex-Governor Lilburn W. Boggs. On 2 August 1842 Governor Thomas Carlin of Illinois signed an order for Joseph Smith's arrest and delivery to a Missouri agent. The Prophet sued for and was granted a writ of habeas corpus by the Nauvoo Municipal Court on 8 August 1842, the day of the arrest. The arresting officers, however, objected to the city court's use of habeas corpus to release prisoners in the custody of state or federal authorities, and left Joseph Smith and Rockwell in the charge of the Nauvoo city marshal, Henry G. Sherwood, while they went for legal counsel. Because of the decision of the court, Sherwood felt no compulsion to hold the prisoners and released them the same day. Attorneys for the Prophet and Rockwell "advised them not to be found on the return of the officers from Quincy (which they observed) believing the prisoners would fall victims to the fury of the populace of Illinois or Missouri, and that the arm of Law would not protect them, nor could they get an impa[r]tial trial by due course of Law" (see George Miller to Governor Thomas Reynolds in Lyndon W. Cook, " 'A More Virtuous Man Never Existed On The Footstool Of The Great Jehovah': George Miller on Joseph Smith," *Brigham Young University Studies* 19[Spring 1979], 402-7). After being freed, the Prophet and Porter Rockwell went into hiding. When the Adams County sheriffs returned to Nauvoo on 10 August 1842 and found the prisoners gone, law-enforcement officers, two governors and a large non-Mormon faction were infuriated. Rewards for the arrest or capture of Joseph Smith and Rockwell were set at $300 or more. When, in the fall of 1842, United States District Attorney Justin Butterfield informed Joseph Smith that it was his opinion that the Missouri requisition was invalid, the Prophet sent messengers to Thomas Ford, the newly elected governor of Illinois, requesting rescission of the demand. Ford refused to rescind his predecessor's official acts but did recommend that Joseph Smith stand trial in Springfield and let judges of the supreme court decide the matter. With the concurrence of Justin Butterfield in this recommendation, the Prophet traveled to Springfield in late December 1842. Judge Nathaniel Pope's opinion, delivered 5 January 1843, was that Joseph Smith could not be a "fugitive from justice" on the assault with intent to kill Boggs and that Boggs's affidavit was imprecise and of questionable validity. The Prophet was discharged on 5 January 1843.

The text refers to one of the Prophet's public appearances during this hiding period.

4. Reference to the massacre of nearly twenty Mormons at Jacob Haun's Mill in Caldwell County, Missouri on 30 October 1838.

5. The Prophet is undoubtedly referring to George W. Robinson, Nancy Rigdon, Martha Brotherton, Orson Pratt, and Sidney Rigdon.

6. See 15 July 1842, note 2.

7. Ephesians 6:17.

8. This statement reflects the sentiment of some non-Mormons at the time regarding the Prophet's being released from arrest three weeks earlier by the Nauvoo Municipal Court on habeas corpus (See 18 June 1842, note 2). Some opposed to the Prophet and Nauvoo's growing prominence as a western city, charged the court with "gross usurpation of power," and demanded that the city's charters be revoked. Since the State of Illinois had authorized Nauvoo's charters, as well as similar charters for Chicago, Springfield, Alton, and Galena, the Prophet knew that they could not be easily disannulled.

9. Lilburn W. Boggs (1798-1861). Governor of Missouri 1836-40. Boggs is particularly remembered by the Mormons for his order of Mormon extermination from Missouri 27 October 1838.

10. Thomas Carlin (1789-1852). Governor of Illinois 1838-42. Although initially friendly to the Mormons, Carlin reversed his position the last year of his governorship.

11. The Prophet not only had not as yet conferred the ordinances of the fulness of the priesthood upon any one in the Church (see 27 August 1843, note 30), but he had only recently received a revelation giving the exact title of the millennial Kingdom of God. Apparently the Prophet had not as yet discussed his understanding of these matters fully even with his closest associates. See Andrew F. Ehat, " 'It Seems Like Heaven Began on Earth': Joseph Smith and the Constitution of the Kingdom of God." *Brigham Young University Studies* 20 (Spring 1980):254-57.

12. George W. Robinson (1814-78) was a native of Pawlet, Rutland County, Vermont. A son-in-law of Sidney Rigdon, Robinson was General Church Recorder 1837-40. Among the first Mormon settlers of Nauvoo, by 1842 he had become disaffected and left the Church.

13. The words enclosed in braces are from the "Book of the Law of the Lord."

31 August 1842

1. See *History of the Church*, 5:139-41, and *Teachings*, pp. 257-60. The source for the entries in *History of the Church* and *Teachings* is the Nauvoo Relief Society Minutes, kept by Eliza R. Snow.

2. See 29 August 1842, note 5.

3. Luke 13:32.

4. Song of Solomon 2:15.

5. Governor Thomas Carlin of Illinois. To counterbalance the acrimonious orations of excommunicated John C. Bennett, members of the Nauvoo Relief Society sent a petition, signed by 1,000 women, to Governor Thomas Carlin. The petition, which spoke in the highest terms of Joseph Smith's virtue, requested the governor to take action against Bennett because there was fear of an "attack upon the peaceable inhabitants of the city of Nauvoo and vicinity, through [the latter's] intrigues and false representations" (see *History of the Church*, 5:71, 82).

6. Matthew 5:11-12.

7. The "foolish things," mentioned in the text, had reference to recent attempts on the part of Missouri to extradite the Prophet as well as the wide publicity given to the John C. Bennett scandal. Despite these grave obstacles Joseph Smith continued to demonstrate his characteristic optimism and did not lose perspective of the magnitude of the latter-day work.

8. On the following day the Prophet wrote a letter presenting the details of what "had been manifested to him" during his exile. He apparently felt that he needed to remain in exile, and so the letter took the place of a discourse on 6 September 1842. On that day, too, in another letter he unfolded further information. Both letters deal with the doctrine of baptism for the dead and are included in the Doctrine and Covenants, as sections 127 and 128 respectively.

9. The day after this discourse was given, Joseph Smith wrote a letter on the subject of the necessity of "eyewitnesses" to baptisms for the dead. This letter has been added to the Church's canon of scripture and is D&C 127.

25 September 1842

1. See *History of the Church*, 5:165. Not in *Teachings*. The original source for the entry in *History of the Church* is most probably the "Book of the Law of the Lord." The William Mendenhall and Wilford Woodruff accounts are here published for the first time. Mendenhall's diary is located in the Church Archives.

2. William Mendenhall (1815-1905) was a native of New Castle County, Delaware. Baptized in December 1841, Mendenhall was ordained a seventy in Nauvoo. He died in Springville, Utah.

3. This is the account of Elijah in hiding when Jezebel sought his life.

4. See 29 August 1842, note 3.

29 October 1842

1. See *History of the Church*, 5:181, and *Teachings*, pp. 267-68. The original source for *History of the Church* and *Teachings* is the "Book of the Law of the Lord," p. 208.

2. See 29 August 1842, note 3.

3. Samuel Bennett, appointed presiding authority of the branch of the Church in Cincinnati, Ohio, in October 1840, was later named associate justice of the Municipal Court of Nauvoo.

4. The words enclosed in braces come from the "Book of the Law of the Lord."

1843

1843

1843

17 January 1843 (Tuesday). Old Homestead.[1]
Wilford Woodruff Journal

This was an interesting day a day that was appointed by general proclamation for humiliation fasting & prayer & thanksgiving for the release & delivery we had received[2] Meetings were appointed in each ward throughout the city I met at President Joseph Smith,s & we had an interesting time Br Joseph spoke to some length on the Kingdom of God & the Baptism of John, he said the Kingdom of God was set upon the earth in all ages from the days of Adam to the present time whenever there was a man on earth who had authority to administer the ordinances of the gospel or a priest of God & unto such a man God did reveal his will concerning the Baptism of John. It was the Baptism of repentance unto the remission of sins for the receiving of the Holy Ghost & it was the gospel Baptism, These were questions which had been in debate for many years & in some degree among the Saints,[3] He also spoke upon the subject of honor & dishonor &c.

22 January 1843 (Sunday). At Temple.[1]
Wilford Woodruff Journal

22d Sunday President Joseph Smith deliverd an interesting discourse at the Temple to an inter large Congregation among other things he treated upon the kingdom of God & the baptism of John, He remarked some say the kingdom of God was not set up on earth untill the day of pentecost & that John did not preach the Baptism of repentance for the remission of sins[2] But I say in the name of the Lord that the kingdom of God was set up on earth from the days of Adam to the present time. Whenever there has been a righteous man on earth unto whom God revealed his word & gave power & authority to administer in his name. And whare their is a Priest of God, A minister who has power & Authority from God to administer in the ordinances of the Gospel & officiate in the Priesthood of God, theire is the kingdom of God & in Consequence of rejecting the gospel of Jesus Christ & the Prophets whom God hath sent, the judgments of God hath rested upon people Cities & nations in various ages of the world, which was the Case with the Cities of Sodom & gomoroah who were destroyed for rejecting the Prophets. Now I will give my testimony I care not for man I speak boldly & faithfully & with authority. How is it with the kingdom of God, whare did the Kingdom of God begin, whare their is no kingdom of God their is no salvation. What Constitutes the Kingdom of God Whare there is a Prophet a priest or a righteous man unto whom God gives his oracles there is the Kingdom of God, & whare the oracles of God are not there the Kingdom of God is not, In these remarks I have no allusion to the Kingdoms of the earth we will keep the Laws of the Land, we do not speak against them we never have & we can hardly make mention of the State of Missouri of our persecutions there &c but what the cry goes forth that we are guilty of larceny Burlary, arson treason & murder &C &C which is fals[3] we speak of the Kingdom of God on the earth not the Kingdom of mem, The plea of many in this day is that we have no right to receive revelations, But if we do not get revelations we do not have the oracles of God & if they have not the oracles of God they are not the people of God But say you what will become of the world or the various professors of religion who do not believe in revelation & the oracles of God as Continued to the Church in all ages of the world when he has a people on earth I Tell you in the name of Jesus Christ they will be damned & when you get into the eternal world you will find it to be so they cannot escape the damnation of hell

As touching the gospel & Baptism that John preached I would say that John Came preaching the gospel for the remission of Sins he had his authority from God & the oricles of God were with him & the Kingdom of [God] for a season seemed to ~~roll~~ be with John alone. The Lord promised Zecheriah[4] that he should have a son, which was a desendant of Aaron & the Lord promised that the priesthood should continue with Aaron & his seed throughout their generations, Let no man take this honour upon himself except he be Called of God as was Aaron, & Aaron received his Call by Revelation.[5] An angel of God Also appeared unto Zecheriah while in the Temple that he should have a son whose name should be John & he should be filled with the Holy Ghost[6] Zecheriah was a Priest of God & officiating in the Temple & John was a priest after his father & held the Keys of the aronic priesthood & was Called of God to preache the Gospel & the Kingdom of God & the Jews as a nation having departed from the Law of God & the gospel the Lord prepared the way for transfering it to the gentiles But Says one the Kingdom of God Could not be set up in the days of John for John said the Kingdom was at hand[7] But I would ask if it could be any nearer to them than to be in the hands of John, the people need not wait for the days of Pentecost to find the Kingdom of God[8] for John had it with him, & he Came forth from the wilderness Crying out repent ye for the Kingdom of heaven is at hand as much as to baul out here I have got the Kingdom of God & I am coming after you, Ive got the Kingdom of God & you Can get it & I am Coming after you & if you dont receive it you will be damned & the Scriptures represent that all Jerrusalem went out unto Johns Baptism[9] Here was a legal administrator, & those that were baptized were subjects for a King & also the laws & oracles of God were there therefore the Kingdom of God was there for no man Could have better authority to Administer than John & our Savior submitted to that authority himself by being Baptized by John[10] therefore the Kingdom of God was set up upon the earth Even in the days of John their is a difference between the Kingdom of God & the fruits & blessings that flow from that Kingdom becaus their was more miracles gifts graces visions healings, tongues &c in the days of Jesus Christ & the Apostles & on the day of pentecost than under Johns Administration, it does not prove by any means that John had not the Kingdom of God, any more than it would that a woman had not a milk pan because she had not a pan of milk, for while the pan might be compared to the Kingdom the milk might be compared to the blessings of the Kingdom John was a Priest after the order of

Aaron & had the Keys of that Priesthood & Came forth preaching repentance & Baptism for the remission of sins but at the same time Crys out there cometh one after me more mighter than I the latchet of whose shoes I am not worthy to unlose,[11] & Christ came according to the word of John, & he was greater than John because he held the Keys of the Melchesedic Priesthood & the Kingdom of God & had before revealed the priesthood to Moses, yet Christ was baptizd by John to fulfill all righteousness & Jesus in his teaching says upon this rock I will build my Church & the gates of hell shall not prevail against it[12] what rock, Revelation[13] Again he says except ye are born of the water & the spirit ye Cannot inter into the Kingdom of God,[14] And though the heavens & earth should pass away my words shall not pass away[15] If a man is born of the water & the spirit he can get into the Kingdom of God[16] it is evident the Kingdom of God was on the earth & John prepared subject[s] for Kingdom by preaching the gospel to them & Baptising them & he prepared the way before the Savior or came as a forerunner & prepared subject for the preaching of Christ, &c. Christ preached through Jerrusalem on the same ground whare John had preached & when the Apostles were raised up they worked in Jerrusalem & Jesus Commanded them to tarry thare untill they were endowed with power from on high[17] had they not work to do in Jerrusalem. they did work & prepared a people for the pentecost The Kingdom of God was with them before the day of pentecost as well as afterwards & it was also with John & he preached the same gospel & Baptism that Jesus & the Apostles preached after him The endowment was to prepare the desiples for their mission into the world.[18] Whenever men can find out the will of God & find an Administrator legally authorized from God there is the Kingdom of God but whare these are not, the Kingdom of God is not All the ordinances Systems, & Administrations on the earth is of no use to the Children of men unless they are ordained & authorized of God for nothing will save a man but a legal Administrator for none others will be acknowledge either by God or Angels[19]

I know what I say, I understand my mishion & business God Almighty is my shield & what Can man do if God is my friend I shall not be Sacrafised untill my time Comes then I shall be offered freely,[20] all flesh is is as grass[21] & a governor is no better than other men when he dies he is but a bag of dung I thank God for preserving me from my enemies I have no enmity I have no desire but to do all men good I feel to pray for all men we dont ask any people to throw away any good they have got we ownly ask them to Come & get more what if all the world should embrace this gospel they would then see eye to eye[22] & the blessings of God would Be poured out upon the people which is my whol soul Amen.

William Clayton Diary[23]

This A.M. Joseph preached in the Temple. subject arose from two questions proposed from a Lyceum.[24] 1st Did John Baptize for remission of sins? 2nd Whether the kingdom of God was set up before the day of Pentecost or not till then? To the 1st Q. he answered, "he did" It is acknowledged of all men that John preached the gospel & must have preached the 1st principles, if so he must have preached the doctrine of Baptism for the remission of sins[25] for that is the 1st principal of the Gospel and was ordained before the foundation of the world.[26] I next give my own testimony because I know it is from God. On the 2nd question He said Where the oracles of God are revealed there is the kingdom of God. Wherever the oracles of God are & subjects to obey those oracles there is the kingdom of God. What constitutes the kingdom of God? an administrator who has the power of calling down the oracles of God, and subjects to receive those oracles no matter if there are but 3,4, or 6 there is the kingdom of God &c.[27]

Franklin D. Richards "Scriptural Items"[28]

Joseph's words 1843 No Generation was ever saved or destroyed upon dead testimony neither can be; but by <u>Living</u>

Wherever the Oracles of God are received & found there is the Kingdom of God

The Kingdom of Heaven was set up before the days of Christ.

Joseph Smith Diary, by Willard Richards

Sunday January 22d Preached at the Temple on the setting up of the Kingdom.

29 January 1843 (Sunday). In Temple.[1]

Joseph Smith Diary, by Willard Richards

Sunday Jany 29 meeting on floor of the Temple Joseph Read the parable of the prodigal Son[2] after prayer by John Taylor, then singing by the Quoir

I feel thankful to Almighty God for the privilege of standing before you this morning it is necessary that the hearers should have good & honest hearts as well as the speaker I aim to address you on the important subject of the Prodigal Son

2 Items I wish to notice Last sabbath.—2 questions saying of Jesus coming John—a greater prophet than John 2d. least in the kingdom of God greater than he.[3]—

some so blind they wont see. I dont expect I can work Miracles enough to open

greatest prophet. What constituted him.—no prophet, if do no miracles John did no miracles.—

How is it John was considered one of the Greatest of Prophets? 3 things

1st he was trusted with a divine mission of preparing the way before the face of the Lord.[4]—Trust before or since? no man!—

2d. He was trusted & it was required at his hands to baptize the son of Man.[5] Who ever did that? who had so great a privilege & glory?—son of God into the waters of baptism & beholding the Holy Ghost—in in the sign[6] the form of a dove—with the sign of the dove. instituted before the creation Devil could not come in sign of a dove.—Holy Ghost is a personage in the form of a personage[7]—does not confine itself to form of a dove—but in sign of a dove. = No man holds this book more sacred than I do.[8]—

3d. John at that time was the only legal administrator holding the keys of Power there was on Earth. the Keys the Kingdom the power the Glory from the Jews Son of Zachariah by the holy anointing decree of heaven these 3 constituted him the greatest born of woman.

He that is least in the Kingdom is greater than he?[9] who did the Jesus have reference to? Jesus was looked upon as having the least claim in all gods kingdom.—

He that is considered the least among you, is greater than John! that is myself.—

another question, Law & prophets were until John—since which time the kingdom of heaven is preached & all men press into it.[10]—

additional proof—to what—I offered you on the last sabbath. that that was the beginning of the Kingdom[11]

Prodigal Son.—when you have heard go & read your bible if the thing are not wring true.—

great deal of speculation. Subject I never dwelt upon—understood by many to be one of the intricate subjects—Elders in this church preach.—no rule of interpretation.—what is the rule of interpretation? Just no interpretation at all. understood precisely as it read.—I have Key by which I understand the scripture—I enquire what was the question which drew out the answer.—

National. Abraham. &c as some suppose 1st place dig up the root—what drew out the saying out of Jesus? Pharisees & scribes murmurred! this man receives sinners & eatheth with them this is the key word.[12]—to answer the murmuring & questioning of [that] Saducees & Pharisees had is it this man as great as he pretends to be. & eat with publicans & sirmers.—Jesus not put to it so but he could have found something of the kind discerned it for nations.—Men in an individual capacity. all straining on this point is a bubble.—Boy Boys say ought to be hanged can tell it to you.

big folks Presbyterians. Methodists. Baptists &c—despise the ignorance & abomination of this world.—

this man receiveth sinners—he spoke this parable. what man of you having an hundred sheep & 100 saducees & Pharisees[13] If you pharisees & saducees. are in the sheepfold. I have no mission for you sent to look up sheep that are lost will back him up—& make joy in heaven.—hunting after a few individuals laying it on his Shoulder—one publican you despise.—one piece of Silver[14]—the piece which was lost—Joy in found of the angels over one sinner that repenteth so righteous they will be damned any how you cannot save them[15]rain off from a gooses back—Great I. little you—

certain man had two sons &c.[16]— am a poor publican a sinner—humbled themselves. spending their bread & living &c Ill return to my fathers house. to Jesus you pharisees so righteous you cannot be touched.—I will arise &c claim not be a pharisee or saducee. I claim not to be a son do not let me starve—nothing about Ephraim Abraham—is not mentioned. all that is meant is brought to bear upon the pharisee. saducee. the publicans & sinners, Eldest son, pharisees & saducees murmuring & complaining—because Jesus sat with publicans & sinners—father came out & entreated when John came baptized all. when Jesus come they were angry & would not go in. dealing of God with individuals men always Righteous always have access to throne of God eats in his fathers home If we interpret this to national, view where is the eldest son?

likened the kingdom to an old womans milk pan—how could Jesus take the kingdom from those who bore no fruit & give it to another.— is an apple tree no longer a tree because it has no apples? parable of Prodigal son spoken to illustrate this distinction—from the moment John's voice was first heard he was the Prunner on the earth entitled to salvation. on the earth.

Servants of God of the last days myself & those I have ordained, have the priesthood & a mission—to the publicans & sinners—& if the Presbyterians & [two lines left blank].

are in the kingdom. if they are not righteous—what is the result. they are sinners & if they reject our voice they shall be damnded.

If a man was going to hell I would not let any man disturb him.—while we will be the last to oppress we will be the last to be driven from our post—peace be still bury the hatchet & the sword.— the sound of war is dreadfull in my ear. any man who will not fight for his wife & children is a coward & a bastard.

Mohemetans, Presbyterians, &c if ye will not embrace our religion embrace our hospitalities.

Franklin D. Richards "Scriptural Items"

the next sabbath he (Joseph) asked and answered
1st How was John the greatest prophet ever born of a woman
2d How ~~was Christ~~ is the least in the Kingdom greater than he
Ans to 1st His greatness consisted in 3 things 1st His appointment to prepare the way before the Lord Jesus Christ 2nd His privilege to Baptise him or induct him into his Kingdom 3d His being the only legal administrator in the affairs of the Kingdom that was then on the Earth consequently the Jews had to obey his instruction or be damned by their own Law & Christ fulfiled all

righteousness in becoming obedient to the the Law which himself had given to Moses[17] on the mount and thereby magnified it and made it honorable instead of destroying it

Ans to 2nd Query Christ was least in the Kingdom in their estimation or least entitled to their credulty as a Prophet but as in Truth greater than John

{The Holy Ghost cannot be transformed into a Dove but the sign of a Dove was given to John to signify the Truth of the Deed as the Dove was an emblem or Token of Truth}[18]

Times and Seasons 4 (15 May 1843):200

The Mormons have not yet completed their great Temple, and have no commodious place of worship, but the apostles and elders preach in private houses on the Sabbath, and at other times, though I seldom attend these latter meetings; but when the weather will admit, they meet in the grove, or on the rough floor of the basement of the Temple, and then the prophet frequently preaches. On one of these occasions I heard him preach concerning the prodigal son.[19]

After naming his text, the prophet remarked, that some one had asked him the meaning of the expression of Jesus, "among those born of the woman there has not arisen a greater than John," [20] and said he had promised to answer it in public, and he would do it then. "It could not have been on account of the miracles John performed, for he did no miracles; but it was,

First, Because he was trusted with a divine mission, of preparing the way before the face of the Lord.[21] Who was trusted with such a mission, before or since? *No man.*

Second, He was trusted, and it was required at his hand, to baptise the Son of Man. who ever did that? Who ever had so great a privilege or glory?[22] Who ever led the Son of God into the waters of baptism, beholding the *Holy Ghost* descend upon him in the *sign* of the Dove?[23] *No man.*

Third, John, at that time, was the only legal administrator, holding the keys of power there was on earth. The keys, the kingdom, the power, the glory, had departed from the Jews; and John, the son of Zachariah, by the holy anointing, and decree of heaven, held the keys of power at that time."[24]

William Clayton Diary

Pres. Joseph Preached in the Temple on the Prodigal Son and showed that it did not refer to any nation, but was mearly an answer to the remark "he recieveth the sinners and eateth with them,"[25] the Temple was crowded with people.

Willard Richards Diary

Meeting. Prodigal Son.

16 February 1843 (Thursday Afternoon). Shokoquon, Henderson County, Illinois.[1]
Joseph Smith Diary, by Willard Richards

3 [P.M.] Elder Hyde prayed I preached to a large & attentive audience 2 hours from 19 Rev—10 verse & shewed them that any man who denied his being a propet was not a preacher of righteousness. they opened their eyes & appeared will pleased. & had good effect.

21 February 1843 (Tuesday Morning). At Temple.[1]
Joseph Smith Diary, by Willard Richards

11 [A.M.] went to Temple found Bro Hawes[2] preaching about Nauvoo house. Mr Woo[d]worth[3] spoke say something in vindicating my own character. {commenced under peculiar circumstances. have made all contracts for Nauvoo house. was employed to build from the commencement. some brick on hand. most ready to start brick work one says can you give me something to eat? I'll try. another says I will have my pay. "Go to hell & get it" said I. I have set me down to a dry Johncake & cold water and the men who have worked with me no man shall go onto my poverty stricken foundation to build himself up. for I began it & will finish it. Not that public spirit here as in other cities dont deny revelation if the Temple and Nauvoo house are not finished you must run away.— when I have had a pound of meat or quart of meal I have divided with the workman. (pretty good Doctrin for paganism said Joseph) have had about 300 men on the job—the best men in the world.

those that have not complained I want them to continue with me. & them who hate Mormonism & every thing else thats good I want them to get their pay & run away}[4]

Joseph say, well the pagan prophet has preached us a pretty good sermon this morning—I dont know as I can better it much—to break off the yoke of oppression, and say what he is a mind to. that the pagans and the pagan prophets to feel more our prosperity is curious. I am almost converted to his doctrine. "he has prophecied if these buildings go down it will curse the place." I verily know it is true. Let us build the temple. there may be some speculations about Nauvoo house. say some—some say because we live on the hill we must build up this fort on the hill. does that coat fit you Dr. Foster?[5] pretty well! put it on then. this is the way people swell like the ox or toad. They come down under the hill among little folks brother Joseph how I love you—and get up opposition & sings names to strangers & scoundrels &c I want all men to feel for me. when I have shook the bush—& bare the burden, and if they do not—I speak in authority in the name of the Lord God he shall be damned,—people on the flats are aggrandizing themselves. by the Nauvoo house. who laid the foundation of the Temple. Bro Joseph in the name of the Lord. not for his aggrandizement but for the good of the whole

Our speculators say our poor folk on the flat are down & keep them down. how the Nauvoo house cheats this man & that man— say the speculators. they are fools ought to hide their heads in a hollow pumpkin & never take it out. the first principle brought into consideration is aggrandizement, some think it unlawful—but it is lawful while he has a disposition to aggrandize all around him. false principle, to aggrandize at the expence of another. every thing God does is to aggrandize his kingdom how does he lay the foundation? build a temple to my great name. and call the attention of the great. but where shall we lay our heads—an old log cabin I will whip Hiram Kimball[6] & esq Wells[7] and every body else over Dr Fosters Head, instead of building the Nauvoo house build a great many little skeletons—see Dr Fosters mammoth skeletons of Dr Foster rising all over town but there is no flesh on them. personal aggrandizement. don't care how many bones—somebody may come along & clothe them. elephants; crocodiles &c eaters. such as grog shop &c—card shops &c—those who live in glass houses should not throw stones. The building of N. House is just as sacred in my view as the Temple.[8]

I want the Nauvoo House built it must be built, our salvation depends upon it. When men have done what they can or will for the temple, let them do what they can for the Nauvoo House. We never can accomplish our work at the expense of another. There is a great deal of murmuring in the Church—about me, but I dont care any thing about it. I like to hear it thunder. to hear the saints grumbling.—the growling dog get the sorest head. If any man is poor and afflicted. let him come and tell of it.—& not complain or grumble

finishing Nauvoo House like a man finishing a fight. if he gives up he is killed—if he holds out a little longer he may live.—a story. a man who will whip his wife is a coward. I fought with a man who had whipped wife. still remembered he was whipped his wife. I whipped him till he said enough.—hang on to the Nauvoo house thus & you will build it. & you will be on Pishagah[9] & the great men who come will pile their gold & silver till you are weary of receiving them. & if you are not careful will be lifted up & fall and they will cover up & cloak all your former sins & hide a multitude of sins & shine forth fair as the sun &c[10]

those who have labored & cannot get your pay be patient, if you take the means which are set apart let him he will destory themselves if any man is hungry let him come to me & I will feed him at my table

if any are hungry or naked dont take away the brick &c but come & tell. I will divided. & then if he is not satisfied I will kick his back side

there cannot be some fire without some smoke. well if the stories about Jose Smith are true, then the stories of J C. Bennet are true about the Ladies of Nauvoo. Ladies that the Relief Society was organized of those who are to be wifes to Jos Smith.[11] Ladies you know whether it is true. no use of living among hogs without a snout. this biting and devouring each other. for Gods sake stop it.

one thing more. political economy. our duty to concentrate all our influence to make popular that which is sound & good. & unpopular that which is unsound Tis right politically for a man who has influence to use it as well as for a man who has no influence to use his, from henceforth I will maintain all the influence I can get. in relation to politics I will speak as a man in religion in authority. if a man lift a dagger to kill me, I will lift my tongue.—when I last preached, heard such a groaning I thought of the paddys ell[?] when he tried to kill him could not contrive any way so he put it [in] the water to drown him. and as he began to come to—see said he what pain he is in how he wigles his tail.—the banks are failing & it is the privilege to say what a currency we want. gold & silver to build the Temple & Nauvoo house. We want your old nose rings & finger rings & brass kettles no longer. if you have old raggs—watches— guns go and peddle them, & bring the hard metal, if we will do this by popular opinion you will have a sound currency. send home bank notes—& take no paper money. & let every man write his neighbor before he starts to get gold and silver.—I have contemplated these things a long time, but the time has not come till now to speak till now

I would not do as the Nauvoo House committee has done, sell stock for an old stone house where all the people who live die. & put that stock into a mans hand to go east and purchase rags[12] to come here & build up Mammoth bones[13] with

as a political man in the name of old Joe Smith I command the Nauvoo committee not to sell a share in the N House without the gold or silver. excuse bro Snider[14] he was in England, when they sold stock for stone house.—I leave it

the meeting was got up by N[auvoo House] Committee the pagans.[15] Roman Catholics. & Methodist & Baptist shall have peace in Nauvoo only they must be ground in Joe smiths mill.—I have been in their mill I was ground in Ohio. & York States a presbyterian smut machine—& last machine was in Missouri & last of all I have been through Illinois smut machine & those who come here must go through my smut machine & that is my tongue.

{Dr Foster[16] remarked much good may grow out of a very little, and much good may come out of this. If any men accuse me of exchanging N[auvoo House]. Stock for Rags &c. I gave a $1000 to this house & $50 to relief society & some to Fulmer[17] to get stone to build Joseph house. & I mean to build Joseph a house & you may build this. & I will help you I mean to profit this. & will divide the mammoth bones with you. I am guilty of all I have been charged.—I have signed my name to a petition to have Wm H. Rolinson[18] to have the Post Office.—I did not know a petition for Joseph Smith.—}

Joseph [said] I thought I would make a coat. it dont fit the Dr. only in the P[ost]. office if it does fit any one let them put it on. The bones are skeleton and as old Ezekiel said I command the flesh & the sinnews to come upon them that they may be clothed.[19]

Blessing by Bro. P. P. Pratt.—

Wilford Woodruff Journal

President Joseph Smith arose & Addressed the meeting as a Christian Prophet &-addressed for about an hour much to our edifycation, many remarks he made were plain & pointed some vary applicable to Dr Foster which he afterwards acknowledged to be true Joseph said the Pagan Prophet had prophesied one thing that was true viz that if we did not build the temple & Nauvoo house it would proove the ruin of the place that if we did not build those buildings we might as well leave the place & that it was as necessary to build one as the other & many other things were said much to the purpose.

12 March 1843 (Sunday Morning). Ramus, Illinois.[1]
Joseph Smith Diary, by Willard Richards

Joseph preached 14 John—in my fathers house are many mansions.

Brigham Young Diary[2]

Br. J. Smith feeles unwell ... Br Joseph Preach from the 14 Chapter of St John at 10 oc am he taut menne grait and glorious things.

2 April 1843 (Sunday Afternoon). Ramus, Illinois.[1]
William Clayton Diary

P.M. Joseph preached on Revelations chap. 5. he called on me to open the meeting. He also preached on the same subject in the evening. During the day president Joseph made the following remarks on doctrine. "I was once praying very ernestly to know the time of the coming of the son of man when I heard a voice repeat the following 'Joseph my son, if thou livest untill thou art 85 years old thou shalt see the face of the son of man, therefore let this suffice and trouble me no more on this matter.' I was left thus without being able to decide wether this coming referred to the beginning of the Millenium, or to some previous appearing, or wether I should die and thus see his face. I believe the coming of the son of man will not be any sooner than that time."[2] In correcting two points in Er Hydes discourse he observed as follows, "The meaning of that passage where it reads 'when he shall appear we shall be like him for we shall see him as he is' is this, When the savior appears we shall see that he is a man like unto ourselves, and that same sociality which exists amongst us here will exist among us there only it will be coupled with eternal glory which we do not enjoy now. Also the appearing of the father and the son in John c 14 v 23 is a personal appearing and the idea that they will dwell in a mans heart is a sectarian doctrine and is false"[3]

In answer to a question which I [William Clayton] proposed to him as follows, 'Is not the reckoning of gods time, angels time, prophets time & mans time according to the planet on which they reside he answered yes "But there is no angel ministers to this earth only what either does belong or has belonged to this earth and the angels do not reside on a planet like our earth but they dwell with God and the planet where he dwells is like crystal, and like a sea of glass before the throne. This is the great Urim & Thummim whereon all things are manifest both things past, present & future and are continually before the Lord. The Urim & Thummim is a small representation of this globe. The earth when it is purified will be made like unto crystal and will be a Urim & Thummim whereby all things pertaining to an inferior kingdom or all kingdoms of a lower order will be manifest to those who dwell on it. and this earth will be with Christ Then the white stone mentioned in Rev. c 2 v 17 is the Urim & Thummim whereby all things pertaining to an higher order of kingdoms even all kingdoms will be made known and a white stone is given to each of those who come into this celestial kingdom, whereon is a new name written which no man knoweth save he that receiveth it. The new name is the key word.[4]

"Whatever principle of intelligence we obtain in this life will rise with us in the ressurection: and if a person gains more knowledge in this life through his diligence & obedience than another, he will have so much the advantage in the world to come.[5]

There is a law irrevocably decreed in heaven before the foundation of this world upon whch all blessings are predicated; and when we obtain any blessing from God, it is by obedience to that law upon which it is predicated.[6]

"The Holy Ghost is a personage, and a person cannot have the personage of the H. G. in his heart. A man receive the gifts of the H. G., and the H. G. may descend upon a man but not to tarry with him.[7]

He also related the following dream. "I dreamed that silverheaded old man came to see me and said he was invaded by a gang of robbers, who were plundering his neighbors and threatening distruction to all his subjects. He had heard that I always sought to defend the oppressed, and he had come to hear with his own ears what answer I would give him. I answered, if you will make out the papers and shew that you are not the agressor I will call out the Legion and defend you while I have a man to stand by me. The old man then turned to go away. When he got a little distance he turned suddenly round and said I must call out the Legion and go and he would have the papers ready when I arrived, and says he I have any amount of men which you can have under your command.

[Note: the above paragraph is crossed through with a penciled line and at the beginning in handwriting that is not William Clayton's, a comment simply says "repeated his of 10 March."[8]]

Er Hyde gave this interpretation "The old man represents the government of these United States who will be invaded by a foreign foe, probably England. The U. S. government will call on you to defend probably all this Western Territory, and will offer you any amount of men you may need for that purpose.[9]

Once when prest. Joseph was praying ernestly to know concerning the wars which are to preceed the coming of the son of man, he heard a voice proclaim that the first outbreak of general bloodshed would commence at South Carolina—see Revelation[10]

The sealing of the 144000 was the number of priests who should be anointed to administer in the daily sacrifice &c.[11] During Prest. Joseph's remarks he said their was a nice distinction between the vision which John saw as spoken of in Revelations & the vision which Daniel saw, the former relating only to things as they actually existed in heaven—the latter being a figure representing things on the earth. God never made use of the figure of a beast to represent the kingdom of heaven—when they were made use of it was to represent an apostate church.

Joseph Smith Diary, by Willard Richards

1. P.M. attended meeting. Joseph read 5th Chapter of ~~Johns~~ revelation. referring particularly to the 6th verse. showing from that the actual existence of beasts in heaven probable those were beasts which had lived on another planet than ours—

God never made use of the figure of a beast to represent the kingdom of heaven.—Beasts 7 eyes Priesthood.[12]—this is the first time I have ever taken a text in Revelation.—and if the young elders would let such things alone it would be far better.—then corrected Elder Hyde as in private. [We here include the text of the corrections made to Orson Hyde]

after breakfast called on Sister Sophronia[13] 10 A. M. to meeting. Elder Hyde Preached 1 epistle John 1. chap 1st 3 verses—when he shall appear we shall be like him &c. he will appear on a white horse, as a warrior, & maybe we shall have some of the same spirit.—our god is a warrior.—John 14.23—it is our privilege to have the father & son dwelling in our hearts.

. . . dined at Sophrona's & soon as we arrived.—Elder Hyde I am going to offer some corrections to you. Elder H. replied—they shall be thankfully received.—When he shall appear we shall see him as he is. we shall see that he is a Man like ourselves.—And that same sociality which exists amongst us here will exist among us there only it will be coupled with eternal glory which glory we do not now enjoy.[14]

14 John 23.—the appearing of the father and of the Son in that verse is a personal appearance.—to say that the father and the Son dwell in a mans heart is an old Sectarian notion. and is not correct.

There are no angels who administer to this earth but who belong or have belonged to this earth. The angels do not reside on a planet like this earth. but they reside in the presence of God—but on a Globe like a sea of glass & fire. "Sea of glass before the throne, &c."[15] where all things are manifest past present & to come.—The place where God resides is a great Urim and Thummin. This earth in its sanctified & immortal state will be a Urim & Thummin for all things below it in the scale of creation, but not above it.[16]—related the Dream written on page 3d Book B[17] Interpretation By O. Hyde—

[The dream referred to is located at the beginning of the second volume of Joseph Smith's Diary under the date 11 March 1843 and is as follows:]

A <u>dream</u>, then related. Night before last I dreamed that an old man come to me and said there was a mob force coming upon him, and he was likely to loose his life, that I was Lieut General[18] and had the command of a large force, and I was also a patriot and disposed to protect the innocent & unoffending. & wanted I should assist him. I told him I wanted some written documents to show the facts that they are the aggressors, & I would raise a force sufficient for his protection, that I would call out the Legion,—He turned to go from me, but turned again and said to me. "I have any amount of men ~~at my command~~ and will put them under your command." [Then follows the] Interpretation by O. Hyde—

old man.—Government of these United States, who will be invaded by a foreign foe. probably England. U. S. Government will call on Gen Smith to defend probably all this western territory and offer him any amount of men he shall desire & put them under his command.[19]

I prophecy in the Name of the Lord God that the commencement of bloodshed as preparatory to the coming of the son of man. will commence in South Carolina,—(it probably may come through the slave trade.)—this the voice declared to me. while I was praying earnestly on the subject 25 December 1832.[20]—

I earnestly desired to know concerning the coming of the Son of Man & prayed, when a voice Said to me, Joseph, my son, if thou livest until thou art 85 years old thou shalt see the face of the son of man. therefore let this suffice & trouble me no more on this matter[21]—

2 April 1843 (Sunday Evening). Ramus, Illinois.[1]
Joseph Smith Diary, by Willard Richards

Meeting 7 eve resumed the subject of the beast.[2]—shewed very plainly that Johns vision was very different from Daniels Prophecy—one referring to things existing in heaven. the other a figure of things which on be on the earth[3] whatever principle of inteligence we attain unto in this life. it will rise with us in the resurrection,—and if a person gains more knowledge and inteligence through his obedience & diligence than another he will have so much the advantage in the world to come.[4]—

There is a law irrevocably decreed in heaven before the foundation of the world upon which all blessings are predicated and when we obtain a blessing it is by obidience to the law upon which that blessing is predicated.

again reverted to Elders Hyde mistake. &c. the Father has a body of flesh & bones as tangible as mans the Son also, but the Holy Ghost is a personage of spirit.—and a person cannot have the personage of the H G in his heart he may receive the gift of the holy Ghost. it may descend upon him but not to tarry with him,[5]—

What is the meaning of the scriptures. he that is faithful over a few things shall be made ruler over Many? & he that is faithful over many shall be made ruler over many more?[6]

What is the meaning of the Parable of the 10 talents?[7] Also conversation with Nicodemus. except a man be born of water & of the spirit.[8]—I shall not tell you?[9]—

Closed by flagellating the audience for their fears.—& called upon Elder Hyde to get up & fulfil his covenant to preach 3/4 of an hour.—otherwise I will give you a good whipping.—

Elder Hyde arose & said Brothers & Sisters I feel as though all had been said that can be said. I can say nothing but bless you.—

6 April 1843 (Thursday Noon). In Temple.[1]
Joseph Smith Diary, by Willard Richards

The first day of the Jubilee, of the Church of Jesus Christ of Latter day Saints. a special Conference assembled on the platform of the Temple, or . . . rough floor of the basement, at 10 o clock A. M. the sun shone clearly. & was very warm & pleasent. Scarce a speck of snow is to be seen except on the north side of Zarahemla Hill.[2] is considerable but the ice was about 2 feet deep in the river west of the temple & north of that point; & south of that the channel is clear of ice,—the walls of the temple are from 4 to 12 feet above the floor of the conference.—

President Joseph was detained by a court . . . President B. Young had charge of the meeting. ~~&~~ during the absence of President Joseph.— . ., O. Pratt read the 3d chap. of 2d Epistle of Peter. & preached on the subject of the resurrection.

10 mi before 12 President Joseph Smith & Elder [Sidney] Rigdon and O. Hyde arrived the floor was about 3/4 covererd with listeners—12 o clock O. Pratt gave way & Joseph. rose to state the object of the meeting. It is my object to ascertain the standing of the first presidency. (as I have been instructed) I present myself for trial, I shall next present my councillors for trial.—3d. to take into consideration the sending out of the twelve or some portion of them or somebody else to get means to build up Nauvoo House & temple 4—Elders will have the privilege of appeals from the different Conferences to this if there are any such cases.[3]—It is important that this conference give importance to the N. House. as a prejudice exists against the Nauvoo House in favor of the Lords House—

There is no place where men of wealth & character & influence can go to repose themselfs. and it is necessary we should have such a place.[4]

Are you satisfied with the first presidency, so far as I am concerned, or will you choose another? If I have done any thing to injure my character in the sight of men & angels—or men & women, come forward tell of it & if not ever after hold your peace.

President B. Young arose & nominated Joseph Smith to continue as the President of the church. Orson Hyde 2 dd it.—voted unanimously.—Such a show of hands was never seen before in the church.—Joseph returned his thanks—to the assembly. & said he would serve them according to the best of his ability.

Next president Joseph Brought forward Elder Rigdon for trial. Br Young nominated Elder Rigdon to continue. 2d by O. Hyde . . . voted, (in general) almost unanimous that Elder Rigdon retained his standing.—

Joseph presented Wm Law for trial. Moved by B. Young. 2d By Heber Kimball in name Lord & voted that Wm Law—retain his standing.—

Voted unanimously that Hyrum Smith retain his office as Patriarch . . . .Hyrum said the Lord bless the people. & Elder Rigdon said so too.—

Joseph said I do not know any thing against the twelve. if I did I would present them for trial.

It is not right that all the burdens of the Nauvoo House should rest on a few individuals—and we will now consider the propriety of sending the twelve to collect means for the Nauvoo House.—

there has been too great latitude in individuals for the building of the Temple to the exclusion of the Nauvoo house. It has been reported that the Twelve have wages $2.00 per day for ~~their services~~ I never heard this till recently. & I do not believe I have never known their having any thing I go in for binding up the twelve, &

Let this conference institute an order to this end & let no man pay money or stock into the hands of the twelve except the payer transmit the account immediately to the Trustee in trust. & no man else but the twelve have authority to act as agents for the Temple & Nauvoo House.—

I will mention one case. he is a good man. thats man's name is Russel.[5] he had been East on business for his brother. & took money belonging to the temple & put it in the bag with his brothers money. 2 or three days after his return he called on his brother for the money, but his brother thought he had paid out too much money— & he would keep the church money to make good his own.—I called to see Russel about the money, and he treated me so politely I concluded he never meant to pay—Bro Russel said, that his brother said he should not be out of money again. There was $20. of the church money, & some dried apple for the Prests.

I propose that you send moneys for the temple by the twelve some or all; or some agent of your choosing & if you send by others & the money is lost, tis lost to yourselves.—I cannot be responsible for it.

It is wrong for the church to make a bridge of my nose in appropriating church funds.—The incorporation required of me securities.—which were lodged in the proper hands—Temple committee ~~have~~ are bound to me in the sum $2,000—& the church is running to them with funds every day—& I am not responsible for it.

so long as you consider me worthy to hold this office,[6] it is your duty to attend to the legal forms belonging to the business.—My desire is that the conference Minutes go forth, to inform all branches of the order of doing business. & the twelve be appointed to this spicial mission of collecting funds for the Nauvoo House.—

When I went to the White House at Washington & presented Letters from Thomas Carlin. Van Buren[7] said Thos Carlin. Thos Carlin Who Thos Carlin? I erred in spirit;—& I confess my mistake, in being angry with Martin Van Buren for saying Thos. Carlin is nobody.—let it be recorded on earth and in heaven that I am clear of this sin.[8]—

There has been complaint against the Temple Committee.—for appropriating the church funds to the benefit of their own children. to the neglect of others who need assistance more than they do.—

I have the complaint, by Wm Clayton.[9] Wm Clayton called, Says I have to say to the conference. I am not so fully preparded to ~~present~~ substantiate the proof as I could wish.—

I am able to prove that property used to a great extent. I am able to prove by the books that Cahoon[10] & Higby[11] have used property for their own families—to the exclusion of others.—Joseph said Let the trial of the Committee be deferred to another day—then let. the Lion & unicorn come together—day after tomorrow. Mr Clayton can have the privilege of bringing his books to the trial.—Moved and Seconded—voted that the twelve be appointed a committee to receive & gather funds to build the Nauvoo House. with this proviso, that the twelve ~~and~~ give bonds for good delivery to trustee in trustee. & payer make immediate report to the trustee in ~~tu~~ trust.—Bro W [illiam] W. Phelps proposed that the twelve give duplicate receipts.

President Young remarked he should never give reciepts for cash. except such as he put in his own pocket for his own use but wished this speculation to stop.—& asked if anyone knew any thing against any one of the Twelve, any dishonesty. I know of one who is not.—And referred to Muzzling the ox that treadethth out the corn.[12]—

Joseph Said, I will answer Bro Brigham,—let the twelve spend the time belonging to the temple for to collect funds—and the remainder of the time they may labor for their support.—The idea of not muzzling the ox that treadeth out the corn is a good old quaker song. I have never taken the first farthing of church funds for my own use till I have first consulted the proper authorities, & when there was no quorum of the twelve or high priests I have asked the Temple Committee who had no business with it.—Elder Cutler[13] said it was so.—Let this conference stop all agents in collecting funds except the twelve.—

William Clayton Diary

This day was a special conference the saints assembled in the

Temple soon after 9. I was appointed to take minutes. About 11 prest Joseph arrived and proceeded to business. He first stated the object of this conference, viz. 1st. To ascertain the standing of the first presidency 2nd. To take into consideration the propriety of sending some of the Twelve into the branches abroad to obtain funds for building the Nauvoo House. 3rd. To give a chance to those Elders who have been disfellowshiped or had their licenses taken away in the branches to have a re-hearing & settle their difficulties[14] He then spake on the importance of building the Nauvoo House stressing that the time had come to build it. and the church must either do it or suffer the condemnation of not fulfilling the commandments of God.

He next presented himself & was unamisiously voted president of the whole church. Next his councillors Ers Rigdon and Wm. Law. and afterwards Er Hyrum who was voted with a hearty aye. He blessed the people in the name of the Lord.

The next business was appointing the Twelve on their mission &c. He showed the injustice of Ers collecting funds for the Temple in as much as they rarely brought them here. The conference must contrive some measures to put the Twelve under bonds, for a true return of monies received by them &c.

6 April 1843 (Thursday Afternoon). In Temple.[1]
Joseph Smith Diary, by Willard Richards

[The meeting began at 3 P.M., and Hyrum Smith spoke before the Prophet arrived.]

Joseph followed. I want the Elders to make hono[ra]ble proclamation abroad what the feelings of the presidency are.—I despise a theif above ground. He would betray me, if he could get the opportunity if I were the biggest rogue in the world, he would steal my horse when I wanted to run away, then read proclamation of the Mayor on Stealing. dated 25 day March 1843.—"Wasp". No. 48"[2] Many observation confirmatory & said, enough Said. for this conferece on this Subject.—

Elders have a privilege to appeal from any decision of a branch to know if they shall retain their office or membership.

Necessary I explain concerning Keokuk[3] it is known that the Gov of Iowa[4] has posted a writ for me on affidavit of Boggs.[5] he still holds that writ as a cudgil over my head. (U.S. Attorney[6] told me all writs issued thus were legally dead.) I said that is a stumper & I will shew them a trick the Devil never did. that is leave them. every man who wishes to cast out economically with regard to futurity.—let them come over. leave as soon as they can settle their affairs without sacrifice let them come & we will protect them & let that government know that we dont like to be imposed upon.—

about the first of August 1842 Mr. Remick[7] came to my house, put on a long face, said he was in distress, about to loose $1400 do a theft of 300 at Sheriffs Sale. said he the sale takes place to-morrow.— I have money in St Louis.—next morning he called. I did not like the looks of him but thought I he is a stranger. I have been a stranger. & better loose 200 than be guilty of sin of ingratitude. took his note. on demand The. day I was taken I asked him for the money.—You ought to have it said he but, I have not got my money from St Louis. I have a curious plan in my mind. I will give you a quit claim deed of the land you bought of Galland[8] & give notes to Gallands notes which I have as his agent" I said Joseph, have not asked you for your property. & would not give a snap for it, but I will accept your offer. but want my money—(1/2 my land in the) state.) said he I will give you deed & he gave me deeds. & I got them recorded.—he called for some more favors. & I let him have some Cloths—to the amount 6 or 7 hundred dollars. I have offered this land to many, if they would go to settle there but nobody will go. I agreed if I found he owned as much as he pretended I would give my influence to build up Keokuk. J. G. Remick is his name he has got most $1100 from me, he looks exactly like a woodchuck, & talks like a woodchuck on a stump with a chaw of tobacco, in his mouth. he tried to get his hands to steal a stove from near my store & carry it off on the raft, he is a theif.—My advice is, if they [the Saints] to choose, come away from Keokuk and not go there more. I am not so much of a christian as many suppose I am, when a man undertakes to ride me I am apt to kick him off & ride him.—I wouldn't buy property in the Iowa. I considered it stooping to accept it as a gift. I wish to speak of the—1/2 breed lands opposite this city.[9] 1/2 breed lands.—1/2 breed lands.—and every man there who is not 1/2 breed had better come away. & in a little time we will call them all 1/2 breed.—I wish we could swap some of our 1/2 breeds here for the 1/2 breeds who lived there. I will give you a key, if any one will growl tomorrow, you will know him to be a 1/2 breed. My opinion is the Legislature have done well in giving the best tittle to settlers & squatters. [10]—

Those who have deeds to those islands from the chancery of Iowa, have as good tittle as any, but the settlers under the Laws of Iowa. ~~th~~ Legislature & chancery of Iowa, are at variance. I believe it a form of swindling ~~from~~ by court of Chancery.

Dr Galland said those Islands dont belong to any body, they were thrown out of U. S. Survey. hence no man had a claim, & it was so considered, when I come here.—

My advice to the Mormons, who have deeds & possessions, is fight it out. you who have no deeds or possessions let them alone.— touch not a stick of their timber. Deeds given by court of chancery, warrants & defend against all unlawful claims.—It is a 1/2 breed, it an anomaly, without form & void, a nondescript. if they have your note, let them come here & sue you then you can carry up your case to the highest court.—So long as the <u>Laws</u> have a shadow of tittle, it is not right for the Mormons to go & carry away the wood In the name of the Lord God, I forbid any man from using any observations of mine, to rob the land of wood.—

Moses Martin[11] has been tried & had fellowship withdrawn by the church at ~~Keokuk~~ Nashville[12]

The question has been asked can a Member not belonging to the church bring a member before the high council, for trial? I answer No! I ask no Jurisdiction in [local] religious matters I merely give my opinion when asked. If there was any feelings at Nashville because I gave my opinion, there is no occasion for it.. I only advice the brethren to come from Iowa, & they may do as they please about coming. If I had not actually got into this work, & been called of God, I would back out. but I cannot back out. I have no doubt of the truth. were I going to prophecy I would prophecy the end will not come in 1844 or 5 or 6. or 40 years ~~more~~ there are those of the rising generation who shall not taste death till christ comes. I was once praying earnestly upon this subject. and a voice said unto me. My son, if thou livest till thou art 85 years of age, thou shalt see the face of the son of man.—I was left to draw my own conclusions concerning this & I took the liberty to conclude that if I did live till that time ~~Jesus~~ he would make his appearance.—but I do not say whether he will make his appearance or I shall go where he is.[13]—

I prophecy in the name of the Lord God.—& let it be written.

that the Son of Man will not come in the heavens till I am 85 years old[14] 48 years hence or about 1890.[15]—then Read 14 Rev. 6 verse another angel fly in the midst of heaven; for the <u>hour</u> of his judgment is come. to extermination—from the commencement. commence when angel commences preaching this gospel 1 day—1000 years. 1000 years as 1 day.[16]—41 yrs 8 months.[17]—only 6 years[18] from the voice, saying, if thou live till thou art 85. years old. Hosea 6th chapter after 2 days &c 2520 years[19] which brings it to 1890.— Gaylor[20] says 45 years according to bible recokening. the coming of the Son of man never will be, never can be till the judgments spoken of for this hour are poured out, which judments are commenced.[21]—

Paul says ye are the children of the light—& not of the darkness, that that day should not overtake us as a theif in the night.[22]—it is not the design of the Almighty to come upon the earth & crush it & grind it to powder) he will reveal it to his servants the prophets.[23] O what wondrous wise men there are going about & braying like— like an ass cry O, Lord, where is Joe Smith—Joe Smith.—whare—O Away up on the top of the topless throne aha.—&c—

Jerusalem must be rebuilt.[24]—& Judah return,[25] must return & the temple[26] water come out from under the temple—the waters of the dead sea be healed.[27]—it will take some time to build the walls & the Temple. &c & all this must be done before Son of Man will make his appearance; wars & rumours of wars.[28] signs in the heavens above on the earth beneath Sun turned into darkness moon to blood.[29] earthquakes in divers places, ~~oceans~~ heaving beyond their bound.[30]—then one grand sign of the son of the son of man in heaven. but what will the world do? they will say it is a planet. a comet, &c. consequently the sun [Son] of man will come as the sign of coming of the son of man; is as the light of the morning cometh out of the east.[31]—10 minutes before 6 singing.

James Burgess Notebook[32]

Remarks on the comeing of the Son of Man by Joseph Smith the Prophet. Made in Nauvoo Christ says no man knoweth the day or the hour when the Son of Man cometh.[33] This is a sweeping argument for sectarianism against Latter day ism. Did Christ speak this as a general principle throughout all generations Oh no he spoke in the present tense no man that was then liveing upon the footstool of God knew the day or the hour But he did not say that there was no man throughout all generations that should not know the day or the hour. No for this would be in flat contradiction with other scripture for the prophet says that God will do nothing but what he will reveal unto his Servants the prophets[34] consequently if it is not made known to the Prophets it will not come to pass;[35] again we find Paul 1st of Thesslonians 5th Chapter expressly points out the characters who shall not know the day nor the hour when the Son of Man cometh for says he it will come upon them as the theif or unawares.[36] Who are they they are the children of darkness or night. But to the Saints he says yea are not of the night nor of darkness of that that day should come upon you unawares. John the revelator says 14 chap 7th verse that the hour of his judgements is come they are precursers or forerunners of the comeing of Christ. read Matthew 24 Chap and all the Prophets. He says then shall they see the Sign of the comeing of the Son of Man in the clouds of Heaven. How are we to see it Ans. As the lighting up of the morning or the dawning of the morning cometh from the east and shineth unto the west—So also is the comeing of the Son of Man. The dawning of the morning makes its appearance in the east and moves along gradualy so also will the comeing of the Son of Man be. it will be small at its first appearance and gradually becomes larger untill every eye shall see it.[37] Shall the Saints understand it Oh yes. Paul says so.[38] Shall the wicked understand Oh no they attribute it to a natural cause. They will probably suppose it is two great comets comeing in contact with each other

It will be small at first and will grow larger and larger untill it will be all in a blaze so that every eye shall see it. Joseph Smith the Prophet.

Franklin D. Richards "Scriptural Items"

Joseph said when he was asking to know of the time of Christs second Coming he obtained for <u>answer</u> my son if thou shalt live untill thou art Eighty five years old thou shalt see the son of man on Earth Joseph was born in Sharon Windsor County Vermont Dec 23 1805. He is therefore now 37 years old last Dec which leaves 48 years yet to transpire untill the tim[e] of Promise that Joseph should see <u>Christ</u>.

7 April 1843 (Friday Morning). In Temple.[1]
Joseph Smith Diary, by Willard Richards

President Joseph rather hoarse from speaking so long yesterday—said he would use the boys lungs to day.—[and after the trial of the Temple Committee] President Joseph stated that the business of the conference had closed. & the remainder of the conference would be devoted to instruction—it is an insult to the meeting to have people run out of meeting Just before we close. if they must go let them go 1/2 an hour before. No Gentleman will go out of meeting Just at close.

7 April 1843 (Friday Afternoon). In Temple.[1]
Joseph Smith Diary, by Willard Richards

4/45 Joseph said to complete the subject of Bro Pratts. I thought it a glorious subject with one ~~additional idea~~ addition their is no fundamental principle belonging to a human System that "ever goes into another in this world or the world to come." the principle of Mr Pratt was correct. I care not what the theories of men are.—we have the testimony that God will raise us up & he has power to do it. If any one supposes that any part of our bodies, that is the fundamental parts thereof, ever goes into another body he is mistaken[2]—5 Choir sung. & notice that Bro Joseph will preach tomorrow morning at 10—

Franklin D. Richards "Scriptural Items"

During Conference Orson Pratt gave a Lecture upon the Second advent of Christ in connexion with the resurrection & to refute the argument of the transition of matter He said that Only about 3/4 of the matter contained in one creature could be converted to the use of another Joseph said No fundamental principle of one creature can be changed to another Creature.

8 April 1843 (Saturday Morning).[1]
William Clayton Report

Pres't Joseph called upon the choir to sing a him and remarked that "tenor charms the ear-bass the heart." After sing the President spoke in substance as follows.

I have three requests to make of the congregation the first is that all who have faith will exercise it, that the Lord may be willing to calm the wind. The next is, that I may have your prayers that the Lord may strengthen my lungs so that, I may be able to make you all hear. And the next is, that I may have the Holy Ghost to rest upon me so as to enable me to declare those things that are true.

The subject I intend to speak upon this morning is one that I have seldom touched upon since I commenced as an Elder of the Church. It is a subject of great speculation as well amongst the Elders of the church as amongst the divines of the day; it is in relation to the beast spoken of in Revelations.[2] The reason why it has been a subject of speculation amongst the Elders, is in conse-quence of a division of sentiment and opinion in relation to it. My object is to do away with this difference of opinion. ~~The knowledge of the subject is not very essential to the Elders.~~ To have knowledge in relation to the meaning of beasts ~~with seven~~ and heads and ~~ten~~ horns and other figure made use of in the revelations is not very essential to the Elders. If we get puffed up by thinking that we have much knowledge, we are apt to get a contentious spirit, and knowledge is necessary to do away contention. The evil of being puffed up is not so great as the evil of contention.[3] Knowledge does away darkness, supense and doubt, for where Knowledge is there is no doubt nor suspense nor darkness. There is no pain so awful as the pain of suspense. this is the condemnation of the wicked; their doubt and anxiety and suspense causes weeping, wailing and gnashing of teeth.[4] In knowledge there is power. God has more power than all other beings, because he has greater Knowledge, and hence he knows how to subject all other beings to him.[5] I will endeavour to instruct you in relation to the meaning of the beasts and figures spoken of. Er (Pelatiah) Brown[6] has been the cause of this subject being now presented before you. He, ~~is~~ one of the wisest old heads we have among us, has been called up before the High Council on account of the beast. The old man has preached concerning the beast which was full of eyes before and behind and for this he was hauled up for trial. I never thought it was right to call up a man and try him because he erred in doctrine, it looks too much like methodism and not like Latter day Saintism. Methodists have creeds which a man must believe or be kicked out of their church. I want the liberty of believing as I please, it feels so good not to be tramelled. It dont prove that a man is not a good man, because he errs in doctrine. The High Council undertook to censure and correct Er Brown because of his teachings in relation to the beasts, and he came to me to know what he should do about it. The subject particularly referred to, was the four beasts and four and twenty Elders mentioned in Rev. ch 5 v. 8. The old man has confounded all Christendom by speaking out that the four beasts represented the Kingdom of God; the wise men of the day could not do any thing with him, and why should we find fault, anything to whip sectarianism and put down priestcraft; a club is better than no weapon for a poor man to fight with, but I could not keep laughing at the idea of God making use of the figure of a <u>beast</u> to represent the Kingdom of God on the earth, when he could as well have used a far more noble and consistent figure. What? The Lord make use of the figure of a creature of the brute creation to represent that which is much more noble and important. The glories of his Kingdom? You missed it that time, old man, but the sectarians did not know enough to detect you.

When God made use of the figure of a beast in visions to the prophets,[7] he did it to represent those Kingdoms who had degenerated and become corrupt—the Kingdoms of the world, but he never made use of the figure of a beast nor any of the brute kind to represent his kingdom. Daniel says when he saw the vision of the four beasts "I came near unto one of them that stood by, and asked him the truth of all this."[8] The angel interpreted the vision to Daniel, but we find by the interpretation that the figures of beasts had no allusion to the Kingdom of God. You there see that the beasts are spoken of to represent the Kingdoms of the world the inhabitants whereof were beastly and abominable characters, they were murderous, corrupt, carnivourous and brutal in their dispositions. I make mention of the prophets to qualify my declaration which I am about to make so that the young Elders who know so much may not rise up and choke me like hornets. there is a grand difference and distinction between the visions and figures spoken of by the prophets and those spoken of in the Revelations of John. None of the things John saw had any allusion to the scenes of the days of Adam or of Enoch or of Abraham or Jesus, only as far as is plainly represented by John and clearly set forth.[9] John only saw that which was "shortly to come to pass" and that which was yet in futurity (He read Rev. ch. 1 v. 1) Now I make this declaration, that those things which John saw in heaven, had no allusion to any thing that had been on the earth, because John says "he saw what was shortly to come to pass" and not what had already transpired. John saw beasts that had to do with things on the earth, but not in past ages; the beasts which he saw had to devour the inhabitants of the earth in days to come. The revelations do not give us to understand any thing of the past in relation to the Kingdom of God. What John saw and speaks of were things which were in heaven, what the prophets saw and speak of where things pertaining to the earth. I am now going to take exception to the present translation of the bible in relation to these matters. There is a grand distinction between the actual meaning of the Prophets and the Present translation. The Prophets do <u>not</u> declare that the[y] saw a beast or beasts, but that the[y] saw the <u>image</u> or <u>figure</u> of a beast.[10] They did not see an actual bear or Lion but the images or figures of those beasts. The translation should have been rendered "image" instead of "beast" in every instance where beasts are mentioned by the Prophets. But John saw the actual beast in heaven, to show to John ~~and to the inhabitants that that being~~ did actually exist there. When the Prophets speak of seeing beasts in their visions, they saw the images; ~~the~~ types to represent certain things and at the same time they received the interpretation as to what those images or types were designed to represent. I make this broad declaration, that where God ever gives a vision of an image, or beast or figure of any kind he always holds himself responsible to give a revelation or interpretation of the meaning thereof, otherwise we are not responsible or accountable for our belief in ~~them~~ it.[11] Dont be afraid of being damned for not knowing the meaning of a vision or figure where God has not given a revelation or interpretation on the subject (He here read Rev. ch 5 v 11 to 13) John saw curious looking beasts in heaven, he saw every creature that was in heaven, all the beasts, fowls, & fish in heaven, actually there, giving glory to God. I suppose John saw beings there, that had been saved from ten thousand times ten thousand earths like this, strange beasts of which we have no conception all might be seen in heaven. John learned that God glorified himself by saving all that his hands had made whether beasts, fowl fishes or man. Any man who would tell you that this could not be, would tell you that the revelations are not true. John heard the words of the beasts giving glory to God and understood them. God who made the beasts could understand every language spoken by them; The beasts were intelligent beings and were seen and heard by John praising and glorifying God.

The popular religionsts of the day say that the beasts spoken of in the revelations represent Kingdoms. Very well, on the same principle we can say that the twenty four Elders spoken of represent beasts, for they are all spoken of at the same time, and represented as all ~~giving~~ uniting in the same acts of praise and devotion. Deacon Homespun[12] said the earth was flat as a pan cake, but science has proved to the contrary. The world is full of technicalities and misrepresentation, but I calculate to overthrow the technicalities of the world and speak of things as they actually exist. Again there is no revelation to prove that things do not exist in heaven as I have set forth, and we never can comprehend the things of God and of heaven but by revelation.[13] We may spiritualize and express opinions to all eternity but that is no authority.

Ye Elders of Israel hearken to my voice and when ye are sent into the world to preach, preach and cry aloud "repent ye for the Kingdom of heaven is at hand repent and believe the gospel."[14] Never meddle with the visions of beasts and subjects you do not understand. Er Brown when you go to Palmyra dont say any thing about the beast, but preach those things the Lord has told you to preach about, repentance and baptism for the remission of sins.

(He here read Rev. ch 13 v 1 to 8) The spiritualizers say the beast that received the wound was Nebuchadnezzar, but we will look at what John saw in relation to this beast. The translators have used the term "dragon" for "devil".[15] Now it was a beast that John saw in heaven, and he was then speaking of "things that were shortly to come to pass." and consequently the beast John saw could not be Nebuchadnezzar The beast John saw ~~as spoken of in the 13th chapter~~ was an actual beast to whom power was to be given. An actual intelligent being in heaven and this beast was to have power given him. John saw "one of the heads of the beast as it were wounded to death; and his deadly wound was healed; and all the world wondered after the beast,"[16] Nebuchadnezzar and Constantine the great not excepted; it must have been a wonderful beast that all human beings wondered after it, and I will venture to say that when God gives power to the beast to destroy the inhabitants of the earth, all will wonder. Verse 4 reads "And they worshipped the dragon which gave power unto the beast; and they worshipped the beast saying, who is like unto the beast? who is able to make war with him? Some say it means the kingdom of the world. One thing is sure, it dont mean the kingdoms of the saints. Suppose we admit that it means the kingdoms of the world, what propriety would there be in saying, who is able to make war with myself. If these spiritualizing interpretations are true, the book contradicts itself in almost every verse, but they are not true. There is a mistranslation of the word dragon in the second verse. The original hebrew word signifies the devil and not dragon as translated. Read ch 12 v 9 it there reads "that, old serpent called the devil, and it, ought to be translated devil in this case and not dragon. Everything that we have not a key word to, we will take it as it reads. The beasts which John saw and speaks of as being in heaven were actually living in heaven, and were actually to have power given to them over the inhabitants of the earth precisely according to the plain reading of the revelations. I give this as a key to the Elders of Israel.

Joseph Smith Diary, by Willard Richards

3 requests.

1st that all who have faith will pray Lord to calm the wind. for as it is now. I cannot speak.

2 that the Lord will strengthn my Lungs.

3d that I may have the Holy Ghost.

The subject which I shall speak from is the beasts spoken of by John.[17]—I have seldom spoken from the revelations & I do it now to do away divisions & not that the knowledge is so much needed.—

knowledge is necessary to prevent division although it may puff up it does away suspence. in knowledge is power, hence Gods knows how to subject all beings he has power—over all.

should not have called up this subject if it had not been for this old white head before Father Brown.[18]—I did not like the old man being called up before the High Council for erring in doctrine.— why I feel so good to have the privilege of thinking & believing as I please.

They undertook to correct him there (whether they did or not I dont care)

Rev. 5 Chap 8 verse.—Father Brown had been to work & confounded all christendom, that these were figure John saw in heaven to represent the different kingdoms of God on earth. he put down Sectarianism, & so far so good.—but I could not help laughing that God should take a figure of a beast to represent his kingdom consisting of Men.—To take a lessor figure to represent a greater. old white head you missed it that time. By figure of Beasts God represented the kingdoms of the world.—Bear. Lion &c. represented the kingdoms of the world. Says Daniel[19] for I refer to the prophets. to qualify my observations. to keep out of the wasp nests or young elders.

The things John saw had no allusion to the day of Adam Enoch Abraham or Jesus—only as clearly specified & set forth to John. I saw that the which was lying in futurity. Rev. 1.1.—read is key to the whole subject

4 beasts. & 24 Elders which was out of every Nation.—it is great stuffing, to stuff all nations into 4 beasts & 24 Elders things which he saw had no allusions to what had been—but what must shortly come to pass.—Rev is one of the plainest books god ever caused to be written—what John saw he saw in heaven—that which the p the prophet[20] saw in vision was on earth, and in Hebrew it is a Latitude & Longitude compared with English version

They saw <u>figures</u> of beasts.—they, Daniel did not see a lion & a bear. he saw an image like unto a bear.—in every place.—John saw the actual beast itself.—it was to let John know that beasts existed there & not to represent figures of things on the earth.—The prophets always had interpretations of their visions &c God always holds himself responsible to give revelations of his visions & if he does it not, we are not responsible.—

speculators read not, fear they shall be condemned. if God has given no Rev

How do you prove John saw creatures in heaven? C 5. V 11. revelation. 13 verse every creature which was in heaven and on the Earth I John saw all beasts in heaven. for I expect he saw the beasts of a 1000 forms from 10,000 worlds like this, the grand secret was to tell what was in heaven. God will glorify himself with all these animals.—

says one I cannot believe in salvation of beasts. I suppose God could understand the beasts &c, in certain worlds== the 4 beasts were angels there. dont know where they come from, they were inteligent inteligent.—but my Darling religion, says, they meant something beside beast.—then the 24 elders must mean something else:—4 beasts meant Buonpart & Cyrus. &c. then the 24 elders meant the kingdoms of the beasts. It is all as flat as a pancake

What do you use such flat and vulgar expressions for being a prophet? because the old women understand it, they make pancakes. the whole argument is flat. & I dont know of any thing better to represent the argument.—

there is no revelation any where to show that the beasts meant any thing but beasts.

O ye Elders of Israel hearken to my voice & when ye are sent into the world to preach, tell them things you are sent to tell. declare the first principles, & let mysteries alone lest you be overthrown.—

Father Brown when you go to palmyra say nothing about the 4 Beasts. Danl. [Revelation] C. 13. 2 verse—some say Deadly wound means Nebuchadnezzar—Constantine & the catholic now for the wasp nest.—preists & Dragon for Devil they have translated beast in heaven—it was not to represent beast in heaven—it was an angel in heaven who has power in the last days to do a work—all the world wondered after the beast, & <u>if the beast was all the world, how could the world wondered after the beast?</u>[21] When the old devil shall give power to the beast to do all his mighty works all the world will wonder—

Who is able to make war with the beast?[22] says the inhabitants of the earth. if it means the kingdom of the world it dont mean the kingdoms of the Saints.—who is able to make war with my great big self.—The Dragon.—we may interpret it.—& it is sometimes Alpelyel [Apollyon]. 9 verse 12 chap.—key word.—independent beast. abstract from the human family.—(25 minutes past 11. lungs failed. the wind blew briskly.) I said more than I ever did before except once at Ramus.[23] & then the little apostates [?] stuffed me like a ~~certain~~ fellows cock turkey with the prophecies of Daniel and crammed down my throat with their fingers[24]—

Franklin D. Richards "Scriptural Items"

Josephs Sayings At the 1843 Conference The reason why God is greater than all others IS He knows how to subject all things to himself Knowledge is Power A beast is never used to represent the Church BUT man in his degenerate state having become like brute Beasts

None of Johns beasts refer or apply to any thing previous to Christ except it is specified (Quoted Rev 4-1)

The Revelator John saw <u>THINGS</u> in Heaven Beasts women &c The Prophets[25] on Earth in vision saw (as the Hebrew says) the <u>images</u> of Beasts Rev 5 13th Proves that John saw <u>Beasts</u> in Heaven and heard them speak praise to God do not know what Language they speak.

William Clayton Diary

Various little items of business attended to and a discourse from the president on Rev.[26]

9 April 1843 (Sunday Morning). Temple Stand.[1]
Joseph Smith Diary, by Willard Richards

Joseph remarkd that some might have expectd him to preach but his heart & lungs would not admit. Joshua Grant[2] will occupy the stand a while followed by Amasa Lyman.

13 April 1843 (Thursday). At Temple.[1]
Joseph Smith Diary, by Willard Richards

I most heartily congratulate you on your safe arrival at Nauvoo. & your safe deliverance from all the dangers & difficulties you have had to encounter but you must not think your tribulations are ended.

I shall not address you on doctrine but concerning your temporal welfare inasmuch as you have come up here assaying to keep the Commandments of God I pronounce the blessings of heaven & earth upon you. & inasmuch as [you] will follow counsel & act wisely & do right these blessings shall rest upon you so far as I have power of with God to seal them upon you I am your servant. & it is only through the Holy Ghost that I can do you good. God is able to do his own work.

we do not present ourselves before you as any thing but your humble servants. willing to ~~be~~ spend & be spent in your services.

we shall dwell on your temporal welfare on this occasion. In the 1st place. where a crowd is flocking from all parts of the world of different minds, religions, &c. there will be some who do not live up to the commandments; & there will be designing characters who would turn you aside & lead you astray. speculators who would get away your property. therefore it is necessary we should have an order here, & when emigrants arrive to instruct them concerning these things.

If the heads of the Church have laid the foundation of this place, & have had the trouble ~~of~~ of doing what has been done—are they not better qualified to tell you how to lay out your money & than those who have had no interest &c—

Some start on the revelations to come here[2] & get turned away & loose all, & then come, and enter their complaints, to us when it is too late to do any thing for them the object of this meeting is to tell you these things & then if you will pursue the same courses you must bear the consequence. There are sevrl objects in your coming here—one object has been to bring you from Sectarian bondage Another from National bondage, where you can be planted in a fertile soil, We have brought you into a free government, not that you are to consider yourselves outlaws, by free government we do not mean that a man has a right to steal rob, &c but free from Bondage. taxation—oppression. free in every thing if he conduct himself honestly & circumspectly with his neighbor—free in a Spiritual capacity.—This is the place that is appointed for the oracles of god to be revealed.[3]

If you have any darkness you have only to ask & the darness is removed. tis not necessary that miracles should be wrought to remove darkness Miracles are the fruits of faith. "how shall we believe of him of whom &c[4] ~~we have not heard. I.E. inasmuch as I have resumed leading before I~~ God may correct the scripture by me if he choose[5] faith comes by hearing the word of God. & not faith by hearing & hearing by the word &c[6] If a man has not faith Enough to do one thing he may do another, if he cannot remove a Mountain he may heal the sick. where faith is there will be some of the fruits. all gift & power which were poured out from heaven were poured out on the heads of those who had faith.[7] You must have a oneness of heart in all things, You shall be satisfied one way or the other with us before you have done with us—there are a great many old huts here but they are all new our city is not 6 or 700 years old as those you come from, it is only a 4 year old not a 4 ~~year old~~ but 3 year old. we commenced building 3 years last fall. there [were] few old setlers—I got away from my keepers in Missouri[8] & run & come on these Shore, & found 4 or 500 families & I went to work to get meat & flour folks were not afraid to trust me, I went to work & bought all this region of country. & I cried Lord what will thou have me to do? "& the answer was build up a city & call my saints to this place!"[9] & our hearts leaped with joy to see you coming here. We have been praying for you all winter,[10] from the bottom of hearts, We are glad to see you—we are poor—& cannot do by you as we would, but will do all we can.—

Tis not to be expected that all can locate in the city.—there are some who have money & will build & hire others. those who cannot purchase. lots can go out in the county. the farmers want your labor.—no industrious man need suffer in this land.—

the claims of the poor on us are such that we have claim on your good feelings for your money, to help the poor. & the church debts also have their demands to save the credit of the church. this credit has been obtained to help the poor. & keep them from starvation &c. those who purchase church lands & pay for it, this shall be their sacrifice.

Men of 50 & 100,000 dollars who were robbed of every thing in the State of Mo.[11] are laboring in this city for a morsel of bread, & there are ~~those~~ who must have starved but for the providence of God through me. If any man say here is land or there is land, believe it not. we can beat all our competitors in lands, price, & ever think. we have the highest prices, best lands. & do the most good with the money we get. our system ~~it~~ is a real smut machine a bolting machine.—& all the shorts brann & smut runs away & all the flour remains with us.—

suppose I sell you land for $10 per acre & I gave 3.4.5.pr acre. then you are speculating says one. yes, I will tell you how. I buy others lands & give them to the widow & the fatherless.—

If the speculators run against me they run against the buckler of Jehovah.—God did not send me up as he did ~~Joshuua~~ Joshua in former days[12] God sent his servants to fight, but in the last days he has promised to fight the battle himself[13]

God will deal with you himself. & will bless or curse you as you do behave yourselves. I speak to you as one having authority that you may know when it come & that you may have faith & know that God has sent me.

The lower part of the town is the most healthy.[14] In the upper part of the town the Merchants will say I am partial &c. but The lower part of the town is much the most healthy. I tell you in the name of the Lord.—I have been out in all parts of the city at all times of night to learn these things.

The Doctors in this region dont know much; & the lawyers[15] when I spoke about them began to say we will renounce you on the stand.—but they dont come up & I take the liberty to say what I have a mind to about them.

Doctors wont tell you <u>where</u> to go to be well. they want to kill or cure you to get your money.—Calomel Doctors[16] will give you Calomel to cure a sliver in the big toe & does not stop to know whether the stomach is empty or not.—& calomel on an empty stomach will kill the patient. & the Lobelia doctors[17] will do the same. point me out a patient & I will tell you whether calomel or Lobelia will kill him or not. if you give it, The river Mississippi is healthy unless they drink it. & it is more healthy than the spring water—dig wells from 15 to 30 feet and it will be healthy.

There are many sloughs on the Islands from were Miasma[18] arises in the summer, and is blown over the upper part of the city. but it does not extend over the lower part of the city.—

All those persons who are not used to living on a river, or lake or large pond of water. I do not want you should stay on the banks of the river. get away to the lower part of the city. back on the hill— where you can get good well water.—if you feel any inconvenience take some mild physic 2 or 3 times & then some good bitters.[19]—

if you can get any thing else take a little salts & cyanne pepper— if you cant get salt take peconia, or gnaw down a butternut tree, eat some boneset or hoarhound.

Those who have money come to me & I will let you have lands & those who have no money if they look as well as I do I will give you advice that will do you good 12 1/4.—I bless you in the name of Jesus Christ Amen ... Joseph gave notice that Bro Gardner[20] wanted 2 or 300 hands ditching—a good job.—

Levi Richards Diary[21]

Spent the day visiting friends & attending Meeting at Temple to hear from Pres Joseph Counsel to Emigrants in relation to settling— &, Speculation &c.

Wilford Woodruff Journal

The New emegrants assembled at the Temple & received an interesting discourse from President Joseph Smith which was truly interesting to the Saints in general.

Willard Richards Diary

Meeting of Emigrants at temple office.

16 April 1843 (Sunday Morning). In Temple.[1]
Joseph Smith Diary, by Willard Richards

Meeting at the Temple. A. M. 10 . o. C

Joseph read Bro Pratts[2] letters to the Editors of "T. & Seasons"[3] concerning the death of Lorenzo Barns.[4] & remarked he read it because it was so appropriate to all who had died in the faith.— Almost all who have fallen in these last days, in the church, have fallen in a strange land, this is a strange land. to those who have come from a distance. we should cultivate sympathy for the afflicted among us.

If there is a place on earth. where men should cultivate this Spirit & pour in the oil & wine in the bosom of the afflicted it is this place. and this spirit is manifest here, and although he is a stranger & afflicted when he arrives, h[e] finds a brother & friend ready to administer to his necessities.—another remark, I would esteem it one of the greatest blessings, if I am to be afflicted in this world, to have my lot cast where I can find brothers & friends all around me. but this is not thing referred to it is to have the privilige of having our dead buried on the land where god has appointed to gather his saints together.—& where there will be nothing but saints, where they may have the privilege of laying their bodies where the Son will make his appearance. & where they may hear the sound of the trump that shall call them forth to behold him, that in the morn of the resurrection they may come forth in a body. & come right up out of their graves, & strike hands immediately in eternal glory & felicity rather than to be scattered thousands of miles apart. There is something good & sacred to me. in this thing. The place where a man is buried has been sacred to me.—this subject is made mention of In Book of Mormon & Scriptures.[5] to the aborigines ~~regard~~ the burying places of their fathers is more sacred than any thing else.[6]

When I heard of the death of our beloved bro Barns it would not have affected me so much if I had the opportunity of burying him in the land of Zion. I believe, those who have buried their friends here their condition is enviable. Look at Joseph in Egypt how he required his friends to bury him in the tomb of his fathers.—see the expence & ~~great company &~~ which attended the embalming and the going up of the great company. to his burial. It has always been considered a gret curse not to obtain an honorable buryal. & one of the greatest curses the ancient prophets could put on any one was that man should go without a burial.[7]

I have said, father, I desire to be buried here, & before I go home, but if this is not thy will ~~not~~ may I return, or find some kind friend to bring me back, & gather my friends, who have fallen in foreign lands, & bring them up hither, that we may may all lie together.—

I will tell you what I want, if to morrow I shall be called to lay in yonder tomb. in the morning of the resurrection, let me strike hands with my father, & cry, my father, & he will say my son, my son,—as soon as the rock rends. & before we come out of our graves.

& may we contemplate these things so? Yes, if we learn how to live & how we die when we lie down we contemplate how we may rise up in the morning and it is pleasing for friends to lie down together locked in the arms of love, to sleep, & locked in each others embrace & renew their conversation.

would you think it strange that I relate what I have seen in vision in relation this interesting theme.[8] Those who have died in Jesus Christ, may expect to enter in to all that fruition of Joy when they come forth, which they have pursued here. so plain was the vision I actually saw men, before they had ascended from the tomb, as though they were getting up slowly, they took each other by the hand & it was my father & my son. my mother & my daughter, my brother & my sister when the voice calls, suppose I am laid by the side of my father.—what would be the first joy of my heart? where is my father—my mother—my sister. they are by my side I embrace them & they me.

It is my meditation all the day & more than my meat & drink to know how I shall make the saints of God to comprehend the visions that roll like an overflowing surge, before my mind.

O how I would delight to bring before you things which you never thought of, but poverty & the cares of the world prevent. but I am glad I have the privilige of communicating to you some things, which if grasped closely will be a help to you when the clouds are gathering. & the storms are ready to burst upon you like peals of thunder. lay hold of these things & let not your knees tremble. nor your hearts faint. what can Earthquakes do. wars. & tornados do? nothing.—all your losses will be made up to you in the resurrection provided you continue faithful. by the vision of the almighty I have seen it.—More painful to me the thought of anhilitation than death. if I had no expectation of seeing my mother Brother & Sisters & friends again my heart would burst in a moment & I should go down to my grave. The expectation of seeing my friends in the morning of the resurrection cheers my soul. and make be bear up against the evils of life. it is like their taking a long journey. & on their return we meet them with increased joy.

God has revealed his son from the heavens. & the doctrine of the resurrection also. & we have a knowledge that these we ~~lay~~ bury here God bring them up again. clothed upon & quickened by the spirit of the great god. & what mattereth it whether we lay them down, or we lay down with them. when we can ~~live~~ keep them no longer

Then let them sink down; like a ship in the storm. the mighty anchor holds the storm so let these truths sink down in our hearts, that we may even here begin to enjoying that which shall be in full hereafter.

Hosanna. Hosanna. Hosanna, to Almighty god that rays of light begin to burst forth upon us even now. I cannot find words to express myself I am not learned. but I have as good feelings as any man. O that I had the the language of the archangel to express my feeling. once to my friends. but I never expect to ~~see~~

when others rejoice I rejoice. when they mourn I would mourn[9]—

to Marcellus Bates.[10] let me administer comfort, you shall soon have the company of your companion in a world of glory[11]— & the friend of Bro. Barns.—& all the saints who are mourning. this has been a warning voice to us all, to be sober & diligent & lay aside mirth & vanity & folly.—& be prepared to die tomorrow. (preached about 2 hours)

 . . . Presst. Joseph said as president of this house. I forbid any man's leaving this house just as we are going to close the meeting. he is no gentleman who will do it. I dont care who it comes from.—if it were from the King of England. I forbid it.—

Wilford Woodruff Journal

 President J. Smith Addressed the assembly of the saints at the temple of the Lord upon the subject of the ~~saints~~ death burial & resurrection of the saints. He had been requested to preach a funeral sermon by several persons who had ~~died~~ lost friends & he had Just Received information that Elder Lorenzo Barnes had died in England we received this information by a letter from Elder P.P. Pratt. After reading the letter he addressed the assembly in a vary feeling interesting & edefying manner among many other remarks he said he should have been more reconciled to the death of Elder barnes Could his bodey have been laid in the grave in Nauvoo or among the Saints, he said he had vary peculiar feelings relative to recieving an honorable burial with his father[12] he Considered Nauvoo would be a burying place of the Saints & Should he die he considered it would be a great Blessing to be buried with the saints & esspecially to be buried with his father yes he wanted to lie by the side of his father that when the trump of God should sound & the voice of God should say ye Saints arise that when the tomb should birst he could arise from the grave & first salute his father & say O my father! & his father say O my son!! as they took each other by the hand he wished next to salute his brothers & sisters & then the Saints & he said it was upon this principle that the ancients were so particular to have an honorable burial with their fathers as in the case of Joseph, before his death he made his kindred promise to carry his bones to the land of Canann & they did so they embalmed his body took it to the land of Canaan & buryed it with his fathers their is a glory in this that many do not comprehend. It is true that in the resurrection ~~that~~ the bodies will be caught up to meet the Lord & the Saints will all be brought together though they were scattered upon the face of the whole earth yet they would not as readily salute each other as though they lay down & rose up together from the same bed, To bring it to the understanding it would be upon the same principle as though two who were vary friends indeed should lie down upon the same bed at night locked in each other embrace talking of their love & should awake in the morning together they could immediately renew their conversation of love even while rising from their bed but if they were alone & in sperate apartments they could not as readily salute each other as though they were together He remarked that should he live & have an opportunity of gathering his friends who had died together he intended to do it but if he should not live to do it himself he hoped that some of his ~~frie~~ friends would. He wished all of the saints to be comforted with the victory they were to gain by the resurrection it is sufficient to encourage the saint to overcome in the midst of evry trial trouble & tribulation though thunders roar & earthquakes bellow, lightnings flash & wars are upon evry hand yet suffer not a joint to tremble nor let not your heart faint for the great Eloheem will deliver you & if not before the resurrection will set you eternally free from all these things from pain sorrow & death. I have labored hard & sought every way to try to prepare this people to comprehend the things that God is unfolding to me In speaking of the resurrection I would say that God hath shown unto me a vission of the resurrection of the dead & I saw the graves open & the saints as they arose took each other by the hand even before they got open while setting up & great Joy & glory rested upon them.

William Clayton Diary

Heard Pres. J preach on the ressurection shewing the importance of being buried with the saints & their relatives in as much as we shall want to see our relatives first & shall rejoice to strike hands with our parents, children &c when rising from the tomb.

Levi Richards Diary

Forenoon meeting in the Temple Pres Smith preached on the resurrection &c.

Rhoda Richards Diary[13]

Brother Wd [Willard Richards] says he has heard the sweetest sermon from Joseph he ever heard in his life.

6 May 1843 (Saturday). Prairie East of Nauvoo.[1]
Joseph Smith Diary, by Willard Richards

9 1/2 Mounted, with staff. Band & about 12 ladies. led by Emma.[2] & proceeded to the General Parade of the Legion east of My farm on the Prairie & had a good day of it except very high wind.— Marched the Legion down Main St. & disbanded about 2 oclock P.M. after a short speech on the Prairie. there were 2 United States officers Present[3] & General Swazey[4] from Iowa.—In my remark told the Legion when we have petitioned those in power for assistance they have always told us they had no power to help us, damn such power.—when they give me power to protect the innocent I will never say I can do nothing.[5] I will exercise that power for their good. So help me God.

Levi Richards Diary

General Joseph Smith addressed the Legion a few m[in]utes with warmth & lively feeling—expressed his perfect satisfattion with the Legion—& noticed the same expressed by two United States officers (names unknown)—Speaking of power in relation to our country & the innocent,—he said that those who held power when applied to by those who were suffering, received in answer "We cant do any thing for you," damn such power,—if I have power, & am called on by the innocent Sufferer I swear I will use by the great God I will use that power for them—& not Say I cant do any thing for you—I can do something—& I will!

Nauvoo Neighbor 1 (10 May 1843)

On Saturday last we had a general parade of the "Nauvoo Legion," according to previous appointment. There were not so many spectators present as there would have been if the weather had been more favorable. It was very cold and windy throughout the day. The Legion however looked well, better than on any former occasion; and they performed their evolutions in admirable style.

General Arlington Bennet[6] was prevented from being present, as was anticipated, in consequence of sickness.

The officers did honor to the Legion, many of whom were equipped, and armed, *cap-a-pie*. Many ladies on horseback honored us with their presence, and we observed that the men were in good spirits; that they had made great improvements, both in uniform and discipline, and from what we saw, we felt proud to be associated with a body of men which in point of discipline, uniform, appearance, and a knowledge of military tactics, are the pride of Illinois, one of its strongest defences, and a great bulwark of the western country.

Two officers of the regular army were present, and expressed great satisfaction at our appearance and evolutions. Lieutenant General Joseph Smith, delivered a spirited and patriotic address on the occasion, which was received with enthusiasm by both officers and men. He was followed by General Swazy of Iowa, in his usual good style.

14 May 1843 (Sunday). Yelrome, Hancock County, Illinois.[1]
Wilford Woodruff Journal

Sunday The meeting was opened by Singing, & Prayer By W Woodruff Then Joseph the Seer arose & said It is not wisdom that we should have all knowledge at once presented before us but that we should have a little then we can comprehend it. He then read the second Epistle of Peter 1st Ch 16 to last vers & dwelt upon the 19th vers with som remarks Ad to your faith Knowledge &c[2] The principl of knowledge is the principle of Salvation the Principle can be comprehended, for any one that cannot get knowledge to be saved will be damned. The Principl of Salvation is given to us through the knowledge of Jesus Christ Salvation is nothing more or less than to triumph over all our enemies & put them under our feet & when we have power to put all enemies under our feet in this world & a knowledge to triumph over all evil spirits in the world to come then we are saved as in the case of Jesus he was to reign untill he had put all enemies under his feet & the last enemy was death[3] Perhaps there are principle here that few men have thought of. No ~~power~~ person can have this Salvation except through a tabernacle Now in this world mankind are naturly selfish ambitious & striving to excell one above another ~~While~~ yet some are willing to build up others as well as themselves[4] so in the other world there is a variety of spirits some who seek to excell, & this was the case with the devil when he fell he sought for things which were unlawful hence he was cast down & it is said he drew away many with him[5] & the greatness of his punishment is that he shall not have a tabernacle this is his punishment So the devil thinking to thwart the decree of God by going up & down in the earth seeking whome he may destroy any person that he can find that will yield to him he will bind him & take possession of the body & reign there glorying in it mightily not thinking that he had got a stolen tabernacle & by & by some one of Authority will come along & cast him out & restore the tabernacle to his rightful owner but the devil steals a tabernacle because he has not one of his own but if he steals one he is liable to be turned out of doors

Now their is some grand secret ther[e] & keys to unlock the subject Not withstanding the Apostle exhorts them to ~~make their Calling~~ Add to their faith virtue Knowledge temperance &C yet he exhorts them to make their Calling & election Shure[6] & though they had herd the audible voice from heaven bearing testinoy that Jesus was the Son of God yet he says we have a more sure word of Prophecy where unto ye do well that ye take heed as unto a light shining in a dark place.[7] Now wherein could they have a more sure word of prophecy than to hear the voice of God saying this is my Beloved Son &C Now for the Secret & grand Key though they might hear the voice of God & know that Jesus was the Son of God this would be no evidence that their election & Calling ~~& election~~ was made shure that they had part with Christ & was a Joint heir with him, they then would want that more sure word of Prophecy that they were sealed in the heavens & had the promise of eternal live in the Kingdom of God then having this promise sealed unto them it was as an anchor to the Soul Sure & Steadfast though the thunders might roll & lightnings flash & earthquakes Bellow & war gather thick around yet this hope & knowledge would support the soul in evry hour of trail trouble & tribulation Then Knowledge through our Lord & savior Jesus Christ is the grand Key that unlocks the glories & misteries of the Kingdom of heaven[8] Compair this principle once with Christondom at the present day & whare are they with all their boasted religion piety & sacredness while at the same time they are Crying out against Prophets Apostles Angels Revelation, Prophesyings, & Visions &C. Why they are Just ripening for the damnation of hell,they will be damned for they reject the more glorious principle of the gospel of Jesus Christ & treat with disdain & trample under foot the main key that unlocks the heavens & puts in our possession the glories of the Celestial world.[9] Yes I say such will be damned with all their professed godliness

Then I would exhort you to go on & continue to call upon God untill you make your Calling & election sure for yourselves by obtaining this more sure word of Prophesey & wait patiently for the promise untill you obtain it Many other vary useful remarks were made on the occasion by Joseph the Seer.

Brigham Young Diary

Herd Br Joseph Smith Preach.

17 May 1843 (Wednesday Morning). Ramus, Illinois.[1]
William Clayton Diary

At 10 Prest. J. preached on 2nd Peter Ch 1. He shewed that knowledge is power & the man who has the most knowledge has the greatest power. Also that salvation means a mans being placed beyond the powers of all his enemies. He said the more sure word of prophecy[2] meant a mans knowing that he is sealed up unto eternal life by revelation & the spirit of prophecy through the power of the Holy priesthood.[3] He also showed that it is impossible for a man to be saved in ignorance. Paul had seen the third heavens and I more.[4] Peter penned the most sublime language of any of the apostles.

Samuel A. Prior[5] Statement, *Times and Seasons* 4 (15 May 1843):198

He commenced preaching, not from the Book of Mormon, however, but from the Bible; the first chapter of the first of Peter,[6] was his text. He commenced calmly and continued dispassionately to pursue his subject, while I sat in breathless silence, waiting to hear that foul aspersion of the other sects, that diabolical disposition of revenge, and to hear that rancorous denunciation of every individual but a Mormon. I waited in vain—I listened with surprise—I sat uneasy in my seat, and could hardly persuade myself but that he had been apprised of my presence, and so ordered his discourse on my account; that I might not be able to find fault with it, for instead of a jumbled jargon of half connected sentences, and a volley of imprecations, and diabolical and malignant denunciations heaped upon the heads of all who differed from him, and the dreadful twisting and wresting of the scriptures, to suit his own peculiar views, and attempt to weave a web of dark and mystic sophistry around the gospel truths, which I had anticipated, he glided along through a very interesting and elaborate discourse, with all the care and happy facility of one who was well aware of his important station, and his duty to God and man, and evidencing to me, that he was well worthy to be styled "a workman rightly dividing the word of truth,"[7] and giving without reserve, "saint and sinner his portion in due season"[8]—and I was compelled to go away with a very different opinion from what I had entertained when I first took my seat to hear him preach.

17 May 1843 (Wednesday Evening). Ramus, Illinois.[1]
William Clayton Diary

In the evening we went to hear a Methodist preacher lecture.[2] After he got through Pres. J. offered some corrections as follows. The 7th verse of C 2 of Genesis ought to read God breathed into Adam his spirit or breath of life,[3] but when the word "ruach"[4] applies to Eve it should be translated lives. Speaking of eternal duration of matter he I said. There is no such thing as immaterial matter. All spirit is matter but is more fine or pure and can only be discerned by purer eyes. We cant see it but when our bodies are purified we shall see that it is all matter.

Samuel A. Prior Statement, *Times and Seasons* 4 (15 May 1843):198

In the evening I was invited to preach, and did so.—The congregation was large and respectable—they paid the utmost attention. This surprised me a little, as I did not expect to find any such thing as a religious toleration among them.—After I had closed, Elder Smith, who had attended, arose and begged leave to differ from me in some few points of doctrine, and this he did mildly, politely, and affectingly; like one who was more desirous to disseminate truth and expose error, than to love the malicious triumph of debate over me. I was truly edified with his remarks, and felt less prejudiced against the Mormons than ever. He invited me to call upon him, and I promised to do so.

21 May 1843 (Sunday Morning). Temple Stand.[1]
Joseph Smith Diary, by Willard Richards

10 1/2—Joseph arrived and after pressing his way through the crowd and getting on the stand said there were some people who thought it a terrible thing that any body should exercise a little power. & said he thought it a pity that any body should give occasion to have power exercised. and requested the people to get out of their alleys, and if they did not keep them clear he might some time run up and down & might hit some of them. & called on Bro Morey[2] to constable to keep the alleys after singing Joseph read 1st chap 2d Epistle of Peter, Wm Law prayed. singing again.

when I shall have the opportunity of speaking in a house I know not. I find my lungs failing—it has always been my fortune almost to speak in the open air to large assemblies.

I have not an idea there has been a great many very good men since Adam There was one good man Jesus.—Many think a prophet must be a great deal better than any body else.—suppose I would condescend. yes I will call it condescend, to be a great deal better than any of you. I would be raised up to the highest heaven, and who should I have to accompany me. I love that man better who swears a stream as long as my arm, and administering to the poor & dividing his substance, than the long smoothed faced hypocrites

I dont want you to think I am very righteous, for I am not very righteous. God judgeth men according to the light he gives them.[3]

we have a more sure word of prophecy, whereunto you do well to take heed. as unto a light that shineth in a dark place[4]

we were eyewitnesses of his majesty and heard the voice of his excellent glory[5]—& what could be more sure? transfigured on the mount[6] &c what could be more sure? divines have been quarreling for ages about the meaning of this.

rough stone rolling down hill.[7]

3 grand secrets lying in this chapter which no man can dig out. which unlocks the whole chapter. What is written are only hints of things which existed in the prophets mind. which are not written concerning eternal glory.

I am going to take up this subject by virtue of the knowledge of God in me. which I have received from heaven.

the opinions of men, so far as I am ~~possessed~~ concerned, are to me as the crackling of the thorns under the pot, or the whistling of the wind.

Columbus and the eggs.[8]—Ladder and rainbow.[9] like precious faith with us—add to your faith virtue &c. another point after having all these qualifications he lays this injunction. but rather make your calling & election sure—after adding all this virtue knowledge &. make your caling & sure.[10]—what is the secret. the starting point.—according as his divine power which hath given unto all things that pertain to life & godliness.

how did he obtain all things? through the knowledge of him who hath called him.—there could not any be given pertaining to life ~~knowledge~~ & godliness without knowledge[11] wo wo wo to christendom.—the divine spirits; &c if this be true.

salvation is for a man to be saved from all his enemies.—until a man can triumph over death. he is not saved. knowledge will do this.

organization of Spirits in the eternal world.—spirits in the eternal world are like spirits in this world. when those spirits have come into this [and] risin & received glorified bodies. they will have an ascendency over spirits who have no bodies. or kept not their first estate like the devil. Devils punishment, should not have a habitation like other men. Devils retaliation come into this world bind up mens bodies. & occupy himself. authorities come alone and eject him from a stolen habitation

design of the great God in sending us into this world and organizing us to prepare us for the Eternal world.—I shall keep in my own bosom. we have no claim in our eternal comfort in relation to Eternal things unless our actions & contracts & all things tend to this end.[12]—

after all this make your calling and election sure. if this injunction would lay largely on those to whom it was spoken. how much more then to them of the 19. century.—

 1 Key Knowledge is the power of Salvation

 2 Key Make his calling and Election Sure

 3. it is one thing to be on the mount & hear the excellent voice &c &c. and another to hear the voice declare to you you have a part & lot in the kingdom.—

Howard and Martha Coray Notebook

 A Sermon by the Prophet Joseph Smith. On Election.

 Every man goes to his own place 2 Peter 1. Ch—Judas transgression by fell that he might go to his own place.[13] there is one glory of the sun another of the moon & another of the stars as one Star differetheth &c. so also is the reserection of the dead.[14] Brethren I am not a very Pieus man. I do not wish to be a great deal better than any body else. If a Prophet was so much better that any body else was he would inherit a glory far beyond what any one else would inherit and behold he would be alone, for who would be his company in heaven. ~~for~~ If I should condesend to be so righteous as the brethren would wish me to be, lo I should be taken from your midst and be translated as was Elijah.[15] Righteousness is not that which men esteem holiness. That which the world call righteousness I have not any regard for. To be righteous is to be just and merciful. If a man fails in kindness justice and mercy he will be damed for many will say in that day Lord, have we not prophecie in thy name and in thy name done many wonderful works but he will say unto them ye workers of iniquity[16] &c we were eye witnesses of his Majesty[17] we have also a more sure word of Prophecy.[18] Now brethren who can explain this no man be [but] he that has obtained these things in the same way that Peter did. Yet it is so plain & so simple & easy to be understood that when I have shown you the interpretation thereof you will think you have always Known it yourselves—These are but hints of those things that were revealed to Peter, and verily brethren there are things in the bosom of the Father, that have been hid from the foundation of the world,[19] that are not Known neither can be except by direct Revelation The Apostle says, unto them who have obtained like precious faith with us the apostles through the righteousness of God & our Savior Jesus Christ, through the knowledge of him that has called us to glory & virtue add faith virtue &c. &c. to godliness brotherly kindness—Charity—ye shall neither be barren or unfruitful in the Knowledge of our Lord Jesus Christ. He that lacketh these things is blind[20]—wherefore the rather brethren after all this give diligence to make your calling & Election Sure Knowledge is necessary to life and Godliness.[21] wo unto you priests & divines, who preach that knowledge is not necessary unto life & Salvation. Take away Apostles &c. take away knowledge and you will find yourselves worthy of the damnation of hell. Knowledge is Revelation hear all ye brethren, this grand Key; Knowledge is the power of God unto Salvation.

What is salvation. Salvation is for a man to be Saved from all his enemies even our last enemy which is death ~~and~~ for David Saith, "and the Lord Said unto my Lord 'Sit thou on my right hand until I make thine enemies thy footstool."[22]

The design of God before the foundation of the world was that we should take tabernacles that through faithfulness we should overcome & thereby obtain a resrection from the dead, in this wise obtain glory honor power and dominion for this thing is needful, inasmuch as the Spirits in the Eternal world, glory in bringing other Spirits in Subjection unto them, Striving continually for the mastery, He who rules in the heavens when he has a certain work to do calls the Spirits before him to organize them. they present themselves and offer their Services—

When Lucifer was hurled from Heaven the decree was that he Should not obtain a tabernacle not those that were with him, but go abroad upon the earth exposed to the anger of the elements naked & bare, but oftimes he lays hold upon men binds up their Spirits enters their habitations laughs at the decree of God and rejoices in that he hath a house to dwell in, by & by he is expelled by Authority and goes abroad mourning naked upon the earth like a man without a house exposed to the tempest & the storm—

There are some things in my own bosom that must remain there.[23] If Paul could say I Knew a man who ascended to the third heaven & saw things unlawful for man to utter, I more. There are only certain things that can be done by the Spirits and that which is done by us that is not done with a view to eternity is not binding in eternity.[24] Oh Peter if they who were of like precious faith with thee were injoined to make their Calling & Election sure, how much more all we There are two Keys, one key knowledge. the other make you Calling & election sure, for if you do these things you shall never fall for so an entrance shall be administered unto you abundently into the everlasting Kingdom of our Lord & Savior Jesus Christ.[25] We made known unto you the power & coming of our Lord & S. J. Christ were Eye witnesses of his Majesty when he received from God the Father honor & glory when there came such a voice to him from the excellent glory, this is my beloved Son in whom I am well pleased. this voice which came from heaven we heard when we were with him in the holy Mount. We have also a more sure word of prophecy whereunto give heed until the day Star arise in your hearts[26] ~~this is~~ It is one thing to receive knowledge by the voice of God, (this is my beloved Son &c.) & another to Know that you yourself will be saved, to have a positive promise of your own Salvation is making your Calling and Election sure. viz the voice of Jesus saying my beloved thou shalt have eternal life.[27] Brethren never cease struling until you get this evidence. ~~T~~ Take heed both before and after obtaining this more sure word of Prophecy.[28]

Franklin D. Richards "Scriptural Items"

Joseph said may 21st Sabbath Salvation is for a man to be saved from all his enemies The 1st chap of 2d Peter is hints of things which are nowhere written. There are things which pertain to the Glory of God & heirship of God with Christ which are not ~~where~~ written in the Bible spirits of the eternal world are diverse from each other as here in their dispositions Aspiring Ambitious &c As man is liable to enemies there as well as here it is necessary for him to be placed beyond their power in order to be saved. This is done by our taking bodies (keeping our first estate)[29] and having the Power of the Resurrection pass upon us whereby we are enabled to gain the ascendancy over the disembodied spirits

The mortification of satan consists in his not being permitted to take a body. He sometimes gets possession of a body but when the proven authorities turn him out of Doors he finds it was not his but a stolen one

Our covenants[30] here are of no force one with another except made in view view of eternity.

James Burgess Notebook

First Chapter second Epistle of Peter. The first four verses are the preface to the whole subject. There are three grand Keys to unlock the whole subject. First what is the knowledge of God, Second what is it to make our calling and election sure. Third and last is how to make our calling and election sure. Ans, it is to obtain a promise from God for myself that I shall have Eternal life. that is the more sure word of prophycy.[31] Peter was writeing to those of like precious faith with them the Apostles First to be sealed with the Holy Spirit of promise that is the testimony of Jesus Second how is he to get that Holy Spirit; Ans except a man be born again he cannot see the Kingdom of God; second except a man be born of water and the spirit he cannot enter into the Kingdom of God.[32] Ques. What is it for a man to obtain salvation Ans, It is to triumph over every foe or ascend far above all enemies for the last enimey to conquor is death and untill that is done you have not obtained salvation J. Smith Prophet. Nauvoo.

Wilford Woodruff Journal

A large Congregation of Saint assembled at the temple & was addressed by President Joseph Smith upon the same subject that he spoke upon at Lima on the 14th[33] in which was interesting in the hiest degree.

Levi Richards Diary

A.M. attended Meeting at the Temple P. Joseph Smith preached from 1 Chap. 2d Peter "we have a more sure word of prophesy &C" spoke about two hours.

11 June 1843 (Sunday Morning). Temple Stand.[1]
Joseph Smith Diary, by Willard Richards

10 A. M. at the Temple Stand. Hymn by the Quire. Read 23 Matthew. P. P. Pratt Prayed. Singing.—
Matt. 23. 37. Subject presented me since I come in this house.—
I a rough stone, the sound of the hammer & chisel was never heard

on me. nor never will be. I desire the learning & wisdom of heaven alone. Have not the least idea but if Christ should come and preach such rough things as he preached to the Jews, but this Generation would reject ~~reject~~ him for being so rough. I never can find much to say in expounding a text.

never is half so much fuss to unlock a door if you have a key or when you have not. or have to cut it out with a jack knife.—

O. Jerusalem. &c. whence are in the curse of Allmighty God that was to be poured out upon the heads of the Jews? That they would not be gathered. because they would not let Christ gather them. It was the design in the Councils of heaven before the world was that the principle & law of that priesthood was predicated upon the gathering of the people in every age of the world. Jesus did every thing possible to gather the people & they would not be gathered and he poured out curses upon them Ordinances were instituted in heaven before the foundation of the world ~~of~~ in the priesthood, for the salvation of man. not be altered. not to be changed. all must be saved upon the same principle.[2]

that is only your opinion Sir—say Sectarians.—when a man will go to hell it is more than my meat & drink to help them to do as they want to.[3]

where there is no change of priesthood there is no change of ordinances says Paul.[4] If god has not changed the ordinances & priesthood, howl ye sectarians, if he has where has he revealed it. have ye turned revelators? then why deny it?

Men have thought many things insoluable, in the last days, that he should raise the dead. Things have been hid from before the foundation of the [world] to be revealed to babes in the last days.

there are a great many wise men & women to in our midst to wise to be taught. & they must die in their ignorance and in the resurrection they will find their mistake.

Many seal up the door of heaven by saying so far god may reveal & I will believe.—heirs of God. ~~&c.~~ upon the same laws ordinance &c of Jesus Christ. & he who will not live it all will come short. of that glory if not of the whole.

ordinance of the baptism.[5] God decreed before the foundation of the world that this baptism should be performed in a house prepared for the purpose.—

Spirits of prison.—the Holy Ghost reveals it. Spirits in the world of ~~prison~~ Spirits.—which Jesus went to preach to. God ordained that he who would save his dead should do it by getting together as with the Jews—It always has been when a man was sent of God with the Priesthood & he began to preach the fulness of the gospel, the [man] was thrust out by his friends.—and they are ready to but[c]her him if he teach things which they had imagined to be wrong. Jesus was crucified upon this principle—

I will turn linguist. Ma[n]y things in the bible which do not, as they now stand, accord with the revelation of the holy Ghost to me.—

Ponder. "this day thou sha[l]t be with me in paradise."[6] Paradise. Modern word. dont answer to the original word used by Jesus.—find the origin of Paradise—find a needle in a hay mow.— here is a chance for a battle ye learned man.—Said Jesus. for there is not time to investigat this matter. for this day you will be with me in the world of Spi[ri]ts. & then I will teach you all about it. & Peter says he went & preached to the world of Spirits.[7] so that they would receive it could have it answered by proxey by those who live on the earth &c.

gathered you for baptism for the dead washing anointings, &c.—said Jesus to Jews. At one time God obtained a house where Peter was[hed] and ano[inte]d &c on the day of pentecost.[8] criticise a little further Hell, modern term. burning lake of fire and Brimstone. I would make you think I was climbing a ladder when I was climbing a rainbow.—who ever revealed it. God never did. Hades. I will hunt after Hades as pat did for woodchuck. Sheol—who are you? God reveals. means a world of spirits.—I dont think so says one. go to my house I will take my lexicon—&c—a world of departed spirits. disembodied spirits all go.—good bad & indiferent.— misery in a world of spirits is to know they come short of the glory others enjoy—they are their own accusers[9] one universal heaven.— & hell. & supose honorable & virtuous & whoremonger—all hudled together.—judged according to deeds done in the body.[10]—shame shame—thus we can mint & anise & cummin and long prayers. but touch not the law, as Peter tells us—[11]

Paul says caught up to 3d heaven, & what tell that Lie for Paul.[12]—Sun Moon & Stars[13]—many mansions[14]—all one say

Sectarians.—They build hay wood & stubble, build on the old revelations without the spirit of revelation or Priesthood. if I had time I would dig into Hell. Hades. Sheol. & tell what exists.—

Heaven of Heavens could not contain him. he took the liberty to go into other heavens.—I thought—Father—Son & H. Ghost all stuck into one person.—I pray for them, father that we may be one[15]—All stuffed into one God—a big God:

Peter[16]—Stephen saw the Son of Man. Saw the son of man standing on the right hand of God.[17]—3 personages—in heaven who hold the keys.—one to preside over all.

If any man attempt to refute. what I am about to say after I have made it plain let him be accursed. as the father hath power in himself so hath the sun [son] power in himself to lay down his life.[18]—

the son doeth what he hath seen the father do. &c[19]—take his body & stuff it into the father.

Gods have an ascendency over the angels angels remain angels.[20]—some are resurrected to become god.[21] by such revelations as god gives in the most holy place.—in his temple.[22] let them who are owing tithing pay it up. & bring stone.—

What did Judge Higby[23]—if those who are owing would bring stone we could get the walls to the roof this fall as easy as to let it down."

closed about 12—

Wilford Woodruff Journal

A large assembly of Saints met at the Temple & were addressed by President Joseph Smith He took for the foundation of his discourse the words of Jesus to the <u>Jews</u> how oft would I have gatherd you togetherd as a hen gathereth her chickens under wings But ye would not &c.[24] He then asked what was the object of Gathering the Jews together or the people of God in any age of the world, the main object was to build unto the Lord an house whereby he could reveal unto his people the ordinances of his house and glories of his kingdom & teach the peopl the ways of salvation for their are certain ordinances & principles that when they are taught and practized, must be done in a place or house built for that purpose this was purposed in the mind of God before the world was

& it was for this purpose that God designed to gather together the Jews oft but they would not it is for the same purpose that God gathers togethe the people in the last days to build unto the Lord an house to prepare them for the ordinances & endowment washings & anointings &c. one of the ordinances of the house of the Lord is Baptism for the dead, God decreed before the foundation of the world that that ordinance should be administered in a house prepared for that purpose. If a man gets the fulness of God he has to get [it] in the same way that Jesus Christ obtain it & that was by keeping all the ordinances of the house of the Lord.[25] Men will say I will never forsake you but will stand by you at all times but the moment you teach them some of the mysteries of God[26] that are retained in the heavens and are to be revealed to the children of men when they are prepared, They will be the first to stone you & put you to death. It was the same principle that Crusified the Lord Jesus Christ. I will say something about the Spirits in prision, theire has been much said about the sayings of Jesus on the Cross to the thief saying this day thou shalt be with me in paradise.[27] The commentators ~~make~~ or translators make it out to say Paradise but what is Paradise it is a modern word it does not answer at all to the original that Jesus made use of, their is nothing in the original in any language that signifies Paradise, But it was this day I will be with thee in the world of spirits & will teach thee or answer thy inquiries. The thief on the Cross was to be with Jesus Christ in the World of Spirits he did not say Paradise or heaven. The doctrin of Baptism for the dead is clearly shown in the new testament[28] & if the doctrin is not good then throw away the new testament but if it is the word of God then let the doctrin be acknowledged & it was one reason why Jesus said how oft would I have gatherd you (the Jews) together[29] that they might attend to the ordinance of the baptism for the dead as well as the other ordinances the Priesthood Revelations &c. This was the case on the day of Pentecost these Blessings were poured out upon the deciples, on that occasion.[30] Their has been also much said about the word Hell & the sectarian world have preached much about it but what is hell, it is annother modern term it is taken from <u>hades</u> the greek, or shaole, the (hebrew) & the true signification is a world of spirits,

Hades shaole paradise, spirits in prision is all one it is a world of spirits, the righteous & the wicked all go to the same world of spirits but says one I believe in one hell & one heaven all are equally miserable or equally happy, but St Paul informs us of three glories[31] & three heavens he knew a man caught up to the third heavens,[32] & Jesus said their were many mansions in my Fathers Kingdom[33] Any man may believe Jesus Christ is good & be happy in it & yet not obey his commands & at last be cut down by his righteous com- mandmends A man of God should be endowed with all wisdom knowledge & understanding in order to teach & lead people, The blind may lead the blind & both fall into the deatch together;[34] Their is much said concerning God the Godhead &c the scripture says their is Gods many & Lords many,[35] the teachers of the day say that the father is God the Son is God & the Holy Ghost is God & that they are all in one body & one God Jesus says or prays that those that the father had given him out of the world might be made one in us as we are one,[36] but if they were to be stuffed into one person that would make a great God, If I were to testify that the world was wrong on this point it would be true Peter says that Jesus Christ sat on the right hand of God[37] any person that has seen the heavens opened knows that their is three personages in the heavens holding the Keys of Power.[38] As the father hath power in himself so the Son hath power in himself,[39] then the father has some day laid down his body & taken it again so he has a body of his own—so has his son a body of his own so each one will be in their own body. Many of the sects cry out O I have the testimony of Jesus, I have the spirit of God But away with Jo Smith he says he is a Prophet But their is to be no Prophets nor revelations in the last days; But stop sir the Revelator says that the testimony of Jesus is the spirit of Prophecy[40] So by your own mouth you are condemned.

But to the text why gather the people together in this place For the same purpose that Jesus wanted to gather the Jews, to receive the ordinances the blessings & the glories that God has in store for his Saints. And I would now ask this assembly and all[41] the Saints if they will now build this house & receive the ordinances & Blessings which God has in store for you, or will you not build unto the Lord this house & let him pass by & bestow these blessings upon another I pause for a reply

Levi Richards Diary

attended Meeting at the Temple weather vary fine moderately warm. heard J. Smith preach from Math "Oh Jerusalem Jerusalem &c, how oft would I have gathered you, as a hen gathereth her chickens under her wings & Ye would not, behold your house is left unto you desolate &c[42]

Pres. J. Smith bore testimony to the same saying that when he was a youth he began to think about these things but could not find out which of all the sects were right he went into the grove & enquired of the Lord which of all the sects were right he received for answer that none of them were right, that they were all wrong, & that the Everlasting Covenant was broken[43]==he said he understood the fulness of the Gospel from beginning to end—& could Teach it & also the order of the priesthood in all its ramifications[44]==Earth & hell had opposed him & tryed to destroy him, but they had not done it==& they never would.

Franklin D. Richards "Scriptural Items"

Joseph said The reason why the Jews were scattered and their House left unto them Desolate was because they refused to be gathered that the fulness of the Priesthood[45] might be revealed among them which never can be done but by the gathering of the People also also The Order & Ordinances of the Kingdom were instituted by the Priesthood in the council of Heaven before the World was The words Prison Paradise & Hell are different translations of the Greek Hades which answers to the Hebrew Shaole the true translation of which is "The world of spirits where the righteous & the wicked dwell together.

Eliza R. Snow Diary

Last sunday I had the privilege of attending meeting and in the forenoon listening to a very interesting discourse by Pres. J. Smith He took for his subject the words of the Savior to wit. "O Jerusalm thou that killest the prophets and stonest them that are sent unto you! How oft would I have gatherred you as a hen gathereth her chickens under her wings and you would not!"[46] He beautifully and in a most powerful manner, illustrated the necessity of the <u>gathering</u> and the building of the Temple that those ordinances may be administered which are necessary preparations for the world to come:[47] he exhorted the people in impressive terms to be diligent— to be up and doing lest the tabernacle pass over to another people and we lose the blessing.

Willard Richards Diary

Meeting all day Joseph P[reached].

24 June 1843 (Saturday). Dixon, Lee County, Illinois.[1]
Manuscript History of the Church

I addressed the assembly for an hour and a half on the subject of marriage; my visitors having requested me to give them my views of the law of God respecting marriage.[2]

30 June 1843 (Friday Afternoon). Temple Stand.[1]
Wilford Woodruff Journal

I require attention. I discoverd what the emotions of the people were on my arival to this City, & I have Come here to say, how do you do to all parties & I do now say How do you do at this time. I meet you with a heart full of gratitude to Almighty God & I presume you all feel the Same I hardly Know how to express my feelings I feel as strong as a Gient[giant] I pulled sticks with the men Coming along & I pulled up the Strongest man theire was on the road with one hand & two Could not pull me up & I continued to pull untill I pulled them to Nauvoo I will pass from that subject then There has been great excitement in the Country & since these men[2] took me I have been cool & dispassionate through the whole: thank God I am now in the hands of the Municipal Court of Nauvoo & not in the hands of Missourians, It has been discussed by the great & wise men ~~layil~~ lawyiers &C O your Powers & legal tribunals are not to be sanctioned & here we will make it lawful to drag away inocent men from their families & friends & have them unlawfully put to death by ungodly men for ther religion. Relative to our Charter Courts right of Hebeas Corpus &C We have all power: And if any man from this time forth says any thing Contrary; Cast it into his teeth Their is a secret in this; if their is not power in our Charters and Courts, then there is not power in the State of Illinois, nor in the Congress or Constitution of the United States for the United States gave unto Illinois her constitution & Charter & Illinois gave unto Nauvoo her Charters which have ceded unto unto us our vested rights & has no right or power to take them from us all the power their was in Illinois she gave to Nauvoo And any man that says to the contrary is a fool. I want you to learn O Israel what is for the happiness & peace of this City & people. If our enemies are determined to oppress us & deprive us of our rights & privileges as they have done & if the Authorities that be on the earth will not assist us in our rights not give us that protection which the Laws & Constitution of the United States & of thi[s] State garrentees unto us: then we will claim them from higher power from heaven & from God Almighty & the Constitution &C I SWEAR I will not deal so mildly with them again for the time has Come when forbearance is no longer a virtue, And if you are again taken unlawfully you are at liberty to give loose to Blood and Thunder But act with Almighty Power. But good luck for me as it always has been in evry time of trouble friends though strangers were raised up unto me & assisted me, The time has come when the veil is torn of from the State of Illinois & they have deliverd me from the State of Missouri: friends that were raised up unto me would have spilt their Blood for me to have delivered me then I told them not I would be delivered By the power of God & generalship & I have brought them to Nauvoo & treated them kindly I have had the privilege of rewarding them good for evil,[3] they took me unlawfully treated me rigorously, strove to deprive me of my rights & would have run me to Missouri to have been murdered if Providence had not interposed: but now they are in my hands, I took them into my house set them at the head of my table & set the best before them my house afforded & they were waited upon by my wife whom they deprived of seeing me when I was taken. I shall be discharged by the Municipal Court of Nauvoo, were I before any good tribunal I should be discharged, But Befor I will bear this unhallowed persecution any longer I will spill my Blood their is a time when bearing it longer is a sin I will not bear it longer I will spil the last drop of Blood I have and all that will not bear it longer say AH And, the Cry of AH rung throughout the Congregation we must stop paying the lawyiers money for I have learned they dont know any thing for I know more than they all. Whosoever believeth that there is power in the Charters of Nauvoo shall be saved he that believeth not shall not come here. If a lawyer shall say their is more power in other places & Charters than in Nauvoo believe it not I have converted this Candidate for Congres Mr Walker[4] I suppose when I see him Converted I will vote for him & not before I have been with these lawyers & they have treated me well But I am here in Nauvoo & the Missourian to[o] & when they will get out I dont know perhaps when some others may, However you may feel about the high hand of oppression, I wish you to restrain your hand from violence. against these men who [are] around me My word is at stake a hair of their heads shall not be harmed, My life is pledged to carry out this great work I know how readily you are to do right you have done great things & manifested your love in flying to my assistance on this occasion I could not have done better myself, And I Bless you in the name of the Lord with all Blessings may you not have to suffer as you have heretofore. I know the Almighty will bless all good men he will bless you: and the time has Come when their shall be such a flocking to the Standard of Liberty as never has been, Nor never shal be hereafter. What an erie [era?] of things has commenced shall the Prophecys be esstablished by the Swords? Shall we allways bear, No. Will not the State of Missouri stay her hand in her unhallowed persecutions against the Saints; if not, I restrain you not any longer, I say in the name of Jesus Christ I this day turn the Key that opens the heavens to restrain you no longer from this time forth. I will lead you to battle & if you are not afraid to die & feel disposed to spill your Blood in your own defence you will not offend me, Be not the aggressor bear untill they strike on the one cheek offer the other[5] & they will be sure to strike that, then defend yourselves & God shall bear you off.[6] Will any part of Illinois say we shall not have our rights treat them as strangers & not friends & let them go to Hell say some we will mob you, mob & be damed, if I [am] under the ne[c]essity of giving up our charte[re]d rights, privileges & freedom which our fathers fought bled & died for & which the Constitution of the United States & & this State garrentee unto us, I will do it at the point of the Bayonet & Sword. Many Lawyiers contend for those thing which are against the rights of men & I can ownly excuse them because of their ignorance. Go forth & Advocate the laws & rights of the people ye lawyiers if not dont get into my hands or under the lash of my tongue Lawyiers say the powers of the Nauvoo Charters are dangerous, But I ask is the Constitution of the United States or of this State dangerous, No neither are the Charters granted unto Nauvoo by the legislator of Illinois dangerous, & those that say they are are fools: We have not our rights those which the Constitution of the U.S.A. grant, & which our Charters grant we have not enjoyed unmolested, Missouri & all wicked men will raise the hugh & cry against us and are not satisfyed, But how are you going to help yourselves what will mobocrats do in the midst of this people, If mobs come upon you any more here, dung your gardings with them, But says one you will get up excitement we will get up no excitement except what we can find an escape from We will rise up Washington like & break of[f] the wait that bears us down & we will not be mobed

To give you an account of my Journey,[7] I will give you an ancedote that may be pleasing A ~~few~~ day before I was taken I rode with my wife through a Neighborhood to visit some friends & I said to Mrs Smith here is a good people I felt this by the spirit of God the next day I was in their hands a prisoner with Wilson[8] who said as he drove up ha, ha ha By God we have got the prophet he gloried much in it, But he is now our prisioner[9] When Reynolds[10] of Missouri & Wilson of Carthage came to take me the first salutation was (instead of taping me on the sholder & saying you are my prisioner) with two cocked pistols to my head God damn you I will shoot you I will Shoot you God damn you I will Shoot you nearly 50 times first & last. I askd them what they wanted to shot me for, if you make any resistance O vary well says I I have no resistance to make they then dragged me away & while on the road I asked them by what authority they did these things they said by a writ from the Govornors of Missouri & Illinois I then told them I wanted a writ of Habeas Corpus the reply was God damn you you shant have it I told a man to Go to Dixon[11] & get me a writ of Habeas Corpus the reply was by Willson God dam you you shant have it. I will shoot you. I sent for a lawyier[12] to Come one Came & Reynolds shut the door in his face & would not let me speak to him & said again God damn you

I will shoot you I turned to him opened my bosom & told him to shoot away & I did it freequently, I told Mr Reynolds that I would have Council to speak to & the Lawyers[13] came to me & I got a writ of Habeas Corpus for myself & got a writ for Reynolds & Wilson for unlawful proceedings towards me & cruel treatment they Could not get out of town that night, I pleged my honor to my Council that the Nauvoo Charter had power to investigate the subject & we came to Nauvoo by Common Consent & I am now a prisioner of higher authority yes higher authority before yourselves The Charter expressly says that the City Council shall have power to enact all laws for the benefit & convenience of said City not Contrary to the Constitution of the United States or of this State & the City ordinances says the Municipal Court shall have Power to give writs of Habeas Corpus arising under the ordinances of the City, Their is nothing but what we have power over excepted restricted by the Constitution of the United States or of this State, It is in accordance with the Constitution of the U.S.A. But says the mob what dangerous powers, But the Constitution of the United nor of this State is not dangerous against good men but bad men the breakers of the law so with the laws of the Country & so with the laws of Nauvoo they are dangerous to mobs but not good men that wish to keep the law We do not go out of Nauvoo to disturb any body or any City town or place why need they be troubled about us let them not meddle with our affairs but let us alone After we have been deprived of our rights & privileges as Citizenship driven from town to town place to place State to State with the sacrifice of our homes & lands & our blood been shed & many murdered & all this becaus of our religion because we worship Almighty God according to the dictates of our own consience Shall we longer bear these cruelties which have been heeped upon us for the last ten years in the face of heaven & in open open violation of the Constitution & laws of these United States & of this State May God forbid I will not bear it if they take away any rights I will fight, for my rights manfully & right-eously untill I am laid up with Blood & thunder sword & pistol. We have done nothing against law or right As touching our City Charter & laws their is a secret in it, What is it our laws go behind the writ & investigate the subject ie of Habeas Corpus while other laws do not go behind the writ You speak of Lawyiers I am a Lawyier to[o] But the Almighty God has taught me the principle of law & the true meaning of the writ of Habeas Corpus is to defend the Innocent & investigate the subject go behind the writ & if the former writ is wright that is issued against an innocent man He should not be dragged to another State & their put to death or in jeapordy life or limbs because of prejudice when he is innocent the benefits of the Constitution & law is for all alike & the great [E]loheem God has given me the prividege of having the benefits of the Constitution & the writ of Habeas Corpus & I am bold to ask for this privilege this day & to ask you to Carry out this privilege principle And all who are in favor of Carrying out this great principle making manifest by raising the right hand & their was a sea of hands a universal vote here is truly a Committy of the whole.

In speaking of my Journey to Nauvoo I will relate a circumstance when Mr Cyrus Walker first Came to me they said I should not speak to any man & they would shoot any man that should speak to me An old man came up[14] & said I should have Council & said he was not afraid of their pistols & they took me from him, & I had an opportunity to have killed him but I had no temptation to do it to him nor any other man, my worst enemy not even Boggs[15] in fact he would have more hell to live in the reflection of his past life than to die. My freedom commenced from that time the old man Came to me & would talk to me we Came direct from Papa grove[16] to Nauvoo we got our writ directed to the nearest Court having authority to try try the Case & we Came to Nauvoo[17] It did my soul good to see your feelings & love manifest towards me I thank God that I have the honor to lead so virtuous & honest people to be your leader & lawyier as Moses to the Children of Israel Hosannah Hosannah Hosannah Hosannah to the name of the Most High God I commend you to his grace & may the Blessings of heaven rest upon you in the name of Jesus Christ Amen

Furthermore if Missouri continues her warfare & continues to Issue her writs against me & this peopl unlawfully & unjustly as they have done & our rights are trampled upon & they undertake to take away my wrights I swair with uplifted hands to Heaven I will spill my Blood in its defence they shall not take away our rights & if they dont stop leading me by the nose I will lead them by the nose & if they dont let me alone I will turn up the world I will make war, when we shake our own bushes we want to ketch our own fruit The Lawyiers themselves acknowledge that we have all power granted us in our Charters that we could ask for, that we had more power than any other Court in the State for all other Courts were restricted while ours was not & I thank God Almighty for it & will not be rode down to Hell by the Missourians any longer, & it is my privilege to speak in my own defence & appeal to your honors

After this interesting & decisive address was delivered in the presence of about seven or eight thousand the multitude dispersed & went to their homes.

Joseph Smith Diary, by Willard Richards

1/2 6. Joseph commenced a lecture on the stand. to Many thousands By how do you do. I meet you with a heart full of gratitude to almighty God. I am well, hearty, strong as a giant. while I was on the road I pulled up the strongest man. Then they got 2 men & they could not pull me up. I have pulled mentally till I have pulled Missouri here.

There has been a great excitement in the country. I have been cool & dispassionate through all. Thank god I am now a prisoner in the hands of the Municipal Court & not of a Missourian

It was not so much my object to tell my afflictions &c as to speak of the Habeus Corpus. so that the minds of all may be corrected & know & publish that we have all power.—there is a secret. the city has all power that the courts have. given by the same authority the Legislature. I want you to hear o Israel this day. if this power is not sufficient we will claim the Cons higher powers. the Constitution of the State & the United.—I have dragged him here by our hand. & will do it again but I swear I will never deal so mildly again.

Be cool be deliberate. be wise, and when you pull do it with sweepstakes. my lot has always been cast among the warmest kind of people.

The time has come when the vail is torn of from this state. & let us mingle with the people of Ills. I should have been torn from with the expense of life & blood if I had asked

I brought them prisoners. and committed them as prisoners not of chains but of kindness to her from whom I was torn[18]

I have no doubt I shall be discharged. by the court the writs are good for nothing. without form & void.—before I will be dragged again ~~bef~~ away among my enemies for trial I will spill the last drop of blood in my veins. see all my enemies in hell. Shall we bear it any longer. & one Universal NO. ran through all the vast assembly like on vast peal of thunder.

I wish the lawyer who says we have no powers in Nauvoo may be choked to death with his own words dont employ ~~any~~ lawyer for their knowledge for I know more [than] they all.

Go ye into all the world preach the gospel. & he that believeth in our chartered right may come here & be saved. & he does not shall remain in ignorance.

one spiritual minded circut Judg—& several fit men.

Esqr. Walker I have converted to the truth of Habeus Corpus. I got here by law write that Just as it should be.

in the midst of all your indignation. use not the hand of violence. for I have pledged my honor.—will you all support my honor. YES universal, by the audience. I have proof of your attachment.

when oppression arises again I have learned we need [not] suffer as we have. we can call others to our aid. Shall the prophecy of our enemies. "we will establish our religion by the sword." be true? No.[19]

If the Missourians oppress us more I this day turn the key by au[tho]rity of the Holy Priesthood—

turn the key unlock the door & motion you not rise up and defend yourselfs—

always act upon the defence but if your enemies oppress you the 2d &, 3 time.[20] let it come. & roar like thunder. & you shall stand forth clean before the tribunal of any citizens of Illinois deny our right. let them go to hell and be damned.—I give up my chartered right at the sword and bayonets.

Legislature like the boy say dady Daddy I have sold my Jackknife got cheated, & want to get it back again.

what can mobocrats do in the midst of Kirkpatrickites.[21]—no better than a hunter being in a bears claw. What could we do with them. dung our garden with them. we dont want any excitme[n]t. but after we have done all.—rise up & ~~tyrann~~ break off the hellish yoke. like Washington. day before I was taken I rode through Dixon & I said to my wife. I said good people I was their prisoner next day Harmon T. Wilson.—said by God we have got the prophet now. I am prison to a higher court than circuit court., defend yoursefs—says a law in our Charter—powers, same charter says Municipal court. has power to enact all laws=. &c dangerous power. because it will protect the innocent, & put down Mobocrats.—constitution of U. S. say "Habeas Corbus shall not be denied"[22] Deny me the right of H. Corpus & I will fight with guns, sword, cannon behind & thunder till I am used up. like Killkenny Cats. we have more power because we have power to go behind the writ. & try the merits of the case.

I ask in the name of J. Christ and all that is sacred that I may have your lives & all to carry out the freedom which is chartered to us.—will you all help me All hands went up.—Mr Walker shall be presented for the Mormons sake—

When at Dixon refused an interview with a lawyer.—turned Markham[23] out doors threatened my life, old gray headed man[24] raised his [indecipherable] his pony, come with Mr Walker.—& I had Lawyers &c enough.—writ for Harmon Wilson damage—assault & Battery.—

Writ Habeas Corpus got up to go to ottawa 22 miles[25] Pawpaw grove. thrust out all but Harmon Wilson. Esq Walker sent Mr Campbell[26] to my rescue.—& came & slept by me.

Morning certain men wanted to see Mr Smith. they would not let me an old man come to talk.[27] Missourian, interupted. stand off you puke Mr Smith we have a committee in Pawpaw grove. a court from whence there is no appeal.—

My liberties began from that hour they lost their pistols.—come come direct to Nauvoo.—when they began to suspect we were coming they remonstrated. B[r]o Grover came.[28]

Hosanna. Do. Do to Almighty God who hath delivered us thus far out of the 7 trouble. 6.25—

(Esqr Walker has introduced as a body of people. the greatest dupes that ever were.—or he is not as big a rouge as he is supposed to be.—1/4 to 7)

Joseph. I told Mr Warren[29] I would not discuss the subject of religion with you. I understand the gospel & you do not. You understand Law I do not

if the Legislature have granted Nauvoo the right of Habeas corpus &c it is no more than they ought to have done.—or more than our fathers fought for.

I swear in the name of Almighty God with uplifted hand the Legislature shall never take away our rights Ill spill my hearts blood first.[30]—

William Clayton Diary

At 4 o clock a large multitude were assembled at the grove & about 5 Prest. J. made his appearance on the stand in company with Cyrus H. Walker Esqr. The general theme of his discourse tended to enlighten the minds of the public concerning the powers of the Municipal Court in relation to Habeas Corpus as granted in the Nauvoo Charter, plainly proving that the municipal court had more power than the circuit courts inasmuch as the latters power was limited while that of the former was unlimited. He also said that he had restrained the saints from using violence in self defense but from henceforth he restrained them no more. The best of feelings prevailed during the whole meeting.

Willard Richards Diary

Lecture at 5 P.M. by Joseph

2 July 1843 (Sunday Evening). Front of Red Brick Store.[1]
Manuscript History of the Church

About 6 p.m. The Maid of Iowa returned to her landing at the nauvoo house, the company who had been on the expedition on board of her, formed in a procession and walked up to my office, where they formed a hollow square and sent in a deputation to me, as soon as I had bid them welcome I opened the window of my office and requested that no man would leave the ground until I had spoken to them. My Brother Hyrum and I went into the hollow square and directed them not to allow their ranks to be broken. I then shook hands with each man, blessing them and welcoming them home.

I then took off my hat and related to them how I was brought home to the midst of my friends, and how I regained my liberty. I feel by the Spirit of the Lord that if I had fallen into your hands that you would either have brought me safe home, or that we should all have died in a heap together, at this time, a well dressed man, a stranger, who had a cloak around him, broke through the South line of the ranks when the orderly sergeant took the strange man by the nape of the neck and kicked him outside the ranks telling him not to come in again; as soon as quiet was resumed I continued my address to the company . . . .

About dusk I dismissed the company, blessing them in the name of the Lord.

3 July 1843 (Monday Afternoon). Grove.[1]
Willard Richards Diary

Joseph spoke. P M.

4 July 1843 (Tuesday Morning). At Stand.[1]
Joseph Smith Diary, by Willard Richards

Elder O. Hyde Lectured Lectured at the Stand at 10 1/2 A.M.— after which Joseph gave a short address concerning his arrest to correct Reports circulated by Renolds[2] [and] Wilson—[3]

Levi Richards Diary

10 A M attended at the grove near the Temple—a large assembly listened to Eld O Hyde—followed by J. Smith a few minutes.

4 July 1843 (Tuesday Afternoon). At the Temple Stand.[1]
Wilford Woodruff Journal

At 2 oclock they were again addressed by Elder Parley P. Pratt in a masterly discourse followed by President Joseph Smith upon the subject of the late arest & persecution who clearly vindicated his innocence & showed the corruption of his pursueers in a tru light. Three Steamers arived in the afternoon—one from St Louis one from Quincy & one from Burlington—bringing altogether about 900 visiting ladies and gentlemen to our City. On the arival of each boat they were escorted to the Stand by the Nauvoo band and the escort Companies whare convenient seats were provided & where they were welcomed by the firing of Cannon which brought to our minds the last words of the Patriot Jefferson:—Let this day be Celebrated by the firing of Cannon &c The legion was not out.

The following is a synopsis of the Address of President Joseph Smith while speaking in his own defence before about 15 000 souls

If the people will give ear a momen I will address them, with few words in my own defence as touching my arest. In the first place I will state to those that can hear me that I never spent more than six months in Missouri except while in prison,[2] while I was there I was at work for the support of my family. I never was a prisoner of war during my stay for I had not made war, I never took a pistol a gun, or sword & the much that has been said on this subject is false I have been willing to go before any governor Judge or tribunal whare justice Could be done & have the subject investigated. I could not have committed treason in that State while there I had no controll any whare in temporal things while there but in spiritual I was driven from that state by force of arms under the exterminating order of Govornor Boggs.[3] I have never commited treason the people know vary well I have Been a peaceable Citizen but their has been a great hugh & cry about ~~Jo Smith~~ Govonor Bogs being shot, No Crime can be done but what it is laid to Jo Smith Here I was again dragged to the United States Court,[4] & was cleared & now it comes again, But as often as God sees fit for me to suffer I am ready But I am as innocent of these Crimes as the Angels in heaven. I am not an enemy to mankind I am a friend to Mankind. I am not an enemy to Missouri nor any any governors or people As to the military station I hold & the Cause of my holding it is as follows: When we came here the State required us to bear arms & do military duty according to law,[5] & as the Church had just been driven from the State of Missouri & robed of all their property & arms they were poor & destitute of armes they were liable to be fined for not doing duty when they had not arms to do it with, they came to me for advice I advised them to organize themselves into independent companies, & demand arms of the State, this they did, Again their were many Elders having licence to preach which by law exhonorated them from Military duty but the officers would not release them on this ground I then told the Saints that though I was clear from Military duty by law in consequence of lameness in one of my legs,[6] yet I would set them the example & would do duty myself, they then said they were willing to do duty if they could be formed into an independent company & I could be at their head & upon this ground came the Nauvoo Legion & I holding the office of Lieutenant General not that I seek for power. & with regard to elections some say we all vote together & vote as I say But I never tell any man how to vote or who to vote for, But I will show you how we have been situated by bringing a Comparison Should their be a Methodist Society here & two Candidates running for office, one says if you will vote for me & put me in govornor I will exterminate the Methodist take away their Charters &c. The other Candidate says if I am Govornor I will give all an equal privilege, which would the Methodist vote for of course they would vote in mass for the Candidate that would give them their rights; thus it has Been with us Joseps Duncan[7] said if the people would elect him he would exterminate the mormons & take away their charters As to Mr Ford[8] he made no such threats, but manifested a spirit in his speaches to give every man their rights, hence the Church universally voted for Mr Ford & he was elected govornor, But he has issued writs against me the first time the Missourians made a demand for me & this is the second one he has issued for me which has caused me much trouble & expense. President Smith Also rehearsed the account of his being taken By Reynolds[9] & Wilson[10] & the unlawful treatment he received at their hands.

The multitude gave good attention & much prejudice seemed to be removed .

Joseph Smith Diary, by Willard Richards

[P.M., after sermon by Parley P. Pratt] President J. Smith gave a brief relation of his capture—detention—treatment & trial. (which will be given in full hereafter.)[11] all of which gave great satisfaction apparently to all parties. & the visitors—as well as saints. appeared highly gratified.

Levi Richards Diary

P M P P Pratt occupied the stand (subject—resurrection & a whole salvation) Some 500 visiters from St. Louis Quincy burlington &c J. Smith spoke about 1/2 hour of his late arrest & trial—& religion &c good order prevailed through the day .

9 July 1843 (Sunday Morning). Temple Stand.[1]
Joseph Smith Diary, by Willard Richards

Joseph remarked that all was well between him and the heavens that he had no enmity against any one. and as the prayer of Jesus or his pattern so prayed Joseph. Father forgive me my trespasses as I forgive those who trespass against me.[2] for I freely forgive all men.—if we would secure & cultivate the love of others we must love others, even our enemies—as well as friends "why is it this babler gains so many followers. & retains them"? because I possess the principle of love, All I can offer the world a good heart & a good hand. Mormons can testify whether I am willing to lay down my life for a Mormon; If it has been demonstrated that I have been willing to die for a Mormon I am bold to declare before heaven that I am just as ready to die for a presbyterian. a baptist or any other denomination.—It is a love of liberty which inspires my soul, civil and religious liberty—were diffused into my soul by my grandfathers. while they dandled me on their knees—and shall I want [for] friends? no!

"Wherein do you differ from other in your religious views?" In reality & essence we do not differ so far in our religious views but that we could all drink into one principle of love One the grand fundamental principles of Mormonism is to recieve thruth let it come from where it may.—we belive in the great Eloheim. who sits enthroned in yonder heavens.—so do the presbyterians. If as a skillful mechanic In taking a welding heat I use a borax & allum &c. an succeed in welding you all together shall I not have attained a good object.

if I esteem mankind to be in error shall I bear them down? No! I will will lift them up. & in his own way if I cannot persuade him my way is better! & I will ask no man to believe as I do. Do you believe in Jesus Chrst &c? So do I. Christians should cultivate the friendship with others & will do it.

"Do you believe in the baptism of infants"? says the presbyterians.—No.—"Why." because it is no where written in the book.

communion is not Baptism. Baptism is for remission of sins. children have no sins.[3]—He Jesus blessed them[4]—do what you have seen me do[5]—all made alive in christ.[6]

faith & repentance.—we are agreed.—baptism. yes by immersion. the Hebrew is the root.—to bury immerse?—Do you believe this no. I believe in being ~~convert~~ converted.[7]—I believe in this tenaciously

Holy Ghost by laying on of hands Evidance. Peter on days of Pentecost.[8] might as well ~~be~~ baptize a bag of sand as a man if not done in view of the getting of the Holy Ghost.—baptism by water is but 1/2 a baptism—& is good for nothing with the other, the Holy Ghost. I am free to day—messenger has returned with offers of peace from the governor[9]

except a man be born again. of water & of the spirit can in no wise enter into the Kingdom.[10]

Though we or an angel from heaven preach any other gospel.[11]

James Burgess Notebook

Remarks on is there to be no more Prophets. John the Revelator says that the testimony of Jesus is the Spirit of prophicy.[12] Now if any man has the testimony of Jesus has he not the spirit of prophecy and if he has the spirit of prophicy I ask is he not a prophet and if a prophet will he can receive revalation And any man that does not receive revelation for himself must be damned for the testimony of Jesus is the spirit of prophicy for Christ says ask and you shall receive.[13] And if he happens to receive anything I ask will it not be a revelation. And if any man has not the testimony of Jesus or the spirit of God he is none of his Christ's[14] namely And if not his he must be damn'd What are we to understand by a Prophet It is his character to predict things that are in the future. I ask what right has any man or set of men or preist or set of preists to say if a man will not do so and so he shall be damn'd. Is he not takeing upon himself or assumeing the character of a Prophet consequently he must either be a true or false Prophet.

In answer to a question asked by a Sectarian preist namely. How is that you Mormons hold that God is an omnipresent being when at the same time he is a personage of Tabernacle.

After God had created the Heavens and the Earth. He came down and on the sixth day said let us make man in our own image.[15] In whose image. In the image of Gods[16] created they them. Male and female: innocent harmless and spotless bearing the same character and the same image as the Gods. And when man fell he did not lose his image but his character still retaining the image of his maker Christ who is the image of man is also the express image of his Fathers person so says Paul.[17] For in him Christ dwelt the fulness of the Godhead bodily. Why because He was the brightness of his glory; and the express image of his person.[18] Ques. What person Gods person. Hebrews 1st chap 3 verse And through the atonement of Christ and the resurrection and obediance in the Gospel we shall again be conformed to the image of his Son Jesus Christ, then we shall have attained to the image glory and character of God. What part of God is omnipresent read the 37 chap of Ezekel. It is the Spirit of god which proceeds from him consequently God is in the four winds of Heaven and when man receives inteligence is it not by the spirit of God[19] J S Prophet

Levi Richards Diary

Sun 9t. July A.M. attended Meeting at the Temple stand—heard Pres Joseph Smith preach shewing the difference between the Latter Day Saints & the ~~Mormons.~~ Sectarians. A conciliatory address to Strangers & all—

16 July 1843 (Sunday Morning). At Stand in Grove, West of Temple.[1]

Letter of Willard Richards to Brigham Young

Sunday 16 Joseph preached all day.—A.M. 27th Matthew & c.—did not hear him.—"Mans foes they of his own house.[2]—the spirit that crucified Christ, same spirit in Nauvoo. refered particularly to—I wont say who—was it Bro Marks?[3]—did not say.—bro Cole [Cowles]?[4] or bro ~~P.P.P.~~?[5] did not hear the sermon, why ask me. nothing new same as when you left.[6]—the spirit was against Christ because of his innocence.—So in the present case.—

Joseph Smith Diary, by Willard Richards

preached all day. or A.M. & P.M. at the Stand, in the grove, near & west of the temple concerning a mans foes being they of his own house.[7] Such as having secret enemies in the city—intermingling with the saints &c.—

Levi Richards Diary

16 July AM at Temple stand heard Pres. Joseph Smith read the 27th Chapt. Math. spoke of the persecution of the innocent the guilty might ~~go free~~ escapes—

Willard Richards Diary

Joseph Pr[eached]—all day—constituted Hyrum prophet

16 July 1843 (Sunday Afternoon). Temple Stand.[1]
Franklin D. Richards "Scriptural Items"

Joseph said July 16th All Blessings that were ordained for man by the Council of Heaven were on conditions of obedience to the Law there of.[2] No man can obtain an eternal Blessing unless the contract or covenant be made in view of Eternity All contracts in view of this Life only terminate with this Life.[3] Case of the woman & 7 husbands Luke 20-29 &c Those who keep no eternal Law in this life or make no eternal contract are single & alone in the eternal world (Luke 20-35) and are only made Angels to minister to those who shall be heirs of Salvation never becoming Sons of God having never kept the Law of God ie eternal Law[4] The earthly is the image of the Heavenly[5] shows that is by the multiplication of Lives[6] that the eternal worlds are created and occupied that which is born of the flesh is flesh that which is born of the Spirit is Spirit.[7]

William Clayton Diary

P.M. went to the Grove and heard Pres. J. preach on the law of the priesthood.[8] He stated that Hyrum held the office of prophet to the church by birth-right & he was going to have a reformation and the saints must regard Hyrum for he has authority.[9] He showed that a man must enter into an everlasting covenant with his wife in this world or he will have no claim on her in the next.[10] He said that he could not reveal the fulness of these things untill the Temple is completed &c.[11]

Levi Richards Diary

P.M. spoke of contracts & covenants made from life end with life![2] the necessity of the Temple that the Servants of God may be sealed in their foreheads.[13]—the 4 Angels not permitted to destroy the earth till it was done[14]—weather warm & dry—

Letter of Willard Richards to Brigham Young

Said he would not prophecy any more.—Hyrum should be the prophet—(did not tell them he was going to be a priest now, nor a King by and by)[15]—told the elders not to prophecy when they went out preaching—

Joseph Smith Diary, by Willard Richards

Proposing Hyrum as a prophet—that he might be (a priest)[16]— so the hearers tell the story.

23 July 1843 (Sunday Afternoon).[1]
Joseph Smith Diary, by Willard Richards

P.M. Law and prophets were until John & 16 Luke 16 v. Joseph preached introduction. It has gone abroad that I was no longer a prophet.—I said it Ironically. I supposed you would all understand. I[t] was not that I would renounce the idea of being a prophet. but that I would renounce the idea of proclaiming myself such. and saying that I bear the testimony of Jesus[2]

No greater love than that a man lay down his life for his friends.[3] I discover 100s & 1000s—ready to do it for me.

In the midst of business. & find the spirit willing but the flesh is weak[4] subject to like passions with other men.[5]—

although I am under the necessity of bearing the infirmities of other men, &c.—on the other hand the same characters when they discover a weakness in brother Joseph. blast his character &c—all that law &c through him to the church.—he cannot be borne with a moment. men mouth my troubles when I have trouble they forget it all I believe in a principle of reciprosiprocity—if we live in a devilish world—&c—

I see no faults in the church.—Let me be resurrected with the saints whether to heaven or hell or any other good place—good society. what do we care if the society is good?[6] dont care what a character is if he's my friend.—a friend a true friend. & I will be a friend to him friendship is the grand fundamental principle of Mormonism, to revolution civilize the world.—pour forth love. friendship like Bro Turley[7] Blacksmith Shop. I do not dwell upon your faults. you shall not upon mine. after you have covered up all the faults among you the prettyest thing is have no faults at all.— meek, quiet, &c.—Presbyterians any truth. embrace that. Baptist. Methodist &c. get all the good in the world. come out a pure Mormon.

Last Monday morning certain men came to me.—Bro Joseph Hyrum is no prophet he cant lead the church. you must lead the Church—if you resign I felt curious—& said—here we learn in a priesthood after the order of Melchisedeck—Prophet priest & king. & I will advance from prophet to priest & then to King[8] not to the kingdoms of this earth but of the most high god.

If I should would there be a great many disappointed in Mo? Law & prophets &c. Suffereth violence & the violent taketh it by force[9]—heaven and earth shall pass away.[10] &c says Christ. he was the rock &c.[11]—gave the law[12] 30 Ex. 30.31. and thou shalt anoint Aron &c. last Chap Ex 15. and thou shalt anoint them &c.[13]—a tittle of law which must be fulfilled.[14]—forever hereditary.—fixed on the head of aron. down to Zachariah—the father of John. Zachariah had no child had not God gave him a son? Sent his angel to declare a son Name John. with the keys.[15]—John King and lawgiver

The Kingdom of heaven suffereth violence & The kingdom of heaven continueth in authority. ~~beareth suffereth violence~~ until John. the authority taketh it by absolute power.. John having the power.—take the kingdom by authority.[16]—

How do you know all this gr[eat] knowledge? by the gift of the H.G. arrested the kingdom from the Jews of these stony Gentils[17]

these dogs to raise up children unto Abraham

John I must be baptized by you. why to answer my decrees John refuses—Jesus had no legal administrator before John.[18] No salvation between the two lids of the bible without a legal administrator

Tis contrary to a governors oath to send a man to Mo. where he is prescribed in his religious opinions.—

Jesus was then the legal administrator.—& ordained his apostles.[19]

I will resume the subject at some future time.—

James Burgess Notebook

Luke 16 chap 16 verse. The Law and the Prophets were untill John since then the Kingdom of Heaven is preached and all men press into it. We will go back to Mount Scinia where Jesus gave the Law to Moses Exodus 30 chap 30 verse also the last chap 15 verse.[20] The preisthood was given to Aron and his posterity throughout all generations We can trace the leanage down to Zachariah he being the only lawfull administrator in his day and the jews knew it well for they always acknowledge the priesthood. and Zachariah having no children. knew that the promise of God must fail, consequently he went into the Temple to wrestle with God according to the order of the preisthood[21] to obtain a promise of a son, and when the Angel told him that his promise was granted he because of unbelief was struck dumb.[22] And when the set time was come John came forth and when he took up his preisthood, he came bounding out of the wilderness saying repent ye for the kingdom of heaven is at hand.[23] he having received the holy anointing was the only lawful administrator and the jews all knew it for the law and the prophets was untill John since then the kingdom of heaven is preached and all men press into it![24] Why! Why ~~John~~ because John was the only lawful administrator and they the Jews well knew it. consequently the only alternative was for them to yeild obedience to mandates of this wild man of the woods, namely John or be damned. For all Jerusalem and all Judea came out to be babtised of John,[25] sadusees, pharasees, Essenees &c For untill John was the law and the prophets, since then the kingdom of heaven is preached and all men press into it.[26] The kingdom of heaven suffereth violence and the violent take it by forse.[27] Now I will translate a little, the kingdom of heaven hath power and authority and by that they take or enter legally and lawfully the kingdom of heaven.

J S Prophet

Franklin D. Richards "Scriptural Items"

July 23 Joseph said after reading Matt 11-12 & Luke 16-16 Heaven & Earth might pass but not a jot or tittle of the Law should read Exodus 40-15 Anointing of Aaron & his sons and shewed that all the Power & Authority & Anointing descended upon the head of John the Baptist or "The Government shall be upon his shoulders"[28] This was virtually acknowledged by all Judea & they of Jersualem coming out to be baptised of him[29] & the rendering the Texts is "The Kingdom continueth in authority or Law & the Authority or legality (which belonged to John) took it by force or wrested it from the Jews to be delivered to a Nation bringing forth the fruits thereof.[30]

Levi Richards Diary

23 July warm & dry ... P.M. J Smith spoke 1 hour & 25 Minutes—Text, Luke 16-16.

Willard Richards Diary

Meeting Hyrum—Joseph.

6 August 1843 (Sunday Morning). Temple Stand.[1]
Joseph Smith Diary, by Willard Richards

Zebedee Coltrin[2] prayed. P. P. Pratt preached on testimony. after Sermon. Joseph (for he came to the Stand soon after Parly commenced.) said he would preach his sermon next Sunday he was not able to day.—would speak of another subject.—the Election[3] he was above the kingdoms of the world for he had no laws.—I have not come to tell you to vote this way, that way, or the other in relation to National matters I want it to abroad to the whole world that every man should stand on his own merits. the Lord has not given me Revelation concerning politics.—I have not asked the Lord for it.—I am a third party stand independent and alone—I desire to see all parties protected in their rights.—as I have to have in relation to Mr Walker.[4] he is a whig candidate a high minded man.

Mr Walker has not hung on to my coat tail to gain his election as some have said. I am going to give a testimony but not for electioneering purposes. before Mr Walker come to Nauvoo rumor come up that he might become a candidate for congress. says I he is an old friend I will vote for him.—when Mr Walker come to my house, I voluntarily told him I was going to vote for him. When I dictated to him the laws of Nauvoo, he received them on my testimony.—the rascals took Walkers & Montgomery[5] security when I was arrested Walker made Reynolds[6] come to me & beg my pardon for abuse he gave me & though his men took the pistols from the rascals, & withdrew all claim to your vote & influence if it will be detrimental to your interest as a people.

Bro Hiram tells me this morning that he has had a testimony that it will be better for this people to vote for hoge.[7] & I never knew Hiram say he ever had a revelation & it failed. Never told Bro Law[8] to tell my private feelings.[9] (Let God speak and all men hold their peace.) and I utterly forbid these polotical demagogues from using my name hereafter forever.—

It is my settled feeling that if gov Ford erred in granting a writ against me it is of the head and not of the heart. and I authorize all men to say I am a personal friend of gov ford.

A Cap to Parleys[10] Sermon

every word that proceedeth from the mouth of Jehovah has such an influence over the human mind the logical mind that it is convincing without other testimony. faith cometh by hearing.[11]

If 10000 men testify to a truth you know would it add to your faith? No, or will 1000 testimonies destroy your knowledge of a fact.? No.—I do not want anyone to tell I am a prophet or attempt to prove my word[12] I Prophecy in the name of God Almighty they shall bear off the palm.

William Clayton Diary

Prest. J. made some remarks on the election showing that he had taken no part in it. stated that Hyrum had had a manifestation that it was for our interest to vote for Hoge.

Levi Richards Diary

6 At the stand near the Temple heard B P Pratt lecture on the principle of evidence—cap_____by Joseph,—that truth carrys its own influence & reccomends itself &c.

Willard Richards Diary

Meeting A.M. Parley. Joseph Hyrum Phelps & Walker.

13 August 1843 (Sunday Morning). Temple Stand.[1]
Joseph Smith Diary, by Willard Richards

Sunday Aug 13th 1843
Joseph Pre. in relation the death of Judge Higby[2]
2d. Peter 3d. C. 10.11.v.—Text said he was not like other. men his mind was continually occupied with the business of the day, and he had to depend entirely upon the living God for every thing he said on such occasions.

The great thing for us to know is to comprehend what God did institute before the foundation of the world.—Who knows it?

It is the constitutional disposition of mankind to set up stakes & set bounds to the works and ways of the Almighty.

we are called this [to] mourn this morning the death of a good man a great man & a mighty man—It is a solemn idea that man has no hope of seeing a friend after he has lost him. but I will give you a more painful thought—the thought is simple and I never design to communicate no ideas but what are simple for to this end I am sent.—suppose we have an idea of a resurrection, &c &c. and yet know nothing at all of the gospel and could not comprehend one principle of the order of heaven. but found yourselves disappointed, yes, at last find your selfes disappointed in every hope or anticipation when decisions goes forth from the lips of the Almighty at last. would not this be a greater disappointment. a more painful thought than annihilation

had I inspiration, Revelation & lungs to communicate what my soul has contemplated in times past there is not a soul in this congregation but would go to their homes & shut their mouths in everlasting silence on religion, till they had learned something.

Why be so certain that you comprehend the things of God. when all things with you are so uncertain. you are welcome to all the knowledge &

I do not grudge the world of all the religion the[y] have got.— they are welcome to all the knowledge they possess.

the sound saluted my ears. we are come unto Mt. Zion.[3] &c. what could profit us to come unto the spirits of Just Men but to learn, and come to the <u>knowledge</u> spirits of the Just.

Where has Judge Higby gone? who is there that would not give all his goods to feed the poor & pour out his gold & silver, to the four winds. to come where Judge Higby has gone.—

that which hath been hid from before the foundation of the world, is revealed to babes and sucklings in the last days.[4]—

The world is reserved unto burning in the last days—he shall send Elijah the prophet. and he shall reveal the covenants of the fathers in relation to the children.—and the children and the covenants of the children in relation to the fathers.[5]—

4 destroying angels holding power over the 4 quarters of the earth. until the the servants of God are sealed in their foreheads.[6] what is that seal. shall I tell you? know No.—

Doctrine Election.—sealing of the servants of God on the top of their heads.[7] tis not the cross as the catholics would have it. doctrine of Election to Abraham was in the relation to the Lord. a man wishes to be embraced in the covenant of Abraham. A man Judge Higby— in world of spirits. is sealed unto the throne, & doctrine of Election sealing the father & children together.[8]

to the mourner. do as the husband and the father would instruct you & you shall be reunited.[9]—

I have been acquainted with Judge Higby a long time & I Never knew a more tenderhearted man.

The president was much exhausted.

Howard and Martha Coray Notebook

Sermon 3thd.
on the death of Judge Higbee.

There is a thought more dreadful than that of total annihilation That thought is the an assurance thought that we shall never again meet with those we loved here on earth[10] Suppose I had died believing that when having some Idea of a resurection and glory beyond the grave which God and angels had secured and yet had not any knowledge intelligence of any Law or any order by which it is to obtained. Well you lose a friend you come up in the resurection hoping to [meet] him again but find yourself separated from them to all eternity and become aware of the fact that through ignorance of the principles of the resurection and reunion you will never behold that dear friend nor ever enjoy his society this thought I say of being disappointed in meeting my friend in the resurection is to me more dreadful than of ceasing to suffer by a cessation of being

~~Were I~~ could I tell the fact as it is all that heard me would go home and never say one word more about God or Christ or religion until they had received that assurance from Heaven which would set their souls at rest by placing all beyond a doubt.[11]

What consolation have we what power what reason to expect one thing more than another in eternity

Hebrews 12 ch 22 ~~& 22~~ v

~~You~~ You have come to an innumerable company of angels to the general assembly and church of the first born And for have were they brought thus far—I answer ~~you~~ that they came to these person-ages to learn of the things of God and to hear revealed through them the order and glory of the kingdoms of God.

I would ask again Is there a word on record that was revealed by those angels and spirits[12] if there is where is it to be ~~found~~ found

Again I enquire what is the order and organization of the Spirits of the just made perfect Let me tell you brethren That which is to be revealed which was kept his from the foundation of the world will be revealed to sucklings and babes[13]

Malachi 4th ch Behold the day cometh that shall burn as an oven and all the proud and they that do wickedly shall be as stubble and they[14] that cometh shall burn them up ~~But~~ although in the beginning God created the Earth standing in the water and out of the water still in the End it shall be burned and few men left[15]—but before that God shall send unto them Elijah the prophet and he shall reveal unto them the covenants of the fathers ~~wi~~ with relation to the children and the covenants of the children in relation to the Fathers that they may have the priviledge of entering into the same in order to effect their mutual salvation[16] And I saw another angel ascending from the east having the Seal of the living God and he cried &c. sayin Hurt not the Earth nor sea nor trees till we have sealed the servants of our Go[d] in their foreheads.[17]—

Now I would ask who know the seal of the living God Behold the ignorance of the World.

A measure of this sealing is to confirm upon their head in common with Elijah the doctrine of election or the covenant with Abraham[18]—which which when a Father & mother of a family have entered into their children who have not transgressed are secured by the seal wherewith the Parents have been sealed.[19] And this is the Oath of God unto our Father Abraham and this doctrine shall stand forever.

Mourners: I exhort you to do as your Father and husband would direct—be sealed by the by the servants of God.[20] Eternal life is to <u>know</u> the only true God and his son Jesus without which there is no salvation.[21]

Franklin D. Richards "Scriptural Items"

Joseph. Translation of Mal 4th-5 . 6 I will send Elijah the Prophet and he shall reveal the covenants of the Fathers to the children and of the Children to the Fathers that they may enter into Covenant with each other lest I come & smite the whole Earth with a curse—

What is the seal spoken of in Rev 7-3 find it out if you can I will not reveal it now but will drop an idea that I have never revealed[22] concerning Election connected with the sealing of the servants of God in the fore or top of the head

Judge Higbee would say that covenants either there or here must be made in view of eternity and the Covenant sealed on the fore heads of the Parents secured the children from falling that they shall all sit upon thrones[23] as one with the God-head joint Heirs of God with Jesus Christ[24]

This principle is revealed also through the covenant of Abraham and his children[25] This is also the blessing and consolation of the Mourners——

William Clayton Diary

Went to meeting heard J. preach on 2 Peter 3. 10 & 11—being a funeral sermon on the death of E. Higbee[26] When speaking of the passage "I will send Elijah the prophet &c" he said it should read and he shall turn the hearts of the children to the covenant made with their fathers[27] Also where it says and they shall seal the servants of God in their foreheads &c it means to seal the blessing on their heads meaning the everlasting covenant thereby making their calling & election sure.[28] When a seal is put upon the father and mother it secures their posterity so that they cannot be lost but will be saved by virtue of the covenant of their father.[29]

Levi Richards Diary

13 AM attended meeting at Temple stand heard Pres. Smith preach Judge Higbee's funeral discourse.

Willard Richards Diary

Meeting Joseph preached Judge Higbys funeral sermon.

13 August 1843 (Sunday Afternoon).[1]
Joseph Smith Diary, by Willard Richards

2. P. M. Joseph as Mayor instructed the Marshall[2] to keep the Ladies camp ground clear of young men.

the city is enlarging very fast. we have so many learned men in this city & the height of knowledge is not to know enough to keep out out of the way. I have been feretting out grog shops, groceries & beer barrels

Mr Bagby of Carthage.[3] who has exercised more despotic power over the inhabitants of this city than any despot of the Eastern country. I met. he gave me some abusive language took up a stone to throw at me I siezed him by the throat to choke him off.

at the Election[4] on the hill they got a Constable name of King.[5]— I dont know what need there was of a constable

Old Father Perry[6] said why you cant vote in this precinct. King took me by the collar ~~to march~~ and told me to go away.

All our wrongs have arisen under the power and authority of democracy and I have sworn that ~~I will~~ this arm shall fall from my shoulder and this tongue cleave to the roof of my mouth. before I will vote for them unless they make me satisfaction & I feel it sensibly.—

I was abused and regulated at the ground, and there was not a man in the crowd to say—this is Bro. Joseph. this is the Mayor—

then spoke of the grog shops and the disturbance of the crowd in the street by Mosseur's grocery.[7] Warned the grog shop to be scarce after this time. and the peace officers to take notice of the grog shops and give him reasonable notice.

closed 20 mi.—3—

William Clayton Diary

P.M. Prest J. offered some complaints of the citizens of Nauvoo 1st because some young men sat on the ladies camp ground and laughed & mocked during meeting He next spake of Walter Bagby & the little skirmish he had with him about a week ago he spoke of Esq Wells[8] interfering when he had no business. He then spake of the abuses he received at the election by King[9] & the board of Judges. also of the Grog & Beer shops & said he should rip them up. He then showed that Sidney Rigdon had bound himself by an oath to Governor Carlin to deliver J into the hands of the Missourians if he could & finally in the name of the Lord withdrew the hand of fellowship from him & put it to the vote of the people. He was cut off by an unamous vote & orders to demand his licence.[10]

Willard Richards Diary

P.M. Joseph found fault with the people of the city. some of them concerning Elections.

27 August 1843 (Sunday Morning). Temple Grove.[1]
Joseph Smith Diary, by Willard Richards

10 A M. President Marks[2] prayed.—

Joseph said 2 weeks to day something said about Elder Rigdon—vote taken to take away his license. on account of a report brought by Elder Hyde[3] from Quincy.—

The letter is one of the most evasive things.—and carries with it a design to hide the truth . . . .

in answer to S. Rigdon of the 15. inst Thom Carlin.—Has any man been concerned in a conspiracy to deliver Joseph Smith to Mo?

if so who?—Read 7th Hebrews. Salem is designed for a hebrew term. it should be Shiloam—which signifies Righteousness & peace.[4] as it is, it is nothing, neither Hebrew, Greek, Latin french or any other To all those who are disposed to say to set up stakes for the almighty—will come short of the glory of god. To becom a joint heir of the heirship of the son he must put away all his traditions.[5]

I bear record this morning that all the combined powers of earth & hell shall not over come this boy.—

If I have sinned I have sinned outwardly—but secretly I have contemplated the things of God.

told an anecdote of the Episcopalian priest—who said he had the priesthood of Aron—but not of Melichisedek—and bore this testimony that I never have found the man who claimed the priesthood of Melchisidek.

The law was given under Aaron for the purpose of pouring out Judments and destructions.

The sectarian world are going to hell—by 100s 1000s 1000 000!

3 grand orders of priesthood referred to here.[6]

1st. King of Shiloam—power & authority over that of Abraham holding the key & the power of endless life.—angels desire to look into it, but they have set up to many stakes. god cursed the children of Israel because they would not receive the last law from Moses.[7]—

by the offering of Isaac.[8]—if a man would attain—he must sacrifice all to attain to the keys of the kingdom of an endless life

What was the power of Melchisedick twas not P. of Aaron &c. a king & a priest to the most high God. a perfect law of Theocracy holding keys of power & blessings. stood as God to give laws to the people. administering endless lives to the sons and daughters of Adam[9] kingly powers. of anointing.[10]—Abram says Melchisedek.—away I have a priesthood.—

Salvation could not come to the world without the mediation of Jesus Christ.

how shall god come to the rescue of this generation. he shall send Elijah law revealed to Moses in Horeb—never was revealed to the C. of Israel and he shall reveal the covenants to seal the hearts of the fathers to the children and the children to the fathers.[11]—anointing & sealing—called elected and made sure[12] without father &c.[13] a priesthood which holds the priesthood by right from the Eternal Gods.—and not be descent from father and mother[14]

2d Priesthood, patriarchal authority finish that temple and god will fill it with power.[15]

3d Priesthood. Levitical[16]

Priests made without an oath but the Priesthood of Melchisedek is by oath and covenant.[17] Holy Ghost.[18]

jesus christ—men have to suffer that they might come up on Mt. Zion. exalted above the heavens[19]—I know a man that has been caught up to the 3d heaven[20]—& saw.

Franklin D. Richards "Scriptural Items"

A sermon of Josephs Heb 7 chap Salem is Shiloam

Those who limit the designs of God as concerted by the grand council of H cannot obtain the Knowledge of God & I do not know but I may say they will drink in the Damnation of their souls—

I Prophecy that all the powers of Earth & Hell shall never be able to overthrow this Boy for I have obtained it by promise—

There are 3 grand principles or orders of Priesthood portrayed in this chapter

1st Levitical which was never able to administer a Blessing but only to bind heavy burdens which neither they nor their father able to bear

2 Abrahams Patriarchal power which is the greatest yet experienced in this church[21]

3d That of Melchisedec who had still greater power even power of an endless life of which was our Lord Jesus Christ which also Abraham obtained by the offering of his son Isaac which was not the power of a Prophet nor apostle nor Patriarch only but of King & Priest[22] to God to open the windows of Heaven and pour out the peace & Law of endless Life to man[23] & No man can attain to the Joint heirship[24] with Jesus Christ with out being administered to by one having the same power & Authority of Melchisedec[25] Joseph also said that the Holy Ghost[26] is now in a state of Probation which if he should perform in righteousness he may pass through the same or a similar course of things that the Son has.

James Burgess Notebook

Hebrewes 7 chap. Paul is here treating of three different

preisthoods, namely the preisthood of Aron, Abraham, and
Melchizedeck, Abraham's preisthood was of greater power than
Levi's and Melchizedeck's was of greater power than that of
Abraham. The preisthood of Levi consisted of cursings and
~~blessings~~ carnal commandments and not of blessings and if the
preisthood of this generation has no more power than that of Levi or
Aron or of a bishhoprick it administers no blessings but cursings for
it was an eye for an eye and a tooth for a tooth.[27] I ask was there any
sealing power attending this preisthood. ~~Oh no~~ that would admit a
man into the presence of God.[28] Oh no, but Abraham's was a more
exalted power or preisthood he could talk and walk with God and
yet consider how great this man was when even this patriarch
Abraham gave a tenth part of all his spoils and then received a
blessing under the hands of Melchesideck[29] even the last law or a
fulness of the law or preisthood[30] which constituted him a king and
preist after the order of Melchesideck or an endless life Now if
Abraham had been like the sectarian world and would not have
received any more revelation, what would have been the consequence it would have damned him. Book of Covenants.[31] The
levitical preisthood was an appendage to the Melchesideck preisthood or the whole law of God when in full face or power in all its
parts and bearings on the earth.[32] It is understood by many by
reading this chapter that Melchesedeck was king of some country or
nation on the earth, but it was not so, In the original it reads king of
Shaloam which signifies king of peace or righteousness and not of
any country or nation.[33]

Malachi says that the sons of Levi shall in the last days offer an
offering in rightousness.[34]

Men will set up stakes and say thus far will we go and no
farther, did Abraham when called upon to offer his son,[35] did the
Saviour,[36] no, view him fulfiling all rightousness again on the banks
of jordon,[37] also on the Mount transfigured before Peter and John
there receiving the fulness of preisthood or the law of God,[38] setting
up no stake but coming right up to the mark in all things here him
after he returned from the Mount, did ever language of such
magnitude fall from the lips of any man, hearken him. All power is
given is given unto me both in heaven and the earth.[39] Offering's
sacrifice's and carnal commandments, was added in consequence of
transgression and they that did them should live by them.[40] View

~~him~~ the Son of God at saying it behoveth me to fulfil all rightous-ness[41] also in a garden saying if it be possible let this cup pass from me nevertheless thy will be done.[42] What was the design of the Almighty in making man, it was to exalt him to be as God,[43] the scripture says yet are Gods and it cannot be broken,[44] heirs of God and joint heirs I with Jesus Christ equal with him possesing all power &c.[45] The mystery power and glory of the preisthood is so great and glorious that the angels desired to understand it and cannot: why, because of the tradition of them and their fathers in setting up stakes and not coming up to the mark in their probation-ary state.[46] J Smith the Prophet.

William Clayton Diary

A.M. at the Grove. Prest. J. preached on Hebrews c 7. After reading a letter from Thos. Carlin to S. Rigdon and making some remarks about it.[47] He shewed that the word "Salem" is a wrong translation it should be "Shalome" signifying peace.[48] He prophecied that "not all the powers of hell or earth combined can ever overthrow this boy" for he had a promise from the eternal God. He spoke concerning the priesthood of Melchisedek shewing that the sectarians never propossed to have it consequently never could save any one and would all be damned together. He showed that the power of the Melchisek P'd was to have the power of an "endless lives."[49] he showed that the everlasting covenants could not be broken, and by the sacrifice requeired of Abraham the fact that when God offers a blessing or knowledge to a man and he refuses to receive it he will be damned.[50]—mentioning the case of the Israelites praying that God would speak to Moses & not to them—in consequense of which he cursed them with a carnal law.[51]

Levi Richards Diary

27 Aug attended meeting at Temple Grove—Letter from Governor Ca[r]lin to Sidney Rigdon read by Joseph Smith ~~attended with~~ remarks on it by J. Smith who afterwards preached from Hebrews 7 upon the priesthood Aaronic, Patriarchal, & Melchisedec.

Willard Richards Diary

Joseph preached.

13 September 1843 (Wednesday).[1]
Joseph Smith Diary, by Willard Richards

2 oclock & 10 minutes Joseph introduced Mr. John Finch[2] of Liverpool England to give an address on his views of the social system. agreeable to Mr. Owens[3] System 1 evils society is suffering. 2 causes which produce them. 3 best means of removing them. Spoke on the first two points Joseph spoke and Finch replied &c all pleasantly.—

14 September 1843 (Thursday Afternoon). Temple Stand.[1]
Joseph Smith Diary, by Willard Richards

2. P.M. at the temple Stand John Finch spoke on the 3d principle mentioned yesterday 10 past 3. Joseph spoke 5 minutes, told an anecdote of Sidney Rigdon. and Al. Cambell[2] got up a community at Kirtland. big fish eat up the little. did not believe the doctrine.—&c.

Levi Richards Diary

... P.M. 2 O'clock at Temple Grove heard Mr Finch's[3] closng Lecture—Answered by Eld John Taylor—& Pres Smith continued 4 hours.

16 September 1843 (Saturday Afternoon).[1]
Joseph Smith Diary, by Willard Richards

20 minutes after 3.—attend the review and inspection of the Legion with my staff. Gen Derby[2] acting inspecter. after which I took my part and gave orders.—after which made a speech to the legion highly satisfied with officers and Soldiers and I <u>felt extremely well myself.</u>

17 September 1843 (Sunday Morning).[1]
Joseph Smith Diary, by Willard Richards

was at meeting. ~~AM~~ gave some directions. & while Almon Babbitt[2] preached I took my part as Mayor outside of the assembly. to keep order & set pattern for the under officers.—after preaching gave some instruction about order in the congregation—men among women & women among men. horses in the assembly Men & boys on the stand &c.

Willard Richards Diary

Babbitt. & Blodget[3] preached and Joseph kept order.

17 September 1843 (Sunday Afternoon).[1]
Levi Richards Diary

17 . . . PM heard the Rev Mr Blodget from Mass. Unitarian Preacher. good discourse of religious Liberty Text "What is Truth"[2] followed by Pres Smith disproving the idea that persecution causes a good work to prosper—continued his discours about 1 1/2 hours speaking of the practice of Medicine[3]—& of Medicine of Quacks & qualified Doctors—of the use of Med & of the abuse of Med.—also spoke decidedly agains Dr Brinks[4] practice—spoke in favor of Doc. Bernhisel[5]—declared that he (J Smith) never lost a patient where he had been the first & only one employed & challenged the congregation to bring instance—they brough none spoke of Lobelia when the patient was too weak to bear it—as being destructive & & said calomel would corrode the stomach when it was empty—said it was a poison—still said it was a med. & useful if used skilfully!!!!!!!!![6]

Joseph Smith Diary, by Willard Richards

P.M. Mr. Blodget the Unitarian Minister preached was gratified with his sermon in general—but differed in opinion on some points—on which I freely expressed myself to his great satisfaction on persecution making the work spread. by rooting up a flower garden or kicking back the sun.

24 September 1843 (Sunday Morning).[1]
Joseph Smith Diary, by Willard Richards

Joseph Preached about 1 hour. from 2d Chapter of Acts—designed to shew the folly of Common Stock[2] In Nauvoo every one Steward over their own.[3]—Amasa Lyman & Geo. J. Adams[4] continued the meeting after preaching Joseph called upon the brethren to draw Stone for the temple. and gave notice for a special conference on the 6th Oct. Meeting adjourned on account of prospect of rain at about 1. P.M.—

7 October 1843 (Saturday Morning).[1]
Times and Seasons 4 (15 September 1843):329-30

Saturday, 10 o'clock A. M.
Conference assembled and proceeded to business.
President Joseph Smith was called to the chair, and Gustavus Hills[2] chosen clerk.
Opened with singing by the choir, and prayer by elder Almon Babbitt.
The president stated the items of business to be brought before the Conference, to be,
1st. The case and standing of elder Sidney Rigdon, counsellor to the First Presidency.
2d. The further progress of the Temple; after which, any miscellaneous business.
Elder Sidney Rigdon addressed the conference on the subject of his situation and circumstances among the saints.
President Joseph Smith addressed the conference, inviting an expression of any charges or complaints which the Conference had to make. He stated his dissatisfaction with elder Sidney Rigdon as a counsellor, not having received any material benefit from his labors or counsels since their escape from Missouri. Several complaints were then brought forward in reference to his management in the Post Office; a supposed correspondence and connection with John C. Bennett, with Ex-Governor Carlin, and with the Missourians, of a treacherous character: also his leaguing with dishonest persons in endeavoring to defraud the innocent.

President Joseph Smith related to the Conference the detention of documents from J. Butterfield, Esq., which were designed for the benefit of himself, (President Smith,) but was not handed over for some three or four weeks, greatly to his disadvantage. Also, an indirect testimony from Missouri, through the mother of Orin P. Rockwell,[3] that said Rigdon and others had given information, by letter, of President Smiths' visit to Dixon, advising them to proceed to that place and arrest him there. He stated that in consequence of those, and other circumstances, and his unprofitableness to him as a counsellor, he did not wish to retain him in that station, unless those difficulties could be removed; but desired his salvation, and expressed his willingness that he should retain a place among the saints.

Elder Almon Babbitt suggested the propriety of limiting the complaints and proofs to circumstances that had transpired since the last Conference.

President Joseph Smith replied, and showed the legality and propriety of a thorough investigation, without such limitation.

Elder Sidney Rigdon plead, concerning the documents from J. Butterfield, Esq., that he received it in answer to some inquiries which he had transmitted to him—that he received it at a time when he was sick, and unable to examine it—did not know that it was designed for the perusal and benefit of President Joseph Smith—that he had, consequently, ordered it to be laid aside, where it remained until inquired for by Joseph Smith. He had never written to Missouri concerning the visit of Joseph Smith to Dixon, and knew of no other person having done so. That, concerning certain rumors of belligerent operations under Governor Carlin's administration, he had related them, not to alarm or disturb any one, but that he had the rumors from good authorities, and supposed them well founded. That he had never received but one communication from John C. Bennett, and that of a business character, except one addressed to him conjointly with Elder Orson Pratt, which he handed over to President Smith[4]—that he had never written any letters to John C. Bennett.

The weather becoming inclement, Conference adjourned until Sunday 10 o'clock A. M.

8 October 1843 (Sunday Morning).[1]
Times and Seasons 4 (15 September 1843):330

President Joseph Smith arose and satisfactorily explained to the congregation the supposed treacherous correspondence with Ex-Governor Carlin, which wholly removed suspicion from elder Sidney Rigdon, and from every other person. He expressed entire willingness to have elder Sidney Rigdon retain his station, provided he would magnify his office, and walk and conduct himself in all honesty, righteousness, and integrity; but signified his lack of confidence in his integrity and steadfastness, judging from their past intercourse.

9 October 1843 (Monday Morning).[1]
Times and Seasons 4 (15 September 1843):330-31

The business pertaining to the Temple was then announced by the President as next in order. . . .

President Joseph Smith presented and read to the Conference, a communication from Col. Frances M. Higbee,[2] whose conduct had been called in question, in connection with elder Sidney Rigdon, and expressed himself satisifed that Col. Frances M. Higbee was free, even of reproach or suspicion, in that matter.

Conference adjourned for one hour.

9 October 1843 (Monday Afternoon).[1]
Times and Seasons 4 (15 September 1843):331-32

Monday, 2 o'clock, P. M.

Conference reassembled, and listened with profound attention, to an impressive discourse from President Joseph Smith, commemorative of the decease of James Adams, Esq.,[2] late of this city, and an honorable, worthy, useful, and esteemed member of the Church of Jesus Christ of Latter Day Saints. He spoke of the importance of our understanding the reasons and causes of our exposure to the vicissitudes of life, and of death; and the designs and purposes of God, in our coming into the world, our sufferings here, and our departure hence—that it is but reasonable to suppose that God would reveal something in reference to the matter—the ignorance of the world in reference to their true condition, and relation. Reading the experience of others, or the revelations given to them, can never give us a comprehensive view of our condition and true relation to God. Knowledge of these things, can only be obtained by experience in these things, through the ordinance of God set forth for that purpose.[3] He remarked that the disappointment of hopes and expectations at the resurrection, would be indescribably dreadful. That the organization of the spiritual and heavenly worlds, and of spiritual and heavenly beings, was agreeably to the most perfect order and harmony—that their limits and bounds were fixed irrevocably, and voluntarily subscribed to by themselves—subscribed to upon the earth—hence the importance of embracing and subscribing to principles of eternal truth. He assured the saints that truth in reference to these matters, can, and may be known, through the revelations of God in the way of his ordinances, and in answer to prayer. The Hebrew church "came unto the spirits of just men made perfect, and unto an innumerable company of angels, unto God the Father of all, and to Jesus Christ the Mediator of the New Covenant;" but what they learned, has not been, and could not have been written.[4] What object was gained by this communication with the spirits of the just, &c.? It was the established order of the kingdom of God—the keys of power and knowledge were with them to communicate to the saints—hence the importance of understanding the distinction between the spirits of the just, and angels. Spirits can only be revealed in flaming fire, or glory. Angels have advanced farther—their light and glory being tabernacled, and hence appear in bodily shape.[5]

Concerning brother James Adams, he remarked, that it should appear strange that so good and so great a man was hated.[6] The deceased ought never to have had an enemy. But so it was, wherever light shone, it stirred up darkness. Truth and error, good and evil, cannot be reconciled. Judge Adams had been a most intimate friend. He had anointed him to the Patriarchal power—to receive the keys of knowledge, and power, by revelation to himself.[7] He had had revelations concerning his departure, and had gone to a more important work—of opening up a more effectual door for the dead. The spirits of the just are exalted to a greater and more glorious work—hence they are blessed in departing hence. Enveloped in flaming fire, they are not far from us, and know and understand our thoughts, feelings and motions, and are often pained therewith.

President Smith concluded with exhortations to the church to renew their exertions to forward the work of the Temple, and in walking before the Lord in soberness and righteousness.

Such is a faint outline of the discourse of President Joseph Smith, which was delivered with his usual feeling and pathos; and was listened to with the most profound and eager attention by the multitude, who hung upon his instructions, anxious to learn and pursue the path of eternal life.

Joseph Smith Diary, by Willard Richards

Conference Cutler[8] Cahoon[9] & Hiram[10] spoke on the temple. P. M. Joseph preached funeral Sermon of Gen James Adams—All men know that all men must die.—What is the object of our coming into existence then dying and falling away to be here no more? This is a subject we ought to study more than any other. which we ought to study day and night.—If we have any claim on our heavenly father for any thing it is for knowledge on this important subject—could we read and comprehend all that has been written from the days of Adam on the relations of man to God & angels. and the spirits of just men in a future state. we should know very little about it. Could you gaze in heaven 5 minutes you would know more than you possibly can know by read all that ever was written on the subject. We are one only capable of comprehending that certain things exist. which we may acquire by certain fixed principles—If men would acquired salvation they have got to be subject to certain rules & principles which were fixed by an unalterable decree before the world was, before they leave this world.[11] what did they learn by coming to the spirits of just men made perfect? is it written. No! The spirits of just men are made ministering servants to those who are sealed unto life eternal. & it is through them that the sealing power comes down— The spirit of Patriarch adam now is one of the spirits of the just men made—and if revealed now, must be revealed in fire. and the glory could not be endured—Jesus shewed himself to his disciples and they thought it was his spirit.[12] & they were afraid to approach his spirit. Angels have advanced higher in knowledge & power than spirits

Judge Adams had some enemies, but such a man ought not to have had an enemy. I saw him first at springfield,[13] when on my way from Mo. to Washington. he sought me out when a stranger. took me to his house. encouraged & cheered me & give me money— when men are prepared. they are better off to go home.—Bro Adams has gone to open up a more effectual door for the dead.—

Flesh and blood cannot go there but flesh and bones quickened by the Spirit of God can[14] If we would be sober, & watch in fasting and prayer, God would turn away sickness from our midst. Hasten the work of the temple. and all the work of the Last Days. Let the elders & saints do away light mindedness and be sober.—

James Burgess Notebook

A great many men suppose there is no difference between ~~a spirit~~ an angel and a spirit of a just man made perfect but Paul makes a distinction in the 12 chap of Hebrews he tells us that the hebrew church had come into the presence of God and Angels and to the spirits of just men made perfect The spirit of a just man made perfect if he made his appearance he would appear or be enveloped in flaming fire and no man in this mortal state could endure it, but an angel could come and appear as an other man for Paul says be careful to entertain ~~an~~ strangers for some have entertained Angels unawares.[15] But to prove spirits view the Saviour after his resurrection when he appeared unto his diciples. they were afraid and thought they had seen a spirit but he convinces them of their mistake by teling them to handle him for says he a spirit has not flesh and bones as ye see me have.[16]J Smith Prophet.

William Clayton Diary

P.M. at the conference Prest. J. preached Judge Adams funeral sermon. The people were well edified and a very good feeling prevailed throughout.

15 October 1843 (Sunday Morning). Temple Stand.[1]
Joseph Smith Diary, by Willard Richards

11 A. M. Cool. calm, cloudy. stand east end of the temple.

singing Prayer By P. P. Pratt. Joseph preached.

It is one of the first principles of my life & one that I have cultivated from my childhood, having been taught it of my father. to allow every one the liberty of conscience.

I am the greatest advocate of the C. of U. S. there is there on the earth. in my feeling the only fault I ~~can~~ find with it is it is not broad enough to cover the whole ground.

I cannot believe in any of the creeds of the different denominations, because they all have some things in them I cannot subscribe to though all of them have some thruth. but I want to come up into the presence of God & learn all things but the creeds set up stakes, & say hitherto shalt thou come, & no further.—which I cannot subscribe to.

I believe the bible, as it ought to be, as it came from the pen of the original writers. as it read it repented the Lord that he had made man.[2] and also God is not a man that he should repent.[3]—which I do not believe.—but it repented Noah that God made man.—this I believe. & then the other quotation stands fair.—if any man will prove to me by one passage of Holy writ, one item I believe, to be false. I will renounce it disclaim it far as I have promulg[at]ed it.—

The first principles of the gospel as I believe. first Faith. Repentance. Baptism for the remission of sins, with the promise of the Holy Ghost.

Heb 6th. contradictions "Leaving the principle of the doctrine of crist. if a man leave the principles of the doctrine of C. how can he be saved in the principles?[4] a contradiction. I dont believe it. I will render it therefore <u>not</u> leaving the P. of the doctrin of crist.[5] &c. Resurrection of the dead & eternal judgment.[6]

one thing to see the kingdom.[7] & another to be in it.[8] Must have a change of heart to see the kingdom of God. & subscribe the articles of adoption to enter therein.

no man can ~~not~~ receive the Holy Ghost without receiving revelations, The H. G. is a revelator.

I prophecy in the name of the Lord God anguish & wrath & [indecipherable] & tribulation and the withdrawing of the spirit of God await this generation. until they are visited with utter destruction. this generation is as corrupt as the generation of the Jews that crucified Christ. and if he were here today & should preach the same doctrine he did then why they would crucify him. I defy all the world & I prophecy they never will overthrow me till I get ready[9]

on the economy of this city.—I think there is to many merchants among you more wool and raw materials & the money be brought here to pay the poor for manufacturing—set our women to work & stop this spinning street yarn and talking about spiritual wives.[10]—Send out your money in the country, get grain, cattle flax.—&c

I proclaim in the name of the Lord God that I will have nothing but virtue & integripity & uprightness.—

We cannot build up a city on merchandize. I would not run after the merchants, I would sow a little flax if I had but a garden and.— lot.

the temporal economy of this people should be to establish manufactoring and not to take usury for ~~his~~ money I do not want to bind the poor here and starve. go out in the county and get food. & in cities. and gird up your loins. & be sober.

when you get food return if you have a mind to.—

some say It is better, say some to give [to] the poor than build the temple.—the building of the temple has kept the poor who were driven from Missouri from starving. as has been the best means for this object which could be devised

all ye rich men of the Latter Day Saints.—from abroad I would invite to bring up some of their money and give to the temple. we want Iron steel powder.—&c—a good plan to get up a forge[?]. bring in raw materials, & manu[f]acting establishments of all kinds.—& surround the rapids—

I never stole the value of a pinhead or a picayune in my life. & when you are hungry and steal, come to me & I will feed you.—

the secrets of masonry is to keep a secret. it is good economy to entertain stranger, to entertain sectarians. come up ye sectarian priests. of the everlasting gospel, as they call it & they shall have my pulpit all day.

wo to ye rich men. give to the poor. & then come and ask me for bread, away with all your meanness & be liberal we need purging, purifying & cleansing you have little faith in your Elders get some little simple remedy in the first stages—if you send for a Dr at all send in the first stages

all ye Drs.—who are fools not well read do not understand the human constitution. stop your practice.—

Lawyers who have no business only as you hatch up. would to God you would go to work or run away.[11]

1/4 past past 2. closed—

Willard Richards Diary

Meeting 1/2 Joseph P[reached]. 3 1/4 economy of Nauvoo.

12 November 1843 (Sunday). At Temple.[1]
William Rowley Diary[2]

As a matter of course we felt a desire to behold the Prophet Joseph—on the following day (Sunday) we proceeded to the Temple (then in an unfinished state) to hear him preach we were gratified in seeing & hearing him on that occasion & we soon felt & knew we were listening to one that had not been taught of men—So different were all his thoughts & language.

29 November 1843 (Wednesday Afternoon). Upper Room, Red Brick Store.[1]
Manuscript History of the Church

Joseph Smith, the Mayor, made some remarks, and his Appeal to the Green Mount Boys[2] was read by William W. Phelps.[3]

... P. P. Pratt offered to deliver the president's appeal to the "Green Mountain Boys" to all the large towns in New York if he could have a copy. The President offered a copy, and it was voted that Elder Pratt shall have the mission granted him, and voted in addition that he go to all the towns in Vermont. . . .

The Mayor spoke; said he rose to make a confession, that he used all his influence to prevent the brethren from fighting when mobbed in Missouri. If I did wrong I will not do so any more. It was a suggestion of the head, he would never do so again, but when the Mobs came upon you, kill them; I never will restrain you again but will go and help you. . . .

Mayor spoke again if I do not stand with those who will stand by me in the hour of trouble and danger, without faltering I give you leave to shoot me.

Mayor read a letter in reply to one he wrote to Henry Clay[4] . . . .
Motioned by Joseph Smith that every man in the meeting who could wield a pen write an address to his mother country—carried

Mayor read the Memorial to Congress[5]—The State rights doctrine are what feed mobs,—they are a dead carcass, a stink and they shall ascend up as a stink offering in the nose of the Almighty.

They shall be oppressed as they have oppressed us, not by Mormons but by others in power, they shall drink a drink offering, the bitterest dregs not from the Mormons but from a meaner source than themselves. God shall curse them.

Adjourned till next Monday evening early candle light.

Joseph Smith Diary, by Willard Richards

4 P.M. A meeting of citizens at the assembly room to appoint a committee to get subscribers to the memorial &c Joseph present.

4 December 1843 (Monday). Upper Room, Red Brick Store.[1]
Joseph Smith Diary, by Willard Richards

I spoke 2 1/2 hours on Missouri persecution. the government in gen. men & measures &c. to a crowded & select congregation Many could not get admission 2 Missourians present.

Nauvoo Neighbor 1 (6 December 1843)

A public meeting was called on Monday evening for the purpose of reading a memorial to congress, for the purpose of seeking redress for grievances sustained in the State of Missouri. . . .

At an early hour the house was crowded to overflowing, and great numbers had to go away for want of room.

As soon as the meeting was opened, they called for the reading of General Smith's "Appeal to the Green Mountain Boys;"[2] which was read by W. W. Phelps after which P. P. Pratt read an address to the "Empire State" of New York, and Dr. Richards[3] was called upon to read the memorial before alluded to.

General Smith then arose, and in his happy eloquent, masterly manner, delivered one of the most powerful interesting addresses that we ever heard; he spoke for two hours and a half, and was listened to with breathless silence by all present. To attempt to give even a faint outline would be superflous, suffice it to say that all were gratified, instructed and riveted to the spot. Two gentlemen from Missouri were present on the occasion and we think that if they possessed the least spark of intelligence, the vivid, glowing color, in which the inhuman deeds of Missouri, was painted, must have made them feel that they were living on a polluted soil, and associated with a degraded bloody herd.

His address to the Green Mountain Boys is a masterly piece, and will be read (as it was listened to) with great interest; we shall probably publish it hereafter.

9 December 1843 (Saturday).[1] Corner of Main and Water Streets.
Wilford Woodruff Journal

Their was a meeting of the Citizens in general & the ordinance passed yesterday[2] was read before the multitude & speaches made by several persons the last of which was President Joseph Smith who gave an interesting address to the assembly spoke of our persecution, the manner that our rights & liberties had been trampled upon & that it was time it was stopped, they all sanctioned the speach of the general & were dismissed in good order & returnd to their homes.

Nauvoo Neighbor 1 (20 December 1843)

[After remarks by John Taylor] General Joseph Smith briefly addressed the meeting; he dissented entirely from the opinion of the Attorney General[3], and observed that it was stated in the charter that the Legion was a part of the militia of Illinois, and that his commission declared that he (General Smith) was the Lieutenant General of the Nauvoo Legion, and if the militia of the State of Illinois, and as such, it was not only his duty to enforce the city ordinances, but the laws of the State when called on by the Governor. He also stated that he had been informed that the Chief Magistrate of Missouri had it in contemplation to make another requisition on the Governor of Illinois for him, Joseph Smith.

18 December 1843 (Monday). Upper Room, Red Brick Store.[1]
Wilford Woodruff Journal

President Smith made an eloquent speech upon the subject manifested mercy towards his enemies when they were in his power but he lifted up his hands towards heaven & declaired that if Missouri Came against us any more he would fight them & defend his rights.

1843 Notes

17 January 1843

1. A meeting held at the Prophet's home is mentioned in *History of the Church*, 5:252, but there is no indication that he spoke to the assembly. Not in *Teachings*. Although the entry in *History of the Church* appears to be based on Wilford Woodruff's Journal, the brief text of the Prophet's sermon is here published for the first time.

2. Woodruff has reference to the Prophet's being discharged by District Court Judge Nathaniel Pope in an extradition case on 5 January 1843 at Springfield, Illinois, wherein the State of Missouri had demanded Joseph Smith on charges of being an accessory to an attempted murder (see 29 August 1842, note 3).

3. It was the contention of Alexander Campbell, one of the principal figures of the Disciples of Christ movement, which started in the late 1820s, that the "Kingdom of God" was not set up on the earth until the day of Pentecost. Hence Joseph Smith's publication of the Book of Mormon and passages from the Book of Moses in the early 1830s regarding the antiquity of gospel ordinances such as baptism led Campbell to denounce Joseph Smith as an imposter. Some of Campbell's previous followers still held to their former notions on this concept even after they had joined the Church. Apparently disagreement over this idea had continued to persist since the time when the Church was centered in Kirtland (1831-37), where many of the Disciples joined the Church.

22 January 1843

1. See *History of the Church*, 5:256-59, and *Teachings*, pp. 271-75. The original source for the reports of this discourse in *History of the Church* and *Teachings* is an amalgamation of the Joseph Smith Diary, by Willard Richards, the William Clayton Diary, and the Wilford Woodruff Journal—the two first-named sources forming the introduction of the sermon and the latter the text. The Franklin D. Richards account is here published for the first time. It was included in the Manuscript History of the Church, (compiled in Nauvoo), but was later replaced by the Woodruff report.

2. Mark 1:4.

3. These were the crimes charged against the Prophet and other members of the Church by the State of Missouri in 1838. Although Joseph Smith escaped from Missouri law-enforcement officers in April 1839, these charges were formally dropped in August 1840. See Boone County Circuit Court Records, August 1840 Term, Columbia, Missouri.

4. Luke 1:5-17; Exodus 40:15 (1-16).

5. Hebrews 5:4.

6. Luke 1:13-15.

7. Matthew 3:1-2.

8. Matthew 3:5-8; Luke 3:7-8.

9. Matthew 3:5-6.

10. Matthew 3:13-17.

11. Luke 3:16.

12. Matthew 3:15; 16:18 (13-20).

13. The full keys for inquiring of the Lord by the sealing power of Elijah (Helaman 10:5-7 [4-10]), which the Prophet received in the Kirtland Temple (D&C 110:13-16), had not as yet been conferred on anyone else (see 27 August 1843 discourse); however, here he is teaching that revelation is the rock of the Church (see D&C 128:10-11), that he saw the conferral of these keys as essential to the completion of his mission (see 5 October 1840, note 19).

14. John 3:5.

15. D&C 1:38.

16. John 3:5.

17. Luke 24:49; Acts 1:4-5.

18. Luke 24:49 (46-49); Acts 1:4-5.

19. See 20 March 1842, note 13.

20. Compare text of discourse dated 28 April 1842, at note 11.

21. 1 Peter 1:24.

22. Isaiah 52:8. See also D&C 84:98.

23. William Clayton 1842-1846 Diaries. Citations from these diaries are used by permission and were provided by Dr. James B. Allen, professor of history at Brigham Young University, Provo, Utah. In sharing with us these quotations, Dr. Allen has substantially assisted this work. (Hereafter cited as William Clayton Diary.)

24. Lyceum meetings apparently were fairly common in Nauvoo—a sort of "school of the Elders" for the Nauvoo era of Church history.

25. Mark 1:4.

26. See 5 January 1841, note 10.

27. Matthew 18:18-20; D&C 90:2-5; 128:10-11. See 5 October 1840, note 19.

28. Franklin D. Richards (1821-99) was baptized in 1838, served several missions for the Church during the Nauvoo period, and was ordained an apostle in 1849. Richards's "Scriptural Items" Notebook is located in the Church Archives.

29 January 1843

1. See *History of the Church*, 5:260-62, and *Teachings*, pp. 275-78. The original source for this discourse as published in the *History of the Church*, and *Teachings* appears to be an amalgamation of the Joseph Smith Diary, by Willard Richards, and the report in *Times and Seasons* (15 May 1843). It is possible that Willard Richards was in fact the author of the *Times and Seasons* account. The reports kept by Franklin D. Richards (except for the words enclosed in braces), William Clayton, and Willard Richards (personal diary) are here published for the first time.

2. Luke 15:11-32.

3. Luke 7:28.

4. Malachi 3:1; Luke 7:27.

5. Matthew 3:13-17.

6. Six months before this discourse Joseph Smith published his book of Abraham. Facsimile 2, figure 7, of the book of Abraham speaks of the Holy Ghost being attended by the "sign of the dove." Though this wording used in the book of Abraham is consistent with the Prophet's discussion of the subject in this discourse, it is unlike the wording used in Matthew 3:16; Mark 1:10; Luke 3:22; John 1:32; 1 Nephi 11:27; 2 Nephi 31:8; and D&C 93:15.

7. Regarding the idea that the Holy Ghost is a personage, see 16 February 1841, note 2.

8. That is, the Holy Bible.

9. Luke 7:28.

10. Luke 16:16.

11. Although he spoke on this subject the previous week, the Prophet did not use the passage cited in note 10 to confirm this idea.

12. Luke 15:1-2.

13. Luke 15:3-7.

14. Luke 15:8-10.

15. Luke 15:7, 10.

16. Luke 15:11-32.

17. John 8:58 (33-59); 3 Nephi 15:5.

18. See note 6, this discourse. The words placed within braces were integrated into the published account of this discourse in the *History of the Church*.

19. Luke 15:11-32.

20. Luke 7:28.

21. Malachi 3:1; Luke 7:27.

22. Matthew 3:13-17.

23. See note 6, this discourse.

24. Exodus 40:15 (1-16); Hebrews 5:4; Luke 1:13-15; Matthew 3:1-12.

25. Luke 15:2, 11-32.

16 February 1843

1. See *History of the Church*, 5:278. Not in *Teachings*. The original source for the *History of the Church* entry is the Joseph Smith Diary, by Willard Richards.

21 February 1843

1. See *History of the Church*, 5:283-87. Not in *Teachings*. The original source for the *History of the Church* account is the Joseph Smith Diary. Wilford Woodruff's report is here published for the first time.

2. Peter Haws (1796-1862). Converted to the Church in Canada, Haws was a member of the Nauvoo House Association.

3. Lucien Woodworth (1799-1867). A native of Orange County, Vermont, he was the architect for the Nauvoo House. Woodworth apparently joined the Church in Nauvoo. The text of Woodworth's speech (enclosed in braces) is included here to provide context for the Prophet's comments.

4. This concludes Lucien Woodworth's speech.

5. Dr. Charles Foster. In 1844 Foster would become a bitter enemy of the Prophet and side with Mormon dissenters seeking to take his life.

6. Hiram S. Kimball (1806-63) was a resident and a land owner at

Nauvoo before the arrival of the Saints. Baptized in 1843, he moved to Utah in 1850.

7. Daniel H. Wells (1814-91) was a resident and landowner at Nauvoo before the arrival of the Saints. Prominent in public affairs, Wells endeared himself to the Mormons and was baptized after the Prophet's death, in August 1846.

8. Based on D&C 124, the completion of the Nauvoo House was recognized as being a divine injunction upon the Saints.

9. *Pisgah* is a Hebrew word meaning a ridge crowning a hill or mountain and which from below or from a distance presents a broken outline. See Numbers 23:14; Deuteronomy 3:27.

10. Psalm 32:1; James 5:20; 1 Peter 4:8; and, Song of Solomon 6:10.

11. John C. Bennett, after he was excommunicated from the Church in mid-1842, published his *History of the Saints*. In it he asserted that there was a French Free Masonic-type cloister of females that, at the asking, the male priesthood of Nauvoo could enjoy. These lurid stories about the purpose of the Relief Society never made the book the bestseller the publishers expected it to be.

12. That is, paper money.

13. The "mammoth bones" apparently referred to numerous buildings then under construction in the upper part of Nauvoo.

14. John Snider.

15. Lucien Woodworth was sometimes called the "pagan prophet."

16. Because the words of Charles Foster provide an essential context for the Prophet's remarks, those words are included, within the braces.

17. John S. Fullmer (1807-83) was a native of Huntington, Luzerne County, Pennsylvania. After his conversion to the Church, Fullmer moved to Nauvoo, where he became intimately associated with Joseph Smith and did some clerical work for the Prophet. After Joseph's death, Fullmer was one of a committee appointed to dispose of the properties of the Saints in Nauvoo.

18. William H. Robinson later became a bitter opponent of Joseph Smith and in the spring of 1844 joined with Mormon apostates seeking to destroy the Prophet's credibility.

19. Ezekiel 37:7, 10 (1-10).

12 March 1843

1. See *History of the Church*, 5:302. Not in *Teachings*. The original source for the *History of the Church* entry is the Joseph Smith Diary. The Brigham Young account is here published for the first time.

2. The Brigham Young Diary is located in the Church Archives.

2 April 1843 (1)

1. See *History of the Church*, 5:323-25. Not in *Teachings*. The William Clayton Diary (as structured and amplified in the Joseph Smith Diary) is the source for all the published versions of these instructions. William Clayton did not segregate the morning and evening instructions as clearly as it is done in the Joseph Smith Diary. We did not break up William Clayton's account into separate entries, because to do so would alter the integrity of the text. Moreover, it is likely that Joseph Smith gave the same instructions in the afternoon and evening. Since Willard Richards was not on this trip to Ramus, undoubtedly either the Prophet or William Clayton had to direct Willard in separating the diary entry into different times of the day. That William Clayton was the original scribe is confirmed by Benjamin F. Johnson in a letter to Anthon H. Lund dated 12 May 1903: "On April 2d and May 16th 1843 the Prophet was at my house with Wm Clayton as *scribe* at which time was written in answer to questions asked all of sections 130 to 131 Doc & Cov" (Johnson to Lund, under date given, Church Archives).

2. William Clayton's Diary is the source for D&C 130:14-17. Compare note 21, this discourse.

3. William Clayton's Diary, as amended in the Joseph Smith Diary, by Willard Richards, is the source for D&C 130:1-2. The combination of both diaries serves as the source for D&C 130:3.

4. William Clayton's Diary is the source for D&C 130:4-11.

5. William Clayton's Diary as amended by the Joseph Smith Diary, is the source for D&C 130:18-19.

6. William Clayton's Diary is the source for D&C 130:20-21. Cf. 5 January 1841, note 10.

7. See note 5 of the 2 April 1843 (2) discourse.

8. On the evening of 9 March 1843 the Prophet had the above dream. It is recorded in Joseph Smith's Diary under the date 11 March 1843. Apparently Clayton recorded it in his diary the morning after the dream, that is, on 10 March 1843.

9. This dream of Joseph Smith and the interpretation by Orson Hyde are here published for the first time. See 5 October 1843, note 8.

10. William Clayton's Diary, as amended by the Joseph Smith Diary, is the source for D&C 130:12-13. Note that the date 25 December 1832 is given in the Joseph Smith Diary but is not given in the Clayton Diary (cf. D&C 87).

11. Revelation 7:4 (1-17); 14:1-5.

12. JST Revelation 5:6 changes the number of eyes to twelve. The number twelve is said to represent "the twelve servants of God, sent forth into all the earth."

13. Sophronia Smith Stoddard McLeary (1803-76) was Joseph Smith's sister.

14. 1 John 3:2. This is the source used for D&C 130:1-2.

15. Revelation 4:6; 15:2. See also D&C 77:1. The William Clayton and Joseph Smith Diaries are the sources for D&C 130:3-7.

16. See note 4, this discourse.

17. That is, the entry for 11 March 1843 in the Prophet's Diary. See note 8, this discourse.

18. Joseph Smith was at this time lieutenant general of the Nauvoo Legion.

19. See 5 October 1843, note 8.

20. The Joseph Smith Diary is the source used for D&C 130:12-13. See note 10, this discourse.

21. The original source for this entry, the William Clayton Diary, is more complete for this statement and is the source for D&C 130:14-15.

2 April 1843 (2)

1. See *History of the Church*, 5:325-26. Not in *Teachings*. See 2 April 1843 (1), note 1.

2. Revelation 4:6.

3. See the William Clayton Diary text of the 2 April 1843 (2) discourse, material after note 11.

4. This is the source used for D&C 130:18-19.

5. Neither the William Clayton Diary, the Joseph Smith Diary here quoted, nor the *draft* Manuscript History of the Church entry for this date, implies the phrasing of D&C 130:22: "Were it not so [that the Holy Ghost is a spirit], the Holy Ghost could not dwell in us." Originally the wording in the

Manuscript History of the Church entry for this date was the same as in the original draft, but in the 1850s the Church historians reworded it to read the way it appears in the Doctrine and Covenants. Other than this alteration, the Joseph Smith Diary is the source for D&C 130:22-23.

6. Matthew 25:21. See note 9, this discourse.

7. Matthew 25:14-30. See note 9, this discourse.

8. John 3:5. See note 9, this discourse.

9. The Prophet would not explain to the congregation at large the meaning of the passages of scripture he quoted, but they did have particular meaning to one listener, Benjamin F. Johnson.

> On the 1st day of April *A.D.* 1843, [Benjamin testified,] President Joseph Smith, Orson Hyde, and William Clayton and others came from Nauvoo to my residence in Macedonia or Ramus in Hancock Co. Illinois, and we[re] joyfully welcomed by myself and family as our guests.
>
> On the following morning, Sunday April, 2nd, President Smith took me by the arm for a walk, leading the way to a secluded spot within the adjacent grove, where to my great surprise, he commenced to offer to me the principle of plural or celestial marriage, but I was more astonished by his asking me for my sister Almera to be his wife.
>
> I sincerely believed him to be a prophet of God, and I loved him as such, and also for the many evidences of his kindness to me, yet such was the force of my education, and the scorn that I felt unvirtuous that under the first impulse of my feelings I looked him calmly, but firmly in the face and told him that, "I had always believed (you) to be a good man, and wished to believe it still, and would try to;" and that, "I would take for him a message to my sister, and if the doctrine was true, all would be well, but if I should afterwards learn that it was offered to insult or prostitute my sister I would take his life." With a smile he replied "Benjamin, you will never see that day, but you shall live to *know* that it is true, and rejoice in it. . . .
>
> He also told me that he would preach a sermon that day for me, which I would understand, while the rest of the congregation would not comprehend his meaning. His subject was the ten talents spoken of by the Savior, "unto him that hath shall be given, and he shall have abundantly, but from that hath not (or will not receive) shall be taken away that which he hath, (or might have had.)" Plainly giving me to understand that the talents represented wives and children as the principle of enlargement throughout the great future, to those who were heirs of Salvation (Joseph F. Smith, "40 Affidavits on Celestial Marriage," book 2, pp. 3-5, Church Archives).

The first two passages of scripture quoted by the Prophet fit into the background Benjamin Johnson gives, but the last does not so readily. Later, in a discourse given 16 July 1843, the Prophet made plainer his reason for quoting John 3:6. Joseph Smith said, "[That] the earthly is the image of the

Heavenly shows that [it] is by the multiplication of Lives that the eternal worlds are created and occuped [for] that which is born of flesh is flesh that which is born of spirit is spirit" (Franklin D. Richards account of 16 July 1843 (2) discourse). Joseph had previously taught that resurrected beings will have "spirit in their [veins] & not blood" (Wilford Woodruff account of 20 March 1842 discourse). The implication is that if your body is not resurrected, your children will be born flesh and bones, but that if your body is resurrected and has spirit in its veins your children will be spirits.

6 April 1843 (1)

1. See *History of the Church*, 5:327-32. Not in *Teachings*. The original source for the entry in *History of the Church* is the *Times and Seasons* account. The close similarity between the *Times and Seasons* report and the Joseph Smith Diary, by Willard Richards, suggests a common source. Because William Clayton's account affirms that he was appointed to take minutes at the conference, it is possible that, his minutes (no longer available) constituted that source. The Prophet made the following remarks at the April 1843 General Conference of the Church.

The *Times and Seasons* (1 April 1843) gave the following description of the conference:

> We have had a very interesting conference, perhaps as much so as any that we have had since our settlement in Nauvoo.
>
> The weather that had been so severe for such a length of time lost its violence; and we were favored all the time with beautiful warm weather, which to us proved very propitious, in consequence of our having to hold our conference in the open air.
>
> The foundation of the Temple was crowded to excess, with thousands of saints, whose faces beamed with gladness as they listened to the Prophet, and others who officiated at the conference. The walls were also covered and the ground outside, for some distance around the Temple. There never was a time perhaps when there was more order, and the most perfect harmony and unity prevailed.

2. Zarahemla Hill was located opposite Nauvoo, on the Iowa side of the Mississippi River. Zarahemla, Lee County, Iowa Territory, was a Mormon settlement.

3. Matters of Church fellowship that were being appealed could go from the branches to a conference of branches and finally to the Nauvoo High Council or the Church's general conference.

4. See D&C 124:56-61.

5. Daniel Russell, born 28 January 1799, was a native of Springfield, Otsego County, New York. His brother, Samuel Russell (also mentioned in the text), was born 25 September 1812 in Erie County, New York.

6. See D&C 107:22.

7. Martin Van Buren (1782-1862) was the eighth president of the U. S. (1837-41).

8. To better appreciate the Prophet's hyperbole, it is essential to understand that it was only after Joseph Smith's famous visit to President Van Buren that Thomas Carlin would say as much as President Van Buren said: "Your cause is just, but I can do nothing for you."

9. William Clayton was serving as temple recorder at the time.

10. Reynolds Cahoon (1790-1861). Baptized in 1830, Cahoon occupied many important positions in the Church and was one of the Prophet's intimate friends.

11. Elias Higbee.

12. Deuteronomy 25:4; 1 Corinthians 9:9; 1 Timothy 5:18.

13. Alpheus Cutler (1784-1864). Converted to the Church in 1833, Cutler was appointed a member of the Nauvoo Temple Committee in 1840.

14. See note 3, this discourse.

6 April 1843 (2)

1. See *History of the Church*, 5:333-37. A small extract is in *Teachings*, pp. 286-87. The original source for the entries in *History of the Church* and *Teachings* is the Joseph Smith Diary. The reports by James Burgess and Franklin D. Richards are here published for the first time. The following remarks were made by the Prophet at the April 1843 General Conference of the Church. James Burgess did not date this discourse, and though he did not arrive in Nauvoo until 13 April 1843 one week after this discourse, his account parallels the Joseph Smith Diary entry so well we have chosen to assign it this date. Although sharing reports of the Prophet's discourses was a common practice in Nauvoo, James Burgess may not have obtained his notes from someone else, therefore this dating of his report of this discourse should be considered very tentative.

2. The letter referred to is included in the *Times and Seasons* report of this discourse.

3. A branch of the Church was located at Keokuk, Lee County, Iowa Territory, and Church members remained there during the entire Nauvoo period. During the heat of the 1842 Missouri extradition attempt, Joseph Smith considered the possibility of strengthening Keokuk as a Mormon settlement. On 15 September 1842 the Prophet counseled his uncle, John Smith, and others to move to Keokuk, and on 19 September 1842 he directed

John Taylor to take a printing press to that city and issue a paper (see *History of the Church*, 5:164-65). These plans did not materialize, but interest in Keokuk and Lee County, Iowa, would continue. In 1843, after Joseph Smith had been acquitted by the Illinois District Court for any wrongdoing in the murder attempt on ex-Governor Boggs, Governor John Chambers of Iowa Territory continued to encourage the Prophet's arrest (if perchance he should enter Iowa). In the text, the Prophet is suggesting that the Saints all come out of Keokuk and Lee County, Iowa Territory, and settle in Illinois. Such an action, or the threat of such an action to Lee County's economy was intended to put pressure on the Iowa Governor to rescind the arrest warrant.

4. John Chambers (1780-1852) was a Whig congressman. He served as territorial governor of Iowa 1841-45.

5. Lilburn W. Boggs, ex-Governor of Missouri.

6. Justin Butterfield (1790-1855). A prominent lawyer from Chicago, Butterfield was appointed United States District Attorney in 1841. He defended Joseph Smith in January 1843 in an extradition case wherein Missouri had demanded the Prophet on charges that he had been an accessory to attempted murder.

7. Joseph G. Remick.

8. Isaac Galland (1791-1858). A land speculator, Galland joined the Church in 1839 after selling thousands of acres of land to the Saints. He served a mission to Pennsylvania and New Jersey 1841-42 but withdrew from the Church by 1843.

9. The Half-Breed Tract, also called the Sac and Fox Indian Reservation, was a 119,000-acre parcel of land lying between the Des Moines and Mississippi rivers in the southeast corner of Iowa.

10. In 1834 Congress passed an act that relinquished the federal government's revisionary interest in the Half-Breed Tract and gave the half-breed Sac and Fox Indians the lands in fee simple. Since Congress failed to specify who the individual owners were, as many as 160 parties came forward to claim the land. In 1838, to remedy this problem, the Wisconsin Legislature required all claimants to file claims with the District Court of Lee County within one year, showing how title was obtained. In the meantime the Territory of Iowa was created, and the first session of the territorial legislature repealed the Wisconsin Act. This action complicated the problem, and suits were filed in the territorial courts, resulting in the sale of the entire tract of land to Hugh T. Reid. Reid, who received a deed executed by the sheriff of Lee County, subsequently sold several small tracts, but his title became involved in litigation. This matter came before the second session of the territorial legislature, but nothing concrete occurred until 1841, when *Spaulding v. Antaya* (U. S. District Court of Iowa Territory) requested partition of the entire tract. A decree of partition was issued, and

commissioners were appointed to divide the 119,000 acres into 101 tracts of equal value. This was done and confirmed by the courts in October 1841.

The Prophet and Church members had a vested interest in the Half-Breed Tract, because in 1839 Church land agents had purchased nearly 20,000 acres (or 17 percent) of the tract from Isaac Galland.

11. Moses Martin (1812-93) was a native of new Lisbon, Grafton County, New Hampshire. Ordained a seventy in 1835, he served several missions for the Church. Martin was subsequently reinstated.

12. Nashville, located three miles below Montrose, Iowa, was founded by Isaac Galland in 1829. A revelation, received in March 1841 (D&C 125), directed members of the Church to settle there.

13. Cf. D&C 130:12-17.

14. The Saints felt it a great advantage to have a prophet. For Joseph Smith's negative prophecy that Christ would *not* come before 1890 was an effective counterpoint to the fanaticism of an equally zealous and very popular millennarian movement led by William Miller. Although the Saints thought that Miller had predicted that the Second Coming would occur on 3 April 1843, just three days before this discourse was delivered (*History of the Church*, 5:326), actually Miller had predicted it could be as much as a year and a half later. Nevertheless, this was still not long enough time, for according to the Lord's voice to Joseph Smith the Second Coming would not be before 1890.

15. Joseph Smith would have been 85 years old on 23 December 1890.

16. See 9 March 1841, note 10.

17. Given "1000 years" equals "a day of the Lord," then "41 yrs 8 months" equals "one hour." ("The *hour* of his judgment is come": Revelation 14:7.)

18. Given the information of note 17, then the start of the "hour of judgment" the "41 yrs 8 months" subtracted from 1890 [1848] was still nearly "6 years" from the time of this discourse.

19. Hosea 6:2.

20. Gaylor. Identification of this man cannot be made.

21. Matthew 24:27-30.

22. 1 Thessalonians 5:2.

23. Amos 3:7.

24. Isaiah 2:2-5; 4:3; 52; Joel 2:32; Zechariah 12:6; 14:2; Acts 1:6-8; 3 Nephi 20:29-46; Ether 13:5, 11; D&C 113:7-9.

25. Isaiah 11:10-16; Ezekiel 37:21-28.

26. Ezekiel 37:26-28; 40-48.

27. Ezekiel 47.

28. Matthew 24:6.

29. Joel 2:31. See also Matthew 24:29 and Joseph Smith-History 1:41.

30. Luke 21:25; D&C 61:4-6, 14-19; 88:90.

31. Matthew 24:27, 29.

32. James Burgess (1818-1904) was converted to the Church in England in 1840 and arrived in Nauvoo 13 April 1843. See note 1, this discourse, for possible dating problem.

33. Matthew 24:36-51; D&C 49:7.

34. Amos 3:7.

35. See text of this discourse for which note 23 applies (the account in the Joseph Smith Diary, by Willard Richards).

36. 1 Thessalonians 5:1-8.

37. Matthew 24:27, 29.

38. 1 Thessalonians 5:1-8.

7 April 1843 (1)

1. See *History of the Church*, 5:337, and *Teachings*, p. 287. The original source for the *History of the Church* and *Teachings* entries is the Joseph Smith Diary. The following remarks were made at the April 1843 General Conference of the Church.

7 April 1843 (2)

1. See *History of the Church*, 5:339. Not in *Teachings*. The original source for the *History of the Church* entry is the Joseph Smith Diary. Franklin D. Richards's report is here published for the first time. The following remarks were made at the April 1843 General Conference of the Church.

2. On 8 October 1875 Brigham Young gave a discourse on the resurrection that taught the same point as the Prophet is here teaching. No doubt Brigham Young based his discourse on this teaching of the Prophet. See Ben E. Rich, *Scrapbook of Mormon Literature* 2 vols. (Chicago: Henry C. Etten & Co., Press, n.d.) 2:40-51. Brigham Young and others often alluded to this concept of the resurrection. See for example *Journal of Discourses* 13:76.

8 April 1843

1. See *History of the Church*, 5:339-45, and *Teachings*, pp. 287-94. The accounts in *History of the Church* and *Teachings* are an amalgamation of reports taken by William Clayton and Willard Richards (Joseph Smith Diary). Franklin D. Richards's report is here published for the first time. The following discourse was delivered at the April 1843 General Conference of the Church.

2. Revelation 5:8.

3. 3 Nephi 11:28-30 (21-41).

4. Matthew 8:12; 13:42, 50; 22:13; 24:51; 25:30; Luke 13:28; Alma 40:13; D&C 19:5; 85:9; 101:91; 133:73; Moses 1:22; Joseph Smith-Matthew 1:54.

5. Abraham 3:15-19.

6. Pelatiah Brown was associated with the Church in Kirtland, and appointed to serve a mission in Palmyra, New York on 7 April 1844.

7. Daniel 7:17 for example.

8. Daniel 7:16.

9. That is, the book of Revelation was a vision of future events without reference to past history, except as "clearly set forth," as for example in Revelation 12 (see JST Revelation 12:1-17).

10. The terms "image(s) of beast(s)" and "figure(s) of beast(s)" are not used by any Old Testament prophet in the King James Version or the Inspired Version. Therefore, Joseph Smith's observations might be part of his incomplete translation of the Bible.

11. In the version of this discourse recorded by Willard Richards, this thought is expressed in the following manner: "The prophets always had interpretations of their visions &c God always holds himself responsible to give revelations of his visions & if he does it not, we are not responsible."

12. Meaning any garden-variety, plain, homely minister.

13. 1 Corinthians 2:9-14.

14. Mark 1:15.

15. Revelation 12:3, 7, 13, 16, 17; 13:2, 4, 11; 16:13; 20:2.

16. Revelation 13:3.

17. Revelation 5:8.

18. Pelatiah Brown.

19. Daniel 7:3-8, 12, 16-28; 8:3-27.

20. Ibid.

21. Revelation 13:3.

22. Revelation 13:4.

23. That is, what he had said on 2 April 1843, just six days before.

24. The *History of the Church* version of this discourse mentions Charles Thompson as the one who opposed the Prophet's teachings on Daniel's prophecies. See *History of the Church*, 5:345.

25. See note 19, this discourse.

26. While this entry from the diary of William Clayton is dated 7 April 1843, the Prophet did not speak on the book of Revelation until 8 April 1843.

9 April 1843

1. See *History of the Church*, 5:346. Not in *Teachings*. The brief remarks in the text were made at the final day of the April 1843 General Conference of the Church.

2. Joshua Grant, Jr., a native of Naples, Ontario County, New York, was born 24 July 1818. With his brother, Jedediah M. Grant, Joshua served a three-year mission to North Carolina and Virginia where the pair baptized two hundred converts. A report of Grant's discourse at the April 1843 General Conference of the Church, mentioned in the text, was published in the *Times and Seasons* 4 (15 June 1843):236-38.

13 April 1843

1. See *History of the Church*, 5:354-57. Not in *Teachings*. The original source for the report in *History of the Church* is the Joseph Smith Diary, by Willard Richards. The reports of Levi Richards, Wilford Woodruff, and Willard Richards are here published for the first time. The following remarks were made to a "great multitude" including a group of British Saints who had arrived from England just the day before.

2. That is, the revelation that the Saints should gather together and form Zion. See 8 April 1840, note 4.

3. That is, the word of the Lord from the Prophet would come from the center place of the Church, which at that time was Nauvoo (see D&C 90:5; 124:126).

4. Romans 10:14.

5. The Prophet had undertaken an inspired translation of the Bible thirteen years before which he still had not published. In this work, according to the research of Robert J. Matthews, more than 3,400 verses of

the Bible underwent revision. See Robert J. Matthews, *"A Plainer Translation:" Joseph Smith's Translation of the Bible—A History and Commentary* (Provo, Utah: Brigham Young University Press, 1975). If Joseph Smith intended to change this passage before his expected publication of the Translation of the Bible (D&C 124:89), it was not altered in the manuscripts of his translation (see Stephen R. Knecht, *The Story of Joseph Smith's Bible Translation—A Documented History*[Salt Lake City: Associated Research Consultants, 1977], p. 228).

6. Romans 10:17.*

7. Hebrews 11; Alma 32:17-43; Ether 12:4-32.

8. The Prophet was alluding to his 1838-39 Missouri imprisonment.

9. D&C 124:2, 30, 56, 145.

10. Nearly 500 English Saints arrived in Nauvoo on 12 April 1843 under the charge of Parley P. Pratt, Lorenzo Snow, and Levi Richards. Some had been detained through the winter at St. Louis and elsewhere.

11. Reference is to the Saints' expulsion from Missouri in 1838-39. New research has shown that the Saints' losses were essentially personal property, not real estate.

12. Joshua 6; 8; 10; 11; 12.

13. D&C 105:14.

14. There was brisk competition among the merchants and land speculators in Nauvoo. Land in the lower part of town was controlled by the Church. The Prophet's comment here is essentially sarcastic—he is suggesting that the lower part of town was spiritually more healthy.

15. Apparently for a year the Prophet amused Nauvoo by making comments about the doctors and lawyers. At last, on 7 April 1844, he unmasked his ruse: "When I say a lawyer I mean a lawyer of the Scrip[tures]. I have done so hither to let the lawyers flutter & let everybody laugh at them" (Thomas Bullock Report, at note 71). He was attacking the doctors but was only poking fun at the lawyers.

16. Calomel was a white, tasteless powder containing mercury used to purge the bowels. "Calomel" doctors were characterized by blood-letting and the use of heroic drugs.

17. The "Lobelia" doctors were also known as Thomsonian herbal practitioners. Samuel Thomson, the founder of Thomsonian medicine, used as his major medication a wild plant, called lobelia, for purging. Capitalizing on the growing opposition to heroic medicine such as calomel, Thomson based his practice on the use of botanic agents. The botanic system of medicine was essentially approved by the Prophet Joseph Smith,

but he warned of the abuses of herbal as well as heroic practitioners as witnessed in the text. See also D&C 42:43. Such uncertainty in the medical practice encouraged self-medication.

18. Miasma was poisonous vapor supposed to arise from swamps.

19. See D&C 42:43; Psalm 104:14.

20. Brother Gardner. This man cannot be properly identified.

21. Levi Richards (1799-1876) a native of Hopkinton, Massachusetts, was an older brother of Willard Richards. A botanical doctor, he served a mission to England 1840-43.

16 April 1843

1. See *History of the Church*, 5:360-63, and *Teachings*, pp. 294-97. The original source for the *History of the Church* account is the Joseph Smith Diary. The reports of Levi Richards and Rhoda Richards are here published for the first time. A variation of the Wilford Woodruff account is published in Matthias F. Cowley, *Wilford Woodruff—Fourth President of The Church of Jesus Christ of Latter-day Saints: History of His Life and Labors as Recorded in his Daily Journal* (Salt Lake City: Bookcraft, 1970), pp. 173-74. The following remarks were intended as a funeral sermon for several of the Saints who had lost loved ones.

2. Parley P. Pratt.

3. See *Times and Seasons* (1 April 1843). The editors of the Church newspaper at the time were John Taylor and Wilford Woodruff.

4. Lorenzo Barnes (1812-42). Baptized in 1833, Barnes was the first missionary of the Church to die while preaching in a foreign land. In 1852 his body was brought from England and interred in the Salt Lake City cemetery.

5. Alma 3:1-3; 30:1-2; 57:28.

6. That is, the Amerindian burial grounds and mounds.

7. Regarding the burial of Joseph, see Genesis 50:22-26; Exodus 13:19; Joshua 24:32. Regarding the curse of the ancient prophets, see Isaiah 14:19-20 (or 2 Nephi 24:19-20).

8. Aside from this discourse and the teachings given in the temple, no other account of Joseph Smith's vision exists.

9. Matthew 5:4; Mosiah 18:9 (8-10).

10. Marcellus L. Bates. A brother-in-law to Orson Pratt, Bates lost his twenty-year-old wife, Jennette, the first week of February 1843. She was buried in Nauvoo.

11. This is the closest allusion to the doctrine of eternal marriage the Prophet had yet made in public discourse. See discourse dated 16 July 1843 (1) for his first explicit reference to this subject.

12. Reference is to Joseph Smith, Sr., the Prophet's father, who died and was buried in Nauvoo in September 1840.

13. Rhoda Richards (1784-1879) was a native of Framingham, Massachusetts. Baptized in 1838, she was a sister of Willard Richards.

6 May 1843

1. See *History of the Church*, 5:383-84. Not in *Teachings*. The *History of the Church* account is an amalgamation of the reports in the Joseph Smith Diary and the *Nauvoo Neighbor*. The report by Levi Richards is here published for the first time. A reminiscent account of this discourse by James Burgess contains the essential details found in the other three accounts published here, and adds that the "Constitution and Government would hang by a *brittle* thread."

> In the month of May 1843. Several miles east of Nauvoo. The Nauvoo Legion was on parade and review. At the close of which Joseph Smith made some remarks upon our condition as a people and upon our future prospects contrasting our present condition with our past trials and persecutions by the hands of our enemies. Also upon the constitution and government of the United States stating that the time would come when the Constitution and Government would hand by a brittle thread and would be ready to fall into other hands but this people the Latter day Saints will step forth and save it.
>
> General Scott and part of his staff on the American Army was present on the occasion.
>
> I James Burgess was present and testify to the above (James Burgess Notebook, Church Archives).

2. Emma Smith.

3. Apparently General Winfield Scott (1786-1866) was one of the United States officers present.

4. Samuel Swazy of Iowa Territory.

5. This is an obvious allusion to the pitiful response President Martin Van Buren gave to the Prophet when he went to Washington D.C. in late 1839 and personally delivered the Saints' petitions for redress of grievances for their Missouri losses of 1838-39. Despite the popular states' rights doctrine, Van Buren's comment, "Your cause is just, but I can do nothing for you," and "If I take up for you I shall lose the vote of Missouri" was unsympathetic if not deplorable (*History of the Church*, 4:80). See Appendix B, at note 9.

6. James Arlington Bennet (1788-?) was elected inspector-general of the Nauvoo Legion in April 1842. Proprietor and principal of the Arlington House, an educational institution on Long Island, New York, Bennet joined the Church in 1843, but withdrew soon after Joseph's death. The *Nauvoo Neighbor* (3 May 1843) gave notice of Bennet's anticipated arrival and the upcoming review of the Legion: "There will be on the 6th inst. a general review of the Nauvoo Legion, General Arlington Bennet of Arlington House, near New York is expected to attend. The Legion will parade and perform the evolutions on the prairie, we hope the day may be favorable, we expect that the Legion on that day will appear to advantage."

14 May 1843

1. See *History of the Church*, 5:387-90, and *Teachings*, pp. 297-99. The entries in *History of the Church* and *Teachings* come from the Wilford Woodruff Journal. "Yelrome" is "Morley" spelled backwards. Now called Tioga, Illinois, this Mormon settlement, located twenty-five miles south of Nauvoo, was presided over by Patriarch Isaac Morley. The Brigham Young report is here published for the first time.

2. 2 Peter 1:5-7.

3. 1 Corinthians 15:26.

4. D&C 93:12; Matthew 10:39.

5. Revelation 12:3, 4, 7-9; D&C 29:36-37.

6. Comparison between 2 Peter 1:5-7 and 2 Peter 1:10.

7. Comparison between 2 Peter 1:16-18 and 2 Peter 1:19.

8. 2 Peter 1:10-11.

9. Ibid.

17 May 1843 (1)

1. See *History of the Church*, 5:392, and *Teachings,* p.301. The original source for the report of this discourse published in *History of the Church* and *Teachings* is the William Clayton Diary. Ramus, also known as Macedonia, was a Mormon settlement twenty miles east of Nauvoo.

2. 2 Peter 1:19.

3. Regarding the phraseology "by revelation, & the spirit of Prophecy," see 27 June 1839, note 3. See also the poetic rendition of D&C 76:53 quoted in note 7 of discourse dated "Before 8 August 1839 (3)."

4. See discourse dated "Before 8 August 1839 (1)," note 4.

5. Samuel A. Prior was a Methodist minister.

6. Actually Joseph Smith quoted 2 Peter 1.

7. 2 Timothy 2:15.

8. Based on Matthew 12:42.

17 May 1843 (2)

1. See *History of the Church*, 5:392-93 and *Teachings*, pp. 301-2. The original source for these entries is the William Clayton Diary.

2. Samuel A. Prior.

3. In his publication of the book of Abraham the year before, Joseph Smith included this translation of Genesis 2:7: "And the Gods formed man from the dust of the ground, and took his spirit [i.e., the man's spirit], and put it into him; and breathed into his nostrils the breath of life, and man became a living soul" (Abraham 5:7).

4. As shown in the last note, Joseph Smith interpreted the phrase *breath of life* in Genesis 2:7 to mean *Adam's [pre-mortal] spirit*, which spirit (ruwach) was put into the body to form a living soul (D&C 88:15: "the spirit and the body are the soul of man."). However the word *ruwach* does not appear in this passage nor in Genesis 3:20, where the name Eve (Chavvah, meaning life-giving) appears. It is clear why Joseph Smith used the word *ruwach* in connection with Genesis 2:17, but his use of this word in connection with Genesis 3:20 is not so clear. Possibly he wanted to emphasize Eve's role as *lives*-giver, which coincides with the usage of *lives* soon to appear in the revelation on eternal marriage (D&C 132:22-24). Parenthetically we note that in the published versions of this discourse, the transliteration of the Hebrew word for "spirit" is given incorrectly as *rauch*. Obviously, Joseph Smith cannot be faulted for scribal errors; however, as seen here, Clayton (as far as phonetic spelling goes) correctly gives the transliteration as *ruach*.

21 May 1843

1. See *History of the Church*, 5:400-403, and *Teachings*, pp. 303-6. The reports in *History of the Church* and *Teachings* are from the Joseph Smith Diary, by Willard Richards. The accounts of this discourse by Martha Jane Knowlton Coray, Franklin D. Richards, James Burgess, Wilford Woodruff, and Levi Richards are here published for the first time.

2. George Morey (1803-?) was appointed high constable in Nauvoo in March 1841.

3. Acts 17:30; Romans 2:12; D&C 45:54; 76:72; 88:99.

4. 2 Peter 1:19.

5. 2 Peter 1:16-18.

6. Matthew 17:1-9.

7. Because there is no source yet found to document the following words, apparently the Church historians, taking the words "rough stone roling down hill" as a clue that the Prophet was making a self-characterization, expanded this to read,

> I am like a huge, rough stone rolling down from a high mountain; and the only polishing I get is when some corner gets rubbed off by coming in contact with something else, striking with accelerated force against religious bigotry, priest-craft, lawyer-craft, doctor-craft, lying editors, suborned judges and jurors, and the authority of perjured executives, backed by mobs, blasphemers, licentious and corrupt men and women—all hell knocking off a corner here and a corner there. Thus I will become a smooth and polished shaft in the quiver of the Almighty, who will give me dominion over all and every one of them, when their refuge of lies shall fail, and their hiding place shall be destroyed, while these smooth-polished stones with which I come in contact become marred.

Apparently the Church historians recalled that Joseph Smith on this or some other occasion made such an autobiographical statement. For whatever reason, they felt justified in inserting this long statement in order to round out the discourse prior to publication. It is obvious though that it would have been impossible for them to recover his exact words more than a decade after the discourse was delivered. The next two notes also deal with considerable expansion of the original text of his discourse. However, in these two cases what was involved was the fleshing out of what were then apparently well known anecdotes and not original concepts by the Prophet.

8. The anecdote of "Columbus and the eggs" referred to in the text, was fleshed out by the Church historians as followers:

> I break the ground; I lead the way like Columbus when he was invited to a banquet where he was assigned the most honorable place at the table, and served with the ceremonials which were observed towards sovereigns. A shallow courtier present, who was meanly jealous of him, abruptly asked him whether he thought that in case he had not discovered the Indies, there were not other men in Spain who would have been capable of the enterprise? Columbus made no reply, but took an egg and invited the company to make it stand on end. They all attempted it, but in vain; whereupon he struck it upon the table so as to break one end, and left it standing on the broken part, illustrating that when he had once shown the way to the new world nothing was easier than to follow it.

See the previous note.

9. The expansions of the original texts (referred to in the previous two notes) deal with the theme of reluctance—the reluctance of others to accept Joseph Smith's teachings. Had the Church historians provided an expansion of "Ladder and rainbow" in the same general theme as given in the previous two notes, it probably would not have been a bad guess. For in his 11 June 1843 discourse, Joseph Smith apparently referred to this anecdote again. However, again the original text does not convey the complete thought, though its context is within the same general theme. Specifically, the text (as we have it) says, "I would make you think I was climbing a ladder when I was climbing a rainbow."

10. Comparison made between 2 Peter 1:1, 5-7 and 2 Peter 1:10.

11. 2 Peter 1:2, 3.

12. Another allusion to the concept of the eternality of the marriage covenant. See note 30, this discourse, and 16 July 1843 (2), notes 7 and 10.

13. Acts 1:25.

14. 1 Corinthians 15:41-42.

15. 1 Kings 2:1-11 (cf. Hebrews 11:5); D&C 110:13.

16. Matthew 7:23.

17. 2 Peter 1:16.

18. 2 Peter 1:19.

19. D&C 124:41.

20. 2 Peter 1:1-9.

21. 2 Peter 1:10-11.

22. Psalm 110:1.

23. 2 Corinthians 12:1-4; D&C 76:5-10, 114-18.

24. See note 30, this discourse.

25. 2 Peter 1:10-11.

26. 2 Peter 1:16-19.

27. Comparison between 2 Peter 1:17 and 2 Peter 1:19. This definition of making one's calling and election sure, the definition given in the 27 June 1839 discourse, and the material at note 31 of this discourse are the clearest and most precise explanations of this important spiritual experience.

28. Confirmation of D&C 132:26-27.

29. Abraham 3:26-28.

30. Notes 12 and 24 and this note represent three distinct contemporary texts of the same discourse that document the most significant doctrinal axiom of the revelation on eternal and plural marriage. Though the revelation was not reduced to writing until seven and a half weeks after this sermon, the core idea of this revelation obviously occupied the Prophet's mind. The fulness of what that revelation implied he had to keep "in his bosom," but he did publicly teach the fundamental concept upon which the revelation rests:

> For all who will have a blessing at my hands shall abide the law which was appointed for that blessing, and the conditions thereof, as were instituted from before the foundation of the world.
>
> And as pertaining to the new and everlasting covenant, it was instituted for the fulness of my glory; and he that receiveth a fulness thereof must and shall abide the law, or he shall be damned, saith the Lord God.
>
> And verily I say unto you, that the conditions of this law are these: All covenants, contracts, bonds, obligations, oaths, vows, performances, connections, associations, or expectations, that are not made and entered into and sealed by the Holy Spirit of promise, of him who is anointed, both as well for time and for all eternity, and that too most holy, by revelation and commandment through the medium of mine anointed, whom I have appointed on the earth to hold this power (and I have appointed unto my servant Joseph to hold this power in the last days, and there is never but one on the earth at a time on whom this power and the keys of this priesthood are conferred), are of no efficacy, virtue, or force in and after the resurrection from the dead; for all contracts that are not made unto this end have an end when men are dead (D&C 132:5-7).

See 27 August 1843, note 43.

31. 2 Peter 1:19. Another specific definition of what it means to make one's calling and election sure. See note 27, this discourse.

32. John 3:3, 5.

33. Wilford Woodruff is referring to the discourse given just the week before, 14 May 1843, at Yelrome, near Lima, Illinois.

11 June 1843

1. See *History of the Church*, 5:423-27, and *Teachings*, pp. 307-12. The original source for the reports of this discourse in *History of the Church* and *Teachings* is an amalgamation of the Joseph Smith Diary, by Willard Richards, and the Wilford Woodruff Journal. The accounts of Levi Richards, Franklin D. Richards, Eliza R. Snow, and Willard Richards (personal diary) are here published for the first time.

2. D&C 130:20-21. See 21 May 1843, note 30.

3. The Prophet had said in an earlier discourse, "I have no enmity. I have no desire but to do all men good. I feel to pray for all men. We don't ask any people to throw away any good they have got. We only ask them to come and get more" (22 January 1843, Woodruff report). He, however, never was interested in engaging in bitter struggles while contending his position. He expressed this idea in another way in his final doctrinal discourse. "When things that are great are passed over with[ou]t. even a tho[ugh]t, I want to see all in all its bearings & hug it to my bosom—I bel[ieve]. all that God ever rev[eale]d. & I never hear of a man being d[amne]d for bel[ievin]g. too much but they are d—d for unbel[ief]" (16 June 1844, Thomas Bullock report).

4. Hebrews 7:12.

5. That is, baptism for the dead. See 5 January 1841, note 10.

6. Luke 23:43.

7. 1 Peter 3:18-20. See also 1 Peter 4:6.

8. Apparently Joseph Smith believed that the place where the apostles received their endowment on the day of Pentecost was a house dedicated to the Lord for the performance of the washing and anointing ordinances. This is not explicitly stated in Acts 2:1-13.

9. The Book of Mormon expresses this thought best—as, for example, in Mosiah 3:25-27. See also Revelation 6:14-17. See 8 April 1843, note 4.

10. Alma 5:15. Cf. Romans 2:6.

11. Matthew 23:23; Luke 11:42.

12. 2 Corinthians 12:1-4.

13. 1 Corinthians 15:41 (40-42).

14. John 14:2.

15. John 17:9-11; see also verses 20-23.

16. See note 37, this discourse.

17. Acts 7:55-56 (54-60).

18. This is John 5:26* as amended by John 10:17-18. Except in the cases of the 5 January 1841 discourse (at note 9) and the Samuel W. Richards account of the King Follett sermon (7 April 1844, at note 119), all other reports have the Prophet, when he quotes John 5:26, substituting the word *power* for the word *life*.

19. John 5:19.

20. This is a confirmation of a part of the revelation to Joseph Smith first recorded a month later and now designated as D&C 132:17.

21. Confirmation of D&C 132:19-20.

22. Confirmation of D&C 132:7, 19-24.

23. Judge Elias Higbee. A member of the Nauvoo Temple Committee, Higbee had served as a judge in Caldwell County, Missouri.

24. Matthew 23:37.

25. Undoubtedly the Church historians decided to amplify this statement based on D&C 124:28, and their knowledge of the Prophet's teachings on temple ordinances: "If a man gets *a* fullness *of the priesthood* of God he has to get *it* in the same way that Jesus Christ obtained it, and that was by keeping *all the commandments and obeying* all the ordinances of the house of the Lord" (*Teachings*, p. 308; changed words italicized). The essence of the Church historians' amplification, which is confirmed by the Franklin D. Richards report, is additionally supported in the following statement of Brigham Young in the Nauvoo Temple which includes the Prophet's teachings on the highest ordinances of the Temple:

> Those who come in here and have received their washing & anointing will [later] be ordained Kings & Priests, and will then have received the fullness of the Priesthood, all that can be given on earth. For Brother Joseph said he had given us all that could be given to man on the earth (Heber C. Kimball Journal kept by William Clayton, 26 December 1845, Church Archives).

See also 27 August 1843, note 30.

26. See 5 October 1840, note 24.

27. Luke 23:43.

28. 1 Corinthians 15:29.

29. Matthew 23:37.

30. See note 8, this discourse.

31. 1 Corinthians 15:40-42.

32. 2 Corinthians 12:1-4.

33. John 14:2.

34. Matthew 15:14.

35. 1 Corinthians 8:5.

36. John 17:9-11.

37. Wilford Woodruff gives us enough context for us to know that Joseph Smith referred to 1 Peter 3:21-22 in support of the concept of separate beings in the Godhead. See text of this discourse at note 16.

38. For example, Acts 7:55-56.

39. See note 18, this discourse.

40. Revelation 19:10.

41. Note that both men and women would receive temple ordinances.

42. Matthew 23:37-38.

43. Isaiah 24:5. This is the only diary reference to the only known public address in which the Prophet bore testimony of his First Vision. It is here published for the first time.

44. Cf. 29 August 1842, note 11.

45. D&C 124:28.

46. Matthew 23:37.

47. Never during the Kirtland period of the Church's history (1831-1837) was it taught that temple ordinances were essential to salvation.

24 June 1843

1. Not in *Teachings*. This sermon on marriage, only briefly mentioned in the text, was delivered to a non-Mormon audience in Dixon. Joseph Smith was at the time in the custody of two law-enforcement officers, one from Illinois and one from Missouri because a third demand from Missouri Governor Thomas Reynolds for the arrest and delivery of the Prophet had been authorized by Thomas Ford, governor of Illinois. See 30 June 1843, note 1.

2. A reminiscent account of this discourse is found in Truman Leonard's Journal: "This day had a long talk with Justin Merril, Phileman's Brother about Josephs arrest at Dixon in Illinois David Town was the man who said by G-d Mr. Smith shall speak on the text we have given him (namely C[elestial] Marriage) you sit down or we will try you by a Court there will be no appeal from" (Truman Leonard Journal, 24 May 1886 [typescript], BYU Special Collections).

30 June 1843

1. See *History of the Church*, 5:465-73. Not in *Teachings*. The report in *History of the Church* is an amalgamation of the accounts in the Wilford Woodruff Journal and the Joseph Smith Diary.

On 17 June 1843, while the Prophet and his family were away from Nauvoo visiting Emma Smith's sister near Dixon, Lee County, Illinois, a third demand from Missouri for the arrest and delivery of Joseph Smith was authorized by the Governor of Illinois. Though he had received advance notice of the warrant, the Prophet was taken by surprise by two officers on 23 June. After being denied counsel, and suffering unwarranted bodily harm from the officers, Joseph feared he might be secreted away to Missouri without any chance of escape. Fortunately Stephen Markham, who was with the Prophet, was successful in enlisting the services of three talented lawyers, who assisted in obtaining a writ of habeas corpus, which was returnable to the nearest court having jurisdiction—i.e., Nauvoo. As was hoped and expected the Prophet was acquitted and discharged by the Nauvoo Municipal Court. The following discourse was delivered by Joseph Smith four hours after his arrival in Nauvoo to a congregation estimated at seven or eight thousand.

2. Joseph Reynolds and Harmon T. Wilson.

3. When the Prophet was arrested by Reynolds and Wilson, he was brutally accosted. However, on their arrival in Nauvoo, Joseph Smith kindly treated them to a sumptuous meal in his own home (*History of the Church*, 5:460).

4. Cyrus Walker (1791-?) was a native of Virginia. He resided in McDonough County, Illinois, where he practiced law. He was defeated by Joseph P. Hoge in his bid for a seat in the United States Congress in 1843.

5. Matthew 5:38-39.

6. D&C 98:13-17, 23-48.

7. On 13 June 1843 Joseph, Emma, and their children left Nauvoo to visit Emma's sister, Elizabeth Hale Wasson, who was residing near Dixon, Lee County, Illinois.

8. Harmon T. Wilson (1816-?) appears to have been a constable from Carthage. The 1850 Federal Census lists him as a Virginia-born merchant.

9. After being arrested by Joseph H. Reynolds and Harmon T. Wilson, the Prophet sent Stephen Markham to find a local constable and secure a warrant to arrest the two above-named officers for false imprisonment and unnecessary force and violence.

10. Joseph Reynolds and Harmon Wilson.

11. The *History of the Church* suggests that an unnamed passer-by was asked by the Prophet to secure him a writ of habeas corpus, but when he did not respond, Joseph sent Stephen Markham instead.

12. Edward Southwick (1812-?), a native of New York, was a lawyer who practiced in Lee County, Illinois.

13. Joseph Smith was finally successful in obtaining the legal services of three lawyers: Edward Southwick, Sheperd G. Patrick, and Cyrus Walker.

14. Undoubtedly John Dixon (1785-?), a native of New York who resided at Dixon.

15. Lilburn W. Boggs.

16. Pawpaw Grove, located in the southeast corner of Lee County, Illinois was 145 miles northeast of Nauvoo.

17. They first were going to Ottawa, Illinois, and were half way there (Pawpaw Grove) when they found out that the judge who was to consider the writ of habeus corpus was in New York. So they returned to Dixon and another writ was issued, ostensibly returnable to Stephen A. Douglas at Quincy, Illinois. Joseph H. Reynolds, Harmon T. Wilson desired to go to Quincy by riverboat and thus avoid Nauvoo. However, the Prophet's wishes were finally followed and they continued the trip by land. Near Nauvoo it was decided, as was hoped all along, that the writ would be returnable at Nauvoo as the "nearest municipal court"—for that was all that was specified in the document. No doubt the general wording of the order was then much to the chagrin of the two officers who had seized the Prophet (*History of the Church*, 5:431-61).

18. Reference is here made to Emma Smith, the Prophet's wife.

19. D&C 63:27-31. See also D&C 58:53.

20. See note 6, this discourse.

21. No identification can be made of the Kirkpatrickites.

22. Article I, Section 9, of the Constitution of the United States.

23. Stephen Markham (1800-78) was baptized in 1837 and was a loyal friend of the Prophet. He often served as the Prophet's private courier.

24. Mr. John Dixon of Dixon, Illinois.

25. On 24 June 1843 a master-in-chancery at Dixon issued a writ of habeas corpus returnable before John D. Caton, Judge of the 9th Judicial Circuit at Ottawa, Illinois. The following day, however, it was learned that Caton was in New York, and the party returned to Dixon, Illinois (see note 17).

26. James Campbell, sheriff of Lee County, Illinois.

27. David Town (1787-?) resided at or near Dixon. He was a native of Massachusetts.

28. Thomas Grover (1807-86), baptized in 1834, was a member of the Nauvoo High Council.

29. Calvin A. Warren (?-1881), a native of New York state, practiced law at Quincy, Illinois.

30. See 29 August 1842, note 8.

2 July 1843

1. See *History of the Church*, 5:481. Not in *Teachings*. The original source for this entry may be the "Book of the Law of the Lord." The following remarks were made to some fifty or sixty men who, under the direction of Jonathan Dunham, had been sent on the *Maid of Iowa* up the Illinois River to assist in rescuing the Prophet. Joseph Smith had been arrested on a charge of being an accessory to an attempted murder of ex-Govenor Lilburn W. Boggs.

3 July 1843

1. The *History of the Church* gives no indication that the Prophet spoke publicly this day. Not in *Teachings*. The account from Willard Richards's diary possibly refers to remarks made by the Prophet to a body of men, under the command of Charles C. Rich, who had just returned to Nauvoo, having been sent to rescue Joseph Smith at Dixon, Illinois.

4 July 1843 (1)

1. Not in *History of the Church*. Not in *Teachings*. Wilford Woodruff's and Levi Richards's reports of the Prophet's remarks on this occasion are here published for the first time.

2. Joseph H. Reynolds.

3. Harmon T. Wilson.

4 July 1843 (2)

1. See *History of the Church*, 5:489-90. Not in *Teachings*. The original source for the report of this discourse in *History of the Church* is the Wilford Woodruff Journal. The reports contained in the Joseph Smith Diary, by Willard Richards, and the Levi Richards Diary are here published for the first time.

2. Although Joseph Smith had taken four short visits to Missouri (in 1831, 1832, 1834, and 1837) he first took up residence in the State of Missouri in mid-March 1838; he continued as a resident of the state until 31 October 1838, when he was imprisoned for six and a half months.

3. Governor Lilburn W. Boggs of Missouri issued the order of Mormon extermination on 27 October 1838.

4. The United States Court refers to the United States District Court, Springfield, Illinois, where the Prophet was discharged in early January 1843. This was the only time he was tried in a federal court.

5. Article 5, Section 1, of the 1818 Illinois State Constitution. "The militia of the State of Illinois shall consist of all free male ablebodied persons, negroes, mulattoes and Indians excepted, resident of the State, between the ages of eighteen and forty-five years, except such persons as now are, or hereafter may be exempted by the laws of the United States or of this State, and shall be armed, equipped, and trained as the General Assembly may provide by law" (*Revised Statutes*, 1845 [Springfield, 1845], p. 36).

6. At the age of seven Joseph Smith contracted typhoid fever, which left complications. First he suffered from a large abscess in his shoulder, followed by pain and swelling in his left leg. Nathan Smith, a well-known surgeon from Dartmouth College, tried in vain to relieve the pain by making a small incision in the Prophet's leg between the knee and the ankle. When the family refused to allow the surgeon to amputate the leg, it was decided to try to remove a large part of the diseased bone. The operation saved the leg but left Joseph with a slight limp the rest of his life (see LeRoy S. Wirthlin, "Nathan Smith [1762-1828] Surgical Consultant to Joseph Smith," *Brigham Young University Studies* 17 [Spring 1977]:319-37).

7. Joseph Duncan (1794-1844). Governor of Illinois 1834-38. He ran unsuccessfully for a second term as governor against Thomas Ford in 1842.

8. Thomas Ford (1800-50) was governor of Illinois 1842-46.

9. Joseph H. Reynolds.

10. Harmon T. Wilson.

11. *Times and Seasons* 4 (1 and 15 July and 1 August 1843):241-78, and *Nauvoo Neighbor* 1(5, 12, 19, and 26 July 1843).

9 July 1843

1. See *History of the Church*, 5:498-500, and *Teachings*, pp. 312-14. The original source for the entries in *History of the Church* and *Teachings* is the Joseph Smith Diary, by Willard Richards. The reports of James Burgess and Levi Richards are here published for the first time.

2. Matthew 6:12, 14-15.

3. Moroni 8:11-12 (4-26). See also JST Genesis 17:6 (3-7).

4. Matthew 19:13-16. See also 3 Nephi 17:21-25.

5. 3 Nephi 27:21 (Cf. 3 Nephi 17:21-25).

6. Moroni 8:12, 19, 22.

7. Matthew 18:3; Luke 22:32; Isaiah 6:10 (cf. Matthew 13:15).

8. Acts 2:37-39.

9. The messenger was Mason Brayman.

10. John 3:5.

11. Galatians 1:8 (6-8).

12. Revelation 19:10.

13. Matthew 7:7. See also Matthew 21:21-22.

14. Revelation 19:10.

15. Genesis 1:26-27.

16. Abraham 4:26, 27.

17. Hebrews 1:3 (1-3).

18. Colossians 2:9 (8-10).

19. Ezekiel 37:9, 14 (1-14).

16 July 1843 (1)

1. See *History of the Church*, 5:510 and 512. Not in *Teachings*. The original source for the entry in *History of the Church* is the Joseph Smith Diary, by Willard Richards. The letter of Willard Richards to Brigham Young, postmarked 19 July 1843, is located in the Church Archives, and is published in *History of the Church*, 5:512. The report of Levi Richards is here published for the first time.

2. Matthew 10:36 (34-39).

3. This was William Marks, president of the Nauvoo Stake. He and others opposed to the principle of plural marriage felt it their duty to prevent the Church from having to endure untold misery and suffering because of the practice. Knowing the Prophet was unable to advocate the principle publicly, they betrayed him by publicly opposing any form of plural marriage. Their technique was to feign ignorance of this doctrinal development, while conducting a campaign ostensibly to rid Nauvoo of the last vestiges of John C. Bennett's "spiritual wifery."

4. Austin A. Cowles, first counselor to William Marks in the Nauvoo Stake presidency. When the revelation on plural marriage was read to the Nauvoo high council a month later (12 August 1843), Cowles rejected it and subsequently resigned his position in the stake presidency (23 September 1843). He prepared an affidavit testifying of these events, and it was published in the *Nauvoo Expositor* (7 June 1844), three weeks before the Prophet's martyrdom.

5. Initially Parley P. Pratt opposed the Prophet on the principle of plural marriage, but near 27 June (just three weeks before this discourse) he and his wife, Mary Ann, accepted the principle. Mary Ann told Vilate

Kimball that although she previously had been "raging against these things . . . the Lord had shown her it was all right" (27-29 June 1843 letter of Vilate Kimball to Heber C. Kimball, Church Archives). Parley's conversion came just before the Prophet's trip to Dixon, Illinois. Willard Richards's awareness of Parley's conversion must have barely preceded this discourse.

6. "Nothing [was] new same as when you left" is an interesting statement in light of the comments made in 16 July 1843, (2), note 15.

7. Matthew 10:36 (34-39).

16 July 1843 (2)

1. See *History of the Church*, 5:510. Not in *Teachings*. The original source for the *History of the Church* account is an amalgamation of the William Clayton Diary, the Joseph Smith Diary, by Willard Richards, and the letter from Willard Richards to Brigham Young, postmarked 19 July 1843. The reports by Franklin D. Richards, Levi Richards, and Willard Richards (personal diary) are here published for the first time.

2. D&C 130:20-21.

3. Confirmation of D&C 132:7, 15-18.

4. Confirmation of D&C 132:6, 16-17.

5. 1 Corinthians 15:46-48.

6. Confirmation of D&C 132:19, 22, 30-32.

7. John 3:6. See 2 April 1843 (2), note 8. At this point in his record, Franklin D. Richards added his conclusions regarding the Prophet's teachings that day: "From the above I deduce that we may make an eternal covenant with our wives and in the resurrection claim that which is our own and enjoy blessings & glories peculiar to those in that condition even the multiplication of spirits in the eternal world." His deduction is a confirmation of D&C 132:19-22.

8. Undoubtedly the "Law of the Priesthood" referred to is D&C 132:6-7. See 21 May 1843, note 30.

9. If the Prophet was not serious about this proposal (see 23 July 1843 discourse), there was nevertheless scriptural precedent for what he had in mind that was consistent not only with the revelations he had received on the temple ordinances, but also with the revelations regarding the organization of the Kingdom of God (see Hyrum L. Andrus, *Doctrines of the Kingdom—Foundations of the Millennial Kingdom of Christ* vol. 3 [Salt Lake City: Bookcraft, 1973], pp. 555-60). See note 15, this discourse.

10. Confirmation of D&C 132:6-7, 15-19.

11. The "fulness of these things," which could not be revealed "until

the Temple is completed," was the relationship of the temple endowment and the temple ordinance of marriage for time and eternity. The Prophet revealed the temple endowment to only nine men (in May 1842). It was another year, however, before his wife, Emma, and his brother Hyrum assented to the implications of the ordinances of eternal marriage. They did so on 23 and 26 May 1843, respectively. Then, on successive days (28 and 29 May 1843), Emma was sealed to Joseph, and Hyrum and his wife, Mary Fielding, were sealed for time and eternity (Joseph Smith Diary, under dates given, Church Archives).

12. Again, confirmation of D&C 132:7, 15-18.

13. Revelation 7:3; 9:4; 14:1; 22:4; D&C 77:9-11, 14. See 13 August 1843 (1), note 7.

14. Revelation 7:2-3. See 13 August 1843 (1), note 7.

15. Apparently sometime between 29 August 1842 (see note 11 that discourse) and the date of this discourse (16 July 1843), the Prophet discussed with Hyrum Smith, Brigham Young, Willard Richards, and others of the Twelve Apostles his full concept of temple ordinances and the plan of the Millennial Kingdom of Christ. However, it was not until 28 September 1843 he was "anointed and ordained to the highest and holiest order of the priesthood" and by common consent "chosen president" of the council to which he was administering the endowment (Joseph Smith Diary, Church Archives). Moreover, it was still not until a month after the 11 March 1844 organization of the Kingdom of God before Joseph was chosen prophet, priest and king over the Council of Fifty. (See D. Michael Quinn, "The Council of Fifty and Its Members, 1844-1945." *Brigham Young University Studies* 20 [Winter 1980]:164-66, 185-86; Andrew F. Ehat, " 'It Seems Like Heaven Began on Earth': Joseph Smith and the Constitution of the Kingdom of God." *Brigham Young University Studies* 20 [Spirng 1980]: 254-57, 263, 267, 268; and Hyrum L. Andrus, *Doctrines of the Kingdom—Foundations of the Millennial Kingdom of Christ* vol. 3 [Salt Lake City: Bookcraft, 1973], pp. 550-60).

16. See note 15, this discourse.

23 July 1843

1. See *History of the Church*, 5:516-18, and *Teachings*, pp. 314-17. The original source for these reports is the Joseph Smith Diary, by Willard Richards. The accounts of this discourse by James Burgess, Franklin D. Richards, Levi Richards, and Willard Richards (personal diary) are here published for the first time. Another version of this discourse, based on the Joseph Smith Diary, was prepared by unknown author and included by Joseph Fielding Smith in *Teachings*, pp. 318-19.

2. Revelation 19:10.

3. John 15:13.

4. Matthew 26:41.

5. James 5:17. See also Acts 14:15 (11-15).

6. The humorous hyperbole the Church historians created from this terse statement apparently was familiar to and not taken so lightly by William Law, the Prophet's first counselor in the First Presidency. In the *Nauvoo Expositor* (7 June 1844), p. 2, Law says, "He often [said] that we [the Saints] would all go to Hell together, and convert it into a heaven, by casting the Devil out" (cf. *History of the Church*, 5:517, or *Teachings*, p. 316).

7. Theodore Turley (1801-71) joined the Church in Upper Canada. He operated a gunsmith shop in Nauvoo.

8. See 16 July 1843 (2), note 15.

9. JST Luke 16:16-23. See Luke 16:16 and Matthew 11:12-13.

10. Luke 16:17. See also D&C 1:38.

11. 1 Corinthians 10:4 (1-4).

12. 3 Nephi 15:15.

13. Exodus 40:15.

14. Matthew 5:18; Luke 16:17.

15. Luke 1:11-17 (5-17); D&C 84:18, 25-28.

16. Matthew 11:12.

17. The JST Luke 3:13* conveys the idea that the promises of Abraham could be extended beyond the house of Israel. Here, however, Joseph Smith goes beyond the manuscripts of the Inspired Version of the Bible identifies the "stones" mentioned in Luke 3:8 as "gentiles." Regarding Joseph's reference to "dogs" as "gentiles," see Jesus' comments to the Greek woman in Mark 7:27 (24-30). Cf. Matthew 15:26 (21-28).

19. Matthew 10:1; John 15:16.

20. Exodus 40:15.

21. Luke 1:8-11. While the Melchizedek Priesthood keys would enable direct intercourse with God, Zacharias holding the Aaronic Priesthood had the keys of access to the ministering of angels (see D&C 84:19-26; 107:18-20). See 21 March 1841, note 26.

22. Luke 1:13, 18, 20 (11-20).

23. Matthew 3:1-2.

24. There is no passage of scripture indicating that John received this

anointing. However, D&C 84:28 states that John "was ordained by the angel of God at the time he was eight days old unto this power, to overthrow the kingdom of the Jews, and to make straight the way of the Lord" (Luke 16:16).

25. Matthew 3:1, 4-6 (1-6).

26. Luke 16:16.

27. Matthew 11:12. See JST Luke 16:16-23.

28. Isaiah 9:6. According to the Willard Richards version of this discourse, Joseph Smith said that "John [was] King and lawgiver." When John's mission was complete, Jesus became "King and lawgiver," to fulfill the Messianic prophecy.

29. Matthew 3:5-6 (1-6).

30. Matthew 11:12; 21:43.

6 August 1843

1. See *History of the Church*, 5:526. Not in *Teachings*. The original source for the *History of the Church* account is the Joseph Smith Diary, by Willard Richards. The reports of William Clayton, Levi Richards, and Willard Richards (personal diary) are here published for the first time.

2. Zebedee Coltrin (1804-87). Baptized in January 1831, Coltrin gave a life of service to the Church.

3. The Illinois State election was held on 7 August 1843, the day after this discourse.

4. Cyrus Walker.

5. Mr. Montgomery was a law student and Cyrus Walker's son-in-law.

6. Joseph H. Reynolds.

7. Joseph Pendleton Hoge (1810-91), a Democrat, served as United States Congressman for Illinois 1843-47. He later served as Judge of the San Francisco Superior Court.

8. William Law.

9. Possibly William Law had informed others that Joseph Smith actually supported Joseph P. Hoge for United States Congressman, even though he had promised his vote to Cyrus Walker in June 1843. Walker refused to give legal aid to the Prophet until the Prophet promised to vote for him. Walker mistakenly believed that he would have the Mormon vote if he had the Prophet's vote.

10. That is, to put finishing touches on Parley P. Pratt's sermon, which had been delivered before the Prophet's.

11. Romans 10:17.

12. See the 16 July 1843 (2) and 23 July 1843 discourses.

13 August 1843 (1)

1. See *History of the Church*, 5:529-31, and *Teachings*, pp. 319-21. The original source of these reports is the Joseph Smith Diary, by Willard Richards. The accounts of this discourse by Howard Coray, Franklin D. Richards, William Clayton, Levi Richards, and Willard Richards (personal diary) are here published for the first time.

2. Judge Elias Higbee died 8 June 1843.

3. Hebrews 12:22-24. See 27 June 1839, note 15.

4. D&C 128:18. See Matthew 11:25; 21:16; and, Luke 10:21 as compared with Matthew 13:35.

5. Malachi 4:3-4.* See note 8, this discourse.

6. Revelation 7:2-3.

7. At this time Joseph Smith was not willing to discuss the temple ordinances of conferral of the fulness of the priesthood, of marriage for time and eternity, or of sealing children to parents; nevertheless, he indicated that the conferral of the fulness of the priesthood was a "sealing . . . on top of the head", of which the phrase "sealed in their foreheads" was symbolic. Furthermore, Joseph Smith here taught that it was through the ordinance of conferral of the fulness of the priesthood that men could be qualified to be a part of the special missionary force of the last days which would number 144,000 high priests (D&C 77:8-11, 14). When Cornelius P. Lott and his wife received these ordinances on 4 February 1844, the Prophet indicated that "the selection of [the] persons to form that number had already commenced." He had already conferred these blessings on at least 17 men (*History of the Church*, 6:196 and Wilford Woodruff Journal, under date given).

8. According to the teachings that the Prophet gave in private (but which he only hinted at in this discourse), to be heir to Abraham's promise that he would head an innumerable posterity, each individual and his children must be sealed for time and eternity. If this sealing was performed, he taught, the covenant relationship would then continue throughout eternity. The Prophet taught, moreover, that such a patriarchal priesthood of kings and priests would have to be established by sealing children and parents back through Abraham to Adam in order to fulfill the mission of Elijah (Malachi 4:5-6). When this was accomplished, the order within the highest degree of the Celestial Kingdom would then be eternally set. Probably no clearer statement of Joseph's theology regarding this concept can be found than what is given in an editorial by Orson Hyde. (The following diagram began the editorial after which came the text.)

A DIAGRAM OF THE KINGDOM OF GOD.

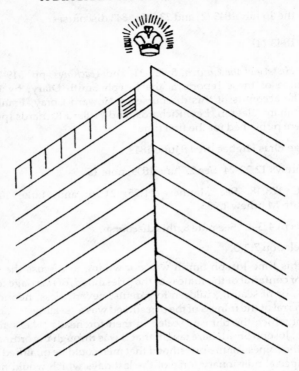

The above diagram shows the order and unity of the kingdom of God. The eternal Father sits at the head, crowned King of kings and Lord of lords. Wherever the other lines meet, there sits a king and a priest unto God, bearing rule, authority, and dominion under the Father. He is one with the Father, because his kingdom is joined to his Father's and becomes part of it.

The most eminent and distinguished prophets who have laid down their lives for their testimony (Jesus among the rest), will be crowned at the head of the largest kingdoms under the Father, and will be one with Christ as Christ is one with his Father; for their kingdoms are all joined together, and such as do the will of the Father, the same are his mothers, sisters, and brothers. He that has been faithful over a few things, will be made ruler over many things; he that has been faithful over ten talents, shall have dominion over ten cities, and he that has been faithful over five talents, shall have dominion over five cities, and to every man will be given a kingdom and a dominion, according to his merit, powers, and abilities to govern and control. It will be seen by the above diagram that there are kingdoms of all sizes, an infinite variety to suit all grades of merit and ability. The chosen vessels unto God are the kings and priests that are placed at the head of these kingdoms. These have received their washings and anointings in the temple of God on this earth; they have been chosen, ordained, and anointed kings and priests, to reign as such in the resurrection of the just. Such as have not received the fulness of the priesthood, (for the fulness of the priesthood includes the authority of both king and priest) and have not been anointed and ordained in the temple of the Most High, may obtain salvation in the celestial kingdom, but not a celestial crown. Many are called to enjoy a celestial glory, yet few are chosen to wear a celestial crown, or rather, to be rulers in the celestial kingdom.

While this portion of eternity that we now live in, called time, continues, and while the other portions of eternity that we may hereafter dwell in, continue, those lines in the foregoing diagram, representing kingdoms, will continue to extend and be lengthened out; and thus, the increase of our kingdoms will increase the kingdom of our God, even as Daniel hath said: "of the increase of his kingdom and government there shall be no end." All these kingdoms are one kingdom, and there is a King over kings, and a Lord over lords. There are Lords many, and Gods many, for they are called Gods to whom the word of God comes, and the word of God comes to all these kings and priests. But to our branch of the kingdom there is but one God, to whom we all owe the most perfect submission and loyalty; yet our God is just as subject to still higher intelligences, as we should be to him.

...These kingdoms, which are one kingdom, are designed to extend till they not only embrace this world, but every other planet that rolls in the blue vault of heaven. Thus will all things be gathered in one during the dispensation of the fulness of times, and the Saints will not only possess the earth, but all things else, for, says Paul, "All things are yours, whether Paul, or Apollos, or Cephas, or the world, or life, or death, or things present, or things to come; all are yours, and ye are Christ's, and Christ is God's" (Orson Hyde, "A Diagram of the Kingdom of God." *Millennial Star* 9 [15 January 1847]: 23-24).

9. The Prophet's words do seem a warning to Elias Higbee's sons, Francis and Chauncey. Both opposed Joseph Smith and teamed with William and Wilson Law to publish the *Nauvoo Expositor*.

10. To Joseph Smith heaven could be desirable only if it did not obliterate the relationships developed here.

11. The idea conveyed in this sentence differs slightly from what is conveyed in the Joseph Smith Diary variant of this discourse. In that version the Prophet is quoted as saying, "Had I inspiration, revelation & lungs to communicate what my soul has contemplated in times past, there is not a soul in this congregation but would go to their homes & shut their mouths in everlasting silence on religion, till they had learned something." Such was the assurance he had of his prophetic calling.

12. Hebrews 12:22-24.

13. See note 4, this discourse.

14. The use of the word *they* rather than the world *day* in Malachi 4:1* agrees with Moroni's variation of this scripture, which he recited during

each of his five visits to Joseph Smith 21-22 September 1823 (see Joseph Smith-History 1:37).

15. Genesis 1:1-2, 6-10; Isaiah 24:6.

16. See notes 7 and 8, this discourse.

17. Revelaton 7:2-3. See 13 August 1843 (1), note 7.

18. Genesis 12:3; 18:8; 22:18; 26:4-5; D&C 110:12; Abraham 2:9-11.

19. When the Church historians amalgamated the entries from the Joseph Smith Diary and the William Clayton Diary to create the version of this discourse that was published, the passage that the blessings conferred by the ordinance of sealing parents and children was unconditional. The wording of the published version suggests that the children of parents who receive the fulness of the priesthood can never fall. This previously unpublished, more complete account of the Prophet's idea *does* contain a conditional. Clearly this is a more reasonable and consistent doctrine: if it were not for such a conditional, the concept would contradict significant doctrines taught by Joseph Smith, not the least of which would be a contradiction of his article of faith that "men will be punished for their own sins."

20. See note 9, this discourse.

21. John 17:3.

22. See note 8, this discourse, regarding Joseph Smith's first teaching the ordinances of sealing parents and children.

23. See note 19, this discourse.

24. Romans 8:17 (14-17).

25. See note 18, this discourse.

26. Elias Higbee.

27. Malachi 4:5-6.*

28. Revelation 7:2-3. See note 7, this discourse. See also note 7 of the discourse dated "Before 8 August 1843 (3)."

29. See note 19, this discourse.

13 August 1843 (2)

1. See *History of the Church*, 5:531-32, Not in *Teachings*. The original sources for the report of this discourse given in *History of the Church* are the Joseph Smith Diary, by Willard Richards and the William Clayton Diary. The brief notation from the Willard Richards Diary is here published for the first time.

2. Henry G. Sherwood (1785-1867) was baptized about 1832 and was appointed Nauvoo marshal in February 1841.

3. Walter Bagby was Hancock County assessor and tax collector, and a bitter non-Mormon.

4. The state election was held the first Monday in August (7 August 1843).

5. This may have been Thomas C. King, sheriff of Adams County, Illinois.

6. Positive identification of this man cannot be made.

7. Frederick J. Moeser was a Nauvoo merchant.

8. Daniel Hamner Wells, a non-member at this time, was justice of the peace in Nauvoo.

9. See note 5, this discourse.

10. Based possibly on the "Law of the Lord," the *History of the Church* amplifies this part of the discourse.

> He [Joseph Smith] then sat down, but resumed—"I had forgotten one thing. We have had certain traders in this city, who have been writing falsehoods to Missouri; and there is a certain man in this city who has made a covenant to betray and give me up to the Missourians, and that, too, before Governor Carlin commenced his persecutions. That man is no other than Sidney Rigdon. This testimony I have from gentlemen from abroad, whose names I do not wish to give.
>
> I most solemnly proclaim the withdrawal of my fellowship from this man, on condition that the foregoing be true; and let the Saints proclaim it abroad, that he may no longer be acknowledged as my counselor: and all who feel to sanction my proceedings and views will manifest it by uplifted hands.
>
> There was a unanimous vote that Sidney Rigdon be disfellowshiped. and his license demanded (*History of the Church*, 5:531-32).

On the following Sunday Sidney denied these charges, but on the Sunday after that, Joseph Smith produced a letter from Thomas Carlin that the Prophet felt was evasive and therefore fell short of absolving Sidney of the charge of treachery. The problem was left unresolved until the October 1843 General Conference. At that time Sidney had his trial and was voted to be retained in his station as a counselor in the First Presidency.

27 August 1843

1. See *History of the Church*, 5:553-56, and *Teachings*, pp. 321-23. The original source for the reports of this discourse in *History of the Church* and *Teachings* is the Joseph Smith Diary, by Willard Richards and the William Clayton Diary. The accounts of Franklin D. Richards, James Burgess, Levi

Richards, and Willard Richards (personal diary) are here published for the first time.

2. William Marks, president of the Nauvoo Stake.

3. Orson Hyde. See 13 August 1843 (2), note 10.

4. Since the King James Version of the New Testament comes from Greek manuscripts, the transliteration of Σαλήμ (given as Salem) in Hebrews 7:1-2 is correct. However, Greek does not have a *sh* equivalent, thus when Shålêm (pronounced shaw-lame') was transliterated from the Hebrew manuscript to the Greek manuscripts of the New Testament, the h was lost. Nevertheless, while authorities say Shalem means *peaceful*, they also say that it may stand for "an early name for Jerusalem." It is this latter point which Joseph Smith disputed.

5. See 5 October 1840, note 24.

6. That is, in Hebrews 7:1-12.

7. See D&C 84:19-25 and JST Exodus 34:1-2. See also 5 October 1840, note 24.

8. That is, when Abraham offered up Isaac (Genesis 22), as repulsive a request as this was, Abraham went ahead and proved his integrity and faith. Consequently God bestowed upon him the highest blessing available to man, the fulness of the priesthood. See D&C 132:36 and note 21, this discourse.

9. At no time before in the history of the Church had the Prophet talked so freely in public of ordinances whereby men were ordained kings and priests. These ordinances were not introduced in Kirtland because Elijah had not come to confer the fulness of the priesthood upon the Prophet before he administered the Kirtland Temple ordinances. Obviously the Prophet could only administer temple ordinances as he then understood them. See 13 August 1843 (1), note 8, and notes 21 and 22, this discourse.

10. The "kingly powers" of the fulness of the priesthood would be conferred by an "anointing." See notes 21 and 22, this discourse, and 13 August 1843 (1), note 8.

11. Malachi 4:5-6*.

12. "Now he which stablisheth us with you in Christ, and hath anointed us, is God; who hath also sealed us, and given the earnest of the Spirit in our hearts" (2 Corinthians 1:21-22). See 27 June 1839, note 11. Apparently it is one thing to receive the anointing and sealing blessings of the priesthood and another thing for them to be called, elected, and made sure.

13. Hebrews 7:3.

14. That is, the fulness of the priesthood comes "not by man, nor the will of man; neither by father nor mother; neither by beginning of days nor end of years; but of God" (JST Genesis 14:28). See also JST Hebrews 7:3.

15. See note 21, this discourse.

16. See note 22, this discourse.

17. Hebrews 7:20-22, 28 (19-28); D&C 84:40 (33-41).

18. See text of this discourse at note 26 for Joseph Smith's comments on the Holy Ghost.

19. Obadiah 21; Revelation 14:1; D&C 76:66.

20. 2 Corinthians 12:1-4.

21. The Prophet here teaches that though Abraham had not yet received the fulness of the priesthood, he had received from the Lord the promise of an innumerable posterity both for this world and in the world to come (D&C 132:28-31). Joseph Smith, however, clarifies that Abraham's endowment (Abraham Facsimile Number 2, figures 3 and 7) was greater than that which his descendants Aaron and Levi would be allowed; and thus "Abraham's" Patriarchal Priesthood (the ordinances of the endowment and patriarchal marriage for time and eternity) comprehended the Aaronic portion of the endowment. Additionally, the Prophet here clarifies that the Patriarchal Priesthood was not the same as the crowning ordinances of the fulness of the Melchizedek Priesthood. Elias returned the authority of promising innumerable posterity, but Elijah restored the authority of the fulness of the priesthood (D&C 110:12-16).

Aside from this theological commentary, it is important to point out that the Prophet's teachings fit perfectly within a historical context. Joseph Smith administered the first ordinances of the Patriarchal Priesthood on 4 May 1842 when he gave both the Aaronic and Melchizedek portions of the endowment to nine men in his store in Nauvoo (see *History of the Church*, 5:1-2, or *Teachings*, p. 137; and H. W. Mills, "De Tal Palo Tal Astilla," *Annual Publications—Historical Society of Southern California* 10 [Los Angeles: McBride Printing Company, 1917]:120-21). By a year later, most of the nine received the ordinances of marriage for time and eternity. In particular, the Prophet and his wife, Emma, and James and Harriet Adams were sealed on 28 May 1843 (Joseph Smith Diary, Church Archives). Similarly, Hyrum Smith and his wife, Mary Fielding, Brigham Young and his wife, Mary Ann, and Willard Richards and his wife, Jennetta, were all sealed the next day. But the higher ordinances that confer the fulness of the priesthood had not as yet been administered. However one month and a day after this 27 August 1843 discourse, Joseph and Emma received the anointing and ordination "of the highest and holiest order of the priesthood" (Joseph Smith Diary, 28 September 1843, Church Archives). Hence by 27 August 1843, "Abrahams patriarchal power . . . [was] the greatest yet experienced in [the] church." As abstract as this may seem, the Prophet was not the only one who understood the relationship between these three orders of priesthood blessings that he said were illustrated in Hebrews 7; they who received these ordinances also understood these relationships. For example, Brigham Young later discussed in public discourse the relationship between the Aaronic and Patriarchal orders of the endowment as follows:

> When we give the brethren their endowments, we . . . confer upon them the Melchizedek Priesthood; but I expect to see the day, when we shall . . . say to a company of brethren, you can go and receive the [endowment] ordinances pertaining to the Aaronic order of Priesthood, and then you can go into the world and preach the Gospel, or do something that will prove whether you will honor that Priesthood before you receive more. Now we pass them through the [temple] ordinances of both Priesthoods in one day. (*Journal of Discourses*, 10:309, quoted in John A. Widstoe, *Discourses of Brigham Young* [Salt Lake City: Deseret Book Co., 1973], p. 396).

Perhaps more important than his later understanding of the relationship between the Aaronic and Melchizedek portions of the endowment is the fact that three weeks before this 27 August 1843 discourse, Brigham Young demonstrates that the Prophet made clear to those who had received the endowment and patriarchal marriage ordinances, that they had not as yet received the fulness of the priesthood. On 6 August 1843, Brigham Young said, "If any in the church [have] the fullness of the Melchizedek Priesthood [I do] not know it. For any person to have the fullness of that priesthood, he must be a king and priest." Since he had received, with eight others, an anointing in 1842 promising him he would, if faithful, eventually receive another anointing actually ordaining him a king and a priest, Brigham Young therefore added, "A person may be anointed king and priest long before he receives his kingdom (*History of the Church*, 5:527, which is quoted verbatim from the contemporary account kept by Wilford Woodruff). Based on his understanding from Joseph the Prophet, Brigham Young said of this third order of priesthood blessings, "Those who . . . come in here [the Nauvoo Temple] and *have received* their washing & anointing *will* [later, if faithful], be ordained Kings & Priests, and will then have received the fullness of the Priesthood, all that can be given on earth. For Brother Joseph said he had given us all that could be given to man on the earth" (Heber C. Kimball Journal, kept by William Clayton, 26 December 1845, Church Archives, italics added). This is the theological and historical context for the Prophet's comments on the three orders of temple blessings outlined in this extremely important discourse.

22. As high and important to the Church as the office of prophet, apostle and patriarch are, nevertheless, these highest ecclesiastical ordinations do not confer the authority of Elijah, the sealing power of the priesthood, or the power of a king and priest. As President Joseph Fielding Smith expressed it best in our own century,

I do not care what office you hold in the Church—you may be an apostle, you may be a patriarch, a high priest, or anything else—but you cannot receive the fullness of the priesthood and the fullness of eternal reward unless you receive the ordinances of the house of the Lord. . . . Then [the door is] open so you can obtain all the blessings which any man can gain. . . . You can have ["the fullness of the Lord's blessings"] sealed upon you as an elder, if you are faithful; and when you receive them, and live faithfully and keep these covenants, you then have all that any man can get. There is no exaltation in the kingdom of God without the fullness of the priesthood" (Joseph Fielding Smith, first address to the Priesthood as President of the Church, 4 April 1970, *The Improvement Era* 73 [June 1970]: 65-66).

Regarding Abraham's receiving the "power of an endless life" after he offered his son Isaac, see note 29, this discourse.

23. Regarding the power "to open the windows of Heaven" (Malachi 3:10), see 5 October 1840, note 19. In regard to the phrase "law of endless Life to man," see D&C 132:19, 22, 24, and 28-32.

24. Romans 8:17 (14-17).

25. See note 38, this discourse.

26. George Laub's report of the 16 June 1844 discourse includes the following similar statement: "But the Holy Ghost is yet a Spiritual body and waiting to take to himself a body, as the Savior did or as God did, or the gods before them took bodies." Franklin D. Richards's account is less vague and represents the clearest statement on the personal identity of the Holy Ghost.

27. Matthew 5:38.

28. While the Levitical order of the endowment would admit only one man, the high priest, within the veil, through the Melchizedek order, all men who prove worthy may be admitted into the presence of the Lord (D&C 107:18-19; see note 23 July 1843, note 21).

29. The apparent discrepancy between the Franklin D. Richards and Martha Coray reports on this point may be reconciled in light of the Prophet's distinction between a man's ordination to the priesthood and his possessing power in the priesthood. Priesthood ordination does not, by itself, assure a man that God will ratify all his acts as a priesthood bearer. Perhaps Abraham received the "anointing and sealing" (the priesthood ordination of king and priest) under the hands of Melchizedek (Genesis 14:17-24 and JST Genesis 14:25-40), but the "election sure"—the absolute assurance of power in the priesthood—came directly from God only after Abraham indicated his willingness to sacrifice Isaac (Genesis 22:1-14).

30. One of the major milestones, if not the major milestone, of the Latter-day work was to be the restoration of the fulness of the priesthood (D&C 124:28). The Prophet's "mission . . . [was to] firmly [establish] the

dispensation of the fullness of the priesthood in the last days, that all the powers of earth and hell [could] never prevail against it" (*History of the Church*, 5:140, or *Teachings*, p. 258). What was this fulness of the priesthood? The most concise but inclusive definition of the authority of the fulness of the priesthood was given by Joseph Smith in his 10 March 1844 discourse when he said, "Now for Elijah; the spirit, power and calling of Elijah is that ye have power to hold the keys of the revelations, ordinances, oracles, powers and endowments of the fulness of the Melchizedek Priesthood and of the Kingdom of God on the Earth and to receive, obtain and perform all the ordinances belonging to the kingdom of God ... [to] have power to seal on earth and in heaven." However, the Prophet had not as yet administered the ordinances that made men kings and priests. Brigham Young said three weeks before this discourse that no one yet in the Church had the fulness of the Melchizedek Priesthood, "For any person to have the fullness of that priesthood, he must be a king and priest" (*History of the Church*, 5:527, which is quoted verbatim from the original source kept by Wilford Woodruff, Church Archives). These ordinances were instituted on 28 September 1843 and in the next five months were conferred on twenty men (and their wives, except for those whose names are asterisked): Hyrum Smith, Brigham Young, Heber C. Kimball, Willard Richards, Newel K. Whitney, William Marks, John Taylor, John Smith, Reynolds Cahoon, Alpheus Cutler, Orson Spencer, Orson Hyde*, Parley P. Pratt*, Wilford Woodruff, George A. Smith, Levi Richards*, Cornelius P. Lott, William W. Phelps, Isaac Morley, and Orson Pratt.* As George Q. Cannon later said,

> Previous to his death, the Prophet Joseph manifested great anxiety to see the temple completed, as most of you who were with the Church during his day, well know. "Hurry up the work, brethren," he used to say, "let us finish the temple; the Lord has a great endowment in store for you, and I am anxious that the brethren should have their endowments and receive the fullness of the Priesthood. ... Then," said he, "the Kingdom will be established, and I do not care what shall become of me."
>
> Prior to the completion of the Temple, [Joseph Smith] took the Twelve and certain other men, who were chosen, and bestowed upon them a holy anointing, similar to that which was received on the day of Pentecost by the Twelve, who had been told to tarry at Jerusalem. This endowment was bestowed upon the chosen few whom Joseph anointed and ordained, giving unto them the keys of the holy Priesthood, the power and authority which he himself held, to build up the Kingdom of God in all the earth and accomplish the great purposes of our Heavenly Father."

Knowing that Sidney Rigdon was the only member of the First Presidency to survive the martyrdom but knowing too that he had not received the ordinances of the fulness of the priesthood, George Q. Cannon added this significant comment: "It was by virtue of this authority, on the death of Joseph, that President Young, as President of the quorum of the Twelve, presided over the Church" (*Journal of Discourses*, 13:49). Joseph

Smith's followers did believe he "firmly established the dispensation of the fullness of the priesthood ... that all ... earth and hell [could] never prevail against it." See notes 21, 22, 29, and 38, this discourse.

31. D&C 107:5,14.

32. D&C 107:13-14.

33. See note 4, this discourse.

34. Malachi 3:1-3.

35. Genesis 22:1-14.

36. For example, Matthew 26:36-46.

37. Matthew 3:15 (13-17).

38. This is the only known record of when, according to Joseph Smith, the Savior received the fulness of the priesthood. Wilford Woodruff's report of the Prophet's 11 June 1843 discourse recorded a significant comment by Joseph Smith regarding this subject: "If a man gets the fulness of God ["priesthood" as in the published version], he has to get [it] in the same way that Jesus Christ obtained it, by keeping all the ordinances of the house of the Lord" (see 11 June 1843, note 9). To Joseph Smith, however, it was not the Lord's will that all have Elijah confer upon them the sealing power of the fulness of the priesthood, for as Franklin D. Richards expressed it, we receive the fulness by "being administered to by one having the same power and Authority of Melchizedek" (D&C 132:7).

Joseph Smith distinguished between the ordination of the twelve disciples as apostles (in Matthew 10) and the bestowal of the sealing power of Elijah upon three of the twelve (in Matthew 17), for he himself received the authority of the apostleship in 1829 (Joseph Smith-History, 1:72; D&C 27:12), but did not receive the sealing power of the fulness of the priesthood until 3 April 1836 (D&C 110:13-16; also text at notes 13-20 of the 10 March 1844 discourse).

39. Matthew 28:18.

40. Galatians 3:12, 19.

41. Matthew 3:15 (13-17).

42. Matthew 26:39 (36-46).

43. In his 21 May 1843 discourse (at note 12), the Prophet, without elaborating on his statement, said he would "keep in [his] own bosom the design of the great God in sending us into this world and organizing us to prepare us for the Eternal world." Joseph Smith did hint though that the doctrine of eternal marriage was related to the implicit question. Here in the James Burgess account of the 27 August 1843 discourse (three months later), the Prophet finally answers his own question: "What was the design of the Almighty in making man? It was to exalt him to be as God." Given that the

Prophet would have answered the question similarly in May, this is remarkable confirmation of the then-unwritten revelation on eternal marriage. When it was written seven and a half weeks later (12 July 1843), this revelation asserted that if couples were sealed by the Holy Spirit of Promise through the authority of the sealing power of the priesthood and later were given the promise that they would come forth in the first resurrection, and if they should continue without commiting the unpardonable sin, "Then shall they be gods ... because they have all power, and the angels are subject unto them" (D&C 132:19-20).

44. John 10:34-35 (32-39).

45. Romans 8:17 and Matthew 28:18.

46. That is Joseph Smith taught that when people deny some commands of God because of their pre-conceived notions and traditions, they actually close the door to their own salvation and exaltation. Given the perplexity he had in teaching certain doctrines at this time of his ministry, it is not hard to understand why he often referred to this characteristic of men and women. Even those within the church had difficulties accepting some of his teachings. See 5 October 1840, note 24, 3 October 1841, note 19 and note 5, this discourse.

47. See 13 August 1843 (2), note 10.

48. See note 4, this discourse.

49. D&C 132:19-24. To have the power of "endless lives" is to have secured before the time of resurrection the promise of exaltation in eternity with the accompanying promise of a continuation of the lives or seed—that is to have the power to have children after the resurrection (see *History of the Church*, 5:391-92).

50. Genesis 22:1-19.

51. Exodus 19, 20:18-21; D&C 84:19-27.

13 September 1843

1. See *History of the Church*, 6:32. Not in *Teachings*. The original source for the entry in the *History of the Church* appears to be the Joseph Smith Diary, by Willard Richards.

2. John Finch from Liverpool, England.

3. Robert Owen was a British utopian socialist who believed in economic as well as political equality, and who considered competition debasing. He decided to establish an ideal society in America at New Harmony, Indiana.

14 September 1843

1. See *History of the Church*, 6:33. Not in *Teachings*. The original source for the entry in *History of the Church* is the Joseph Smith Diary, by Willard Richards. The report by Levi Richards is here published for the first time.

2. Alexander Campbell (1788-1866), with whom Sidney Rigdon associated was one of the founders of the Disciples of Christ. He established and became first president of Bethany College.

3. John Finch.

16 September 1843

1. See *History of the Church*, 6:34. Not in *Teachings*. The original source for the entry in *History of the Church* is the Joseph Smith Diary, by Willard Richards.

2. Erastus H. Derby, born 14 September 1801, was a native of Hawley Township, Franklin County, Massachusetts. He is best remembered for his friendship and aid to the Prophet during the latter's attempts to avoid illegal arrest in 1842.

17 September 1843 (1)

1. See *History of the Church*, 6:34. Not in *Teachings*. The original source for the entry in *History of the Church* is the Joseph Smith Diary, by Willard Richards. The brief notation in Willard Richard's personal diary is here published for the first time.

2. Almon W. Babbitt (1812-56). An active and talented man, Babbitt was baptized in 1833 and given numerous important assignments in the Church. His incorrigible nature, however, often placed him in disfavor with Church leaders.

3. Reverend Blodgett was a Unitarian minister from Massachusetts.

17 September 1843 (2)

1. See *History of the Church*, 6:34. Not in *Teachings*. The original source for the entry in the *History of the Church* is the Joseph Smith Diary, by Willard Richards. The Levi Richards report is here published for the first time.

2. John 18:38.

3. See 13 April 1843, notes 16 and 17.

4. William B. Brink was a botanical doctor who resided in Nauvoo. A

member of the Church, Brink probably was baptized in Nauvoo.

5. John M. Bernhisel (1799-1881) was a doctor of medicine. Converted to the Church in New York, he was a close friend of the Prophet and was later elected Utah's first delegate to Congress.

6. See 13 April 1843, note 17.

24 September 1843

1. See *History of the Church*, 6:37-38. Not in *Teachings*. The original source for the entry in *History of the Church* is the Joseph Smith Diary, by Willard Richards.

2. Several communitarian groups sprung up in the United States in the first half of the nineteenth century. Converts to the Church living in the Kirtland area in 1830 (formerly associated with Alexander Campbell) had participated in such orders.

3. The 1831-33 phase of the Church's Law of Consecration and Stewardship did not secure private ownership of property to Church members in Kirtland, Ohio or Jackson County, Missouri. From 1834 to 1838 consecration consisted of donation of surplus property only—Church members retained title to personal and real property. In 1838 (with the reception of D&C 119) the law of consecration required the donation of surplus properties plus 10% annual increase. This 1838 development of consecration, with some minor modifications, continued during the Nauvoo period. Thus the Prophet could say that Church members were private stewards, having private ownership of property.

4. George J. Adams (1819-80). Baptized in 1840, Adams was an able and aggressive missionary for the Church. After the Prophet's death he refused to be controlled by the Quorum of the Twelve and left the Church.

7 October 1843

1. See *History of the Church*, 6:47-48. Not in *Teachings*. The original source for the entry in *History of the Church* is *Times and Seasons* (15 September 1843). The following remarks by the Prophet were made at the October 1843 General Conference of the Church.

2. Gustavus Hills, born 29 January 1804, was a native of Chatham, Middlesex County, Connecticut. A watchmarker by trade, Hills was an associate justice of the municipal court of Nauvoo.

3. Orrin Porter Rockwell (1813-78). A colorful personality baptized in 1830, Rockwell was charged by Missourians with assault with intent to kill ex-Governor Lilburn W. Boggs. He remained a close friend of the Prophet.

4. The letter referred to is published in *History of the Church*, 5:250-51.

8 October 1843

1. See *History of the Church*, 6:48-49. Not in *Teachings*. The original source for the entry in *History of the Church* is *Times and Seasons* (15 September 1843). The following remarks were made at the October 1843 General Conference of the Church.

9 October 1843 (1)

1. See *History of the Church*, 6:49-50. Not in *Teachings*. The original source for the entry in *History of the Church* is *Times and Seasons* (15 September 1843). The following remarks were made at the October 1843 General Conference of the Church.

2. Francis M. Higbee (1820-?) was the son of Elias Higbee.

9 October 1843

1. See *History of the Church*, 6:50-52, and *Teachings*, pp. 324-26. The account of this funeral sermon in *History of the Church* and *Teachings* is an amalgamation of the reports in *Times and Seasons* (15 September 1843) and the Joseph Smith Diary. The reports of James Burgess and William Clayton are here published for the first time.

2. James Adams (1783-1843) was a prominent probate court judge from Springfield, Illinois. He ran unsuccessfully for governor of Illinois in 1834. After joining the Church he won the admiration and love of the Prophet and was one of nine men upon whom the endowment was first bestowed in May 1842.

3. Regarding the "ordinance of God set forth for [the] purpose" of revelation, see 5 October 1840, note 19.

4. In his 27 June 1839 discourse (Richards's Pocket Companion account), Joseph Smith said that when the ancients obtained the blessings of the Second Comforter— "Isaiah, Ezekiel, John upon the Isle of Patmos, St. Paul in the three heavens, and all the Saints who held communion with the general assembly and Church of the Firstborn"—the Lord taught them face to face and gave them a perfect knowledge of the mysteries of the Kingdom of God. While the Prophet stated there were things they received that were unlawful to utter (2 Corinthians 12:4[1-4]; 3 Nephi 17:17; 19:34 [32-34]; 28:12-14; D&C 76:115), yet there was a general theme revealed to all. That theme pertained to the future destiny of man before and during the earth's millennial state.

See passages refered to in 27 June 1839, note 15. For specific passages in the Book of Mormon confirming the idea of one general revelation for those who attain to these blessings, see 1 Nephi 14:20-28; 2 Nephi 27:6-23; Ether 3:25-27; 4:4-9, 13-16.

5. See note 4 of the discourse dated "Before 8 August 1839(3)."

6. James Adams, a staunch Illinois Democrat was, politically speaking, a very active man. Over the years his activity drew attention and he did not escape the slander that often attends party politics. In 1837, for example, he had a run-in with the young Abraham Lincoln. According to historian Harry E. Pratt, this bitter political feud was one of the "four events in the early career of Abraham Lincoln which he probably wished later could be forgotten" (Harry E. Pratt, "Lincolniana Notes." *Journal of the Illinois State Historical Society* 48 [1955]:456.

7. James Adams was one of the nine men to whom the Prophet gave the patriarchal priesthood keys of revelation in May 1842 (see 5 October 1840, note 19).

8. Alpheus Cutler.

9. Reynolds Cahoon.

10. Hyrum Smith.

11. See text of the discourse dated 2 April 1843(1), at note 6.

12. Luke 24:37, 39 (36-39).

13. This was 4 November 1839 (see *History of the Church*, 4:20).

14. 1 Corinthians 15:50.

15. Hebrews 13:2.

16. Luke 24:39 (36-39). See 27 June 1839, note 21.

15 October 1843

1. See *History of the Church*, 6:56-59, and *Teachings*, pp. 326-29. The original source for the reports in *History of the Church* and *Teachings* is the Joseph Smith Diary. The brief notation concerning this discourse in the Willard Richards Diary is here published for the first time.

2. Genesis 6:6.

3. 1 Samuel 15:29.

4. See King James Version, Hebrews 6:1.

5. JST Hebrews 6:1.

6. See 27 June 1839, note 5.

7. John 3:3.

8. John 3:5.

9. The Prophet made a similar remark on two other occasions. See discourse dated 28 April 1842 at note 11, and 27 August 1843 after notes 5 and 48.

10. Spiritual wives; that is, rumors about plural marriage, which was not yet taught publicly.

11. See 13 April 1843, note 15.

12 November 1843

1. Not in *History of the Church* or *Teachings*. The following report by William Rowley is here published for the first time.

2. William Rowley was born 21 June 1798 at Litchfield, Staffordshire, England. Coverted to the Church in England, Rowley arrived with a group of Saints in Nauvoo on 11 November 1843. The William Rowley Diary is located in Manuscripts Division, J. Willard Marriott Library, University of Utah, Salt Lake City, Utah.

29 November 1843

1. See *History of the Church*, 6:88, 93-95. Not in *Teachings*.

2. The Green Mountain Boys had been formed in 1770 by settlers in present-day Vermont. Commanded by Ethan Allen, they sought to protect their land holdings from claim by New York. The regiment fought in the American Revolution.

3. William W. Phelps (1792-1872) was baptized in 1831 and remained a prominent Church leader until 1838, often assisting with the printing of Church literature. In Nauvoo, after being rebaptized because of apostasy, Phelps remained close to the Prophet and assisted him in several writing endeavors.

4. Henry Clay (1777-1852). Clay was a U.S. stateman with whom Joseph Smith corresponded in 1843 and 1844. Since Clay was a candidate for the presidency, the Prophet asked him what his "rule of action" would be towards the Mormon people if he were elected. See *History of the Church*, 6:64-65 and 376-77.

5. The memorial referred to is published in *History of the Church*, 6:84-88. Colonel John Frierson, political representative of John C. Calhoun, agreed to present the memorial for a redress of Missouri grievances to Congress in exchange for Mormon support of Calhoun in his presidential bid.

4 December 1843

1. See *History of the Church*, 6:99. Not in *Teachings*. This meeting of the citizens of Nauvoo was a continuation of the meeting held on 29 November 1843. The original source for the report in *History of the Church* is based on the Joseph Smith Diary, by Willard Richards, and the *Nauvoo Neighbor* (6 December 1843).

2. The Prophet's appeal to the Green Mountain Boys of Vermont is found in *History of the Church*, 6:88-93.

3. Willard Richards.

9 December 1843

1. See *History of the Church*, 6:107-8. Not in *Teachings*. The source for the entry in *History of the Church* is the *Nauvoo Neighbor*. The Wilford Woodruff report is here published for the first time.

2. The Nauvoo city ordinance referred to is cited in *History of the Church*, 6:105-6. The ordinance stated, "If any person or persons shall come with process, demand, or requisition, founded upon the aforesaid Missouri difficulties, to arrest said Joseph Smith, he or they so offending shall be subject to be arrested . . . and if found guilty, sentenced to imprisonment for life . . . pardoned [only] by the Governor" (*History of the Church*, 6:105).

3. Josiah Lamborn (1819-1847) was Attorney General of Illinois 1840-1843. Lamborn gave it as his opinion that the Nauvoo Legion was a creation of the City of Nauvoo, and not part of the regular militia of the state.

18 December 1843

1. Not in *History of the Church* or *Teachings*. The following report by Wilford Woodruff is here published for the first time.

1844

1844

7 January 1844 (Sunday Afternoon). Cornelius P. Lott's Home.[1]
Joseph Smith Diary, by Willard Richards

Rode out to my farm & Preached at Bro. Lots.[2] also D Spencer[3] & Reynolds Cahoon preached.

19 January 1844 (Friday). Mansion House.[1]
Joseph Smith Diary, by Willard Richards

In the evening gave a Lecture on the constitution & candidates for the presidency &c. Backenstos.[2] Clerk of Co Court. present Bro Phelps[3] & a great Co. in Bar Room.

21 January 1844 (Sunday). Front of Robert D. Foster's Hotel, Near Temple.[1]
Wilford Woodruff Journal

A large assembly of Saints met at the Temple and herd an interesting discours deliverd by President Joseph Smith. The following is a synopsis of his discourse upon the occasion

When I Consider the surrounding Circumstances in which I am placed this day, standing in the open air with week lungs &

somwhat out of health I feel that I must have prayers & faith of my brethren that God may strengthen me & pour out his special blessings upon me if you get much from me this day. Their are many people assembled here to day & throughout this City & from various parts of the world who say that they have received to a certainty a portion of knowledge from God by revelation in the way that he has ordained & pointed out I shall take the broad ground then that if we have or Can receive a portion of knowledge from God by immediate revelation by the same source we can receive all knowledge. What shall I talk about today I know what Br Cahoon[2] wants me to speak about, he wants me to speak about the Comeing of Elijah in the last days I Can see it in his eye, I will speak upon that subject then, The Bible says "I will send you Elijah before the great & dredful day of the Lord Come that he shall turn the hearts of the fathers to the Children & the hearts of the Children to their fathers lest I Come & smite the whole earth with a Curse,"[3] Now the word turn here should be translated (bind or seal)[4] But what is the object of this important mission or how is it to be fulfilled, The keys are to be deliverd[5] the spirit of Elijah is to Come, The gospel to be esstablished the Saints of God gatherd Zion built up, & the Saints[6] to Come up as Saviors on mount Zion[7] but how are they to become Saviors on Mount Zion by building thair temples erecting their Baptismal fonts & going forth & receiving all the ordinances, Baptisms, Confirmations, washings anointings ordinations & sealing powers[8] upon our heads in behalf of all[9] our Progenitors who are dead & redeem them that they may Come forth in the first resurrection & be exhalted to thrones of glory with us, & here in is the chain that binds the hearts of the fathers to the Children, & the Children to the Fathers which fulfills the mission of Elijah & I would to God that this temple was now done that we might go into it & go to work & improve our time & make use of the seals[10] while they are on earth & the Saints have none to much time to save & redeem their dead, & gather together their living relatives that they may be saved also, before the earth will be smitten & the Consumption decreed falls upon the world[11] & I would advise all the Saints to go to with their might & gather together all their living relatives to this place that they may be sealed & saved that they may be prepared against the day that the destroying angel goes forth & if the whole Church should go to with all their might to save their dead seal their posterity & gather their living friends & spend none of their time in behalf of the world they would hardly get through before night would Come when no man Could work[12] & my ownly trouble at the present time is concerning ourselves that the Saints will be divided & broken up & scattered before we get our Salvation[13] Secure for thei[r] is so many fools in the world for the devil to operate upon it gives him the advantage often times, The question is frequently asked Can we not be saved without going through with all thes ordinances &c[14] I would answer No not the fulness of Salvation, Jesus said their was many mansions in his fathers house & he would go & prepare a place for them.[15] House here named should have been translated (Kingdom)[16] & any person who is exhalted to the highest mansion has to abide a Celestial law & the whole law to[o],[17] But their has been a great difficulty in getting anything into the heads of this generation it has been like splitting hemlock knots with a Corn doger for a wedge & a pumpkin for a beetle,[18] Even the Saints are slow to understand I have tried for a number of years to get the minds of the Saints prepared to receive the things of God, but we frequently see some of them after suffering all they have for the work of God will fly to peaces like glass as soon as any thing Comes that is Contrary to their traditions,[19] they Cannot stand the fire at all, How many will be able to abide a Celestial law & go through & receive their exhaltation I am unable to say but many are Called & few are Chosen.[20]

Joseph Smith Diary, by Willard Richards

Preached in front of Dr Foster Mammoth Hotel to several thousand people.—although the weather was somewhat unpleasant. on sealing the hearts of the fathers to the children & the heart of the children to the fathers.

8 February 1844 (Thursday Evening). Upper Room, Red Brick Store.[1]
Wilford Woodruff Journal

I met with a congregation of the Citizens in the room over Joseph Store for the purpose of hearing the views of General Joseph Smith given concerning the affairs of Government his views were written & were read by Wm W Phelps & were in the highest degree interesting.[2] Gen Smith gave his reasons for permitting his name to go forth as a Candidate for the Presidency of the United States. which were as follows

I would not have suffered my name to have been used by my friends on any wise as president of the United States or Candidate for that office If I & my friends could have had the privilege of enjoying our religious & civel rights as American Citizen even those rights which the Constitution guarantee unto all her Citizens alike but this we as a people have been denied from the beginning Persecution has rolled upon our heads from time to time from portions of the United States like peels of thunder because of our religion & no portion of the government as yet has steped forward for our relief & under view of these things I feel it to be my right & privilege to obtain what influence & power I can lawfully in the United States for the protection of injured innocence & If I loose my life[3] in a good cause I am will to be sacrificed on the alter of virtue rightousness & truth in maintaining the laws & Constitution of the United States if need be for the general good of mankind.

Joseph Smith Diary, by Willard Richards

evening had a political Meeting in the assembly room & Bro Phelps publicly read my views of the Gen Government for the first time—Elders Hyde & Taylor made a speech—& myself also.

18 February 1844 (Sunday). At Temple.[1]
Joseph Smith Diary, by Willard Richards

I Preached at the Temple to a Large Collection.

Thomas Bullock Diary[2]

Attd the first meeting at the temple, Joseph spoke, to an immense congregation.

21 February 1844 (Wednesday Evening). Upper Room, Red Brick Store.[1]
Joseph Smith Diary, by Willard Richards

Rev Mr De.Wolf,[2] Churchman, Lectured in the assembly room

in the eve. I attended & after sermon—at his request, spoke to the people to show them that to get salvation we must not only do somethings but every thing which God had commanded to get salvation.[3]

25 February 1844 (Sunday). At Temple.[1]
Joseph Smith Diary, by Willard Richards

I preached at or near the Temple. Hiram also preached.

Wilford Woodruff Journal

President Smith Preached at the Temple.

Thomas Bullock Diary

Went to the Temple with my wife[2]—heard Joseph preach on Cardinal points—an immense congregation.

7 March 1844 (Thursday Morning). At Temple.[1]
Joseph Smith Diary, by Willard Richards

9 A. M. I Joseph presented to the meeting the proceedings of O. F. Bostwick[2] & the Lawyers &c—for the people to speak out, say whether such men should be tolerated and supported in our midst.—and from this time I design to bring such characters before the committee of the whole.—and if these things cannot be put a stop to. I will give them in to the hands of the mob.—the hands of the officers of the city falter, and are palsied by the conduct of such men.

There is another I will speak about he is a mormon.—a certain man who lived here before we come here. the two first letters of his name are Hiram Kimball—when the city had passed an ordinance to tax steam boats. He goes and tells the captains of the steam boats that he owned the landing. and they need not to pay tax—and I am determined to use up such men if they will not stop their efforts. If this is not true. Let him come forward & throw of[f] the imputation.—when ~~they~~ people appeal to carthage I will appeal to this people—the highest court—I despise the Lawyers who lag on their law suits. Kimball & Morrison[3] say they own the wharfs. but the city own the wharf.—64 ft. from high water mark from printing office to the northern limits of the city.—

annother thing. I want to speak about. the Lawyers of this city. I have good feelings & and I will reprove them—and the prophets always did say wo unto you ye Lawyers.—the Maratime laws of the U. S. have ceded up the tolls wharfage &c to the respective corporations who have jurisdiction. &c.

Shallow drafts intoxicate the brain &c.

Look at the reason.—no vessel could land any where if Subject to individuals laws.—Corporation owns the streets of the city, and have a right to tax the Boats to make wharfs. the same as to tax citizens to make roads—want every man in this city to stay at home & let the Boat Captains. peace officers and every body alone.—

How are we to keep peace in this city. & defend our selves against mobs—disgrace every man by preaching—him on the house top, who will, who not be still, and mind their own business.—Let them alone to use themselves up.—

A couple of merchants in this city. I was ~~visi~~ told by an old gentleman this morning who told me that the spirit of Mobocracy was almost subsiding.—These mobocrats have as the people abroad say.—told the people that they need not bring butter eggs &c—to Nauvoo will not tell their names. if they will not let the people bring in their produce.—the people will not buy their goods

another Man. will not call his name. has been writing to the New York Tribune⁴ some of the ~~greatest~~ most disgraceful things possible to name.—he has stated in that article that there are a great many appropriations to the temple—applied some where else &c.— to stigmatize the Trustee⁵ & turn prejudice against us abroad.—if any man who has appointed any thing.—old harness horses waggon ~~&c~~ let him come forward the first farthing and we cannot show where it has been appropriated. I will give him my head for a foot ball.—

he also states that the Temple cannot be build it costs so much. who dont know that we can put the roof on this building this season? by turning all the means of the N. House & doubling our diligence we can do it.

The best way for such men is to be still. If I did not love men I would not reprove them. but work in the dark as they do—read the Tribune & you see for yourself.—

he is not a Lawyer. he is nearer related to a Doctor. a small man.—"Mr McNiel[6]—enquired if he was the man.—" No did not know you—you are a stranger. Joseph rested [during Hyrum Smith's remarks].

Chas Foster asked if Joseph meant him Joseph said. I will ask you a question—[F.] that is no way. [J.] yes that is the way the Quakers do. Why did you denominate yourself.—Jesus said—whose image & superscription is it[7]—[F.] Did you mean me.—[J.] Why did you denominate yourself. did [F.] then I understand you meant me.—[J.] You said it.—[F.] You shall hear form me.—Mayor I fine you $10.00 for that threat, and disturbing the meeting Doctor [Robert] Foster spoke to palliate and exhort him to await—&c doctor said he has not threatened you.—Joseph says he has—Doctor no one has heard him threaten you—and hundreds cried I have. Doctor continued to speak & Mayor said stop order or I will fine you—

W W. Phelps read Gen Smiths views of the powers & policies of the Gen Government, after which it was voted unanimously with one exception, to uphold Gen Smith for the Presidency.

"A voice of Innocence from Nauvoo" was then read by W W Phelps.—and all the people assembly said Amen. twice

Doctor Foster read a letter from Thomas Ford Governor

30 minutes past 12. adjourned till 2. P. M.

Wilford Woodruff Journal

The Prophet arived & took the stand. and arose in the midst of people & said (Orson Pratt come & take your post) & further remarked I do not know whether the object of the meeting has been told or not I apologize for not comeing sooner. I have had so much on my mind since I saw you that I hardly know whare to begin or to say but one of the grand objects that I had in view in calling this meeting was in making a few remarks relative to the laws & ordinances and building the temple, the reason I want to speak of the laws is the Officers have difficulty in administering the laws. We are republican & wish to have the people rule but rule in righteousness, Sone [Some] would complain with what God himself would do, the laws are enacted by petition and they can all be repealed if they wish it but the people ought not to complain of the officers but to complain of the law makers, I am instructed by the

City Council to tell this people that if you do not like any law we have passed we will repeal it for we are your servants, Any that Complain of our rights and Charters it is because they are wicked the devil is in them. the reason I called it up is we have a simple gang of fellows who does not know whare their elbows or head is if you preach virtue to them they will oppose that if you preach the Methodist God to them they will oppose that or any thing els & if their is any Case tried they want it appealed to Carthage Mr Boswick's case had to go to Carthage our Lawyers will send any thing to Carthage. I want to know if the Citizens will sustain me when my hands are raised to heaven for the people, I will areign the person before the people that act against the interest of the City & I will have the voice of the people which is republican and as likely to be the voice of God And ~~as long as long~~ as long as I have a tongue to speak I will expose the iniquity of the Lawyiers and wicked men I fear not their boiling over nor the boiling over of Hell their thunders & forked lightning. I despise the man that will betray you with a kiss. Here is Hiram Kimball has set at naught the ordinances of the City. By saying that He owns the wharf & steem boats need not pay them. wharefore this body is the highest Court what appeal to Carthage I would not appeal there if i died a thousand deaths. Kimball nor Morrison does not own the wharfage water street runs along the beach & belongs to the City & not individuals I will reprove the lawyers & doctrs anyhow Jesus did[8] & evry prophet has & if I am a prophet I shall do it, at any rate I shall do it for i profess to be a prophet. The laws & Constitution of the United States has ceded up the right to Corporate Cities to regulate all wharfage of shiping & Steem Boats &c all laws of taxation is subject to the City & not individuals, And I want from this time forth evry fool to stay at home & let the steem Boats & Captain alone and let the peace officers alone. How can we keep off mobs & keeping innocent Blood from being shed, By striking a blow at evry thing that rises up in disorder & I will war an eternal war with those that oppose me while I am labouring in behalf of the City. A man has been writing to the New York Tribune I will not mention his name.[9] He says that much has been appropriated for the building the Temple that has been spent for other purposes. But I pledge myself that any man that has paid any old shoes, harnesss, horses, or any thing els if he will come I will show him on Book that evry farthi[n]g has gone on Book & been appropriated for the building of the Temple ~~if not so~~ I will pled[g]e my head for a foot ball that this is true. their are men in our midst who are trying to build up themselves at our expense & others in our midst that are watching for iniquity & will make a man an offender for a word,[10] But I will rest myself & give way for others.

Willard Richards Diary

Great Meeting at Temple all day.

7 March 1844 (Thursday Afternoon). At Temple.[1]
Joseph Smith Diary, by Willard Richards

Joseph said in relation to those who give property on the temple. be careful into whose hands it come into that it may be entered into the church books. that those whose names are found in the church books[2] shall have the first claim in that house. I intend to keep the door at dedication myself—& not a man shall pass who had not paid his bonus

I do not care 1/2 so much about the Pres election as I do the office I have got we have as good a right to make a political party to gain power to defend ourselves as for ~~mormons~~ demagogues to make use of our religion to get power to destroy ourselves.—we will whip the mob by getting up a president. when I look into the Eastern papers & see how popular I am I am afraid I shall be president.—

on the annexation of Texas—some object—the anti-Mormons are good fellows—I say it in anticipation they will repent object to Texas on account of slavery.—Tis the very reason why she should be received.—

Houston[3] says "gentlemen if you refuse to receive us we must go to the British" and the first thing they will do will be to set the negroes free & Indians & they will use us up.

British officers running all over Texas to pick a quarrel with us.—more honorable for us to receive them. & set the negroes free & use the negroes & indians against our foes.

dont let Texas go out.[4] Our Mother & the daughter of the land, will laugh us in the teeth.—and if these things are not so—God never spoke ~~with~~ by any prophet since the world began.—I have been [thought not completed] south held the balance of power &c—by annexing Texas.—I can do away this evil liberate 2 or 3 states & if that was not sufficient, call in Canida—

Send the negroes to Texas. from Texas to Mexico where all colors are alike.—Notice was given for the relief Society to meet saturday 2 P. M. to adopt "the voice of Innocence from Nauvoo."[5]

Joseph stated the Mormon Zion has endured all animus
Singing & prayer by B. Young.

Wilford Woodruff Journal

President Smith remarked in relation to those who give in property for the temple we want it brought to the proper source that it may be put on the Church Book[6] So that in the endowment those whose names are on Book shall have the prefference. As to politics I care but little about the Presidential Chair., I would not give half as much for the office as I would for the one I now hold, but as the world have used the power of Goverment to oppress & persecute us it is right for us to use it for the protection of our rights. when I get hold of the eastern paper & see how popular I am I am afraid myself that I shall be elected, But if I should be I would not say that your cause is just & I could not do anything for you.[7] What I said in relation to the annexation of texas is with some unpopular the people are opposed to it, I will take this objection away. the opposition is because it is filled up with Slavery,[8] now I wish to turn the argument it is the vary reason why it ought to be received in order to watch over them of the ~~greatest~~ two evils we should reject the greatest The president of Texas sayes if you do not receive us in the United States we will go to the British[9] this would certainly be bad policy for this Nation the British are now throughout that whole Country trying to bribe all they can. How much better it is to be to a little expens than to have the indians & British upon us & destroy us all, we should grasp all the territory we can[10] and I know, much that I do not tell I have had bribes offerd me, but I have rejected them. The government will not receive any thing from me they are self sufficient, but they must go to Hell & work out their own salvation with fear & trembling. as soon as texas was annexed I would liberate two or three states & pay them for their salves & let them go to Mexico whare they are mixed blacks &c I would also receive Canida & stand by them & many other usful remarks He made.

Thomas Bullock Diary

At the temple all day—the Prophet, Patriarch, B. Young, Taylor &c spoke—both large meetings. a most splendid day—& an attentive congregation—received much instruction.

Nauvoo Neighbor 1 (13 March 1844)

On Thursday last a large concourse of people assembled at the Temple, according to previous appointment. Gens. Joseph Smith and Hyrum Smith, Elder Young, and others, addressed the meeting at considerable length, and were listened to with profound attention. Upwards of five thousand persons were present on the occasion.

10 March 1844 (Sunday). At Temple.[1]
Wilford Woodruff Journal

A large assembly of the Saints met at the temple & was addressed by President Joseph Smith upon one of the most important & interesting subjects ever presented to the saints & the principles presented were of the greatest importance to be understood it was as follows the work & calling & spirit of Elias, Elijah, & Mesiah The following is a synopsis of the discourse

Their is a differance between the spirit & office of Elias & Elijah it is the spirit of Elias[2] I wish first to speak of. And in order to come at the subject I will bring some of the testimony from the scripture & give my own, in the first place suffice it to say I went into the woods to inquire of the Lord by prayer his will concerning me—& I saw an angel & he laid his hands upon my head & ordained me to be a priest after the order of Aaron[3] & to hold the keys of this priesthood which office was to preach repentance & Baptism for the remission of sins & also to baptise but was informed that this office did not extend to the laying on of hands for the giving of the Holy Ghost that that office was a greater work[4] & was to be given after wards but that my ordination was a preparetory work or a going before which was the spirit of Elias for the spirit of Elias was a going before to prepare the way for the greater, which was the Case with John the Baptist he Came balling through the wilderness prepare ye the the way of the Lord & make his paths strait[5] & they were informed if they Could receive it it was the spirit of Elias[6] & John was vary particular to tell the people He was not that light but was sent to bear witness of that light, He told the people that his mission was to preach repentance & baptize with water,[7] but it was he that should Come after him that should baptise with fire & the Holy Ghost[8] if he had been an imposture he might have gone to work beyound, his bounds & undertook to have performed ordinances that did not belong to that office & calling under the spirit of Elias. The spirit of Elias is to prepare the way for a greater revelation of God which is the priesthood of Elias or the Priesthood that Aaron was ordained unto. And when God sends a man into the world to prepare for a greater work holds the keys of the power of Elias it was called the doctrin of Elias even from the early ages of the world.[9] John,s mission was limited to preaching & Baptizing but what he done was legal & when Jesus Christ Came to any of John,s deciples He baptized them with fire & the Holy Ghost, we find the Apostles endowed with greater power than John their office was more under the spirit & power of Elijah than Elias. In the Case of Philip when he went down to Samaria was under the spirit of Elias he baptised both men & women, when Peter & John herd of it they went down & lade hands on them & they received the Holy Ghost this shows the distinction between the two powers.[10] when paul came to Certain Deciples He asked if they had received the Holy Ghost they said no, who baptized you then we were Baptizd unto Johns Baptism No John did not baptized you for he did his work right, & so Paul went & baptized them for He knew what the true doctrin was & he knew that John Had not Baptised them,[11] & these principles and [it] is strange to me that men who have red the scriptures of the New Testament are so far from it. What I want to impress upon your minds is, the difference of power in the different parts of the Priesthood, so that when any man comes among you saying I have the spirit of Elias you can know whether he be true or fals, for any man that comes having the spirit & power of Elias he will not transend his bounds, John did not transend his bound but faithfully performed that part belonging to his office, and evry portion of the great building should be prepared right & assigned to its proper place,[12] & it is necessary to know who holds the keys of power & who dont, or we may be likely to be decieved, That person who holds the keys of Elias hath a preparitory work, But if I spend much more time in conversing about the spirit of Elias I shall not have time to do justice to the spirit & power of Elijah, this is the Elias spoken of in the last days & here is the rock upon which many split thinking the time was past in the days of John & Christ & no more to be, but the spirit of Elias was revealed to me & I know it is true therefore I speak with boldness for I know varily my doctrin is true. Now for Elijah, the spirit power & calling of Elijah is that ye have power to hold the keys of the revelations ordinances, oricles powers & endowments of the fulness of the Melchezedek Priesthood[13] & of the Kingdom of God on the Earth & to receive, obtain & perform all the ordinances belonging to the Kingdom of God even unto the sealing of the hearts of the ~~hearts~~ fathers unto the children & the hearts of the children unto the fathers even those who are in heaven.[14] Malachi says I will send Elijah before the great and dreadful day of the Lord come & He shall turn the hearts of the Fathers to the Children and the hearts of the Children to the Fathers lest I come & smite the earth with a Curse, Now what I am after is the knowledge of God & I take my own Course to obtain it, what are we to understand by this in the last days, in the days of Noah God destroyed the world by a flood & has promised to destroy it by fire in the last days[15] but before it took place Elijah should first come & turn the hearts of the Fathers to the Children &c now comes the point what is this office & work of Elijah, it is one of the greatest & most important subjects that God has revealed, He should send Elijah to seal the children to the fathers & fathers to the Children, Now was this merely confined to the living to settle difficulties with families on earth, by no means, it was a far greater work Elijah what would you do if you was here would you ~~confine~~ confine your work to the living alone. No I would ~~confine~~ refer you to the scriptures whare the subject is manifest, i.e, without us they could not be made perfect, nor we without them,[16] the fathers without the children nor the children without the fathers. I wish you to understand this subject for it is important & if you will receive it this is the spirit of Elijah that we redeam our dead & connect ourselves with our fathers which are in heaven & seal up our dead to come forth in the first resurrection & here we want the power of Elijah to seal those who dwell on earth to those which dwell in heaven this is the power of Elijah & the keys of the Kingdom[17] of Jehovah. Let us suppose a case; suppose the great God who dwells in heaven should reveal himself to Father Cutler[18] here by the opening heavens and tell him I offer up a decree that whatsoever you seal on earth with your decree I will seal it in heaven,[19] you have power then, can it be taken of[f] No, Then what you seal on earth by the Keys of Elijah is sealed in heaven, & this is the power of Elijah, & this is the difference between the spirit & power of Elias and Elijah, for while the spirit of Elias is a forerunner the power of Elijah is sufficient to make our calling & Election sure,[20] & the same doctrin whare we are exhorted to go on unto perfection not laying again the foundation of repentance from dead works but of laying on of hands, resurrection of the dead &c.[21] we cannot be perfect without the fathers, &c[22] we must have revelations then & we can see that the doctrin of revelation as far transcends the doctrin of no revelation as knowled[g]e is above ignorance for one truth revealed from heaven is worth all the sectarian notions in exhistance. This spirit of Elijah was manifest in the days of the Apostles in delivering certain ones to the buffitings of Satan that they may be saved in the day of the Lord Jesus, they were sealed by the spirit of Elijah unto the damnaton of Hell untill the day of the Lord or revealtion of Jesus Christ[23] Here is the doctrin of Election that the world have quarreled so much about, but they do not know any thing about it, The doctrin that the Prysbeterians & Methodist have quarreled so much about once in grace always in grace, or falling away from grace I will say a word about, they are both wrong, truth takes a road between them both. for while the Presbyterian says once in grace you cannot fall the Methodist says you can have grace to day, fall from it to morrow, next day have grace again & so follow it, but the doctrin of the scriptures & the spirit of Elijah would show them both fals & take a road between them both for according to the scriptures if a man has receive the good word of God & tasted of the powers of the world to come if they shall fall away it is impossible to renew them again, seeing they have Crucified the son of God afresh & put him to an open ~~frame~~ shame[24], so their is a possibility of falling away you could not be renewed again, & the power of Elijah Cannot seal against this sin, for this is a reserve made in the seals & power of the priesthood,[25] I will make evry doctrin plain that I present & it shall stand upon a firm bases And I am at the defiance of the world for I will take shelter under the broad ~~sheler~~ cover of the wings of the work in which I am ingaged, it matters not to me if all hell boils over

I regard it ownly as I would the crackling of thorns under a pot A murderer; for instance one that sheds innocent Blood Cannot have forgiveness, David sought repentance at the hand of God Carefully with tears, but he could ownly get it through Hell, he got a promise that his soul should not be left in Hell,[26] Although David was a King he never did obtain the spirit & power of Elijah & the fulness of the Priesthood,[27] & the priesthood that he received[28] & the throne & kingdom of David is to be taken from him & given to another by the name of David in the last days, raised up out of his linage[29] Peter refered to the same subject on the day of pentecost,[30] but the multitude did not get the endowment that Peter had but several days after the people asked what shall we do, Peter says I would ye had done it ignorantly speaking of crucifying the Lord &c He did not say to them repent & be baptized for the remission of your sins but he said repent therefore & be converted that your sins may be blotted out when the times of refreshing shall come from the presence of the Lord, Acts iii,19 this is the case with murderers they could not be baptized for the remission of sins for they had shed innocent Blood.

Again the doctrin or sealing power of Elijah is as follows if you have power to seal on earth & in heaven then we should be Crafty, the first thing you do go & seal on earth your sons & daughters unto yourself, & yourself unto your fathers in eternal glory, & go ahead and not go back, but use a little Craftiness & seal all you can; & when you get to heaven tell your father that what you seal on earth should be sealed in heaven[31] I will walk through the gate of heaven and Claim what I seal & those that follow me & my Council The Lord once told me that what I asked for I should have,[32] I have been afraid ~~to aske~~ to ask God to kill my enemies lest some of them should peradventure ~~should~~ repent I asked a short time, since for the Lord to deliver me out of the hands of the Govornor of Missouri & if it must needs be to accomplish it to take him away, & the next news that Came pouring down from their, was Governor Reynolds had shot himself,[33] and I would now say beware O earth how you fight against the Saints of God & shed innocent Blood, for in the days of Elijah his enemies came upon him & fire was Called down from heaven & destroyed them,[34] the spirit of Elias is first Elijah second, & Masiah last. Elias is a fore runner to prepare the way, & the spirit & power of Elijah is to come after holding the keys of power building the Temple to the Cap stone, placing the seals of the Melchezedeck priesthood[35] up on the house of Israel & making all things ready then Mesiah comes to his Temple which is last of all. Mesiah is above the spirit & power of Elijah, for he made the world & was that spiritual rock unto Moses in the wilderness.[36] Elijah was to come & prepare the way & build up the kingdom before the coming of the great day of the Lord Although the spirit of Elias might begin it, I have asked of the Lord concerning his coming & while asking, the Lord gave me a sign & said in the days of Noah I set a bow in the heavens as a sign & token that in any year that the bow should be seen the Lord would not come, but their should be seed time—harvest during that year, but when ever you see the bow withdraw, it shall be a token that their shall be famin pestilance & great distress among the nations.[37] But I take the responsibility upon myself to prophesy in the name of the Lord, that Christ will not come this year as [William] Miller[38] has prophecyed, for we have seen the bow. And I also Prophecy in the name of the Lord that Christ will not Come in forty years & if God ever spake by my mouth he will not come in that length of time & Jesus Christ never did reveal to any man the precise time that he would come,[39] go & read the scriptures & you cannot find any thing that specified the exact [time] he would come & all that say so are fals teachers. Their are some important things concerning the office of the Mesiah in the organization of the worlds which I will speak of hereafter.[40] May God Almighty bless you & pour out his spirit upon you is the prayer of your unworthy servant Amen.

James Burgess Notebook

Showing the difference between the Spirit of Elias, Elijah and the messiah.

J Smith P[rophet].

of the spirit of Elias I must go back to the time at Susquehannah river when I retired in the woods pouring out my soul in prayer to Almighty God.[41] An Angel came down from heaven and laid his hands upon me and ordained me to the power of Elias and that authorised me to babtise with water unto repentance. It is a power or a preparatory work for something greater. you have not power to lay on hands for the gift of the holy ghost but you shall have power given you hereafter, that is the power of the Aronick preisthood.[42] this is the power which John the babtist was clothed with when he came bounding out of the wilderness saying repent ye for the kingdom of heaven is come unto you or is at hand, For there standeth one among you whose shoes latchett I am not worthy to unloose. he has greater power than I have he will babtise you with fire and with the holy ghost.[43] Jesus said of John this is Elias which was for to come if you will receive me otherwise he cannot do the work of an Elias, for Elias is preparatory for something greater to prepare my way before me I have power to restore all things and establish my kingdom amongst you, but if you will not receive me and my doctrine, he is not that Elias which was for to come for he cannot accomplish that for which he was sent, see 1st chap of John 19 to 22 verse for he confessed that he was not Elias why because they would not receive him that was coming after him namely Christ. Philip was clothed with the power of Elias when he went to samaria he could babtise for remission of sins, but could not lay on hands for the gift of the holy ghost, but sent for Peter and John who had the power of Elijah &c[44] Acts 19 chap Paul when he came to Corinth found certain diciples and asked them if they had received the holy ghost since they bleived, and they said we have not so much as heard of the holy ghost and with what surprise says he unto them. unto what were you babtised and they said unto Johns babtism. not so not so my friends if you had you would have heard of the holy ghost but you have been duped by some designing knave who has come in the name of John an imposture. how do you know it Paul why John verilly babtised with water unto repentance always telling the people that they should beleive on him that should come after him. he would babtise with fire and with the holy ghost. Johns babtism stood good but these had been babtised by some imposture. The spirit of Elijah is to turn the hearts of the fathers to the children and the hearts of the children to the fathers lest I come and smite the earth with a curse[45] the babtism for the dead and the ordinances that is to be administered by us for them for paul says that they without us cannot be made perfect neither can we without them be made perfect.[46] Now we come to talk about election a great deal is said about it. one way or another. The prespetary says once in grace always in grace, the methodist says once in grace can fall from grace and be renewed again. there is some truth in both of these statements Paul says in the 6 chap of hebrews that after arriving at a certain knowledge and then fall away it is impossible to renew them again, well paul the prespratarian says once in grace always in grace I say it is not so the methodist says once in grace can fall from grace and be renewed again I Paul say it is impossible seeing that they crucify to themselves the son of God afresh and put him to an open shame.

Make your calling and election sure go on from grace to grace untill you obtain a promise from God for yourselves that you shall have eternal life. this is eternal life to know God and his son Jesus Christ, it is to be sealed up unto eternal life and obtain a promise for our posterity.[47] Whatever you shall bind on earth shall be bound in heaven, this is the power of Elijah to seal or bind or turn the hearts of the fathers to their children sealed against all sin but the sin of sheding innocent blood and the Sin against the holy ghost. David was one of the promised seed yet he was guilty of murder see Acts Chap 2&3 other sins will go to judgement before hand.[48]

Joseph Smith prophet.

Revelation given through Joseph Smith in answer to a certain question Son of Man if you live untill you are 85 years of age you shall see the face of the Son of Man and so long as you see the rainbow strethching across the heavens there will be seed time and harvest and the son of Man will not come that year.[49]

Joseph Smith was born in the year 1805

$$\begin{array}{r} 1805 \\ \underline{85} \\ 1890 \end{array}$$

Franklin D. Richards "Scriptural Items"

On Sunday March 10 Joseph the Priest[50] delivered the following concernin the Spirits & Powers of Elias Elijah & of Messiah

The power of Elias is not the power of Elijah related the vision of his ordination to the priesthood of Aaron on the Susquehannah river to preach the preparatory gospel. This said the Angel is the Spirit of Elias

The spirit of Elias is to prepare the way for one greater to come

The spirit of Elijah is that degree of power which holds the sealing power of the Kingdom to seal the hearts of the fathers to the children & of the children their fathers not only on earth but in Heaven both the living & the Dead to each other for they (the dead) cannot be made perfect without us Heb 11-40

This power of Elijah is to that of Elias what in the architecture of the Temple of God those who seal or cement the Stone to their places are to those who cut or hew the stones the one preparing the way for the other to accomplish the work By this we are sealed with the Holy Spirit of promise ie <u>Elijah</u>

To obtain this sealing is to make our calling and election sure which we ought to give all diligence to accomplish[51]

there are two sins agains which this power does not secure or prevail they are "The sin against the Holy Ghost" And "shedding of innocent Blood" which is equivelant to "crucifying the Son of God afresh & putting him to an open shame"[52] Those who do these it is impossible to renew unto repentance for they are delivered to the buffettings of satan untill the <u>day of redemptions</u>[53]

illustrated the case of David said he could not obtain celestial glory and the reason why he had any hope or obtained a Promise that of his seed one should be raised up to reign over Israel forever was because that he had not spoken against the spirit & because he had not done this he ~~was renewed unto repentance and~~ obtained promise that God would not leave his soul in Hell[54]

Also spake of the rulers of the Jews & Peters preaching I wot (wish) that through ignorance ye did it as did those over whom ye ruled Acts 3-17 Peter did not preach repentance & Baptism but repent & be converted that your sins may be blotted out when the times of redemptions shall come from the presence of God Promised to treat upon the Spirit of Messiah <u>some future time</u>

A Revelation So long as we see the bow in the cloud seed time & harvest shall continue that year when the bow shall cease[55] then shall come famine wars &c after which the sign of the son of man shall be seen in heaven.[56]

Joseph Smith Diary, by Willard Richards

I attended meeting A M at the Stand by the Temple and preached on the Subject of the Spirit of Elias Elijah. ~~Elias~~ & Mes[si]ah clearly defining the offices of the 3 personages.

The Savior will not come this year. nor 40 yrs to come. The bow has been seen in the cloud & in that year that the bow is seen seed time and harvest will be. but when the bow ceases to be seen look out for a famine.[57]

Thomas Bullock Diary

Frost in the night—day most beautiful—went to the temple Joseph & Hyrum spoke. Joseph spoke on the Spirit of Elias the Spirit of Elijah and the Spirit of Messiah the Spirit of Elias is a forerunner same as John the Baptist—the Spirit of Elijah is the sealing power—to seal the hearts of the Fathers to the children—and the children to the Parents[58] as Paul declared that the Saints of the last days could not be perfect without them—neither can they be perfect without us[59]—the Spirit of Messiah is all power in Heaven and in Earth[60]—Enthroned in the Heavens as King of Kings and Lord of Lords[61]—the Rainbow is not to be seen—it is a sign of the commencement of famine & pestilence[62] &c &c and that the coming of the Messiah is not far distant—the Messiah will not come this year—upsets Millerites[63] the Messiah will not come for 40 years and he told the people to write[64] it a very large and attentive congregation—

John Solomon Fullmer Papers[65]

Prophesy delivered by President
Joseph Smith, March 10th 1844.

While enquiring of the Lord concerning the End of time, it was made known to him by the Holy Spirit, that there should be prosperity, seed time and harvest every year in which the Rainbow was seen, for to that was Noah refered as a surety on this subject,—But in the year when the Bow was not to be seen, would commence desolation, calamity and distress among the Nations, without seed time or harvest,[66]—And that the Revelation of the Son of Man from Heaven, would not be in this year, nor the next;[67] and he would say to his Millerite friends, that it would not be in forty years to come. He uttered all this in the name of the Lord, and said we should go home and write it—

J.S.F.

24 March 1844 (Sunday). At Temple Stand.[1]
Wilford Woodruff Journal

I have been informed by two gentleman[2] that a conspiracy is got up in this place for the purpose of taking the life of President Joseph Smith his family and all the Smith family; the heads of the Church, one of the gentleman will give his name unto the public & the other wishes it to be hid for the present they will both testify to it on oath & make an affidavit upon it the names of the persons revealed at the head of the Conspiracy are as follows (Chancy Higby[3] Dr Foster,[4] Dr Jackson,[5] Wm & Wilson Law) and the lies that Higby has hatched up as a foundation to work upon is, he says that I had mens heads Cut off in Missouri & that I had a Sword run through the hearts of the people that I wanted to kill & put out of the way[6] I wont swear out a warrent against them for I dont fear any of them they would not scare of[f] and old Setting hen. I intend to publish all the iniquity that I know of If I am guilty I am ready to bear it their is honor among enemies I am willing to do any thing for the good of the people, I will give the names of one of the gentleman who have divulged the plot his name is Eaton,[7] he will sware to it he is a bold fellow. Jackson said a Smith should not be alive 2 weeks not over two months any how. As concerning the Character of these men I will say nothing about it now, but If I hear any thing more from them on this subject I will tell what I know about them.

[After addresses from Orson Spencer and Sidney Rigdon] (President Joseph Smith again arose & said in relation to the power over the minds of ~~the~~ mankind which I hold, I would say it is in consequence of the power of truth in the doctrins which I have been an instrument in the hands of God of presenting unto them & not because of any Compulsion on my part. I will ask if I ever got any of it unfair. If I have not reproved you in the gate,[8] I ask did I ever exerise any compulsion over any man. did I not give him the liberty of disbelieveing any doctrin I have preached if he saw fit, why do not my enemies strike a blow at the doctrin, they cannot do it, it is truth, And I am as the voice of one Crying in the wilderness repent of your sins & prepare the way for the Coming of the Son of Man, for the Kingdom of God has Come unto you and hence forth the ax is laid unto the root of the tree and evry tree that bringeth not forth good fruit, God Almighty (and not Jo Smith) shall hew down & cast it into the fire.)[9]

Joseph Smith Diary, by Willard Richards

10 A M. I preached at the Temple stand, followed by O. Spencer[10] & Prest Rigdon

On the Stand I related what was told me yesterday by Mr Eaton.

that Wm. Law. Wilson Law. R.D. Foster, Chauncey L. Higbee, & Joseph Jackson had held a caucus, designing to destroy all the Smith family in a few weeks.

Thomas Bullock Diary

Went to the Temple Joseph spoke about a conspiracy to kill him—he said he would not say anything about the characters of the Laws, Jackson, D̲r̲ Foster, or Higbee—but if he was driven to it, he would tell all he knew ... Joseph again spoke [after Orson Spencer and Sidney Rigdon] and shewed that his Power was in the Doctrines he taught and defied all men to upset it—he called aloud "as the voice of one bawling in the wilderness Repent ye Repent ye for the Kingdom of God is at hand"—[11]

5 April 1844 (Friday Morning). Near Temple.[1]
Nauvoo Neighbor 2 (1 May 1844)

At 10 o'clock I attended near the Temple, where the word of God was proclaimed by Mr. A. M. Lyman, and others, and at the close of whose addresses Joseph Smith in a plain and familiar style satisfactorily closed. The text was 104th verse of 119th Psalm (through thy precepts I get understanding &c).

6 April 1844 (Saturday Morning). In Grove.[1]
Times and Seasons 5 (1 May 1844):522

Conference Minutes.
Conference met pursuant to appointment, on Saturday the 6th of April, 1844.

Present, President Joseph Smith, Hyrum Smith, Sidney Rigdon and William Marks.

Of the Twelve, Brigham Young, Heber C. Kimball, Willard Richards, Wilford Woodruff, John Taylor, and George A. Smith.

The members of the High Council, an immense number of elders, and an innumerable concourse of people

Saturday, April 6, 1844.

Presidents Joseph, and Hyrum Smith came to the stand at 1/4 past 10 o'clock, when the meeting was called to order by elder

Brigham Young. The choir sung a hymn, after which President Joseph Smith rose to state to the congregation the nature of the business which would have to come before them. He stated that it had been expected by some that the little petty difficulties which have existed, would be brought up and investigated before this conference, but it will not be the case; these things are of too trivial a nature to occupy the attention of so large a body. I intend to give you some instruction on the principles of eternal truth, but will defer it until others have spoken, in consequence of the weakness of my lungs. The elders will give you instruction, and then, (if necessary) will offer such corrections as may be proper to fill up the interstices. Those who feel desirous of sowing the seeds of discord will be disappointed, on this occasion. It is our purpose to build up, and establish the principles of righteousness, and not to break down and destroy. The great Jehovah has ever been with me, and the wisdom of God will direct me in the seventh hour; I feel in closer communion, and better standing with God than ever I felt before in my life, and I am glad of this opportunity to appear in your midst. I thank God for the glorious day that he has given us. In as large a congregation, it is necessary that the greatest order and decorum be observed; I request this at your hands, and believe that you will all keep good order.

William Clayton Report

10 1/2 A. M.

Pres. Joseph & Hyrum came to the stand Meeting called to order by Er B. Young

The choir sung an Hymn after which Pres. Joseph Smith arose to state to the congregation the business which would have to come before them. It had been expected that the little petty difficulties which had existed would be brought up, but it would not be the case. He intended to give them some instruction on the principles of eternal truth but would defer it untill the last in consequences of the weakness of his lungs. The Elders would give instruction and then if necessary he would offer such corrections as might be necessary to fill the interstices. Those who wanted to sow the seeds of discord will be disapointed for the wisdom of God will direct him in the seventh hour He feels in closer communion and better standing with God than ever before in his life. He was glad of the opportunity to appear in their midst. He thanked God for the glorious day that God had given us. He believe they will keep good order.

Joseph Smith Diary, by Willard Richards

I made a few introductory remarks to an immense number of the saints assembled on the 14th Anniversary of Church in the grove 1/4 miles east of the temple on Young St.—10 A.M. weather warm. brisk air from the south.—

Wilford Woodruff Journal

Conference assembled at 10, oclock AM April 6 President (B. Young, Called the Conference to order. (President Joseph Smith Said He Should not occupy time in Speaking of any difficulties that might have occured in our midst, Said He was not a fallen prophet, & never in any nearer relationship to God than at the present time, & would show before the Conferen[ce] closed that God was with him.)[2]

Willard Richards Diary

Special [meeting] at the stand 1/4 m E [of] Temple.

7 April 1844 (Sunday Morning). At Temple[1]
Joseph Smith Diary, by Willard Richards

A very pleasant morning. the people began to assemble. and by 10 oclock there was the largest congregation ever seen in Nauvoo. . . .

Prest. J. Smith requested that the congregation would keep good order—and in the name of the constitution, continental congress & God Almighty I command the public to keep good order.

7 April 1844 (Sunday Afternoon). At Temple.[1]
Joseph Smith Diary, by Willard Richards

3 1/4 P. M.—Joseph commenced speaking on the subject of the Dead—relative to the death of elder King Follet[2] who who was crushed in a well. by the falling of a tub of rock on him.—

If men do not comprehend the character of God[3] they do not comprehend themselves. what kind of being is God?—Eternal life to know God.[4]—if man does not know God, has not Eternal life.—if I am so fortunate as to comprehend and explain the [incomplete thought] let evry one sit in silence and never lift your voice against the servants of God again.

Every man has a right to be a false prophet. as well as a true prophet.—in the beginning. before the world was.—Is a man like one of yourselves.—should you see him to day. you would see a man in fashion and in form. Adam was formed in his likeness.[5]—

refute the Idea that God was God from all eternity—Jesus said as the father had power in himself even so hath the son power[6] to do what the father did. Lay down his body. & take it up again.—you have got to learn how to make yourselves God, Kings, Priests, &c.[7]—by going from a small to great capacity. Till they are able to dwell in everlasting burning[8] & everlasting power.—

how consoling when called to part with a dear friend. to know their very being will rise to dwell in everlasting burning.—heirs of God.[9] and ascend a throne as those who have gone before.—I saw the father work out his kingdom with fear & trembling.[10]—god is glorified in salvation Exaltation—of his ancestors &c.—not all to be comprehended in this world.—the head, or the head one—The head one of the Gods,[11] brought forth the Gods.—Dr & Lawyers that have persecuted.—The head one called the Gods together in grand council—to bring forth the world.—Example of error as yocabem Jacob—the son of Zebedee—& James James the son of Zebedee[12] 4 Mat. 21. Greek Hebrew. German. & Latin.—In the begining the head of the gods called a council of the Gods—and concocted a scheme to create the world.—Soon as we begin to understand the character of the Gods he begins to unfold the heavens to us.[13]—Doctors say.—created the earth out of nothing. Borau.[14]—creates.—it means to organized.[15]—God had materials to organise the world. Elements[16]—nothing can destroy. no beginning no end.—

The soul. Doctors of Divinity. God created in the beginning—he never the character of man.[17] dont believe it.—who told you God was self existent? correct enough.—in hebrew put into him his spirit.[18]—which was created before. Mind of man coequal with God himself. friends seperated for a small moment from their spirits. coequal with God. and hold converse when they are one with another—[19]

If man had a beginning he must have an end.—might proclaim. God never had power to create the spirit of man

Inteligence exist upon a self existent principle no creation about it.[20] all mind & spirit God ever sent into the world are susceptible of enlargement.—all things God has seen fit proper to reveal while dwelling in mortality, are revealed. precisely the same as though we were destitute of bodies.[21]—

what will save our spirits will save our bodies—our tabernacles—for our spirits—All spirits who have not obeyed the Gospel must be damned.—who have not obeyed the decrees of son of man.

We are looked upon by God as though we were in Eternity—the greatest resonsibility resting upon us is to look after our dead.—they without us cannot be made perfect without us.[22] Meet Paul 1/2 way.—Hence the saying of Elijah.—God made provisions before the world was for every creature in

All sin shall be forgiven in this world or world to come—except one

Salvation for all men who have not committed a certain sin can save any man who has not committed the unpardonable sin.[23] cannot commit the unpardonable sin after the ~~diss~~ dissolution of the body. Knowledge save a man.—

No way for a man to come to understanding but give his consent to the commandment[24] Damned by mortification—a lake as of fire of brimstone—as exquisite the disappointment of the mind of man[25]—

Why? Must commit the unpardonable sin in this world. will suffer in the eternal world until he will be exalted.—

work of the devil. the plans the devil laid to save the world.—

Devil said he could save them all[26]—Lot fell on Jesus.—All sin &c[27] forgiven except the sin against the Holy Ghost.—Got to deny the plan of salvation. &c. with his eyes open. Like many of the apostates of christ of the Church of Jesus Christ of last Days.

Let All be careful.—lest you be deceived. best man brings forth best works.

To the mourners your friend has gone to wait the perfection.—of the reunion.—the resurrection of your friend in felicity while worlds must wait myriads of years before they can receive the like blessings.—leave the subject. bless those who have lost friends. only gone for a few moments.—

Shall mothers have their Children? Yes. they shall have it without price. redemption is paid possessing all the inteligence of a god. the child as it was before it died out of your arms thrones upon thrones. Dominion upon dominion just as you[28]—

Baptism of water fire & Holy Ghost. are inseperably connected.[29]—found in the German Bible to prove what I have taught for 14 years about baptism.—I baptize you with water. but when Jesus comes having the keys—he shall baptize you with the baptism of fire & Holy Ghost.[30]—

Leaving the principles of doctrine of baptism &c[31]—one god. one baptism. & one baptism[32]—I.E. all three.

called upon all men. Priests and all to repent and obey the gospel.—if they do not they will be damned.—those who commit the unpardonable sin are doomed to Gnaolom.[33] without end.— God dwells in everlasting burnings.[34]—Love all men but hate your deeds.—

You dont know me—you never will[35] I dont blame you for not believing my history had I not experienced it could not believe it myself

5 1/2 closed.

Wilford Woodruff Journal

3 o clock P M April Sunday 7th 1844

The following important edefying & interesting discourse was deliverd by President Joseph Smith to about ~~twenty~~ ten thousand souls upon the subject of the death of Elder King Follet

I now call the attention of this congregation while I addres you upon the subject of the dead The case of our Beloved Brother King Follet, who was crushed to death in a well, as well as many others who have lost friends will be had in mind this afternoon, & shall speak upon the subject in general as far as I shall be inspired by the Holy Spirit to treat upon ~~the subject~~ it, I want the Prayers & faith of the saints that I may have the Holy Ghost, that the testimony may carry conviction to your minds of the truth of what I shall say, & pray that the Lord may strengthen my lungs, there is strength here & your prayers will be herd. Before I enter upon an investigation of this subject, I wish to pave the way, and bring up the subject from the beginning that you may understand. I do not intend to please you with oritory but with the simple truths of heaven to Edify you. Go to the morn of creation to understand ~~of~~ the decrees of the Eloheem at the Creation. It is necessary for us to have an understanding of God at the beginning, if we get a good start first we can go right, but if you start wrong you may go wrong. But few understand the character of God. they do not know they do not understand their relationship to God. the world know no more than the brute beast, & they know no more than to eat drink and sleep & this is all man knows about God or his exhistance, except what is given by the inspiration of the Almighty. go then to the beginning that you may understand. I ask this congregation what kind of a being is God? turn your thoughts in your hearts, & say have any of you seen or herd him or communed with him this is a question that may occupy your attention The scriptures inform us that this is eternal life to know the ownly wise God & Jesus Christ whom He has sent.[36] If any inquire what kind of a being God is, I would say If you dont know God you have not eternal life, go back & find out what kind of a being God is. If I am the man that shows you what kind of a being God is, then let evry man & woman sit in silence and never lift up his hand against me again if I do not do it, I will not make any further pretentions to inspiration or to be a prophet, I would be like the rest of the world, fals teachers & you would want to take my life. But you might just as well take the lives of other fals teachers as mine if I was fals, But meddle not with any man for his religion, evry goverment ought to permit evry man to enjoy his religion, I will show the world is wrong by showing what God is. I am going to inquire after God so that you may know God, that persecution may cease concerning me, I go back to the beginning to show what kind of a being God was, I will tell you & hear it O Earth! God who sits in yonder heavens is a <u>man like yourselves</u> That God if you were to see him to day that holds the worlds you would see him like a man in form, like yourselves. Adam was made in his image and talked with him & walkd with him.[37] In order to understand the dead for the consolation of those that mourn, I want you to understand God and how he comes to be God. We suppose that God was God from eternity. I will refute that Idea, or I will do away or take away the veil so you may see. It is the first principle to know that we may converse with him and that he once was a man like us, and the Father was once on an earth like us, And I wish I was in a suitable place to tell it <u>The scriptures inform us mark</u> it that Jesus Christ said As the <u>Father hath power in</u> himself so hath <u>the son</u> power in himself to do what the father did[38] even to lay down my body & take it up again do you believe it, if not, dont believe the bible. I defy all Hell and earth to refute it. And you have got to learn how to make yourselves God, king and priest, by going from a small capacity to a great capacity to the resurrection of the dead to dwelling in everlasting burnings,[39] I want you to know the first principle of this law, how consoling to the mourner when they part with a friend to know that though they lay down this dody [body]. it will rise & dwell with everlasting burnings to be an heir of God & joint heir of with Jesus Christ[40] enjoying the same rise exhaltation & glory untill you arive at the station of a God. What did Jesus Christ do, the same thing as I se the Father do, see the father do[41] what, work out a kingdom, when I do so to I will give to the father which will add to his glory, he will take a Higher exhaltation & I will take his place and am also exhalted. Those are the first princples of the gospel. It will take a long time after the grave to understand the whole If I should say anything but what was in the bible the cry of treason would be herd I will then go to the Bible, Barasheet[42] in the beginning, Analize the word in and through the head, an old Jew added the word Bath, it red the head one of the Gods, broat forth the Gods, I will transpose it in the english language. I want you to know & learn that the Holy Ghost knows somthing. The grand Council set at the head and contemplated the creation of the world, some will say, the scriptures say so & so, but I will show you a text out of an old book containing the four languages, the german is here what does this text say, yoakabeam, the son of Zebedee, the bible says James the son of Zebedee, but this says Jacob son of Zebedee 21 ch 4th ver Matthew The Dr says (I mean Dr of Law not of physic) If you say any thing not according to the Bible we will cry treason, But if ye are not led by revelation how can ye escape the damnation of Hell, here we have the testimony of four I have the oldest Book in the world & the Holy Ghost I thank God for the old Book but more for the Holy Ghost. The Gods came together & concocked the plan of making the world & the inhabitants, having an knowledge of God we know how to Approach him & ask & he will answer[43] An other thing the learned Dr says the Lord made the world out of nothing,[44] you tell them that God made the world out of somthing, & they think you are a fool. But I am learned & know more than the whole world, the Holy Ghost does any how, & I will associate myself with it. Beaureau,[45] to organize the world out of chaotic matter, element they are principles that cannot be disolved they may be reoganized. Another subject which is calculated to exhalt man I wish to speak of The resurrection of the dead The soul the mind of man, whare did it come from? The learned says God made it in the beginning, but it is not so, I know better God has told me so. If you dont believe it, it wont make the truth without effect, God was a self exhisting being, man exhists upon the same principle. God made a tabernacle & put a spirit in it and it became a Human soul,[46] man exhisted in spirit & mind coequal with God himself, you who mourn the loss of friends are ownly seperted for a moment, the spirit is seperated for a little time, they are now conversant with each other as we are on the earth. I am dwelling on the immutibility of the spirit of man, is it logic to say the spirit of man had a begining & yet had no end, it does not have a begining or end, my ring is like the Exhistanc of man it has no begining or end, if cut into their would be a begining & end, so with man if it had a begining it will have an end, if I am right I might say God never had power to create the spirit of man, God himself could not create himself. Intelligence is Eternal & it is self exhisting,[47] All mind that is susseptible of improvement, the relationship we have with God places us in a situation to advance in knowledge. God has power to institute laws to instruct the weaker intelligences that thay may be exhalted with himself this is good d doctrin, it taste good, I can taste the principles of eternal life, so can you, they are given to me by the revelations of Jesus Christ and I know you believe it. All things that God sees fit to reveal to us in relation to us, reveals his commandments to our spirits, and in saving our spirits we save the body, the same as though we had no Body how comes the awful responsibility if in relation to our dead, if they do not be baptized they must be damned, (I wish I had 40 days to talk) what promises are made, what can be said if in the grave, God dwells in eternity, and he does not view things as we do, the greatest responsibility lade upon us in this life, is in relation to our dead Paul said we cannot be made perfect without us [them],[48] for it is necessary that the seals are in our hands to seal our children & our dead for the fulness of the dispensation of times,[49] A dispensation to meet the promises made by Jesus Christ befor the foundation of the world for the salvation of man. All sins and blasphemy, were to be forgiven except the sin against the Holy Ghost.[50] God has made provision for evry spirit in the eternal world, and the spirits of our friends should be searched out & saved, Any man that has a friend in eternity can save him if he has not committed the unpardonable sin, He cannot be damned through all eternity, their is a possibility for his escape in a little time, If a man has knowledge he can be saved, if he has been guilty of great sins he is punished for it, when he consents to obey the gospel whether Alive or dead, he is saved, his own mind damns him[51] I have no fear of hell fire that dont exhist No man can commit the unpardonable sin, untill He receives the Holy Ghost, All will suffer untill they obey Christ himself, even the devil said I am a savior and can save all, he rose up in rebelion against God and was cast down,. Jesus Christ will save all except the sons of perdition. What must a man do to commit the unpardonable sin they must receive the Holy Ghost have the heavens opened unto them,[52] & know God,[53] & then sin against him, this is the case with many apostates in this Church, they never seease to try to hurt me, they have got the same spirit the devil had, you cannot save them, they make open war like the devil, stay all that hear, dont make any hasty mooves you may be saved, if a spirit of Bitterness is in you, dont be in haste, say you that man is a sinner, well if he repents he shall be forgiven. I could go back and trace evry subject of interest concerning the relationship of man to God if i had time, their is many mansions in my fathers Kingdom,[54] what have we to console us in relation to our dead, we have the greatest hope in relation to our dead, of any people on earth we have seen them walk worthy on earth and those who have died in the faith are now in the selestial kingdom of God, they have gone to await the resurrection of the dead, to go to the celestial glory, while there is many who die who will have to wait many years, But I am authorized to say to you my friends in the name of the Lord, that you may wait for your friends to come forth to meet you in eternity in the morn of the celestial world, those saints who have been murdered in the persecution shall triumph in the celestial world, while their murderers shall dwell in torment untill they pay the utmost farthing.[55]

I have Fathers, Brothers, children, that are gone to eternity soon to meet me, the time will soon be gone, the trump will soon be blown. A question will Mothers have their children in Eternity yes, yes, you will have the children But as it falls so it will rise, It will never grow,[56] It will be in its precise form as it fell in its mothers arms. Eternity is full of thrones upon which dwell thousands of children reigning on thrones of glory not one cubit added to their stature I will leave this subject here and make a few remarks upon Baptism, I will read a tex[t] in Jerman [German] upon Baptism, John says I Baptise you with water But when Jesus Christ Comes He shall adminster the baptism of fire & the Holy Ghost,[57] John said his baptism was good for nothing without the Baptism of Jesus Christ, Many talk of any baptism not being essential to salvation but this would lay the foundation of their damnation, There has also been remarks made concerning all men being redeemed from Hell, But I say that any man who commits the unpardonable sin must dwell in hell worlds without end.[58]

Thomas Bullock Report

The President having arrived—the Choir sung an hymn Elder Amasa Lyman prayed.

The Prophet while I address you on the subject which was contempd in the fore pt. of the Con.[59]—as the Wind blows very hard it will be hardly possible for me to make you all hear it is of the greatest importance & the mo solemn of any that cod. occupy our attentn. & that is the subj of the dead on the dece of our bror. Follit who was crushed to death in a well—& inasmuch as there are a great many in this congre who live in this city & who have lost friend I shall speak in genl. & offer you my ideas so far as I have ability & so far as I shall be inspd. by the H S. to dwell on his subjt. I want your prayer faith the inspn. of Alm God to say things that are true & shall carry the testimony to your hearts & pray that he may streng my lungs—stay the winds—& let the pray of the Saints to heaven appear—for the prayers of the righteous avail much[60] & I verily believe that your prayers shall be heard before I enter in this investign. fully of the subjt. that is lying before us I wish to make a few preliminaries in order that you may understand when I come to it I do not calculate to please your ears with oratory with much leang. but I calculate to edify you with simple truths from Heaven. I wish to go back to the begin: of creation—it is necessary to know the mind decree & ordinatn. of the great Eloi beging at the creatn. & it is necy. for us to have un understandg. of God in the beging. if we start right it is very easy for us to go right all the time but if we start wrong it is hard to get right There are very few who understand rightly the char of God—They do not comprehend any thing that is past or that which is to come & com: but little more than the brute beast if a man learns know nothing more than to eat, drink, sleep, &

does not comprehend any of the desn. of God the Beast com the same thing eats drin sleeps—[k]noes nothing more & how are we to do it by no or. way than the inspn of A. God.

I want to go back to the begin & so get you into a more lofty sphere than what the human being generally understands I want to ask this cong: every man wom: & child to ansr. the questn. in their own heart what kind of a being is God I agn. rept. the questn. what kind of a being is God does any man or woman know have any of you seen, him heard him, communed with him, here is the questn. that will peradventure from this time henceforth occupy your attentn.—The Apos: says this is Eternal life to know God & J.C. who he has sent[61]—that is eternl. life if any man enquire what kind of a being is God if he will search deligently his own heart that unless he knows God he has no eternal life—my first object is to find out the character of the true God & if I shod. be the man to com: the God & I com: them to your heart let every man & woman henceforth shut their mouths & never say anything agst. the man of God & If I do not do it I have no right to revn. inspn. if all are [indecipherable word] to the God they will all be as bad off as I am. they will all say I ought to be d d. there is not a man or wom who wod not breath out an anathema on my head & some wod feel authd. to take away my life—if any man is authd. to take away my life who say I am a false teacher so I shod. have the same right to all false teacher & where wod. be the end of the blood & there is no law in the heart of God that wod. allow any one to interfere with the rights of man every man has the right to be a false as well as a true prophet—If I shew verily that I have the truth of God & shew that ninety nine of 100 are false prop. it wod. deluge the whole world with blood. I want you all to know God to be familiar with him & if I can bring you to him all persecut. agst. me will cease & let you know that I am his servt. for I speak as one havg. authy. and not as a scrib[e][62] open your ears & eyes all ye Ends of the Earth & hear & I am going to prove. it to you with the Bible & I am going to tell you the desns. of God to the human race & why he interferes with the affairs of man God himself who sits enthroned in yonder Heavens is a man like unto one of yourselves who holds this world in its orbit & upholds all things by his power if you were to see him today you wod. see him a man for Adam was a man like in fashion & image like unto him Adam wakd talked & convd. with him as one man talks & com: with anor.[63] in order to speak for the consoln. of those who mourn for the loss of their friend it is necy. to understand the char. & being of God for I am going to tell you what sort of a being of God. for he was God from the begin of all Eternity & if I do not refute it—truth is the touchstone they are the simple and first princ: of truth to know for a certainty the char. of God that we may conv[erse] with him same as a man & God himself the father of us all dwelt on a Earth same as Js. himself did & I will shew it from the Bible—I wish I had the trump of an Arch An. I cod. tell the story in such a manner that pers: shod cease for ever—J.Sd. as the Far. hath power in himself even so hath the Son power to do what[64] the Far. did that ansr. is obvious in a manner to lay down his body & take it up—J—did as my Far. laid down his body & take it up agn. if you don't believe it you don't believe the Bile the Scrip says & I defy all hell all learng. wisdom & records of hell togr to refute it here then is Etl. life to know the only wise and true God you have got to learn how to be a God yourself & be a K. & ~~God~~ Priest[65] to God same as all have done by going from a small capy to anr. from grace to grace until the resn. ~~of~~ & sit in everlasting power as they who have gone before & God in the L D. while certn. indivals are proclaimg. his name is not trifling with us—how consoling to the mourner when they are cald. to part with a wife, mother, father dr. relative to know that all Earthly taber shall be dissolved that they shall be heirs of God & jt. hrs of J. C.[66] to inherit the same power exaltn. until you ascd. the throne of Etl. power same as those who are gone bef. what J. did I do the things I saw my Far. do[67] before worlds came rolld. into existence I saw my Far. work out his K with fear & trembling[68] & I must do the same when I shall give my K to the Far. so that he obtns K rollg. upon K. so that J treads in his tracks as he had gone before. It is plain beyond comprehensn. & you thus learn the first prin of the Gospel when you climb a ladder you must begin at the bottom run[g] until you learn the last prin of the gospel for it is a great thing to learn Saln. beyond the grave & it is not all to be com in this world. I sup I am not alld. to go into investign. but what is contd. in the Bible & I think is so many wise men who wod. put me to death for treason I shall turn commentator today. I shall go to the first Hebrew word in the Bible the 1st sen: In the beginning—Berosheat[69]—In by thro. & every thing else. Roshed[70] the head when the Inspd. man wrote it he did not put the 1st pt. to it. a man a Jew witht. any authy. thot. it too bad to begin to talk about the head of any man. "The Head one of the Gods brought forth the Gods" is the true meang. of the word—if you do not believe it you do not believe the learned man of God—no man can tell you more than I do thus the H God brot. forth the Gods in the Head council—I want to bring it to English. Oh ye lawyers ye doctors I want to let you know that the H G. knows something as well as you do—the Head God called togr. the Gods & set in Grand Council &c when I say a lawyer I mean a lawyer of the Scrip.[71] I have done so hither to let the lawyers flutter & let everybody laugh at them. some learned Dr. mit. take a notn. to say thus & so—& are not to be altd. & I am going to shew you an error I have an old book in the Latin Greek Hebrew & German & I have been readg. the Germ: I find it to be the most correct that I have found & it corresponds the nearest to the revns. that I have given the last 16 yrs[72] years it tells about Jachabod[73] means Jacob—in the English James— & you may talk about James thro all Eternity in the 21 v. of 4th Mat: where it gives the test. that it is to Jacob & how can we escape the dn. of hell witht. God reveal to us. Latin says that Jackobus means Jacob—Hebrew says means Jacob—Greek says Jacks Jacob German says Jacob thank God I have got this book & I thank him more for the gift of the H G. I have all the 4 Test. come here ye learned men & read if you can. I shod. not have brot. up this word ~~unt~~ only to shew that I am right when we beg to learn this way we beg to learn the only true God & when we be[g]in to know how to come to him—he begins to unfold the heavens to us & tell us all abt. it bef our prayers get to his ears[74] at the bo now I ask all the learned men who hear me wher. the learned men who are preachg. Saln. say that God created the Heavens & the Earth out of nothing & the reason is that they are unlearned & I know more than all the world put togr. & If the H.G. in me com: more than all the world I will associate with it—What does Boro[75] mean it means to organize same as you wod. organize a Ship.—God himself had materials to org. the world out of chaos which is Element & in which dwells all the glory[76]—that nothing can destroy they never can have an ending they coexist eternally—I have anor. to dwell on & it is impossible for me to say much but to touch upon them—for time will not permit me to say all—so I must come to the resn. of the dead—the soul the in[ne]r Spirit—of God man says created in the beging. the very idea lessens man in my idea—I don't bel. the doct: hear it all ye Ends of the World for God has told me so I am going to tell of things more noble—we say that God himself is a selfexisting God, who told you so, how did it get it into your head who told you that man did not exist in like manner— how does it read in the Heb. that God made man & put into it Adams Spirit & so became a living Spirit[77]—the mind of man—the mind of man is as immortal[78] as God himself—hence while I talk to these mourners—they are only separated from their bodies for a short period—their Spirits coexisted with God & now converse one another same as we do—does not this give your satisfactn. I want to reason more on the Spirit of Man for I am dwelling on the body of man on the subjt. of the dead—the SP of man I take ring from my finger and liken it unto the mind of man, the im[mor]t. Sp. bec. it has no beging. Suppose you cut it into but as the D[evil] lives there wod. be an end all the fools & wise men from the beging. of creation who say that man had begin—they must have an end & then the doc of annihilitn. wod. be true—but if I am right I mit. with boldness proclaim from the housetop that God never had power to create the Sp of Man at all—it is ne God himself cod. not create himself— intelligence is self existent[79] it is a sp. from age to end & there is no creatn abt. it

the first principles of man are self exist with God—that God himself finds himself in the midst of Sp & bec he saw proper to institute laws for those who were in less intelligence that they mit. have one glory upon another in all that knowledge power & glory & so took in hand to save the world of Sp: you say honey is Sweet & so do I. I can also taste the Sp of Eternal life I know it is good & when I tell you of these things that were given me by Insp of the H S. you are bound to rece it as sweet & I rej more & more. Mans rel. to God & I will open your eyes in rel to your dead all things which God of his inf reason has seen fit to reveal to us in our mortal state in regard to our mortal bodies are revd. to us as if we had no bodies & those revns. which will save our dead will save our bodies. & God reveals them to us in the view of no eternal dissn. of the body—hence the awful responsibility that rests upon us for our dead—for all the Spirits must either obey the gospel or be d—d solemn thot. dreadful thot. is there nothing to be done for those who have gone before us without obeyg the decrees of God Wod. to God that I had 40 days & nights—to tell you all to let you know I am not a faln prop—what kind of characters are those who can be saved altho their bodies are decaying in the grave—the greatest responsibility that God has laid upon us to seek after our dead—the apostle says they without us cant be Perfect[80]—now I am speaking of them I say to you Paul, you cant be perfect witht. us.—those that are gone before & those who come after must be made perfect—& God has made it obligatory to man—God said he shall send Elijah &c I have a declarn to make as to the provn. which God made from before the foundn. of the world. what has J. sd. All sins & all blas. every trans. that man may be guilty of there is a Saln. for him or in the world to come[81]—every Sp in the Et. world can be ferreted out & saved unless he has comd. that Sin which cant be remd to him—that God has wrot. out saln. for all men unless they have comd. a certn. sin.[82] a friend who has got a friend in the world can save him unless he has comd. the unpard sin & so you can see how far you can be Savior there is no thing that a man can commit the unpardonable sin after the dissn of the body & there is a way possible for escape. not Part[icul]arly st[ate]d those that are witht. wisdom until they get exalted to wisdom ~~so long as man will not give acct. of his sins~~ a sinner has his own mind & is in his own comdemner ~~for the G~~ will the torment of the mind of man is as exquisite as a lake burng. with fire & brimstone[83]—I know the Scriptures I understand them—no man can commit the unpardonable sin after the dissn. of the body but they must do it in this World—hence the Saln. of J. C was wrought out for all men to triumph over the devil—for he stood up for a Savior—J. contd. that there wod. be certn. souls that wod. be condemned & the d[evi]l sd. he cod. save them all[84]—as the grand council gave in for J. C. so the d l fell & all who put up their heads for him. All sin shall be forgiven except the sin agt. the H. G. he has got to say that the Sun does not shine while he sees it he has got to deny J. C. when the heavens are open to him. & from that time they begin to be enemies like many of the apostates of the Church of J. C. of L.D.S.—when a man begins to be an enemy he hunts him—for he has the same Sp. that they had who crucd. the Lord of life—the same Sp. that Sin agt. the H. G. I advise all to be careful what you do—stay—do not give way—you may find that some one has laid a snare for you be cautious—await—when you find a Sp. wants bloodshed murder same is not of God but is of the devil out of the abundance of the heart man speaks—the man that tells you words of life is the man that can save you—I warn you agt all evil characters who sin agt. H. G. for there is no redempn. for them in this world nor in the world to come I can enter into the mysteries—I can enter largely into the eternal worlds—for J. sd. ~~where my~~ In my Fars. mansion there are many mansions &c[85] There is one glory of the moon sun & star &c[86] we have the reason to have the greatest hope & consoln. for our dead— for we have aided them in the 1.st princ for we have seen them walk in the midst & sink asleep in the arms of J. & hence is the glory of the Sun—you mourners have occn. to rejoice for your husband has gone to wait until the redn. & your expn. & hope are far above what man can conceive—for why God has revd. to us—& I am authd. to say by the authy. of the H. G. that you have no occasn. to fear for he is gone to the home of the just—don't mourn don't weep—I know it by the test of the H. G. that is within me—rejoice O Israel—your friends shall triumph gloriously—while their murderers shall welter for years.—I say for the benefit of strangers I have a Far. Bror. Friends who are gone to a world of Sp—they are absent for a momt.—they are in the Sp. then shall we hail our Mor. Fars. Friends & all no fear of mobs—&c but all one Eternity of felicity—Mothers you shall have your Children for they shall have it—for their debt is paid there is no damn. awaits them for they are in the Spirits—as the Child dies so shall it rise from the ded & be living in the burng. of God.[87]—it shall be the child as it was bef it died out of your arms Children dwell & exercise power in the same form as they laid them down

The Bap of Water witht. the B of Fire & the H G. attg. it are necy he must be born of W. & Sp[88] in order to get into the K of God & in the German text bears me out same as the revns. which I have given for the 14 years—I have the test to put in their teeth that my test has been true all the time You will find it in the declar of John the Bap (reads from the German) John says I bap you with Water but when J comes who has the power he shall adm the bap of F & the H. G. Gt.[89] God now where is all the Sect. world. & if this is true they are all d——d as clearly as any Anathama ever was—I know the text is true—I call upon all to say I—(shouts of I) Alex Campbell[90]—how are you going to save them with water—for John sd. his bapm. was nothing witht. the bap of J. C. One God, Far., Jesus, hope of, our calling, one baptism[91]—all three bap make one. I have the truth & I am at the defiance of the world to contradict.

I have preached Latin Hebrew Greek German & I have fulfilled all I am not so big a fool as many have taken me for—the Germans know that I read the German correct—Hear it all ye Ends of the Earth—all ye Sinners Repent Repent—turn to God for your reln. wont save you & ye will be d—d but I do not say how along—but those who Sin agt. the H. G. cannot be forgiven in this world or in the world to come but they shall die the 2nd. death[92]—but as they concoct scenes of bloodshed in this world so they shall rise to that resurn. which is as the lake of fire & brimstone—some shall rise to the everlasting burning of God[93] & some shall rise to the dn. of their own filthiness—same as the lake of fire & brimstone—I have intd. my remarks to all—to all rich & poor bond & free great & small I have no enmity agst any man. I love you all—I am their best friend & if persons miss their mark it is their own fault—if I reprove a man & he hate me he is a fool—for I love all men especially these my brethren & sisters—I rejoice in hearing the test of my aged friend—You never knew my heart. No man knows my hist—I can not do it. I shall never undertake—if I had not experienced what I have I should not have known it myself—I never did harm any man since I have been born in the world—my voice is always for peace—I cannot lie down until my work is finished—I never think evil nor think any thing to the harm of my fellow man—& when I am called at the trump & weighed in the balance you will know me then[94]—I add no more God bless you. Amen—The choir sung an hymn at 1/2 p 5.

William Clayton Report

Choir sun an Hymn Prayer by Er. A. Lyman.

Prest. J. Smith called the attention of the con. upon the subjects contemplated in the fore part of this con.[95]—as the wind blows hard it will be impossible to make hear unless profound attention—Subject of the greatest importance and most solemn that could occupy our attention. the subject of the dead been requested to speak on the subject on the decease of bro Follet who was crushed to death &c—I have been requested to speak by his friends & relatives & inasmuch as great many here in con—who live in this City as well as elsewhere who have deceased friends feel disposed to speak on the subject in general and offer my ideas as far as ability & as far as inspired by H.S. Want your prayers faith the inspiration of Almighty God the Gift of H.S. that I may set forth truth things that can easily be comprehended and will carry the testimony to your hearts. Pray that the L may strengthen my lungs control the mind that it may enter into the the ear of the L of Sabaoth. The fervant effectual prayer of righteous men availeth much[96]—. Will speak in order to hold out Before enter fully into the investigation wish to pave the way—make a few preliminaries—bring the subject from the beginning in order that you may understand the subject when I come to it. Do not calculate to please your ears with superfluity of words oratory much learning, but edify you by the simple truths of heaven. First place wish to go back to the beginning of creation. There the starting point in order to fully aquainted with purposes decrees &c of the Great Eloheim that sits in the hev. for us to take up beginning at the creation necessary to understand something of God himself in the beginning. If we start right easy to go right all the time—start wrong hard matter to get right. Few beings in the world who understand the character of God and do not comprehend their own character. They cannot compre[he]n the beginning nor the end neit[her] their own relation and is but little above the beast. If a man comprehends nothing more than to eat sleep arise and not any more and what the designs of Jehov what better than the beast it does the same thing—eat drink sleep & comprehends present and knows as much as we, unless we are able to com by the inspiration of A. God. Go back to beginning to lift you minds into a more exalted standing than the human mind is want Want to ask this this congregation every man, woman, &c what kind of a being is God. ask yourselves. I repeat the question what kind of a being is God. Any man or woman that know, any of you seen him? heard him? communed with him? Here a subject that will peradventure occupy your attention while you live—The apostle says this is eternal life to know &c''[97] that is eternal life if any man inquires what kind of being is God casts his mind to know—if the declaration of the ap[ostle] be true he will realize that he has not eternal life. There can be eternal life on no other principle. 1st object to find the character of the only wise & true God.

I comprehend so that the spirit seals it upon you hearts, let every man and woman put his hand on his mouth & never say any thing against the [indecipherable] of God again. But if I fail it becomes my duty to renounce all my pretensions to inspiration &c and if I should do so should I not be as [indecipherable] as all the rest of the world. Not a man would not breath anathema if they knew I was a false prophet. Some would take my life. If any man is authorized to take my life because I am a false teacher then upon the same principle am I authorized to take the life of every false teacher and who would not be the sufferer—but no man is authorized to take away life in consequence of their religion. All laws and governments ought to tolerate whether right or wron. If I show that I have the truth of God & 99/100 are false teachers while they pretend to hold the keys of God & go to killing them because &c would it not deluge the world in blood. Want you should all now God—be familiar—If I can get you to know I can bring to him.& if so you will cease to persecute me. I speak in authority. What kind of a being was God in the beginning. Hear all ye ends of the earth. I am going to prove it by the bible & the relation the human family sustains with God. 1st God that sits enthroned is a man like one of yourselves. That is the great secret. If the veil was rent to day & the great God who holds this world in its sphere or its orbit—the planets—if you were to see him to day you would see him in all the person image, very form of man, For Adam was created in the very fashion of God. Adam recieved instruction walked talked as one man with another.[98] In order to understand the subject of the ded for the consolation of those who mourn for the loss of their friends necessary they should understand Going to tell you how God came to be God. We have imagined that God was God from all eternity— These are incomprehensible to some but are the first principle of the gospel—to know that we may converse with him as one man with another & that he was once as one of us and was on a planet as Jesus was in the flesh—If I have the privilege could tell the story in such a manner as persecution would cease forever. Said Jesus (mark it Br. Rigdon)[99] What did Jesus say—as the father hath power in himself even so hath the son power to do[100] what why what the father did, to lay down his body and took it up again. Jesus what are you going to do—to lay down my life as my father did that I might take it up again. If you deny it you deny the bible. I defy the [indecipherable] and wisdom & all the combined powers of earth and hell to refute it. [indecipherable] You have got to learn how to be a god yourself in order to save yourself—to be priests & kings[101] as all Gods has done—by going from a small degree to another—from exaltation to ex—till they are able to sit in glory as with those who sit enthroned. I want you to know while God is being proclaimed that he is not trifling with you nor me. 1st principles of consolation how consoling to the mourner when called to part with husband father wife child to know that those being shall rise in immortal glory to sorrow die nor suffering more. & not only that to contemplate—the saying they shall be heirs of God &c.—what is it—to inherit the same glory power & exaltation with those who are gone before. What did Jesus do. Why I do the things that I saw the father do[102] when worlds came into existence. I saw the father work out a kingdom with fear & trembling[103] & I can do the same & when I get my K[ingdom] work[ed out] I will present to the father & it will exalt his glory and Jesus steps into his tracks to inherit what God did before. This is some of the first principles of the gospel about which so much hath been.—You have got to find the beginning of this history & go on till you have learned the last—will be a great while before you learn the last. It is not all to be comprehended in this world. I suppose that I am not allowed to go into an investigation of anything that is not in the Bible—you would cry treason. So many learned and wise men here—will go the the old Bible the very Berosheit.[104] make a comment on the first sentence of the history of creation. Berosheit want to annalize the word—Be[105]—in by through & everything else—rosh[106] [indecipherable]—the head. sheit[107]—where do it come from—when they inspired man wrote he did not put the Be there—But a jew put it there. It read in the first—the head one of the Gods brought forth the Gods—is the true meaning—rosheet signifies to bring forth the Eloheim. Learned men cannt learn any more than what I have told you hence the head God brought forth the head God in the grand council. Will simplify it in the English language. The learned Doctors who have persecuted me I want to let you know that the H.G.—

The grand councilers set in yonder heavens and contemplated the creation of the worlds that was created at that time. When I say Doctor & Lawyer I mean the D & L of the scriptures.[108] Some learned doctor might say the scriptures say thus & so and we must believe the scriptures He referred to an old book (N.T.) in the Hebrew, Latin, German & Greek—find it to be the most correct—find it to correspond with the revelations I have received. It talks about Yachaubon the son of Zebedee—means Jacob.[109] The N.T. says James—now if Jacob had the keys you might talk about James and never get the keys. Matthew 4-21 verse it gives the word Jacob instead of James How can we escape the damnation of hell unless God be with us—Men bind us with chains—Read from the Hebrew Yingacoub—Jacob. Greek Ichobon—Jacob. German He has got the oldest book in the world—but he has got the oldest book in his heart. Latin Yacobus—Jacob too—Should not have introduced this testimony were it not to back up the word rosh—the head father of the Gods. When we begin in this way we begin to find out God— what kind a being we have got to worship. When we begin to know how to come to him he begins to come to us. When we are ready to come to him he is ready to receive us. Learned Doctors tell us God created the heavens & earth out of nothing. They account it blasphemy to contradict the idea—They will call you a fool—You ask them why they say don't the Bible say he created the world & they infer that it must be out of nothing. The word create came from the word Barau[110]—don't mean so—it means to organize—same as man would use to build a ship—hence we infer that God had materials to organize from—chaos—chaotic matter.—element had an existence from the time he had. The pure pure principles of element are principles that never can be destroyed—they may be organized and re organized=but not destroyed.

It is as[o]ciated with the subjects in question the resurrection of the dead. Another subject—the soul—the mind of man—they say God created it in the beginning. The idea lessens man in my estimation. Don't believe the doctrine—know better—God told me so—Make a man appear a fool before he gets through if he dont believe it. We say that God was self—existant who told you so? It's correct enough but how did it get into your heads—who told you that man did not exist upon the same principle (refer to the bible) Don't say so in the old Hebrew—God made man out of the earth and put into him his spirit and then it became a living body[111] The mind of man—the intelligent part is coequal with God himself. I know that my testimony is true. hence when I talk to these mourners what have they lost—They are only separated from their bodies for a short season but their spirits existed coequal with God and they now exist in a place where they converse together as much as we do on the earth. Is it logic to say that a spirit is immortal and yet have a beginning because if a spirit have a beginning it will have an end—good logic—illustrated by his ring. All the fools learned & wise men that comes and tells that man has a beginning proves that he must have an end and if that doctrine is true then the doctrine of annihilation is true. But if I am right then I might be bold to say that God never did have power to create the spirit of man at all. He could not create himself—Intelligence exists upon a selfexistent principle[112]—is a spirit from age to age & no creation about it—All the spirits that God ever sent into this world are susceptible of enlargement. That God himself—find himself in the midst of spirit and glory because he was greater saw proper to institute laws whereby the rest could have a privilege to advance like himself. I know that when I tell you those words of eternal life that are given to me I know you taste it and I know you believe it. Wants to talk more of the relation of man to God—in relation to your dead. All things whatsoever God has seen proper to reveal to us while we are dwelling in mortality are revealed to us in the abstract & independent of affinity of this mortal tabernacle—but they are revealed as though we had no bodies at all—tho revealed to our spirits and those revelations must of necessity—save our spirits with them. Hence the responsibility, the awful res. that rests upon us in relation to our dead—for all spirits who have not obeyed the gospel in the flesh must obey the gospel or be damned. Is there no preparation—no salvation for our fathers & friends who have died and not obeyed the decrees of the son of man—Would to God I had 40 days & nights I would let you know that I am not a fallen prophet—What kind of beings can be saved although their bodies are mouldering in the dust. When his commandments teach us it is in view of eternity. The greatest responsibility in this world is to seek after our dead. They without us cannot be made perfect[113]—It is necessary that those who come after us should have salvation in common with us—& thus hath God laid this upon the [indecipherable] of the world hence the saying of Elijah. Speak in relation to the provisions God hath made to suit the conditions of man. What hath Jesus said? All sins & all blasphemies every transgression except one there is a provision either in this world or in the world of spirit.[114] Hence God hath made a provision that every spirit can be ferreted out in that world that has not sinned the unpardonable sin neither in this world or in the world of spirits. Every man who has a friend in the eternal world who hath not committed the unpardonable sin you can save him. A man cannot commit the unpardonable sin after the dissolution of the body there is a way for his escape. Knowledge saves a man and in the world of spirits a man can't be exalted but by knowledge. So long as a man will not give heed to the commandments he must abide without salvation. A man is his own torment.[115] Hence the saying they shall go into the lake that burns with fire & is as exquisite as a lake & so is the torments of a man—I said no man could commit the unpardonable sin after the dissolution of the body—Hence the salvation that the saviour wrought out for the salvation of a man if it did not [indecipherable] him in one place it would another—The contention in heaven was Jesus said there were certain man would not be saved the devil said he could save them.[116] he rebelled against God and was thrust down. After a man has sinned the sin againt the H.S. there is no repentence for him. Hence like many of the apostates of the C of J.C. L.D.S. They go to far the spirit leaves them hence they seek to kill me they thirst for my blood—they neve[r] cease—he has got the same spirit that crucified Jesus. You cant renew them to repentence[117]— awful is the consequence. Advise all to be careful what they do— you may by and by find out that you have been decieved. He continued his discourse—& told of parents receiving their children—concluded his remarks by Baptism—Choir sang—

Samuel W. Richards Record[118]

Must know the only living and true God and Jesus Christ. to have eternal life, God: a man like one of us, even like Adam. Not God from all Eternity. Once on a planet with flesh and blood, like Christ. As the father hath life in himself &c.[119] To know God learn to become God's. Exalted by the addition of subjects to his family, or kingdom.[120]

Create (Burrau,[121] in Hebrew,) which means organize from Element Chaos, or Element, All things revealed to us as though we had no bodies. for the exaltation of our Spirits, hence our bodies being connected, cannot commit the unpardonable sin after the disolution of the body.

Joseph Fielding Journal[122]

I have evidence enough that Joseph is not fallen ... April 6th-44 Our anual Conference bigan and continued 4 Days Joseph,s

Discourse on the Origin of Man, the Nature of God and the Resurrection was the most interesting Matter of this time and any one that could not see in him the Spirt of Inspiration of God must be dark, they might have known that he was not a fallen Prophet even if they thought he was fallen.

Willard Richards Diary

10.000[123] people special conference.

William Clayton Diary

Joseph discoursed on the dead.

8 April 1844 (Monday Morning). Temple Stand.[1]
William Clayton Report

9 3/4 A. M. Prest. J. Smith took his seat on the stand. and requested choir to sing an Hymn. His lungs having failed he would call upon Er B. Young to read 1 Cor 15 Ch.

Er B. Young said to cont the sub of Prest. S discourse yesterday shall com by read 18 Cor.—from an old Bible—W. W. Phelps read

Prayer by Er B. Young. choir sung an Hymn

Prest. J. said impos. to continue the subject as to raise the dead Lungs is gone—time to do things must wait—give it up and leave the time to those who can make you hear—will do it some other time. Make a proc to the Ers—Wanted you to stay in order I might make this Proc. you know the Ld has lead the Church from rev. Has another rev. in rel to economy in the Church Shall not be able as largely as some other. time will give 1st prin—has ben great discourse in rel to Zion—prophets—make a proc that will cover a broad gd. the whole America is ~~the~~ Zion itself—from North to South—that is the Zion where the Mountain of the Ld shd be[2]— when Ers take up br will see it[3]—dec. this morning are calculating soon as Temple finished washing & anointing &c when those last & most impt ordinance can be done[4]—must be in a house—prov made during time of laying found: where men may rec endowment to make K & Pts[5] unto the Most H G. having nothin to do with temporal things but K of G. G has provided for a house to be built where we can get a House this the central place & where we can be baptized for dead—it is nec. when we want to save our dead we go through all the ordinances same as for ourself from bap to ordination & endt. From henceforth I have rec—inst from Ld that Ers shall build churches where ever they raise branches through the States then build stakes—in the gt cities Boston &c[6] there shall be stakes—reserved the pro. to the last. all this to be und. that this work shall commence after the washing anointing & endowment here

The Ld has an est law in relation to the matter. there must be a particular spot for the sal, of our dead. I verily believe this will be the place, hence men who want to save their dead can come and bring their families do their work and return to live and wait till the go to receive their reward.[7] Shall leave the rest for the brethren—tis my duty to teach the doctrine—spt is willing flesh is weak.[8] God is not willing to let me gratify you— but I must teach the Ers and they should teach you He will make me to be God in your stead[9] & they be mouth for me. Have been giving some inst to Er Adams[10] to speak to you & when he makes a mistake will get up and correct him.

Wilford Woodruff Journal

Conference met at 10 oclck April 8th

President J Smith arose and said it is impossible to continue the subject that I spoke upon yesterday in Consequence of the weekness of my lungs. Yet I have a proclamation to make to the Elders you know the Lord has led the Church untill the present time I have now a great proclamation for the Elders to teach the Church hereafter which is in relation to Zion, The whole of North and South America is Zion, the mountain of the Lords House is in the Centre of North & South America, when the House is done, Baptism font erectd and finished & the worthy are washed, anointed, endowed & ordained Kings & priests,[11] which must be done in this life, when the place is prepared you must go through all the ordinances of the house of the Lord so that you who have any dead friends must go through all the ordinances for them the same as for yourselves; then the Elders are to go through all America & build up Churches untill all Zion is built up, but not to commence to do this untill the Temple is built up here and the Elders endowed then go forth & accomplish the work & build up stakes in all North and South America, Their will be some place ordained for the redeeming of the dead I think this place will be the one, so their will be gathering fast enough here. President Smith lungs failed him and he appointed Elder G. J. Adams to occupy the time during the foornoon He however remarked that his proclamation just made was the greatest ever made as all could not come here;[12] but it was necessary that enough should come to build up the temple & get an endowment so that the work could spread abroad.

Thomas Bullock Report

Monday morning
Prayer by Pres Young—after which choir sung an hymn
Prophet it is just as impossible for me to continue the subject as to raise the dead—my lungs are worn out—I will do so anor. day. has led this Church by revn. I have anr. revn. a great grand & glorious revn. & this is what I am going to declare—you kno there has been great discusn. where Zion is & when the gathg. of the D is & which I am to—the whole America is the Land itself N. & S itself & is descd. by the Prophets that it shod. be in the centre of the land. the declan. is that as soon as the temple & B font is prepd. & so as we can wash & anoint the El of Israel there must be a place prepd for that purpose—there are provins made until the work is compd. to be as K & P of the mos H. God but as all to do with the hs of God—but there must be an express place built for that purpose & for men to be B for their dd for every man who wishes to save the F & M. B. S & F. must go thro the same—B—A. W. & all the protectn. of the powers of the Priesthood same as for themselves—the Elders of Israel shall build Churches unto the Ld. & there shall they build Churches unto the Ld: there shall be a Stake of Zion—it is a glorious pro—& I reserved it to the last & desn. it to be understd. that it shall be after the washg. & anointg. here—the place that the Ld. has estd. for the Sn. of the dead—there must be a parlar place. I verily belive this to be the place—& men who wish to save their dead must come here to be B for their dead—& then may go back agn.—& I shall leave m Brern to enlarge—it is my duty to teach those who err in doctrine—the Sp is willg. but the flesh is weak[13]—if God made Aaron to be their mouthpiece & Made me to be their K. & their God[14] & if you dont

like it you must lump it—I have give instron to El Adams in some principles—if he makes a mistake I will tell it.

Joseph Smith Diary, by Willard Richards

Prest. J. Smith said he must give up the subject of yesterday.

Made a proclamation.—I have another great and grand Revelation—great discussion where Zion is.—The whole America is Zion that is the Zion where the Mountain of the Lords house shall be. about the central part of N. & South America.—

soon as the Temple is finished.—Lord hath ordained where these last & most important ordinances must be in a house.—provided for the purpose.—when we can get a house built first there is the place.—Bap. washed. anointed, sealed &c for the dead the same as for themselves.—

from henceforth the elders shall build churches where ever the people receive the gospel sufficient. then build stakes to this place. I verily believe that God will establish this place for the salvation of the dead.—those who want to save their dead can come hither. those who do not wish to come hither to live can bring their families and attend the ordinances and return.

23 April 1844 (Tuesday). Masonic Hall.[1]
Thomas Bullock Diary

Meeting—Joseph & others speaking.

5 May 1844 (Sunday Afternoon and Evening). Mansion House.[1]
Joseph Smith Diary, by Willard Richards

A large co in Bar Room P.M. & eve Joseph spoke a long time on petitions read Friersons[2] letter, Clays letter &c.[3]—

12 May 1844 (Friday Morning). Temple Stand.[1]
Thomas Bullock Report

The Savior has the words of Eternal life[2]—nothing else can profit us—there is no salvation in believing an evil report against our neighbor—I advise all to go on to perfection and search deeper and deeper into the mysteries of Godliness[3]—a man can do nothing for himself unless God direct him in the right way, and the Priesthood is reserved for that purpose—the last time I spoke on this stand, it was on the resurrection of the dead; when I promised to continue my remarks upon that subject.[4] I still feel a desire to say something on this subject—let us this very day begin anew, and now say with all our hearts, we will forsake our sins and be righteous—I shall read the 24th. ch of Matthew and give it a litteral rendering and reading, and when it is rightly understood it will be edifying (he then read & translated it from the German) I thought the very oddity of its rendering would be edifying any how—"And it will preached be; the Gospel of the Kingdom in the whole world, to a witness over all people, and then will the end come."[5] I will now read it in German—(which he did, and many Germans who were present said he translated it correct) the Savior said, when those tribulations should take place, it should be committed to a man, who should be a witness over the whole world, the keys of knowledge, power, and revelations, should be revealed to a witness who should hold the testimony to the world;[6] it has always been my province to dig up hidden mysteries, new things, for my hearers— just at the time when some men think that I have no right to the keys of the Priesthood[7] just at that time, I have the greatest right—the Germans are an exalted people. the old German translators are the most correct; most honest of any of the translators, and therefore I get testimony to bear me out in the revelations that I have preached for the last 14 years—the old German, Latin, Greek and Hebrew translations all say it is true, they cannot be impeached, and therefore I am in good company—all the testimony is, that the Lord in the last days would commit the keys of the Priesthood to a witness over all people—has the Gospel of the Kingdom commenced in the last days? and will God take it from the man, until he takes him, himself?[8] I have read it precisely as the words flowed from the lips of Jesus Christ—John the Revelator saw an angel flying thro' the midst of heaven, having the everlasting Gospel to preach unto them that dwell on the earth, &c.[9] the Scripture is ready to be fulfilled when great wars, famines, pestilence, great distress, judge-ments, &c are ready to be poured out on the Inhabitants of the Earth—John saw the angel having the holy Priesthood who should preach the everlasting gospel to all nations,—God had an angel, a special messenger, ordained, & prepared for that purpose in the last days—Woe! Woe! be to that man, or set of men, who lift up their hands against God and his Witness in these last days.[10]—for they shall deceive almost the very chosen ones—my ~~apostate~~ enemies say that I have been a true prophet—& I had rather be a fallen true prophet, than a false prophet; when a man goes about prophesying and commands men to obey his teachings, he must be either a true or false prophet; false prophets always arise to oppose the true prophets, and they will prophesy so very near the truth that they will deceive almost the very chosen ones—the doctrine of eternal judgments belong to the 1st. principles of the Gospel in the last days[11]—in relation to the Kingdom of God[12]—the devil always sets up his Kingdom at the very same time in opposition to God,—every man who has a calling to mininster to the Inhabitants of the world, was ordained to that very purpose in the grand Council of Heaven before this world was[13]—I suppose that I was ordained to this very office in that grand Council[14]—it is the testimony that I want, that I am God's servant, and this people his people—the Ancient Prophets declared in the last days the God of Heaven shall set up a Kingdom which should never be destroyed, nor, left to other people;[15] & the very time that was calculated on; this people was struggling to bring it out[16]—he that arms himself with Gun, sword, or Pistol except in the defense of truth, will some time be sorry for it[17]—I never carry any ~~thing~~ weapon with me bigger than my Pen Knife—when I was dragged before the Cannon and muskets in Missouri, I was unarmed. God will always protect me until my mission is fulfilled.[18] I calculate to be one of the Instruments of setting up the Kingdom of Daniel, by the word of the Lord, and I intend to lay a foundation that will revolutionize the whole world[19]—I once offered my life to the Missouri Mob as a sacrifice for my people—and here I am—it will not be by Sword or Gun that this Kingdom will roll on—the power of truth is such that—all nations will be under the necessity of obeying the Gospel the prediction is that army will be against army[20]—it may be that the Saints will have to beat their Ploughes into Swords.[21] It will not do for men to sit down and see their women & children destroyed patiently,—my text is on the resurrection of the dead, which you will find in the 14 ch. of John In my Fathers house are many mansions &c it should be

In my Father's Kingdom are many Kingdoms[22]—in order that ye may be heirs of—God and joint heirs with me[23]—I do not believe the methodist doctrine of sending honest men, and noble minded men to hell, along with the murderer and adulterer—they may hurl all their hell and fiery billows upon me, for they will roll off me as fast as they come on—but I have an order of things to save the poor fellows at any rate, and get them saved for I will send men to preach to them in prison and save them if I can. There are many mansions for those who obey a celestial law[24]—& there are other mansions for those who come short of that law—every man in his own order there is baptism &c for those to exercise who are alive, and baptism for the dead, who died without the knowledge of the gospel I am going on in my progress for eternal life—it is not only necessary that you should be baptized for your dead, but you will have to go thro' all the ordinances for them, same as you have gone through, to save yourselves; there will be 144,000 Saviors on Mount Zion,[25] and with them an innumerable host, that no man can number—Oh! I beseech you to forward, go forward and make your calling and your election sure[26]—and if any man preach any other gospel with that which I have preached, he shall be cursed,[27] and some of you who now hear me, shall see it & know that I testify the truth concerning them; in regard to the law of the Priesthood[28]—there should be a place where all nations shall come up from time to time to receive their endowments, and the Lord has said, this shall be the place for the baptism for the dead[29]—every man that has been baptized and belongs to the Kingdom, has a right to be baptized for those who are gone before, and, as soon as the Law of the Gospel is obeyed here by their friends, who act as proxy for them, the Lord has administrators there to set them free—a man may act as proxy for his own relatives—the ordinances of the Gospel which was laid out before the foundation of the world has been thus fulfilled, by them, and we may be baptized for those who we have much friendship for, but it must be first revealed to the man of God, lest we should run too far[30]—as in Adam all die, so in Christ shall all be made alive,[31] all shall be raised from the dead—the Lamb of God hath brought to pass the resurrection so that all shall rise from the dead—God Almighty himself dwells in Eternal fire,[32] flesh and blood cannot go there for all corruption is devoured by the fire[33]—our God is a consuming fire[34]—when our flesh is quickened by the Spirit, there will be no blood in the tabernacles,[35]—some dwell in higher glory than others—those who have done wrong, always have that wrong knawing them—Immortality dwells in everlasting burnings[36]—I will from time to time reveal to you the subjects that are revealed by the Holy Ghost to me—all the lies that are now hatched up against me are of the devil & all the influence of the devil & his servants will be used against the kingdom of God—the Servants of God teach nothing but the principles of eternal life—by their works ye shall know them[37]—a good man will speak good things, & holy principles and an evil man, evil things;—I feel in the name of the Lord, to rebuke all such bad principles, liars &c and I warn all of you to look out who you are going after—I exhort you to give heed to all the virtue and the teachings which I have given you; all men who are immortal, dwell in everlasting burnings;[38] you cannot go any where, but where God can find you out;[39] all men are born to die & all must rise, all must enter eternity—in order for you to receive your children to yourself, you must have a promise, some ordinance some blessing in order to assend above principalities or else it may be an angel[40]—they must rise just as they died—we can there hail our lovely infants with the same glory, the same loveliness in the celestial glory where they all enjoy alike—they differ in stature, in size—the same glorious spirit gives them the likeness of glory and bloom[41]—the old man with his silvery hairs will glory in bloom & beauty[42]—no man can describe it to you—no man can write it[43]— when did I ever teach any thing wrong from this stand? when was I ever confounded? I want to triumph in Israel before I depart hence and am no more seen[44]—I never told you I was perfect—but there is no error in the revelations which I have taught—must I then be thrown away as a thing of nought?—I enjoin for your consideration, add to your faith, virtue, love &c[45] I say in the name of the Lord, if these things are in you, you shall be fruitful.[46] I testify that no man has power to reveal it, but myself, things in heaven, in earth and hell[47]—and all shut your mouths for the future—I commend you all to God, that you may inherit all things—& may God add his blessings. Amen.

George Laub Journal

Concerning Gods Witness

24th chapter of ~~Revelations of John~~ Mathew, Mathew 6 & 7 14 verses, & the orriginal translation Reads thus and I will Send you a nother witness & he shall preach this gospel to all nations to the ends of the world But woe to that man or woman who Shall lift up their or his hands against god's witness for the[y] are rasing their hands or arms against the power of god and the[y] will be cursed. But in these times in the last days there will many fals prophets arise and false teachers and decieve many the[y] Shall have many followers by their deceit.[49] the[y] Strive to have power and by their pernitious ways lead of[f] many—for Brother Joseph Smith was chosen for the last dispensation or Seventh Dispensation The time the grand council Set in heaven to organise this world Joseph was chosen for the last & greatest Prophet to lay the foundation of gods work of the Seventh Dispensation therefore the Jews asked John the Baptist if he was Elias or Jesus or that great prophet that was to come.[50]

the Devil lusifer also organised his kingdom in oposition to overthrow gods kingdom & he became the Son of perdition[51]

also concerning the kingdoms in my fathers house or kingdom are many kingdoms or worlds I will goe to prepare a place for you.[52] and according to your works you shall be rewarded.[53] These who will not obey the gospel will goe to the world of spirits there to stay till the[y] have paid the utmost farthing or till some person pays their depts they owe.[54] Now all those die in the faith goe to the prison of Spirits to preach to the ded in body, but they are alive in the Spirit & those Spirits preach to the Spirits that they may live according to god in the Spirit and men do minister for them in the flesh and angels bare the glad tidings to the Spirits & the[y] are made happy by these means.[55] therefore those who are baptised for their dead are the Saviours on mount Zion[56] & the[y] must receave their washings and their anointings for their dead the same as for themselves till the[y] are connected to the ones in the dispensation before us and trace their leniage to connect the priesthood again

and if any other man preach any other gospel then this and the Baptism for the remission of sins and the laying on of hands for the reception of the holy ghost let him be anathamised or acursed[57] The curs of god shall be upon him or them.

Concerning Resurection Flesh and Blood cannot inherit the kingdom of god or the kingdom that god inherits or inhabits.[58] But the flesh without the blood and the Spirit of god flowing in the vains in Sted of the blood for blood is the part of the body that causes corruption.[59] therefore we must be changed in the twinkle of an Eye or have to lay down these tabernacles and leave the blood vanish away[60] Therefore Jesus Christ left his blood to atone for the Sins of the world that he might assend into the presents of the father for god dwels in flaming flames and he is a consuming fire[61] he will consume all that is unclean and unholly and we could not abide his presents unless pure Spirits in us.[62] for the Blood is the corruptible part of the tabernacles.

for the resurrection is devised to take away corruption and make Man perfect or in the glory which he was created for The body is Sowen in corruption & raised in Incorruption[63] Then we will be able to goe in the presents of god Br. Joseph Smith was sent to remind the world of Sin or rituousness & of the Judgments to come But this is that of what John Says in his 14th Chapter, but he Says of sin or rituousness and of a Judgment to come to reprove the world This is rong Translation for to remind is correct.[64]

Samuel W. Richards Record

The Prophet Joseph said May 12th 1844 After reading the 24th Chap of Math[65] from from an Ancient German Bible Text: "The Kingdom must preached be to a witness over all Nation People." "preached to a man who should be a witness to all people, is the meaning of the text." quoted Rev. 14-6 having the Gospel saying the hour of his Judgment is come.

At the general & grand Council of heaven, all those to whom a dispensation was to be commited, were set apart & ordained at that time, to that calling.

The Twelve also as witnesses were ordained.[66]

Subject changed to Resurrection of the Dead. John 14:2d "in my Fathers Kingdom are many Kingdoms. I go to prepare a Kingdom for you, that the exaltation that I receive you may receive also."

The sectarians have no Charity for me but I have for them. I intend to send men to prison to preach to them, and this is all on the Principle of entering in by Water and Spirit.[67] Then you must not only be baptized for them but they must receive the Holy Ghost by Proxy and be sealed by it unto the day of their redemption as all the other ordinances by proxy.[68]

All persons who have been Baptized and who have received the

Holy Ghost may be baptized for their ancestors or near relatives. God has administrators in the eternal world to release those spirits from Prison the ordinances being administered by proxy upon them the law is fulfilled.

All resurected bodies dwell in flaming fire for our God is a consuming fire.[69]

With what body do they rise?

You must obtain promises for them as Abraham. They rise with the same sized and shaped bodies, but to have the same glories as full grown bodies.[70]

Joseph Fielding Journal

On Sunday the 13th [12th] of May Joseph spoke on the Gospel of the Kingdom and shewd that when God set up his Kingdom on the Earth Satan always set up his in Opposition alluding to Appostay at this [time] working in this Place[71], I never felt more delighted with his discourse than at this time, It put me in Mind of Herod when they said at his Oration It is the voice of a God and not of a Man,[72] The Circumstances were widely different, he also spoke some on the Resurrection.

Joseph Smith Diary, by Willard Richards

10 A.M. preached at the Stand touching many things.

Thomas Bullock Diary

I and wife went to Temple stand Joseph preached on the resurrection and baptism for the dead he translated 24 ch Matthew—I learned a great deal.

14 May 1844 (Tuesday Evening). Temple Stand.[1]
Joseph Smith Diary, by Willard Richards

This P.M. My Old Lawyer[2] gave a lecture on the stand. stating the difficulties I had formerly encountered. I spoke after he had closed & continued my history to the present time.—

17 May 1844 (Friday). Upper Room, Red Brick Store.[1]
Nauvoo Neighbor 2 (22 May 1844)

When Gen. Smith was called upon, he spoke with much talent, and ability and displayed a great knowledge of the political history of this nation, of the cause of the evils under which our nation groans, and also the remedy.

26 May 1844 (Sunday Morning).[1]
History of the Church, 6:408-12

President Joseph Smith read the 11th Chapter II Corinthians. My object is to let you know that I am right here on the spot where I intend to stay. I, like Paul have been in perils,[2] and oftener than anyone in this generation. As Paul boasted, I have suffered more than Paul did. I should be like a fish out of water, if I were out of persecutions. Perhaps my brethren think it requires all this to keep me humble. The Lord has constituted me so curiously that I glory in persecution. I am not nearly so humble as if I were not persecuted. If oppression will make a wise man mad, much more a fool. If they want a beardless boy to whip all the world, I will get on the top of a mountain and crow like a rooster: I shall always beat them. When facts are proved, truth and innocence will prevail at last. My enemies are no philosophers: they think that when they have my spoke under, they will keep me down; but for the fools, I will hold on and fly over them.

God is in the still small voice.[3] In all these affidavits, indict-ments, it is all of the devil-all corruption. Come on! ye prosecutors! ye false swearers! All hell, boil over! Ye burning mountains, roll down your lava! for I will come out on the top at last.[4] I have more to boast of than ever any man had. I am the only man that has ever been able to keep a whole church together since the days of Adam. A large majority of the whole have stood by me. Neither Paul, John, Peter, nor Jesus ever did it. I boast that no man ever did such a work as I. The followers of Jesus ran away from Him; but the Latter-day Saints never ran away from me yet. You know my daily walk and conversation. I am in the bosom of a virtuous and good peole. How I do love to hear the wolves howl! When they can get rid of me, the devil will also go. For the last three years I have a record of all my acts and proceedings, for I have kept several good, faithful, and efficient clerks in constant employ: they have accompanied me everywhere, and carefully kept my history, and they have written down what I have done, where I have been, and what I have said; therefore my enemies cannot charge me with any day, time, or place, but what I have written testimony to prove my actions; and my enemies cannot prove anything against me.[5] They have got wonderful things in the land of Ham. I think the grand jury have strained at a gnat and swallowed the camel.[6]

A man named Simpson[7] says I made an affidavit against him, &c. Mr. Simpson says I arrested him. I never arrested Mr. Simpson in my life. He says I made an affidavit against him. I never made an affidavit against him in my life. I will prove it in court. I will tell you how it was: Last winter I got ready with my children to go to the farm to kill hogs. Orrin P. Rockwell was going to drive. An Englishman came in and wanted a private conversation with me. I told him I did not want any private conversations. "I demand one of you!" Such a one I am bound to obey anyhow. Said he—"I want a warrant against the man who stabbed Brother Badham.[8] He said it was a man who boarded at Davis'.[9] He said it was Mr. Simpson—it answered his description. I said I had no jurisdiction out of the city. He said—"The man must be arrested, or else he will go away." I told him—"You must go to Squire Wells,[10] Johnson,[11] or Foster."[12] Mr Lytle[13] stepped up and said—"I am a policeman." I jumped into my carriage, and away I went.

When I came back I met Mr. Jackson.[14] He said—"You did wrong in arresting Mr. Simpson." I told him I did not do it. I went over and sat down, and related the circumstances. He turned round and said—"Mr. Smith, I have nothing against you; I am satisfied." He went and supped with me. He declared in the presence of witnesses, that he had nothing against me. I then said—"I will go over to Esquire Johnson, and testify what the Englishman told me." I told him not to make out that I believe he is the man, but that I believe he is innocent. I don't want to swear that he is the man. Messrs. Coolidge,[15] Rockwell, Hatfield,[16] and Hawes[17] were present.

Mr. Johnson made one out in due form: and as I sat down in a bustle the same as I do when one of the clerks brings a deed for me to sign. Johnson read it. I said—"I can't swear to that affidavit; I don't believe it: tear up that paper." Mr. Simpson agreed to come before Badham and make it up. I did not swear to it.

After a while, Dr. Foster and others came in. They called me up to testify. I told it all the same as I do here. Mr. Simpson rose up, and asked—"Do you believe now that I am the man who stabbed Mr. Badham?" I replied—"No sir, I do not now, nor ever did: the magistrate says I did not swear to it." He considered, and made a public declaration that he was satisfied with me.

Aaron Johnson went before the grand jury and swore I did not swear to it, when Dr. Foster goes and swears that I swore to it, and that he was in the room when he was not in. Chauncey wanted me to stay and have a conversation. Dr. Foster asked Aaron Johnson for the writ and affidavit. He handed them to Dr. Foster, who read them, and then threw them into the fire. I said—"Doctor, you ought not to have burned it; it was my paper." Dr. Foster goes to the grand jury and swears he did not burn only one; but I say he burnt both. This is a fair sample of the swearing that is going on against me.

The last discharge was the 40th; now the 41st, 42nd, 43rd; all through falsehood.[18] Matters of fact are as profitable as the Gospel, and which I can prove. You will then know who are liars, and who speak the truth I want to retain your friendship on holy grounds.

Another indictment has been got up against me. It appears a holy prophet has arisen up,[19] and he has testified against me: the reason is, he is so holy. The Lord knows I do not care how many churches are in the world. As many as believe me, may. If the doctrine that I preach is true, the tree must be good.[20] I have prophesied things that have come to pass, and can still.

Inasmuch as there is a new church, this must be old, and of course we ought to be set down as orthodox. From henceforth let all the churches now no longer persecute orthodoxy. I never build upon any other man's ground. I never told the old Catholic that he was a fallen true prophet God knows, then, that the charges against me are false.

I had not been married scarcely five minutes, and made one proclamation of the Gospel, before it was reported that I had seven wives. I mean to live and proclaim the truth as long as I can.

This new holy prophet has gone to Carthage and swore that I had told him that I was guilty of adultery. This spiritual wifeism!

Why, a man dares not speak or wink, for fear of being accused of this.

William Law testified before forty policemen, and the assembly room full of witnesses, that he testified under oath that he never had heard or seen or knew anything immoral or criminal against me. He testified under oath that he was my friend, and not the "Brutus." There was a cogitation who was the "Brutus." I had not prophesied against William Law. He swore under oath that he was satisfied that he was ready to lay down his life for me, and he swears that I have committed adultery.[21]

I wish the grand jury would tell me who they are—whether it will be a curse or blessing to me. I am quite tired of the fools asking me.

A man asked me whether the commandment was given that a man may have seven wives; and now the new prophet has charged me with adultery. I never had any fuss with these men until that Female Relief Society brought out the paper against adulterers and adulteresses.[22]

Dr. Goforth[23] was invited into the Laws' clique, and Dr. Foster and the clique were dissatisfied with that document, and they rush away and leave the Church, and conspire to take away my life; and because I will not countenance such wickedness, they proclaim that I have been a true prophet, but that I am now a fallen prophet.

Jackson has committed murder, robbery, and perjury; and I can prove it by half-a-dozen witnesses. Jackson got up and said—"By God, he is innocent," and now swears that I am guilty. He threatened my life.

There is another Law, not the prophet, who was cashiered for dishonesty and robbing the government. Wilson Law also swears that I told him I was guilty of adultery. Brother Jonathan Dunham[24] can swear to the contrary. I have been chained. I have rattled chains before in a dungeon for the truth's sake. I am innocent of all these charges, and you can bear witness of my innocence, for you know me yourselves.

When I love the poor, I ask no favors of the rich. I can go to the cross—I can lay down my life; but don't forsake me. I want the friendship of my brethren.—Let us teach the things of Jesus Christ. Pride goes before destruction, and a haughty spirit before a downfall.[25]

Be meek and lowly, upright and pure; render good for evil. If you bring on yourselves your own destruction, I will complain. It is not right for a man to bear down his neck to the oppressor always. Be humble and patient in all circumstances of life; we shall then triumph more gloriously. What a thing it is for a man to be accused of committing adultery, and having seven wives, when I can only find one.

I am the same man, and as innocent as I was fourteen years ago; and I can prove them all perjurers. I labored with these apostates myself until I was out of all manner of patience; and then I sent my brother Hyrum, whom they virtually kicked out of doors.

I then sent Mr. Backenstos,[26] when they declared that they were my enemies. I told Mr. Backenstos that he might tell the Laws, if they had any cause against me I would go before the Church, and confess it to the world. He [William Law] was summoned time and again, but refused to come. Dr. Bernhisel[27] and Elder Rigdon know that I speak the truth. I cite you to Captain Dunham, Esquires Johnson and Wells, Brother Hatfield and others, for the truth of what I have said. I have said this to let my friends know that I am right.

As I grow older, my heart grows tenderer for you. I am at all times willing to give up everything that is wrong, for I wish this people to have a virtuous leader, I have set your minds at liberty by letting you know the things of Christ Jesus. When I shrink not from your defense will you throw me away for a new man who slanders you? I love you for your reception of me. Have I asked you for your money? No; you know better. I appeal to the poor. I say, Cursed be that man or woman who says that I have taken of your money unjustly. Brother Babbitt[28] will address you. I have nothing in my heart but good feelings.

Joseph Smith Diary, by Willard Richards

10 A M. preached at the stand about Joseph Jackson and the mobocrats.

Thomas Bullock Diary

At the Stand recording J. Smith's sermon.

13 June 1844 (Thursday Afternoon). At Seventies Hall.[1]
Joseph Smith Diary, by Willard Richards

P.M. attend meeting in 70s Hall G. J. Adams Preached—after which I made some observations—

16 June 1844 (Sunday Morning). Grove East of Temple.[1]
Thomas Bullock Report

Prayer by N Whitney choir sang "Mortals Awake" The Prophet read the 3rd Rev. text 6th. v. & made us K & P. unto God & his Far. to him be glory & dom. for evermore[2]—

It is altogr. correct in the translatn.[3]—now you know that of late some have sprung up & apostat. & they declare that Pro bel[ieves]. in a plurality of Gods[4]—&c. & behold a very great secret they cry it has been my intentn. to take up this subjt. & show what my Faith is in the matter—I have contemplated the saying of Je[sus] as it was in the days of Noah so shall it be at his 2nd. coming & if it rains I'll preach—the plurarlity of Gods—I have selected this text I wish to declare I have allways—& in all congregats. when I have preached it has been the plurality of Gods it has been preached 15 years—I have always decld. God to be a distinct personage—J.C. a sep. & distinct pers from God the Far. the H.G was a distinct personage[5] & or Sp & these 3 constit. 3 distinct personages & 3 Gods—if this is in accordance with the New Test.—lo & behold we have 3 Gods any how & they are plural any how—our text says

the apost[les] have disc[overe]d. that there were Gods above—God was the Far. of our Ld. J.C.[6]—my object was to preach the Scrip—& preach the doctrine there being a God above the Far. of our Ld. J.C.—I am bold to declare I have taut. all the strong doctrines publicly—& always stronger that what I preach in private—John was one of the men & the apos. declare they were made K. & P. unto God the Fatr. of our Ld. J.C.[7] it reads just so hence the doctrine of a plurality of Gods is as prominent in the Bible as any doctrine—it is all over the face of the Bible, it stands beyond the power of controversy—a wayfaring man tho a fool need not fail—Paul says there are gods many & Lords many[8]—I want to set it in a plain simple manner—but to us there is but one God pertaining to us, in all thro all,[9]—but if J. Smith says there is Gods many & Lds. many they cry away with him crucify him mankind verily say that the Scrip [i]s with them—Search the Script & & they testify of things that apostates wod blaspheme—Paul if Jo Smith is a blasphemer you are—I say there are Gods many & Lds many but to us only one & we are to be in subject to that one & no man can limit the bounds, or the eternal existence of eternal time—hath he beheld the et[erna]l. world. & is he authd. to say that there is only God he makes himself a fool—& there is an end of his career in knowledge he cannot obtn. all knowledge for he has sealed up the gate to[10]

some say I do not interpret same as you—they say it means the heathen God.[11] Paul says there are Gods many &c it makes a plurality of Gods any how—witht. a revn. I am not going to give the God of Heaven to them any how—you know & I testify that Paul had no allusions to it—I have it from God & get over it if you can—I have a witness of the H.G—& a test. that Paul had no allusion to the Heathen G. in the text—Twice I will shew from the Heb. Bible & the 1st. word shews a plurality of Gods—& I want the apostate & learned men to come here—& prove to the contrary an unlearned boy must give you a little Hebrew—Berosheit &c[12] In the begin. rosheit—the head—it shod. read the heads of—to organize the Gods—Eloiheam Eloi. God in sing. heam,[13] reanders Gods I want a little learning as well as other fools

Popes quot: Drink deep[14]

all the confusion is for want of drinking and draught the head God—organized the heavens & the Earth—I defy all the learning in the world to refute me—

In the begin the heads of the Gods organized the heaven & the Earth—now the learned Priest—the people rage—& the heathen imagine a vain thing—if we pursue the Heb further—it reads

The Head one of the Gods said let us make man in our image[15] I once asked a learned Jew[16] once—if the Heb. language compels us to render all words ending in heam in the plural—why not render the first plural—he replied it would ruin the Bible—he acknowledged I was right. I came here to investigate these things precisely as I believe it—hear & judge for yourself—& if you go away satisfied— well & good—in the very beginning there is a plurality of Gods— beyond the power of refutation—it is a great subject I am dwelling on—the word Eloiheam ought to be in the plural all the way thro[17]— Gods—the heads of the Gods appointed one God for us[18]—& when you take a view of the subject it sets one free to see all the beauty holiness & perfection of the God—all I want is to get the simple truth—naked & the whole truth—Men say there is one God—the Far. Son & the H.G. are only 1 God—it is a strange God any how 3 in 1. & 1 in 3. it is a curious thing any how—Far. I pray not for the world but I pray for those that thou givest me &c &c[19] all are to be crammed into 1 God—it wod. make the biggest God in all the world—he is a wonderful big God—he would be a Giant I want to read the text to you myself—I am agreed with the Far. & the Far. is a greed with me & we are agreed as one[20]—the Greek shews that is shod. be agreed[21]—Far. I pray for them that thou hast given me out of the world &c &c[22] that they may be agreed & all come to dwell in unity & in all the Glory & Everlasting burngs of God & then we shall see as we are seen[23] & be as God—& he as the God of his Far.—I want to reason—I learned it by translating the papyrus now in my house[24]—I learned a test. concerning Abraham & he reasoned concerng. the God of Heaven—in order to do that sd. he—suppose we have two facts that supposes that anotr. fact may exist two men on the earth—one wiser than the other—wod. shew that antr. who is wiser than the wisest may exist—intelligences exist one above anotr. that there is no end to it[25]—if Abra. reasoned thus—if J.C was the Son of God & John discd. that god the Far. of J.C had a far. you may suppose that he had a Far. also—where was ther ever a Son witht. a Far.—where ever did tree or any thing spring into existence witht. a progenitor—& every thing comes in this way—Paul says that which is Earthyly is in likeness of that which is Heavenly[26]— hence if J. had a Far. can we not believe that he had a Far. also—I despise the idea of being scared to death—I want you all to pay particr. attent. J. sd. as the Far. wrought precisely in the same way as his Far. had done bef[27]—as the Far. had done bef.—he laid down his life & took it up same as his Far. had done bef—he did as he was sent to[28] lay down his life & take it up again & was then committed unto him the keys &c I know it is good reasoning—I have reason to think that the Church is being purged—I saw Satan fall from heaven[29]—& the way they ran was a caution. all these are wonders & marvellous in our eyes in these last days—so long as men are under the law of God they have no fears, they do not scarce themselves—I want to stick to my text—to shew that when men open their lips—

they do not injure me—but injure themselves—To the law & to the testimony[30]—they are poured all over the Scrip

when things that are great are passed over witht. even a thot I want to see all in all its bearings & hug it to my bosom—I bel. all that God ever revd. & I never hear of a man being d[amne]d for belg. too much but they are d—d for unbel.

they found fault with J.C. bec. he sd. he was the Son of God & made himself equal with God[31]—they say like the apost. of old I must be put down[32]—what Je. say—it is written in your law I said Ye are Gods[33]—it was thro' him that they drink of the rock[34]—of course he wod. take the honor to himself—J. if they were called Gods unto whom the word of God why shld. it be thot incredible that I shod. say I am the Son of God.[35] Oh Apostates did ye never think of this bef. these are the quotations that the apostates take to the Scrip— they swear that they bel the Bible & the Book of Mormon[36] &c & then you will get filth & slander & bogus makers plenty—& one of the Church members prophesied that Jo Smith shld. never preach any more—& yet I am now prachg.—go & read the vision[37]—there is glory & glory—Sun, moon & Stars—& so do they differ in glory & every man who reigns is a God—& the text of the Do & Covt damns themselves—Paul what do you say—they impeached Paul & all went & left him[38]—Paul had 7 churches & they drove him off from among them—& yet they cannot do it by me—I rej. in that—my test. is good—Paul—says there is one Glory of the Sun the moon & the Stars—& as the Star differs &c[39]—They are exalted far above princ. thrones dom. & angels—& are expressly decld. to be heirs of God & jt. heirs with J.C.[40] all havg. et[erna]l. power—the Scrip are a very strange doct.—I have an[othe]r. Scrip—now says God when visited Moses in the Bush—moses was a stutt[er]ing sort of a boy like me—God said thou shalt be a God unto the children of Israel—God said thou shalt be a God unto Aaron & he shall be thy spokes.[41] I bel. in these Gods that God reveals as Gods—to be Sons of God[42] & all can cry Abba Father[43]—Sons of God who exalt themselves to be Gods even from bef. the foundatn. of the world & are all the only Gods I have a reverence for—[44]

John sd. he was a K[ing].[45]—J.C. who hath by his own blood made us K & P to God.[46] Oh thou God who are K. of K's & Ld. of Lds.[47]—we cannot bel. thee—old Catholic Church is worth more than all[48]—here is a princ. of logic—that men have no more sense—I will illustrate an old apple tree—here jumps off a branch & says I am the true tree. & you are corrupt—if the whole tree is corrupt how can any true thing come out of it—the char[acte]r of the old ones have always been sland[ere]d. by all apos[tates] since the world began—I testify again as God never will acknowledge any apost: any man who will betray the Catholics will betray you—& if he will betray one anothr. he will betray you—all men are liars who say that they are of the true—God always sent a new dispensatn.[49] into the world—when men come out & build upon o[the]r men's foundatn.—did I build on anotr. mans foundtn. but my own—I have got all the truth & an indepent. rev[elatio]n. in the bargain[50]— & God will bear me off triumphant—I will drop this subjt. I wish I cod. speak for 3 or 4 hours it is not expedt. on acct. of the rain—I will still go on & shew you proof on proof. all the Bible is as equal one part as another

George Laub Journal

The Scripture Say I and my father are one[51] & again that the father son & holy ghost are one 1 John 5 ch. 7 vers But these three agree in the Same thing[52] & did the Saviour pray to the father. I pray not for the world but those [w]home he gave me out of the world that we might be one, or to Say be of one mind in the unity of the faith.[53]

but Every one being a diffrent or Seperate person & So is god & is god & Jesus Christ & the holy ghost. Seperate persons.but the all agree in one or the Self Same thing But the holy ghost is yet a Spiritual body and waiting to take to himself a body. as the Savior did or as god did or the gods before them took bodies[54] for the Saviour Says the work that my father did do i also & those are the works[55] he took himself a a body & then laid down his life that he might take it up again[56] & the Scripture Say those who will obey the commandments shall be heirs of god & Joint heirs with of Jesus Christ[57] we then also took bodys to lay them down, to take them up again & the Sperit itself bears witness with our Spirits that we are the children of god & if children then heirs and Joint heirs with Jesus Christ if So be that we Suffer with him in the flesh that we may be also glorified to gether. See Romans 8 ch 16 & 17 Vers.

McIntire Minute Book

Sunday the 16th of June 1844 Gen. Joseph Smiths Last public Discorce on Doctrine he comenced By Reading Rev. 1st Ch 6 verse— "And hath made us Kings & priests unto God & his father &c He then preceded to show the plurality of Gods By Refering to the 1st Gen. as in the origanel Hebrew—that it Read that in the Begining the Head Gods organized the Earth & the heavens[58] &—and that God was a distinct in of himself & the Son also was a distinct personage But in the image of the Father—he quoted the 17th of St John 20, 21, 22, 23 that the apostles & the Desciples may all agree in one—or be agreed in the one principal as thou father & me are agred—Jesus said that all things that He saw the father do he did—and also the 82 psalm 1st verse God standith in the Congragations of the Mighty; he Judgeth among the Gods—

Joseph Smith Diary, by Willard Richards

Preached at the stand 10 o'clock A.M.

William Clayton Diary

Preached at the stand.

16 June 1844 (Sunday Afternoon). Grove East of Temple.
William Clayton Diary

4 o clock at the stand stated the design of the meeting & ordered the Major General to have the Legion in readiness to suppress all illegal violence in the City.

18 June 1844 (Tuesday Afternoon). Frame Building, Near Mansion House.[1]
William Clayton Diary

After Phelps got through Genl. J. Smith addressed the multitude. He briefly explained the object of the mob and showed that they waged a war of extermination upon us because of our

religion. He called upon all the volunteers who felt to support the
constitution from the Rocky Mountains to the Atlantic Ocean to
come with their arms, ammunition & defend the constitution. He
called upon them as the Lieutenant General of the N. L and Illinois
Militia in the name of the Constitution of the U.S. the people of the
State of Ill. and the citizens of Nauvoo. He called upon the Citizens
to defend the lives of their wives & children, fathers and mothers,
brothers & sisters from being murdered by the mob. He urged them
in strong terms not to shed innocent blood.—not to act in the least
on the offensive but invariably in the defensive and if we die—die
like men of God and secure a glorious resurrection. He concluded by
invoking the Great God to bless the people.—

. . .In the above address he advised all to arm themselves those
who had no rifles, get swords, scythe and make weapons of some
kind He informed them that he had 5000 Elders minute men who
would come with volunteers as soon as he would inform them. He
said there were many from Iowa waiting to come when requested.

McIntire Minute Book

Joseph Smith to the Nauvoo Legion his Last adress in which he
called for all philanthropic men from Main to the Rocky Mountains
& from the East & the west & from the North & the south to the help
of this people also he cursed the Mob.—with thunder & lightning &
the sword plague Earthquakes & pestilence & devouring fire.

1844 NOTES

7 January 1844

1. See *History of the Church*, 6:171. Not in *Teachings*. The original source for the entry in *History of the Church* is the Joseph Smith Diary.

2. Cornelius P. Lott (1798-1850). A native of New York City, Lott joined the Church in Luzerne County, Pennsylvania, before 1834. In 1842 he moved onto Joseph Smith's farm, four miles east of Nauvoo, to manage it.

3. Daniel Spencer (1794-1868) was converted to the Church sometime in 1840. He was a member of the Nauvoo City Council, and was appointed in August 1844 to fill the remainder of Joseph Smith's term as mayor of Nauvoo.

19 January 1844

1. See *History of the Church*, 6:180. Not in *Teachings*. The original source for the entry in *History of the Church* is the Joseph Smith Diary.

2. Jacob B. Backenstos, a friendly non-Mormon, served as clerk of the circuit court in Hancock County. In 1844 he was elected to the Illinois legislature, and in 1845 he was elected sheriff.

3. William W. Phelps.

21 January 1844

1. See *History of the Church*, 6:183-85, and *Teachings*, pp. 329-31. The original source for the reports in *History of the Church* and *Teachings* is the Wilford Woodruff Journal except for the introduction which comes from the Joseph Smith Diary.

2. Reynolds Cahoon.

3. Malachi 4:5-6.

4. Malachi 4:5-6*; D&C 128:17-18.

5. This refers to the appearance of Elijah in the Kirtland Temple on 3 April 1836. See D&C 110:13-16.

6. The Saints, meaning both males and females, could serve as "Saviors on Mount Zion."

7. Obadiah 21.

8. All ordinances of the temple that are done for the living, including marriage for time and eternity and the fulness of the priesthood, can also be done for the dead (see James E. Talmage, *The House of the Lord* [Salt Lake City:

Deseret Book Company, 1968], pp. 163 and 211, and B. H. Roberts, *A Comprehensive History of The Church of Jesus Christ of Latter-day Saints—Century 1* 6 vols. [Provo, Utah: Brigham Young University Press, 1965] 6:495).

9. It is uncertain whether the Prophet was announcing a change of practice that ordinance work would be done for the Saints' progenitors further back than those individuals for whom they "believed would have accepted the Gospel" (which was at most four generations). In this regard Apostle Melvin J. Ballard (commenting on the policy announced by the Prophet on 19 October 1840 [*Teachings* p. 179]) said:

> That limitation given to Latter-day Saints at that time was, baptism for their dead whom they believed would have received the Gospel. That is all. And no others. Now since we are not prepared to pass judgment on our dead ancestors whom we did not know, the church has gone further and has permitted members of the church to do the work for all their immediate ancestors except they are murderers. There can be no work done for those who have committed murder. We are to do the work for our dead, whether we know they will receive it or not (*The Three Degrees of Glory—A Discourse by Melvin J. Ballard* [Salt Lake City: Deseret Book Company, n.d.], p. 20).

10. That is, the power of Elijah and Elias.

11. Isaiah 10:22-23. See also D&C 87:6.

12. John 9:4.

13. The Prophet feared that the Saints would be scattered again before they could obtain their temple blessings at the central place. Matthew 23:37-38 (34-39).

14. See 11 June 1843, note 25.

15. John 14:2.

16. John 14:2*.

17. See 11 June 1843, note 25.

18. Using more current terminology, this sentence translates: "It has been like splitting the knots of hemlock trees using a piece of corn bread for a wedge and a pumpkin for the sledge hammer."

19. See 5 October 1840, note 24; 3 October 1841, note 19; and, 27 August 1843, note 5.

20. Matthew 22:14 (1-14). See also D&C 121:34 (34-40).

8 February 1844

1. See *History of the Church*, 6:210-11, and *Teachings*, pp. 331-32. The original source for the reports of this address in *History of the Church* and

Teachings is the Wilford Woodruff Journal except for the introduction which comes from the Joseph Smith Diary.

2. The Prophet's "Views on the Powers and Policy of the Government of the United States," published in pamphlet form, is given in full in *History of the Church*, 6:197-209.

3. See Joseph Smith Diary report of the 9 July 1843 discourse (after note 2), for a similar remark by the Prophet.

18 February 1844

1. See *History of the Church*, 6:221. Not in *Teachings*.

2. Thomas Bullock (1816-85). A trained stenographer, Bullock was scribe to Joseph Smith and wrote nearly 700 pages of the manuscript of Joseph Smith's history.

21 February 1844

1. See *History of the Church*, 6:223, and *Teachings*, p. 332. These reports are based on the Joseph Smith Diary, by Willard Richards.

2. The Reverand DeWolf, an Episcopalian minister, had preached in Nauvoo the previous year on 11 June 1843.

3. See 11 June 1843, note 25.

25 February 1944

1. See *History of the Church*, 6:225. Not in *Teachings*. The entry in *History of the Church* is based on the Joseph Smith Diary. The brief reports of Wilford Woodruff and Thomas Bullock are here published for the first time.

2. Thomas Bullock's wife was Henrietta Rushton Bullock.

7 March 1844 (1)

1. See *History of the Church*, 6:236-40. Not in *Teachings*. The original source for the report of this discourse in *History of the Church* is an amalgamation of the Joseph Smith Diary, by Willard Richards and the Wilford Woodruff Journal.

2. Orsimus F. Bostwick. The text has reference to Bostwick's being fined $50 for slanderous language concerning himself and certain females of Nauvoo. Hyrum Smith was complainant. Francis M. Higbee, Bostwick's attorney, informed the Prophet that he would appeal the case to the municipal court and then to the circuit court at Carthage.

3. Arthur Morrison was a friendly non-Mormon who greatly assisted the Saints in Clay County, Missouri 1834-36. He subsequently moved to Nauvoo.

4. The Prophet was referring to Charles A. Foster. A land speculator in Nauvoo, Foster subsequently joined other dissidents in opposing the leadership and influence of Joseph Smith.

5. Joseph Smith was the Trustee-in-Trust for the Church.

6. Dr. James McNeil had a small drug business and botanical medicine practice in Nauvoo.

7. Matthew 22:20.

8. See 13 April 1843, note 15. Regarding Jesus reproving the "lawyers and doctors," see Matthew 23.

9. Charles Foster. See note 4, this discourse.

10. Isaiah 29:21.

7 March 1844 (2)

1. See *History of the Church*, 6:243-44, and *Teachings*, pp. 333-35. The original source for the reports of this discourse in *History of the Church* and *Teachings* is an amalgamation of the Joseph Smith Diary, by Willard Richards and the Wilford Woodruff Journal. The brief report by Thomas Bullock is here published for the first time.

2. That is, the "Book of the Law of the Lord" wherein donations to the temple were recorded.

3. Samuel Houston (1793-1863) was a United States statesman and general. He was president of the Republic of Texas 1836-44.

4. When Texas declared its independence in 1836, an overwhelming majority favored annexation by the United States. To take Texas could result in war with Mexico, and would unavoidably stir sectional controversy over slavery. With 1844 (an election year) coming, northern and western senators refused to vote for annexation, and Texas began developing friendly ties with Great Britain. In the spring of 1844 presidential hopefuls Henry Clay (Whig) and Martin Van Buren (Democrat) announced their opposition to the annexation of Texas. At the Democratic convention in Baltimore, however, southern Democrats and a few northern expansionists demanded Texas be in the campaign and nominated James K. Polk instead of Van Buren on the basis of the latter's opposition to annexation. Joseph Smith is here advocating annexation at a time when both Whigs and Democrats were opposed to it.

5. "The Voice of Innocence from Nauvoo" was a document prepared

by a large number of the female part of Nauvoo to decry the nefarious activities of Orsimus F. Bostwick. It was published in the *Nauvoo Neighbor* on 20 March 1844. See 7 March 1844 (1) note 2.

6. The "Book of the Law of the Lord."

7. This is what President Martin Van Buren informed the Prophet during the latter's visit to Washington, D.C., in the fall of 1839. Joseph Smith and others were seeking for redress of their Missouri grievances.

8. Sectionalism between the northern and southern states was becoming more and more pronounced. The Prophet is here referring to northern concerns that the annexation of Texas would upset the balance between slave and non-slave states.

9. See note 4, this discourse. Texas was establishing ties with the British at the time, and there was fear that if the independent republic was not annexed by the United States it would be dominated by Great Britain.

10. The Prophet is here advocating an aggressive, expansionist view.

10 March 1844

1. See *History of the Church*, 6:249-54, and *Teachings*, pp. 335-41. The original source for the report of this discourse in *History of the Church* and *Teachings* (with the exception of the introductory statement which is from the Joseph Smith Diary) is the Wilford Woodruff Journal. The accounts by James Burgess, Franklin D. Richards, Thomas Bullock, and John Solomon Fullmer are here published for the first time.

2. Luke 1:17; Matthew 11:12-14. See also JST Matthew 17:10-14.

3. D&C 13.

4. Joseph Smith-History 1:72.

5. Matthew 3:3.

6. See note 2, this discourse.

7. Mark 1:4.

8. Matthew 3:11.

9. See text of "Before 8 August 1839 (1)" after note 12. See also D&C 27:6-7; 77: 9, 14; 110:12 for occasions when the title "Elias" is applied.

10. Acts 8:5-20.

11. Acts 19:1-6.

12. D&C 124:145.

13. See 27 August 1843, note 30.

14. Malachi 4:5-6.

15. Genesis 9:8-17 (see also JST Genesis 9:21-25); Malachi 4:1-6.

16. Hebrews 11:40.

17. See text of this discourse at note 13. See also 27 August 1843, note 30.

18. Alpheus Cutler. Incidentally, "Father" Cutler had received these blessings (see 27 August 1843, note 30).

19. See 27 August 1843, note 30.

20. 2 Peter 1:10. See 27 June 1839, note 11.

21. Hebrews 6:1-2.

22. Hebrews 11:40.

23. 1 Corinthians 5:1-5; 1 Timothy 1:20. See also D&C 78:12; 104:10 (9-10); 132:26. The expression "buffetings of Satan" is not used in the King James Version of the Bible (see, however, 2 Corinthians 12:7).

24. Hebrews 6:4-6.

25. Confirmation of D&C 132:19, 26-27.

26. Acts 2:25-29, 34.

27. Although David was anointed a king by the Prophet Samuel, it was not, according to this teaching of Joseph Smith, after the order of the fulness of the Melchizedek Priesthood (see 1 Samuel 16:12-13). For this reason, when David ordered the murder of Uriah (2 Samuel 11), he did not commit the unpardonable sin.

28. 2 Samuel 6:12-13, 17-19 does not mention whether David had an attending priest offer the sacrifices in his behalf, which would seem likely because David was not of the lineage of Levi. Nevertheless the Prophet seems clear that David held the priesthood. See also 2 Samuel 24:18-25.

29. Concerning the David of the Last Days to rule in Jerusalem see 2 Samuel 7:8-29 (esp. v. 8-19); Ezekiel 34:23-25; 37:21-28; Zechariah 3; Isaiah 55:3-5; Jeremiah 30:4-9; Psalms 89:1-4; and D&C 113:5-6.

30. Acts 2:29, 34.

31. See 27 August 1843, note 30.

32. In conjunction with making your calling and election sure, the Lord grants this privilege of asking and receiving. See JST Genesis 14:31 (26-32); Isaiah 65:24; John 21:20-23; Helaman 10:5(4-10); 3 Nephi 28:1, 3, 10 (1-14); D&C 7:1 (1-8), 50:26-29; 76:55,59 (51-61); 101:27 (cf. 27 June 1839, note 9); 124:95, 97; 132: 40 (40-49).

33. Thomas Reynolds (1796-1844) was a chief justice of the Supreme Court in Illinois before becoming the sixth governor of Missouri 1840-44. As governor he made several demands on the state of Illinois to extradite the Prophet Joseph Smith. He committed suicide 9 February 1844 in his executive office in Jefferson City, Missouri.

34. 2 Kings 1:10, 12 (5-17).

35. That is, the fulness of the priesthood. See 27 August 1843, note 30.

36. 2 Corinthians 10:4 (1-4).

37. Genesis 9:8-17; JST Genesis 9:21-25.

38. William Miller (1782-1849) was founder of the Millerite movement. See 6 April 1843 (2), note 14.

39. Matthew 24:36; D&C 39:21; 49:7.

40. Only the Thomas Bullock report records the essence of what the Prophet meant in this statement: "The Spirit of Messiah is all power in Heaven and in earth [post-resurrection power of Christ in Matthew 28:18], enthroned in the Heavens as King of Kings and Lord of Lords [Revelation 17:14; 19:16 (11-16)]."

41. No other account speaks so vividly of his intensity on this occasion—"I retired in the woods pouring out my soul in pray[e]r to Almighty God." (see D&C 13 and Joseph Smith-History 1:68.)

42. Joseph Smith-History 1:72.

43. Luke 3:16.

44. Acts 8:5-20.

45. Malachi 4:5-6.

46. Hebrews 11:40.

47. John 17:3. See text of the 13 August 1843 discourse, at note 19.

48. 2 Samuel 11.

49. This and the Franklin D. Richards' account are the most complete versions of this revelation from contemporary records.

50. See 16 July 1843 (2) discourse, note 15.

51. Cf. 27 June 1839, text at notes 6-12. Regarding the Prophet's equating the sealing by the "Holy Spirit of Promise" to making your calling and election sure, see note 7 of discourse dated "Before 8 August 1839 (3)."

52. Hebrews 6:4-6.

53. See note 23, this discourse.

54. Acts 2:25-29, 34.

55. See text at note 49, this discourse.

56. Matthew 24:30.

57. See text at note 49, this discourse.

58. Malachi 4:5-6.

59. Hebrews 11:40.

60. Matthew 28:18. Thomas Bullock is the only recorder of this discourse who identifies some aspect of the Prophet's understanding of the "spirit of Messiah." See next scripture referenced in note 61, this discourse.

61. Revelation 17:14; 19:16 (11-16). See also Deuteronomy 10:17.

62. See text at note 49, this discourse.

63. See 6 April 1843 (2), note 14.

64. Of the six contemporary accounts of this discourse, four of the reporters recorded this prophecy.

65. The John Solomon Fullmer papers are located in the Church Archives.

66. See text at note 49, this discourse.

67. See 6 April 1843 (2), note 14.

24 March 1844

1. See *History of the Church*, 6:271-73. Part of this discourse is in *Teachings*, p. 341. The original source for the reports of this address in *History of the Church* and *Teachings* is the Wilford Woodruff Journal. The account by Thomas Bullock is here published for the first time.

2. Marenus G. Eaton and Abiathar B. Williams.

3. Chauncey L. Higbee (1821-84). Son of Elias Higbee. After his father's death in 1843, Chauncey turned against Joseph Smith and was excommunicated from the Church. Later he became a prominent politician in Illinois, serving as state representative, state senator, and circuit judge.

4. Robert D. Foster (1811-?) was converted to the Church by 1839. A land speculator at Nauvoo, Foster was excommunicated for apostasy in April 1844.

5. Joseph H. Jackson, a stranger to the Saints in Nauvoo, attempted to endear himself to the Smith family. After being denied the right to marry

Hyrum Smith's daughter, Lavina, Jackson became embittered and sided with William Law and other apostates opposed to Joseph Smith. Although Jackson, in his scurrilous *Narrative of the Adventures and Experiences of Joseph H. Jackson in Nauvoo* (Warsaw: August 1844), claimed to be a close confidant of the Prophet until his rupture with Church leaders in the spring of 1844, in fact, only shortly after Jackson arrived in Nauvoo, in 1843, Joseph Smith expressed to his scribe, William Clayton, his lack of confidence in the man.

6. The Prophet is here alluding to the so-called order of Danites of the Missouri period.

7. Marenus G. Eaton (1811-?). Eaton, though not a member of the Church, became a member of the Council of Fifty shortly after this time.

8. Isaiah 29:21.

9. John 1:23; Matthew 3:2, 8, 10.

10. Orson Spencer.

11. Matthew 3:2.

5 April 1844

1. Not in *History of the Church* or *Teachings*. The reporter is unnamed in the newspaper, but circumstantial evidence shows him to be Dr. G. W. Goforth. An announcement in the *Nauvoo Neighbor* (20 March 1844) indicated that Joseph Smith would preach King Follett's funeral sermon this day, but it was deferred until Sunday.

6 April 1844

1. See *History of the Church*, 6:287-88. Not in *Teachings*. The original source for the *History of the Church* account is *Times and Seasons* (1 May 1844), and it appears that the *Times and Seasons* report is based on William Clayton's minutes of the Prophet's remarks. The accounts of the Prophet's brief remarks on this occasion in the Joseph Smith Diary, the Wilford Woodruff Journal, and the Willard Richards Diary are here published for the first time.

2. The Prophet is here alluding to a vocal group of apostates, headed by William Law, that accused Joseph Smith of being a fallen prophet. They specifically opposed his teachings on the plurality of Gods, priesthood sealings, and plural marriage.

7 April 1844 (1)

1. See *History of the Church*, 6:297. Not in *Teachings*. The entry in *History of the Church* is based on the Joseph Smith Diary, by Willard Richards.

7 April 1844 (2)

1. See *History of the Church*, 6:302-17, and *Teachings*, pp. 342-62. The report of this discourse in *History of the Church* and *Teachings* is an amalgamation of the accounts of Willard Richards (Joseph Smith Diary), Wilford Woodruff, Thomas Bullock, and William Clayton. The reports of Samuel W. Richards, Willard Richards (personal diary) and William Clayton (personal diary) are here published for the first time.

Traditionally considered the Prophet's greatest sermon, the King Follett discourse was delivered at a time when both anti-Mormon and apostate sentiment was intensifying. "Accusations were repeatedly being made," notes B. H. Roberts, "that President Smith was a fallen prophet." On this occasion he coolly claimed that this single discourse would vindicate his prophetic calling. Although the sermon contains no new doctrine, never before had Joseph Smith so thoroughly, eloquently, and with such power presented what by now had become the very life-blood of Mormon theology. B. H. Roberts added that "The Prophet lived his life in a *crescendo*. From small beginnings, it rose in breadth and power as he neared its close. As a teacher he reached the climax of his career in this discourse (*Teachings*, pp. 355-56). Joseph Fielding, one who knew all that the dissenters knew of the Prophet's private teachings, including plural marriage, the endowment, and the Council of Fifty, had "evidence enough [from the discourse] that Joseph [was] not fallen." So affected was he by this sermon that he asserted "any one that could not see in him the Spirit of Inspiration of God must be dark. They might have known that he was not a fallen Prophet even if they thought he was fallen."

A special issue of *Brigham Young University Studies* 18 (Winter 1978) included three indepth studies of the King Follett discourse. Donald Q. Cannon presented the historical context of the address. A newly amalgamated text of the four major reports of the sermon was prepared by Stan Larson. Finally, Van Hale analyzed the doctrinal antecedents that are synthesized in this and the 16 June 1844 discourses.

2. King Follett (1788-1844) was baptized in Ohio in 1831. On the morning of 9 March 1844, Follett was walling up a well in Nauvoo when a bucket of rock fell on him, crushing him to death.

3. D&C 88:49, 67 (48-50, 63-69).

4. John 17:3.

5. Genesis 1:26-27.

6. See 11 June 1843, note 18.

7. Revelation 1:6; 5:10; 20:6.

8. Isaiah 33:14 (13-17).

9. Romans 8:17.

10. Philippians 2:12.

11. See note 70, this discourse.

12. See text of discourse at note 73 and note 73.

13. D&C 88:63 (48-50, 63-69); see text of 9 March 1841 discourse at note 8.

14. See note 75, this discourse.

15. See 5 January 1841, note 8.

16. See note 4 of discourse dated "Before 8 August 1839 (1)."

17. Ibid.

18. See 17 May 1843 (2) note 3.

19. The thought is rounded out in the text after footnote 78.

20. D&C 93:23, 29, 33; Abraham 3:18.

21. See text of discourse in paragraph after note 79.

22. Hebrews 11:40.

23. D&C 76:43-44.

24. John 7:17.

25. See 8 April 1843, note 4.

26. Moses 4:1 (1-4).

27. Matthew 12:31-32 (cf. JST Matthew 12:26).

28. See text of this discourse at notes 56 and 87, and the text after 117. See also 20 March 1842, note 22.

29. See Moses 6:59-60.

30. Matthew 3:11.

31. Hebrews 6:1-2.

32. Ephesians 4:5-6.

33. The only time the word *gnolaum* appears in the scriptures is in Abraham 3:18: Concerning spirits, "Notwithstanding one is more intelligent than the other, [they] have no beginning; they existed before, they shall have no end, they shall exist after, for they are gnolaum, or eternal." Thus, this discourse suggests that the fate of the sons of perdition is eternal doom.

34. Isaiah 33:14 (13-17).

35. See note 94, this discourse.

36. John 17:3.

37. Genesis 1:26-27.

38. See 11 June 1843, note 18.

39. Isaiah 33:14 (13-17).

40. Romans 8:17.

41. Clearly the Prophet is here quoting John 5:19. However, when Jonathan Grimshaw amalgamated the texts to prepare this discourse for inclusion in the Manuscript History of the Church (and consequently what appeared in the *History of the Church*, 6:304, or *Teachings*, pp. 346-47), the final text obscured the fact that the Prophet made an allusion to this passage of scripture. It was so obscured that B. H. Roberts, when he edited this discourse, observed that the Prophet's argument based on John 5:26 (in the text at notes 38, 64 and 100) could have been "very much strengthened by" quoting John 5:19. Thus Roberts could not tell that the original text actually quoted John 5:19. Roberts' note was reproduced verbatim in *Teachings*, p. 346. See text at notes 67 and 102.

42. See note 70, this discourse.

43. See 5 October 1840, note 19.

44. See note 4, discourse dated "Before 8 August 1839 (1)."

45. See note 75, this discourse.

46. See 17 May 1843 (2), note 3.

47. D&C 93:23, 29, 33; Abraham 3:18.

48. Hebrews 11:40.

49. D&C 128:18; Ephesians 1:10.

50. Matthew 12:31-32.

51. See 8 April 1843, note 4.

52. Taken together, Ezekiel 1:1, Matthew 3:16; Mark 1:10; Acts 7:56; 1 Nephi 1:8; 11:14, 27, 30; 12:6; Helaman 5:48; 3 Nephi 17:24; 28:13; Ether 4:9; D&C 76:12, 19; 93:15; 107:19; 110:1, 11; 137:1, 138:11, 29; Moses 7:3 (cf. Moses 1:2-11, 24-41) Joseph Smith-History 1:16-20, 43 (27-43), 68; and *Teachings*, pp. 9, 51, 151, 312, 328, 338, 339, 345, 350, and 371 show that the phrase "heavens opened" usually refers to a direct heavenly vision on the order of the blessings attending the visitation of the Second Comforter (see 27 June 1839, note 15). Compare the two visions of Newel Knight recorded in *History of the Church*, 1:83 and 85.

53. See 1 May 1842, note 7.

54. John 14:2.

55. Matthew 5:26.

56. See text of this discourse at notes 28 and 87, and the text after note 117. See also 20 March 1842, note 22.

57. Matthew 3:11.

58. D&C 76:31-49; Matthew 11:32; Hebrews 6:4-6.

59. See note 1, this discourse.

60. James 5:16.

61. John 17:3.

62. Matthew 7:29.

63. Genesis 3:8.

64. See 11 June 1843, note 18.

65. Revelation 1:6; 5:10; 20:6.

66. Romans 8:17.

67. See note 41, this discourse.

68. Philippians 2:12.

69. It should be remembered that these are reports of what the Prophet said and not his transliterations of the original language. The transliteration for the first word in Genesis 1:1 is B^{e}rê'shîyth (pronounced bray-sheeth'). According to the "Dictionary of the Hebrew Bible" in *Strong's Exhaustive Concordance* this word means "the first, in place, time, order or rank—beginning, chief, first (-fruits, part, time), principal thing."

70. The word given here phonetically transliterates from the Hebrew as Rê'shîyth (pronounced ray-sheeth'). The word, which when transliterated is re'sh, means "the head" as the Prophet applied it here (see note 107). Joseph Smith claimed the prefix "B^e"—(of B^{e}rê'shîyth—see last note) was not required. While in fact, the Dâgêsh' [or point] in the bosom of the letter Bêyth (‫ב‬) that begins Genesis 1:1 removes the aspiration of the first vowel, the Prophet says the B (meaning "in, by, through and everything else") should also be dropped. If this is followed, then he is free to form a translation "The Head one of the Gods organized the heaven and the earth" which comes from "rê'shîyth / bârâ' / 'ĕlôhîym / 'êth / hashâmayim / v'êth / ha'arts."

71. See 13 April 1843, note 15.

72. That is, revelations he had received since 1828.

73. Jakobum, would be the proper transliteration. See note 69, this discourse. The James mentioned in Matthew 4:21, from the Hebrew (Matthew 17:1) transliterates as Ya°ăqôb; from the Greek (Matthew 4:21) as Iakōbŭs; and, from the Latin (Matthew 4:21), Iacobus.

74. Isaiah 65:24.

75. The word transliterated from the Hebrew is bârâ (pronounced baw-raw'). See notes 69 and 70, this discourse. See also 5 January 1841, note 8.

76. D&C 93:28-29, 32-39.

77. See 17 May 1843 (2), note 3.

78. See note 4, discourse dated "Before 8 August 1843 (1)."

79. D&C 93:23, 29, 33; Abraham 3:18.

80. Hebrews 11:40.

81. Matthew 12:31-32.

82. D&C 76:31-49.

83. See 8 April 1843, note 4.

84. Moses 4:1 (1-4).

85. John 14:2.

86. 1 Corinthians 15:41 (40-42).

87. Isaiah 33:14 (13-17). See text of this discourse at notes 28 and 56, and the text after note 117. See also 20 March 1842, note 22.

88. John 3:5.

89. Matthew 3:11.

90. Alexander Campbell, founder of the Disciples of Christ.

91. Ephesians 4:5-6.

92. Revelation 2:11; 20:6, 12-15; 21:8 (cf. Jacob 3:11; D&C 63:17-18); D&C 29:41, 44; 76:37.

93. Isaiah 33:14 (13-17).

94. See 6 April 1843 (2), after note 2.

95. See note 1, this discourse.

96. James 5:16.

97. John 17:3.

98. Genesis 3:8.

99. Apparently Sidney Rigdon and Joseph Smith did not see "eye to eye" on the concept of a once-mortal God.

100. See 11 June 1843, note 18.

101. Revelation 1:6; 5:10; 20:6; D&C 76:56 (50-56). See also 27 August 1843, note 30.

102. See note 41, this discourse.

103. Philippians 2:12.

104. See notes 69 and 70, this discourse.

105. This is confirmation that Joseph Smith was scrutinizing the prefix "B^e" in his analysis of the word *Bere'shıyth*. See notes 69 and 70, this discourse.

106. The transliteration should be *rê'shîyth*. See notes 69 and 70, this discourse.

107. If we are following the Prophet's reasoning correctly, he believed that the word *rê'shîyth* should have been the two words *re'sh* and *shîyth*; that the two words were originally there, and the letter **ש**, which is both the last letter of the first word and the first letter of the second word, was somehow dropped from one of the words thus fusing the two words into one. As Joseph Smith indicates, one meaning of the word *shîyth* is "to bring," and the word *re'sh* means "head."

108. The Prophet, after a year of poking fun, finally reveals his ruse (see 13 April 1843, note 15).

109. See note 73, this discourse.

110. See note 75, this discourse.

111. See 17 May 1843 (2), note 3.

112. D&C 93:23, 29, 33; Abraham 3:18.

113. Hebrews 11:40.

114. Matthew 12:31-32.

115. See 8 April 1843, note 4.

116. Moses 4:1 (1-4).

117. Hebrews 6:4-6.

118. Samuel W. Richards (1824-1909) was baptized at the age of fourteen and in 1842 moved to Nauvoo, where he worked as a carpenter on the Nauvoo Temple.

119. John 5:26. See commentary on the Prophet's variation of this passage in 11 June 1843, note 18.

120. See 2 April 1843 (2), note 9.

121. See note 75, this discourse.

122. Joseph Fielding (1797-1863). Converted to the Church in Upper Canada, Fielding served an important mission to England 1837-41.

123. This is probably the most reliable estimate of the conference attendance. The *Nauvoo Neighbor* (10 April 1844) report of the April 1844 General Conference of the Church was not as conservative in its estimate of the number present as was Willard Richards. The Church newspaper, like the Thomas Bullock account, estimated an attendance of between 15,000 and 20,000.

> The weather was most favorable. We do not remember that we ever saw so large an audience before, any where in the western country. The number that composed it is variously estimated from fifteen to twenty thousand. We were particularly attracted by the respectable and gentlemanly deportment of the whole multitude. Many spectators were present from Quincy, Alton, Warsaw, Fort Madison, and other towns of less notoriety. The good order that was preserved, when we consider the immense number that were present, speaks much in favour of the morality of our city.

Although historians have been skeptical of these large attendance figures the presence of spectators from several nearby communities conceivably could have swelled the size of the assembly to unusual proportions.

8 April 1844

1. See *History of the Church*, 6:381, and *Teachings*, pp. 362-63. The account of this discourse in *History of the Church* and *Teachings* is an amalgamation of the reports by William Clayton, Wilford Woodruff, Thomas Bullock, and Willard Richards (Joseph Smith Diary).

2. Isaiah 2:2-3 (2-5). See text of a discourse reported by Martha Coray in Appendix B, at note 4.

3. In preparation for publication this sentence was fleshed out to read "when *the* Elders, *shall* take up *and examine the old prophecies in the Bible, they* will see it" (italicized words added).

4. The last and most impressive ordinances of the Gospel are designed to be administered in the House of the Lord.

5. Revelation 1:6; 5:10; 20:6; D&C 76:56 (50-56).

6. The first stakes to be organized in the large cities of the United

States were Los Angeles (1923), San Francisco (1927), New York (1934), Chicago (1936), and Washington D.C. (1940). The Boston Stake was organized in 1962.

7. Here Joseph Smith emphasizes that some ordinances of the priesthood have to be performed in the temple of the Lord and cannot be performed in public places. See 1 May 1842 discourse and 12 May 1844, note 28.

8. Matthew 26:41.

9. Exodus 4:16 (10-17).

10. George J. Adams.

11. See 27 August 1843, note 30.

12. This was a significant statement in light of the Church's principle of "the gathering of Israel." In Nauvoo, not only did Joseph Smith start a new phase of the "gathering" by establishing Nauvoo as the hub of a wheel of outlying gathering places called stakes, but as was indicated here, all of North and South America would be the place for the "gathering to Zion in the last days." The previous policy emphasized a concept of gathering to a single location. See D&C 124:36 and the text of discourse reported by Martha Coray in Appendix B, after note 3.

13. Matthew 26:41.

14. Exodus 4:16 (10-17). This statement may have meant much more to the men who were members of Joseph Smith's private Council of Fifty. Three days later, on 11 April 1844, they chose Joseph as their "Prophet, Priest and King" (see 16 July 1843 (2), note 15).

23 April 1844

1. There is no mention of an address by the Prophet on this day in *History of the Church* or *Teachings*. This brief note by Thomas Bullock is here published for the first time.

5 May 1844

1. See *History of the Church*, 6:356. Not in *Teachings*. The original source for the entry in *History of the Church* is undoubtedly the Joseph Smith Diary, by Willard Richards.

2. Colonel John Frierson, of Quincy, was a government surveyor. A Democrat, he served in the original territorial legislature of Iowa.

3. Henry Clay's letter to Joseph Smith was dated 15 November 1843. It is not known when the Prophet received the letter, but he replied on 13 May 1844. See *History of the Church*, 6:376-77.

12 May 1844

1. See *History of the Church*, 6:363-67, and *Teachings*, pp. 364-68. The original source for the account of this discourse in *History of the Church* and *Teachings* is the Thomas Bullock report. The accounts of Thomas Bullock (personal diary) and Samuel W. Richards are here published for the first time.

A reminiscent account of this discourse by David Osborn (1807-93) parallels certain parts of the Bullock report.

> I will mention a few instances of his commenting on or explaining the scriptures: On the stand (Upon the bench at Nauvoo) he read the 24th chapter of Math. in the German Bible. When he came to the 14th v. he read it thus "And this Gospel of the Kingdom shall be preached for or against all Nations and then shall the end come" he called on a learned German in the congregation to say whether he had read the verse correctly, he said he had. Joseph then observed that he considered the German translation of the Scriptures more correct than any other and furthermore he believed the German people were more honest than many other nations. Again in commenting on 1st. Cor. 12th ch. 31st. v. he read it thus "Thus I have shown unto you a more excellent way," for says he the Translators make the Apostle swerve from the truth in order to do away or invalidate the true organization of the gospel ordinances with its spiritual Gift and office (David Osborn Journal, Church Archives).

2. John 6:68 (66-71). See also John 17:8; D&C 59:23; Moses 6:59.

3. That the mysteries of godliness were a desirable subject of righteous pursuit is suggested by the following passages: Psalm 25:14; Daniel 2:28; Matthew 13:11; 1 Corinthians 4:1; 1 Nephi 2:16; 10:19; Alma 12:9-11; D&C 6:7; 19:8-10 (4-22); 42:61; 50:24-30; 76:5-10, 114-119; 84:19; 88:49-50, 63-69 (49-69); 93:1, 19-22, 26-28, 36-39; 107:18-19; 121:26-28; 132:23; 27 June 1839 text, paragraph with note 5. Nevertheless, this important attribute of godliness is only part of the attribute of charity (1 Corinthians 13:2; 2 Peter 1:5-7).

4. He last spoke at length on 7 April and only briefly on 8 April. On both occasions he promised to continue the subject of the King Follett sermon.

5. Matthew 24:14*.

6. In the Prophet's word for word translation of Matthew 24:14 the key word *zu* he chose to translate as *to* rather than *for*.

7. William Law, who was only recently excommunicated, claimed that Joseph Smith was a fallen prophet because he was practicing plural marriage. Here Joseph Smith asserts that despite these objections, he still possessed the keys given to him by revelation (see D&C 28:7; 64:5; 90:1-5; 112:15; 115:19; 128:10-11; 132:7, 19, 45).

8. See D&C 90:1-5; 112:15.

9. Revelation 14:6-7.

10. Cf. the discourse dated "Before 8 August 1839 (2)," the sentence after note 6.

11. See 27 June 1839, note 5.

12. See note 71, this discourse.

13. Abraham 3:23.

14. Regarding pre-mortal priesthood appointments, see Jeremiah 1:4-5; Abraham 3:22-23 and Alma 13:3-5 (1-9).

15. Daniel 2:44.

16. No doubt a calculation based on the words "in the days of these kings" of Daniel 2:44. Also based on a comparison between Revelation 12:6 (1-6) and three passages: JST Revelation 12:1-7; D&C 5:14; and, D&C 33:5.

17. Matthew 26:52.

18. See 22 January 1843, note 20.

19. This he was doing specifically by organizing the "Kingdom of God" or "Council of Fifty." See D. Michael Quinn, "The Council of Fifty and Its Members, 1844-1945." *Brigham Young University Studies* 20 (Winter 1980) and Andrew F. Ehat " 'It Seems Like Heaven Began on Earth': Joseph Smith and the Constitution of the Kingdom of God." *Brigham Young University Studies* 20 (Spring 1980), and Hyrum L. Andrus, *Doctrines of the Kingdom—Foundations of the Millennial Kingdom of Christ* vol. 3 (Salt Lake City: Bookcraft, 1973), pp. 352-401, 550-60.

20. Matthew 24:7 is the closest approximation to this statement in the scriptures.

21. Joel 3:10 (cf. Joseph Smith-History 1:41, for the time of the fulfillment of this prophecy).

22. John 14:2*.

23. Romans 8:17.

24. Admittedly, D&C 130:1 could be interpreted as "In the heavens there are the three glories: celestial, terrestrial and telestial." However, Joseph Smith clearly indicates in this sentence that there are differences of glory *within* the Celestial Kingdom. This, therefore, effectively eliminates this possible alternate interpretation.

25. Revelation 14:1 (cf. Obadiah 21, Revelation 7 and D&C 77:8-11, 14).

26. 2 Peter 1:10.

27. Galatians 1:8 (6-8).

28. Here he calls it a "law of the priesthood" that certain ordinances can only be performed in the house of the Lord. See text of 8 April 1844 at note 7.

29. D&C 124:29-39.

30. This is perhaps the clearest statement of the procedure of proxy work for the dead—how it is that those who have died are informed that their descendants have done their ordinances work by proxy. Agreeable to D&C 132:7, the proxy work (done at that time) for other than blood kin ("those who we have much friendship for") must be approved by the Prophet on a case by case basis.

31. 1 Corinthians 15:22 (21-22).

32. Isaiah 33:14 (13-17).

33. 1 Corinthians 15:50.

34. Hebrews 12:29.

35. See text of 20 March 1842 discourse at note 21.

36. Isaiah 33: 14 (13-17). According to Thomas Bullock's report of this discourse, Joseph Smith twice indicated that "all men who are immortal, dwell in everlasting burnings." The celestial, terrestrial and telestial kingdoms however are of varying degrees of "everlasting burnings."

37. Matthew 7:20 (15-20).

38. See note 36, this discourse.

39. Psalm 139:7 (1-16); Jeremiah 23:24 (23-24).

40. Confirmation of D&C 132:16-17, 19. On children being sealed to parents, see 13 August 1843 (1), note 8.

41. See 20 March 1842, note 22.

42. According to his own account, Zebedee Coltrin saw with Joseph Smith and Oliver Cowdery a vision of the resurrected Adam and Eve. "They were the two most beautiful and perfect specimens of mankind [I have] ever seen." "Their heads were white as snow, and their faces shone with youth." (The first quotation is from the Salt Lake School of the Prophets Minute Book, 1883, p. 70 [meeting of 11 October 1883]. The second quotation is from an extract of the Spanish Fork, Utah High Priests Quorum Minutes for 5 February 1878, extract in the Zebedee Coltrin Papers. Both of these manuscripts are located in the Church Archives.)

43. See description of the resurrection given in the 16 April 1843 discourse.

44. See 28 April 1842, note 11.

45. 2 Peter 1:5-7.

46. 2 Peter 1:8; D&C 107:30-31.

47. D&C 28:7 (1-7).

48. George Laub (1814-80), a native of Earl, Lancaster County, Pennsylvania, was baptized in 1842. In Nauvoo he was ordained a seventy and received his endowment on 19 December 1845.

49. Matthew 24:5.

50. Laub did not transcribe his original notes of this discourse in his journal until nearly a year after the death of Joseph Smith; thus, this reference to John 1:21 may be Laub's interpolation.

51. D&C 76:26.

52. John 14:2.

53. Revelation 20:12-13.

54. Matthew 5:26.

55. 1 Peter 4:6.

56. Obadiah 21.

57. Galatians 1:8 (6-8); 1 Corinthians 16:22.

58. 1 Corinthians 15:50.

59. See 20 March 1842, note 21.

60. 1 Corinthians 15:51-53.

61. Isaiah 33:14 (13-17); Hebrews 12:29.

62. Ephesians 5:5. See also 3 Nephi 27:19.

63. 1 Corinthians 15:42.

64. John 16:8*.

65. Matthew 24:14.

66. This is the only known reference in the Prophet's teachings concerning the pre-mortal ordination of the Twelve Apostles.

67. John 3:5.

68. That all temple ordinances for the living are also performed for the dead, see James E. Talmage, *The House of the Lord,* pp. 163, 211 and B. H. Roberts, *Comprehensive History of the Church* 6:495.

69. Hebrews 12:29. See also note 36, this discourse.

70. See 20 March 1842, note 22.

71. Joseph Fielding, who was a member of the "Kingdom of God" or "Council of Fifty," stated that the Prophet was very specific in his allusions made at this point of the discourse. He was referring to the fact that while the "Kingdom" was organized on 11 March 1844, William Law soon thereafter organized an opposition church (see Andrew F. Ehat, " 'They Might Have Known That He Was Not a Fallen Prophet'—The Nauvoo Journal of Joseph Fielding." *Brigham Young University Studies* 19 (Winter 1979):146-148.

72. Acts 12:22.

14 May 1844

1. See *History of the Church*, 6:377. Not in *Teachings*. The original source for the entry in *History of the Church* is the Joseph Smith Diary, by Willard Richards.

2. John S. Reid. He had given legal assistance to the Prophet in New York in 1830.

17 May 1844

1. The following remarks of the Prophet at a political convention in Nauvoo are not in *History of the Church* or *Teachings*. At this convention Joseph Smith was unanimously nominated a candidate for President of the United States, and delegates were chosen to represent the decisions of the convention at the Baltimore Convention in July 1844.

26 May 1844

1. Not in *Teachings*. The report of this discourse published in *History of the Church* was made by Thomas Bullock, but has either been lost or misplaced. The brief accounts by Willard Richards (Joseph Smith Diary) and Thomas Bullock (personal diary) are here published for the first time.

2. 2 Corinthians 11:26. See D&C 122:5.

3. 1 Kings 19:12.

4. On 27 August 1843, Joseph Smith (as reported by Franklin D. Richards) said, "I prophesy that all the powers of Earth and Hell shall never be able to overthrow this Boy, for I have obtained it by promise."

5. Several clerks were employed in keeping his diaries, letterbooks and accounts. For example, Willard Richards and James Mullholland kept regular diaries for the Prophet, and William Clayton and Robert B. Thompson recorded letters, revelations and diary entries into the "Book of the Law of the Lord."

6. Matthew 23:24.

7. Mr. Alexander Simpson, a land speculator from Kentucky.

8. Richard Badham. The *Nauvoo Neighbor* (13 December 1843) reported the stabbing: "On Sunday night last the house of Richard Badham, who resides about five miles east of this city, was visited by two ruffians who sought for money, and threatened the lives of Mr and Mrs Badham if they would not give it to them. They obtained four dollars and fifty cents a gun and a watch, and stabbed Mr. Badham in the abdomen."

9. Amos Davis.

10. Daniel H. Wells.

11. Aaron Johnson (1806-77) was baptized in 1836 and was a justice of the peace in Nauvoo.

12. Robert D. Foster.

13. John Lytle (1803-92) was baptized in 1836 and was a Nauvoo policeman.

14. Joseph H. Jackson.

15. Joseph Wellington Coolidge, born 31 May 1814, was a native of Bangor, Maine. A carpenter by trade, Coolidge was the administrator of Joseph Smith's estate.

16. John Hatfield, born 29 November 1819, was a native of Washington, Wayne County, Indiana. A seventy, Hatfield served a mission in 1844 and is numbered among a group of men who accompanied the Prophet to Carthage in May 1844 when the Prophet was charged with adultery. He operated a cabinet shop on Parley Street in Nauvoo.

17. Peter Haws.

18. That the Prophet was involved in from forty to fifty lawsuits is not an exaggeration.

19. Reference is here made to William Law. Law and other disaffected Mormons organized a church in Nauvoo on 28 April 1844.

20. Matthew 7:17-19 (15-20).

21. The indictment based on the sworn testimony of William and Wilson Law, filed on 23 May 1844 before the May term of the Hancock Circuit Court, State of Illinois, identifies Joseph Smith's plural wife, Maria Lawrence, as one with whom the Prophet, from 12 October 1843 to 23 May 1844, supposedly "liv[ed] together . . . in an open state of adultery." The case was labeled by the prosecutor during the May term of 1844 circuit court "nolle prosequi," meaning that the indictment would not be prosecuted.

408 *The Words of Joseph Smith*

22. The Prophet is apparently referring to "The Voice of Innocence from Nauvoo" published in the *Nauvoo Neighbor* (20 March 1844). See 7 March 1844 (1), note 2 and 7 March 1844 (2), note 5.

23. Dr. W. G. Goforth, as a non-Mormon sought to have Joseph Smith nominated as a candidate for president of the United States. He was baptized and ordained a High Priest on 8 April 1845.

24. Jonathan Dunham was a Nauvoo policeman.

25. Proverbs 16:18.

26. Jacob B. Backenstos.

27. John M. Bernhisel.

28. Almon W. Babbitt.

13 June 1844

1. See *History of the Church*, 6:461. Not in *Teachings*. The *History of the Church* account is based on the Joseph Smith Diary.

16 June 1844 (1)

1. See *History of the Church*, 6:473-79, and *Teachings,* pp. 369-76. The original source for the account of this discourse in *History of the Church* and *Teachings* is the Thomas Bullock report. The William P. McIntire account is here published for the first time.

2. Revelation 1:6.

3. JST Revelation 1:6*.

4. In the first and only issue of the *Nauvoo Expositor*, William Law and others claimed in Resolution 2 (p. 2, col. 3) that Joseph Smith, Hyrum Smith and others taught "false and damnable doctrines . . . such as plurality of Gods above the God of this universe . . . the plurality of wives, for time and eternity, [and] the doctrine of unconditional sealing up to eternal life, against all sins except that of shedding innocent blood."

5. See, for example, the paragraph of the discourse dated 27 June 1839 ending with note 15.

6. See Romans 15:6; 2 Corinthians 1:3; 11:31; Colossians 1:3; 1 Peter 1:3; 1 John 2:22; 2 John 3; Revelation 1:6; 2:27; 3:5, 21.

7. Revelation 1:6.

8. 1 Corinthians 8:5 (4-6).

9. 1 Corinthians 8:6.

10. See 5 October 1840, note 24; 3 October 1841, note 19; and, 27 August 1843, note 5.

11. This is the standard orthodox interpretation.

12. See notes 69 and 70 of the 7 April 1844 discourse.

13. The transliteration should be 'elôhîym (pronounced el-o-heem'). The singular for god is simply 'êl (pronounced ale). According to the Hebrew dictionary, the plural form means "gods in the ordinary sense; but specifically used (in the plural, thus, especially with the article) of the supreme God."

14. A little learning is a dangerous thing.
> Drink deep, or taste not the Pierian spring,
> There shallow draughts intoxicate the brain,
> And drinking largely sobers us up again.
—Alexander Pope (1688-1744)

15. Genesis 1:26-27*. At this point of the text, the Utah editor of this discourse made the error of requoting the faulty transliteration of Genesis 1:1, placing it here as a transliteration of Genesis 1:26. Thomas Bullock did not even attempt to record the Prophet's reading of the Hebrew; however, the transliteration should have been vayi'mer 'elôhîym n'eseh 'âdâm betsalemênûw keidemûwtheûw.

16. Joseph Smith is possibly referring to Joshua Seixas who, for a few weeks, taught Hebrew to the Prophet and others in Kirtland, Ohio (1836). The word 'elôhîym is the first plural in the Bible.

17. In the Old Testament the word 'elôhîym is found translated either God or gods 2674 times. Only 8 percent of the time is it translateds gods. The word 'el is found translated God 179 times and only once translated gods. Thus the singular form is found only 6 percent of the time. Other Hebrew words are translated God, most particularly the word yehôvîh appearing 266 times (but yehôvâh only appears 3 times).

18. While this appears arbitrary it is consistent with previous revelation to Joseph Smith regarding the true nature of worship. See D&C 93:1-39.

19. John 17:9-11.

20. 1 John 5:7-8.

21. Cf. 1 John 5:7-8.

22. John 17:9-11.

23. John 17:9-11; Isaiah 33:14 (13-17); D&C 76:94. The American Translation of the New Testament uses the word *union* in place of the word *one* used in the King James Version.

24. Since the summer of 1835 Joseph Smith possessed relics and mummies excavated in Egypt including some treasured papyri texts. In 1842, he published his translation of these records entitled The Book of Abraham.

25. Abraham 3:18.

26. 1 Corinthians 15:46-48.

27. John 5:19. See 7 April 1844, note 41.

28. John 9:4.

29. Luke 10:18 (17-20).

30. Isaiah 8:20.

31. John 10:33; 5:18.

32. See for example, Matthew 9:3; Luke 15:2; 19:14; John 7:15, 9:16; 11:47; 19:12.

33. John 10:34.

34. 1 Corinthians 10:4 (1-4).

35. John 10:34-36.

36. For example, Joseph Fielding says that William Law used Jacob 2 of the Book of Mormon to combat the Prophet's practice of plural marriage, and in the Nauvoo Expositor Resolution 6 (p. 2, col. 4), the followers of William Law quoted the Doctrine and Covenants to contradict Joseph Smith's financial practices. Ironically, both books of scripture were revealed through Joseph Smith.

37. D&C 76.

38. Joseph Smith is apparently referring to the seven churches Paul wrote to, namely, Rome, Corinth, Galatia, Ephesus, Philippi, Colosse and Thessalonica.

39. 1 Corinthians 15:40-42.

40. Romans 8:17.

41. Exodus 3:16.

42. Job 38:7; John 1:12; Romans 8:14, 19; 1 John 3:1-2; 3 Nephi 9:17; Moroni 7:26, 48; D&C 11:30; 39:4; 45:8; 76:24, 58 (50-60); Moses 6:68 (57-68); 7:1; 8:13-22 (cf. Genesis 6:1-8).

43. Romans 8:15 (14-17).

44. Abraham 3:22-4:1.

45. Revelation 1:6.

46. Ibid.

47. Revelation 17:14; 19:16.

48. In light of the Prophet's teachings in this discourse and elsewhere, this observation is clear. For example, Reverend William J. Logan's comments on Extreme Unction in his *A Catechism for Adults* (Chicago: Adult Catechetical Teaching Aids Publications, n.d.), pp. 92-94, are illuminating.

49. See, for example, the "Before 8 August 1839 (1)" and 5 October 1840 discourses.

50. The Prophet would no doubt agree that all the world's knowledge he had available to him was an indirect *catalyst* for his revelations. In the chemical formula for revelation, so to speak, the catalysts aided the reaction, but did not figure in the final results.

51. John 10:30.

52. 1 John 5:8.

53. John 17:9-11.

54. Cf. the text of the 27 August 1843 discourse at note 26.

55. John 9:4.

56. John 10:18 (14-18).

57. Romans 8:17.

58. Genesis 1:1*. See 7 April 1844, notes 69 and 70.

16 June 1844 (2)

1. See *History of the Church*, 6:479. Not in *Teachings*.

18 June 1844

1. See *History of the Church*, 6:498-500. Not in *Teachings*. The account of this discourse in *History of the Church* is a reminiscent report based on the recollections of several men who were present and heard the address. The reports by William Clayton and William P. McIntire are here published for the first time.

Appendix A[1]

Willard Richards Pocket Companion

A ⊙—⊞ Key. Finding fault with the Church (A final key deliverd by Joseph in the following Language)

I will give you one of the keys of the mysteries of the kingdom. It is an eternal principle that has existed with God from all Eternity that that man who rises up to condemn others, finding fault with the Church, saying that they are out of the way while he himself is righteous, then know assuredly that that man is in the high road to apostacy and if he does not repent will apostatize as God lives The principle is as correct as the one that Jesus put forth in saying that he who seeketh a sign is an adulterous person,[2] & that principle is Eternal, undeviating & firm as the pillars of heaven, for whenever you see a man seeking after a sign you may set it down that he is an adulterous man.[3]

---

1. See *History of the Church*, 3:383-85, *Teachings*, pp. 155-56, and discourse dated 2 July 1839. This account, which parallels the Prophet's 2 July 1839 discourse, was copied by Willard Richards in England. Although the report has earmarkings of being taken from the Wilford Woodruff Journal, it is not found there, and we see three possible explanations for its existence: (1) It was part of Wilford Woodruff's original report of the 2 July 1839 discourse, but was somehow overlooked when it should have been

transcribed into his journal, (2) It is a separate report of the 2 July 1839 discourse by John Taylor (copied by Willard Richards), which is no longer extant, or (3) Willard Richards extrapolated on the Woodruff report of the 2 July 1839 discourse when he copied it into his "Pocket Companion" in England.

2. Matthew 12:39; D&C 63:7-14.

3. See *Teachings*, p. 278.

Appendix B[1]

Howard and Martha Coray Notebook[2]

A few Item from a discourse delivered by Joseph Smith July 19 1840

Read a chap in [Ezekiel] concluding with this saying and when all these things come to pass and Lo they will come then shall you know that a Prophet hath been among you[3]

Afterwards read the parable of the 12 olive trees[4] and said speaking of the Land of Zion ~~that~~ It consists of all N. & S America[5] but that any place where the Saints gather is Zion which every righteous man will build up for a place of safety for his children ~~that~~ The olive trees are 12 stakes which are yet to be built not the Temple in Jackson [County, Missouri] as some suppose for while the 12 ~~olive~~ stakes are being built we will be at peace but the Nations of the Earth will be at war.

our cry from the 1st has been for peace and we will continue pleading like the Widow at the feet of the unjust judge but we may plead at the feet of Majistrates and at the feet of Judges At the feet of Governors and at the feet of senators & at the feet of ~~the~~ Pre[s]idents for 8 years it will be of no avail. We shall find no favor in any of the courts of this government.[6] The redemption of Zion is the redemption of all N & S America and those 12 stake must be built up before the redemption of Zion can take place and those who refuse to gather and build when they are commanded to do so cease to be Saviours of men and are henceforth good for nothing but shall be cast out and trodden underfeet of men for their transgression as Reed Peck[7] was when he aplied in the name of an apostate for business in a store in Quincy They told him that they wanted no apostates round them and showed him the door At this same store the Authorities of this Church could have obtained almost any amount of credit they could have asked—

We shall build the Zion of the Lord in peace untill the servants of that Lord shall begin to lay the foundation of a great and high watch Tower and then shall they begin to say within themselves what need hath my Lord of this tower seeing this is a time of peace &c—Then the Enemy shall ~~brak~~ come as a thief in the night and scatter the servants abroad when the seed of these 12 Olive trees are scattered abroad they will wake up the Nations of the whole Earth[8] Even this Nation will be on the very verge of crumbling to peices and tumbling to the ground and when the constitution is upon the brink of ruin this people will be the Staff up[on] which the Nation shall lean and they shall bear ~~away~~ the constitution away from the very verge of destruction[9]—Then shall the Lord say go tell all my servants who are the strength of mine house my young men and middle aged &c come to the Land of my vineyard and fight the battle of the Lord—Then the Kings & Queens shall come then the rulers of the Earth shall come then shall all saints come yea the Foreign saints shall come to fight for the Land of my vineyard for in this thing shall be their safety and they will have no power to choose but will come as a man fleeeth from a sudden destruction—But before this the time shall be ~~when~~ these who are now my friends shall become my enemies and shall seek to take my life and ~~shall be m~~ there are those now before me who will more furiously pursue me ~~and~~ the more dilligently seek ~~to~~ my life and be more bood thirsty upon my track than ever were the Missouri Mobbers You say among yourselves as did them of old time it is I & is it I But I know these things by the visions of the Almighty.[10]

But brethren come ye yea come all of you who can come and go to with your mights and build up the cities of the Lord and whosoever will let him come and partake of the poverty of Nauvoo freely for those who partake of her poverty shall also ~~shall also~~ partake of her prosperity. And it is now wisdom in God that we should enter into as compact a city as posible[11] for Zion and Jerusalem ~~and~~ must both be built up before the coming of Christ ~~This will near a half of a century~~ How long will it take to do this 10 years Yes more than 40 years will pass before this work will be accomplished and when these cities are built then shall the coming of the Son of man be[12]

Now let all who can coolly and deliberately dispose of their property come up and give of their substance to the [poor?] that the hearts of the poor may be comforted and all may worship god together in holiness of heart Come brethren come all of you.—And I prophecy in the name of the Lord that the state of Illinois shall become a great ~~mountain~~ and mighty mountain as [a] city set upon a hill that cannot be hid and a great that giveth light to the world ~~and~~ The city of Nauvoo als shall become the greatest city in the whole world.—

Curse that man who says to his neighbor you are a mean man because you do not believe as I do I now invite all liberall minded men to come up to Nauvoo and help to build up the city of our God We are not greatly distressed no nor ever will be This is the principle place of gathering therefore let the brethren begin to roll in like clouds and we will sell you lots if you are able to pay for them and if not you shall have them without money and without price

The greater blessing is unto those who come in times of adversity. For many will come to us in times of prosperity that will stand at the corners of the street saying with long pharisaical faces ~~don~~ to those that come after them dont go near Bro Joseph dont go near the authorities of the church for they will pick your pockets they will rob you of all your money Thus will they breed in our midst a spirit of dissatisfaction and distrust that will end in persecution and distress—

Now from this hour bring every thing you can bring and build a Temple unto the Lord a house into the mighty God of Jacob.[13] We will build upon the top of this Temple a great observatory a great and high watch tower and in the top thereof we will Suspend a tremendous bell ~~whi~~ that when it is rung shall rouse the inhabitants of Madison wake up the people of Warsaw and sound in the ears of men [in] Carthage Then comes the ancient records yea all of them dig them yea bring them forth speedily

Then shall the poor be fed by the curious who shall come from all parts of the world to see this wonderful temple Yea I prophecy that pleasure parties shall come from England to see the Mamoth and like the Queen of Sheba shall say the half never was told them. School houses shall be built here and High schools shall be established and the great men of the [earth] shall send their sons here to board while they are receiving their education among us And even Noblemen shall crave the priviledge of educating their children with us and these poor saints shall chink in their pockets the money of these proud men received from such as come and dwell with us

Now brethren I obligate myself to build as great a temple as ever solomon did if the church will back me up. Moreover it shall not impoverish any man but enrich thousands I prophecy that the time shall be when these saints shall ride proudly over the mountains of Missouri and no Gentile dog nor Missouri dog shall dare lift a tongue against them but will lick up the dust from beneath their feet[14] and I pray the father that many here may realize this and see it with their eyes. And if it should be (Stretching his hand towards the place and in a melancholly tone that made all hearts tremble) will of God that I might live to behold that temple completed and finished from the foundation to the top stone I will say Oh Lord it is enough Lord let thy servant depart in peace, which is my ernest prayer in the name of the L Jesus Amen on this day the Stake of Macedonia over which Father Jhon Smith presided was publicly appointed.

---

1. Not in *History of the Church* or *Teachings*. Although the report of this discourse in the Coray Notebook is dated 19 July 1840, there are reasons to believe that this dating is incorrect, and that Martha Coray integrated ideas she later learned into her final copy, in Utah, ideas she learned after the original discourse. Some possible reasons are: (1) The date "19 July 1840" is penned in a darker ink color and may have been an afterthought, not part of the original notes; (2) The notation at the end of the discourse suggests two possibilities: (a) the discourse was given on the date that the Stake of Macedonia (Ramus) was organized (4 July 1840) or (b) the discourse was given on the day John Smith was appointed president over the Church in Macedonia (5 October 1843); (3) Reference to government of the United States eventually coming to the "verge of crumbling" and the "constitution [approaching] the brink of ruin" fits more consistently with 1843 than 1840. Similarly, the idea that the Second Coming would not come for another "40

years" and the notion that Zion comprehends all of North and South America were teachings of the Prophet in 1843 and 1844. Because of these problems the integrity of this report is in question, and we have chosen to place it here in the appendix. The following report was first published by Dean C. Jessee in *Brigham Young University Studies* 19 (Spring 1979):390-94.

2. Howard Coray (1817-1908) was baptized in 1840 and served as scribe to Joseph Smith 1840-41. Martha Jane Knowlton Coray (1822-81) was a native of Covington, Kentucky. The wife of Howard Coray, Martha Jane was baptized in February 1840. She was a member of the Nauvoo Relief Society, and in Utah she served on the board of directors of Brigham Young Academy. The Coray Notebook was acquired by the Church sometime after 10 July 1902, and is located at Church Archives.

3. The chapter read was Ezekiel 33, and the passage specifically referred to was verse 33.

4. D&C 101:43-62.

5. It is generally supposed that the Prophet first described North and South America as the land of Zion in his 8 April 1844 discourse.

6. D&C 101:81-93.

7. Reed Peck (1814-94) was originally part of the Colesville, New York, branch in 1830. He turned against the Church during the Missouri persecutions in 1838.

8. A revelation to Joseph Smith states, "The decree hath gone forth from the Father that [the elect] shall be gathered in unto one place upon the face of this land [America]" (D&C 29:8), but the Book of Mormon states that though the "church of the Lamb ... were few, ... nevertheless, ... the Saints of God were also upon all the face of the earth" (1 Nephi 14:12). Thus to fulfill both of these prophecies, the gathering of Israel had to have at least two phases: an initial consolidation, and then a more universal orientation.

9. This is the only known contemporary account of this well-known prophecy of Joseph Smith (cf. 2 April 1843 (1), note 9, and 6 May 1843, note 1; see also *Journal of Discourses* 6:152; 7:15; 12:204; 21:8, 31; 23:104, 122-23).

10. This concern for a compact pattern of settlement is consistent with an 1831 revelation instructing the Saints to settle "together as much as can be." The revelation added that the "church [branches] shall be organized in as close bodies as they can be; and this for a wise purpose." (*Book of Commandments*, 44, verse 57.) Compare this idea with the 8 April 1840 discourse, note 5. A possible explanation of this seeming contradiction is that while the Saints could locate in various settlements near Church headquarters (Nauvoo), each individual community should remain as compact as possible.

11. Because of the revelation he received 25 December 1832, Joseph Smith knew that the Savior would not come before the year 1890 (see D&C 130:12-17 or the 2 April 1843 (1), discourse, note 10).

12. Isaiah 2:2-5.

13. Based on this sentiment, Brigham Young said often that when the Saints returned to Jackson County, Missouri, there would not be as much as a "yellow dog [a persecuting gentile settler] to wag his tail" (see J. Golden Kimball address in *Conference Report*, (October 1930): 59).

Scripture Index

Index